Railway Problems

Railway Problems

EDITED, WITH AN INTRODUCTION

By

William Z. Ripley, Ph.D.

Revised Edition

In Two Volumes

Volume II

BeardBooks
Washington, D.C.

Boston: Ginn and Company

Reprinted 2000 by Beard Books, Washington, D.C.

ISBN 1-58798-076-2

Printed in the United States of America

XVI

RATES TO COMPETING LOCALITIES

The Danville, Va., Case[1]

Prouty, *Commissioner:*

* * * * * * * *

The rates complained of are divided in the complaint into four groups. First, those to Danville from northern and eastern cities; second, rates on sugar, molasses, rice, and coffee from New Orleans to Danville; third, rates from certain western points to Danville; fourth, the rate on tobacco from Danville to western points.

1. Freight from northern and eastern cities may come to Danville either all rail or by rail and water. This case does not show to what extent all rail competition exists, but it fairly appears from the testimony that the great bulk of such traffic is brought by water to Norfolk, or to some point in that vicinity which may be conveniently designated as Norfolk, and is from thence carried by rail to its destination. Taking New York as a type of these cities, the class rates to Lynchburg and Danville are as follows:

Rates in Cents per 100 Pounds, except Class F, which is per Barrel

From New York to	Classes												
	1	2	3	4	5	6	A	B	C	D	E	H	F
Lynchburg, Va., water and rail	54	47	38	25	22	18	18	22	18	18	22	25	36
Danville, Va., water and rail	66	58	47	33	29	24	24	27	24	22	29	33	46

[1] Decided February 17, 1900. Interstate Commerce Reports, Vol. VIII, pp. 409–442. Resumed in *Ibid.*, Vol. VIII, pp. 571–583. Finally disposed of in the Chattanooga decision. See Ripley's Railroads: Rates and Regulation, p. 483.

The map on the following page gives a general idea of the location of the points in question and the lines of transportation involved.

This traffic comes by boat to Norfolk. From Norfolk the Southern Railway leads directly to Danville, distance 205 miles. The short line from Norfolk to Lynchburg is by the Norfolk & Western 204 miles. The distance by the Chesapeake & Ohio is 231 miles. Lynchburg is upon the Southern road, 66 miles north of Danville, and a third route from Norfolk to Lynchburg is by the Southern to Danville 205 miles and from Danville to Lynchburg 66 miles, making 271 miles in all. Lynchburg is upon the main line of both the Chesapeake & Ohio and the Norfolk & Western.

There are three lines of railway leading north and east from Danville, which were formerly independent, but are now all controlled by the Southern. These are the Atlantic & Danville to Norfolk, the Richmond & Danville to Richmond, and the Lynchburg & Danville to Lynchburg.

* * * * * * * *

Rates from eastern cities to Richmond are much lower than to Lynchburg, due probably to the fact that Richmond has by the James river direct water communication with the Atlantic seaboard. All other rates appear to be uniformly the same to Norfolk, Richmond and Lynchburg, certainly to Richmond and Lynchburg. For the purpose of avoiding unnecessary repetition, only the rate to Lynchburg will be given.

2. The rates on sugar, molasses, rice, and coffee from New Orleans to Lynchburg and Danville are as follows:

FROM NEW ORLEANS TO	SUGAR	MOLASSES	COFFEE	RICE
Lynchburg	32	26	40	32
Danville	43	37	51	43

The Southern alone carries this traffic into Danville, but it may bring it either from the North *via* Lynchburg or from the South. The Chesapeake & Ohio, Norfolk & Western,

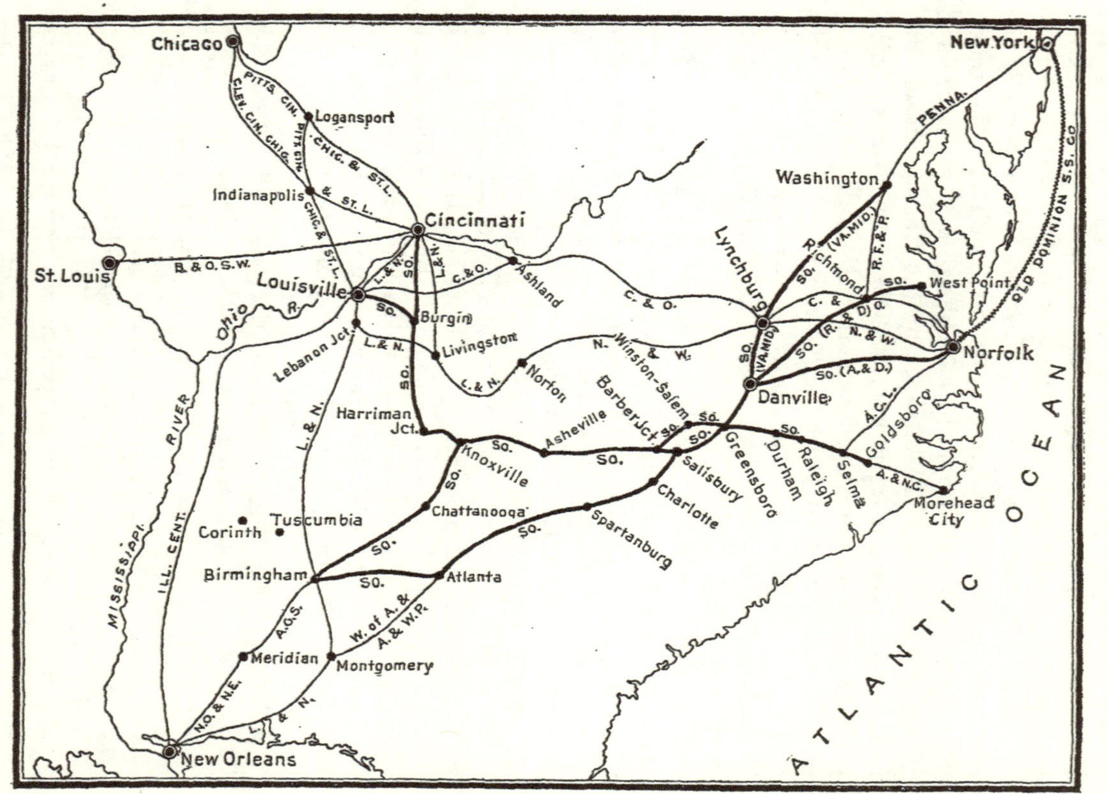
Chicago
New York
PENNA.
Logansport
Washington
Indianapolis
Cincinnati
St. Louis
Louisville
Lynchburg
Richmond
West Point
OLD DOMINION S.S. CO.
Norfolk
Burgin
Livingston
Ashland
Lebanon Jct.
Norton
Winston-Salem
Barber Jct.
Danville
Harriman Jct.
Asheville
Knoxville
Greensboro
Durham
Raleigh
Selma
Goldsboro
Salisbury
Charlotte
Morehead City
Chattanooga
Spartanburg
Corinth
Tuscumbia
Birmingham
Atlanta
Meridian
Montgomery
New Orleans
Ohio R.
MISSISSIPPI RIVER
ILL. CENT.
B.&O.S.W.
L.&N.
C.&O.
N.&W.
C.&N.
A.C.L.
A.&N.C.
R.F.&P.
A.G.S.
N.O.&N.E.
W. of A.& A.&W.R.
ATLANTIC OCEAN

and Southern all compete for this same traffic to Lynchburg, Richmond, and Norfolk. Such traffic may leave New Orleans by various routes. It may reach the Southern road over either the Louisville & Nashville, the Queen & Crescent, or the Illinois Central, and it may also reach the Chesapeake & Ohio and Norfolk & Western over either of those lines. In going by the Southern to either Lynchburg or Richmond it passes through Danville, by whatever route it starts.

* * * * * * * *

3. Rates from Cincinnati and Louisville are the same to Lynchburg and also to Danville. Those rates, together with the rates from Chicago and East St. Louis, are given below:

RATES IN CENTS PER 100 POUNDS, EXCEPT CLASS F, WHICH IS PER BARREL

	CLASSES															
	1	2	3	4	5	6	A	B	C	D	E	H	F	Grain	Flour	Packing-House Products
From Louisville, Ky., and Cincinnati, O., to																
Lynchburg, Va. . .	62	53½	40½	27½	23	18½	—	—	—	—	—	—	—	16	16	23
Danville, Va. . . .	68	56	45	33	28	21	19	22	22	21	30	30	—	21	22	22
From Chicago, Ill., to																
Lynchburg, Va. . .	72	62	47	32	27	22	—	—	—	—	—	—	—	19	19	27
Danville, Va. . . .	108	90	70	50	43	33	31	39	34	31	43	45	68	31	34	39
From East St. Louis, Ill., to																
Lynchburg, Va. . .	84	72½	55	37½	32	26	—	—	—	—	—	—	—	22½	22½	32
Danville, Va. . . .	106	89	70	50	43	33	28	39	34	29	43	45	68	29	34	39

The Southern Railway reaches in effect with its own iron Louisville and Cincinnati from Lynchburg and Danville. Traffic from either of these cities to Lynchburg by that route would necessarily pass through Danville. The Chesapeake & Ohio also reaches both Louisville and Cincinnati. The Norfolk & Western by its connections takes traffic from these two cities. The distances by the several routes are as follows:

From Cincinnati
To Lynchburg
via the Chesapeake & Ohio 474 miles;
via the Norfolk & Western 510 miles;
via the Southern 742 miles.

To Danville
via the Southern 676 miles.

From Louisville
To Lynchburg
via the Chesapeake & Ohio 537 miles;
via the Norfolk & Western 551 miles;
via the Southern 722 miles

To Danville
via the Southern 656 miles.

* * * * * * * * *

Traffic from Chicago, St. Louis and other parts of the West and Southwest passes through Cincinnati and Louisville, reaching those points by various lines. It might be expected that the same difference in rate would prevail between Lynchburg and Danville in case of traffic originating beyond and passing through Cincinnati and Louisville as in case of traffic originating at those cities, but an inspection of the rates above given shows that the discrimination against Danville is very decidedly greater with freight starting at St. Louis or Chicago than it is with the same freight when it originates at Louisville or Cincinnati. The reason for this will be stated later.

4. The rate on leaf tobacco from Danville to Louisville is 40 cents per hundred pounds, while the rate from Lynchburg and Richmond to the same point is 24 cents per hundred pounds. The Southern road makes this rate and carries this traffic from Richmond, Lynchburg and Danville, that from Richmond or Lynchburg passing through Danville *en route* for Louisville. Tobacco rates from Danville to other western destinations are correspondingly higher than those from Richmond and Lynchburg.

All the rates above referred to are made and participated in by the Southern Railway. In case of all those rates, no matter from what direction the traffic comes, it is carried through Danville to Lynchburg or Richmond. The complainants insist that by thus making the lower charge to the more distant point the defendant violates the 4th section and is also guilty of an unjust discrimination under the 3d section.

The defendant justifies the difference in rates between Danville upon the one hand and Richmond and Lynchburg on the other by showing the existence of competitive conditions at the two last-named .points. The claim, briefly stated, seems to be this:

Baltimore is an important commercial center, and is so situated and has such railroad connections that it competes both in domestic business and as a port of export and import with other commercial centers upon the Atlantic seaboard, like New York, Philadelphia, etc. The lines of railway connecting these centers with the West are strong trunk lines, and are so situated that competition between them has been unusually active. The Erie Canal to New York has been and is an important factor in fixing the Baltimore rate, especially the export rate, which has generally been the same as the domestic rate. From all these causes it had resulted, previous to the construction of the Chesapeake & Ohio Railway, that the Baltimore rate from almost all directions was an extremely low one.

When the Chesapeake & Ohio Railway was completed from Cincinnati through to Richmond and Norfolk, these points were put into communication with the West in the same manner that Baltimore was by its lines of railway, and that company at once adopted the policy of making its rates from the West to Richmond and Norfolk the same as the Baltimore rate. This was probably done for two reasons: First, to enable Richmond and Norfolk to compete with Baltimore for the wholesale trade in intermediate territory; second, that the Chesapeake & Ohio might conduct through the port of Norfolk an export and import business.

After the passage of the Act to Regulate Commerce, the Chesapeake & Ohio, under its interpretation of the 4th section of that Act, applied no higher rate to intermediate points than was applied to Norfolk upon business moving east, and, in most cases,. to Cincinnati upon business moving west; and this had the effect of giving intermediate points as low a rate as Norfolk or Cincinnati. The original line of the Chesapeake & Ohio did not pass through Lynchburg, but about 1886 it acquired a line of railway leading from Clifton Forge through Lynchburg to Richmond, and the effect of this was to give Lynchburg the Richmond rate.

Still later, when the Norfolk & Western Railway was completed through Lynchburg to Norfolk, that company was obliged to adopt those rates of the Chesapeake & Ohio to Richmond, Lynchburg and Norfolk which were then in effect. It also placed the same construction upon the 4th section which the Chesapeake & Ohio, together with most northern roads, had, and charged no more to the intermediate than to the distant point in either direction. This gave all stations upon the main line of the Norfolk & Western the same rate as Norfolk. The Southern came into this field of competition last of all. When that company determined to compete for this traffic it simply met the rates of the Chesapeake & Ohio and the Norfolk & Western which were already in effect, and this is all it has ever done. It has not reduced the Richmond or Lynchburg or Norfolk rate. It has not raised the Danville rate. It has in no way intensified the discrimination against Danville, but has simply left the situation where it found it. By entering this competitive field it did not injure Danville; to withdraw from it would not benefit Danville. The business is a source of some profit to the Southern Company; therefore that company should be allowed to continue in it.

The above is the claim of the Southern Railway Company defendant, as we understand it. The facts stated in that claim are for the most part correct. The Baltimore rate, owing to various competitive influences, was, previous to the construction of the Chesapeake & Ohio Railway, an extremely low rate. We find from the testimony in this case that the Chesapeake & Ohio determined to place Richmond and Norfolk upon an equality with Baltimore in the matter of rates, and that subsequently, upon the passage of the Interstate Commerce Act, it so interpreted the 4th section of that Act as to give to all intermediate points as low a rate as the more distant point. When the Norfolk & Western entered Richmond, Lynchburg and Norfolk it found this relation in rates in effect, and that relation has ever since been maintained. The Southern was the last competitor to enter this territory, and we find upon the testimony of Mr. Culp, its Traffic Manager, that the policy of that line has been to meet at Richmond, Lynchburg and Norfolk the rates made by other lines.

We do not find, as claimed by the Southern Railway, that the Baltimore rate has fixed the Richmond and Norfolk rate. Upon the other hand, these two rates have mutually interacted the one upon the other, and while the Baltimore rate has been subject to reductions by influences from the north as well as from the south, we think that the Norfolk rate may have operated to reduce the Baltimore rate quite as frequently as the reverse. Neither do we find, as claimed by this same defendant, that the Chesapeake & Ohio has been responsible all along for the Richmond, Lynchburg and Norfolk rates, and that the Norfolk & Western upon entering the field, and subsequently the Southern, have simply met those rates. These three lines of railway are in competition for this business, and there is no evidence which satisfies us that any one of them has been in the past, or will be in the future, entirely responsible for fluctuations in the competitive rates. * * * * * *

The Southern Railway Company was organized in July, 1894, for the purpose of effecting the consolidation of certain railway properties. As a result of that consolidation that company almost or quite from the first owned a through line from the Ohio river to Norfolk, as well as to Richmond and Lynchburg. Previous to this time the roads composing the Southern had not competed for western business to these three points, but the Southern decided at once to become such competitor, and has been since.

The lines of railway composing the Southern had, previous to the consolidation, formed a through route for the transportation of merchandise from New Orleans to Richmond, Lynchburg and Norfolk. It does not very clearly appear to what extent such lines north of Danville had engaged in traffic between northern cities and Lynchburg.

What has been said sufficiently states the competitive conditions existing at Richmond and Lynchburg as compared with Danville. There is, however, still another phase of this situation which should be especially referred to.

It has been already seen that the Chesapeake & Ohio, the Norfolk & Western, and Southern all compete for business from Louisville and Cincinnati to the three cities in question. It has been further noticed that the difference in rates on traffic originating north of the Ohio river is much greater than in case of traffic originating at Cincinnati & Louisville, although the competition between these rival lines is through Cincinnati & Louisville. The reason seems to be this:

In the making of rates between the West and the Atlantic seaboard the New York-Chicago rate is taken as a base. The rate from Chicago to Baltimore is a certain differential below that from Chicago to New York. Rates from various sections in the West to New York are a percentage of the Chicago rate. Thus, Louisville is a 100 per cent point, and the rate from there to New York or Baltimore is the same as Chicago. Cincinnati is an 87 per cent point, and the rate from Cincinnati would be 87 per cent of the rate from Chicago to Baltimore. Now, Richmond and Lynchburg take the Baltimore rate, and upon the rule above stated the rate from Cincinnati to Richmond and Lynchburg ought to be less than the rate from Louisville. It seems, however, that at some time in the past the lines leading from Louisville insisted upon making the same rate from that city as from Cincinnati. It further appears that the same lines, working probably through Southern territory, insisted that the Danville rate should approach quite nearly the Lynchburg rate on Louisville and Cincinnati business.

The rate from Chicago to Danville is made by adding to the Louisville and Cincinnati rate the local rate from Chicago to those cities; that is, traffic which has come from Chicago to Louisville pays exactly the same rate from Louisville to Danville as does traffic which originates at Louisville. The local first-class rate from Chicago to Louisville is 40 cents, which, added to the first-class rate from Louisville to Danville, makes a through rate of $1.08; but the rate from Chicago to Baltimore, first class, is 72 cents, and since Lynchburg takes the Baltimore rate the rate from Chicago to Lynchburg is also 72 cents. This rate of 72 cents is divided, from Chicago to the north bank of the Ohio river 23 cents, and from the river to Lynchburg 49 cents.

The testimony was that Danville merchants bought largely in the markets of Chicago and St. Louis, and but little in those of Cincinnati and Louisville, so that the Chicago and St. Louis rates are the ones which especially concern that city.

It will be seen from an examination of the foregoing facts that through rates to and from all directions, whether north, east, south, or west, are higher to Danville than to Richmond and Lynchburg. The complainants insist that this discrimination in favor of the two cities last named is most detrimental to the material interests of Danville. * * *

It appears from the testimony that it has been possible to ship tobacco from Danville to Richmond, store it for a time at Richmond, and send it along to market upon the same rate that it could have been shipped from Danville itself in the first instance, although the first carriage from Danville to Richmond was by the Southern, and the final shipment from Richmond may have passed back through Danville over the same line.

The complainants insist that not only does this discrimination in freight rates cripple the business industries already located at Danville, but that it prevents the establishment of new industries at that point. . . .

The complainants further insist that, in addition to the specific injuries previously pointed out, the general effect is most baleful. This, as we have often remarked in previous cases, must also be true. The cost in Danville of everything into which the freight rate enters is more than in the favored localities, and unless there are some compensating circumstances the effect of this must be to decrease the value of property and to depress all kinds of business in that city.

Twenty years ago Danville was a town of some 3000 inhabitants. To-day it is a place of nearly 20,000. Most of this growth had taken place previous to the last ten years. In the whole period it has developed more than Lynchburg, but it is not at the present time as thriving as its rival. It will be remembered that Lynchburg only received the Richmond rate when the Chesapeake & Ohio obtained possession of the Richmond & Allegheny Railroad, about 1886. * * *

The Southern Railway was organized in 1894 for the purpose of consolidating certain railroad properties, and it has since its organization, from time to time, taken on additional properties. The lines which it now controls into Danville were originally built and operated by independent companies. . . . In 1886 or thereabouts the Richmond & Danville Company leased the Virginia Midland, which it continued to operate from then on until absorbed by the Southern. The complainants insist that previous to the lease of the Virginia Midland and while these roads were in competition for business, Danville enjoyed substantial equality in freight rates with Lynchburg and Richmond.

The Traffic Manager of the Southern Railway testified that he had been familiar with the rate situation in this vicinity since 1875, and that during that time rates had been uniformly higher to Danville than to either Richmond or Lynchburg. . . . Generally speaking the difference was greater than now exists in amount and perhaps equally great in percentage. Since 1887 the published rates to Danville have been higher by about the present degree than to Richmond and Lynchburg.

While this is true of the established rate, the testimony of numerous witnesses introduced by the complainants leaves as little doubt, and we find, that previous to 1886 the actual rate paid by Danville was not materially higher than that of its competitors, Lynchburg and Richmond. It is well understood that published rates previous to 1887 were not observed. Special rates, rebates, and all kinds of concessions to shippers were in those days the rule, not the exception; and we are satisfied that merchants at Danville then obtained much better rates in comparison with their competitors at Richmond and Lynchburg than they do to-day. It is not probable that these rates were in all cases equal. The average was probably higher, but the effect of any difference against Danville was not felt as it now is, for the reason that business is now transacted upon smaller margins than it then was. From about 1886, when there ceased to be effective competition, the rates were better maintained, and since then the business interests of Danville have suffered more from the effect of these discriminations.

The defendant Southern Railway insisted that, if compelled to reduce its rates at Danville, it must make corresponding reductions throughout its intermediate territory, and that the effect of this would be to seriously cripple its revenues. An examination of rates from the points in question to other points upon the lines of the Southern Railway reveals the fact that those rates are usually higher at the present time than the Danville rate. Rates from northern and eastern cities are considerably higher to Greensboro and Raleigh than to Danville, being first class from New York to Danville 66 cents, Raleigh 84 cents, and Greensboro 84 cents. The same is true of rates from New Orleans and from the West. Thus, the rate on molasses is 37 cents to Danville against 47 cents to Raleigh and 44 cents to Greensboro. The first-class rate from Chicago is $1.08 to Danville, and $1.33 to Raleigh and Greensboro. Flour from Chicago takes a rate of 19 cents to Lynchburg, 34 cents to Danville, and 43 cents to Raleigh and Greensboro. This is true with respect to rates from all directions in Southern Railway territory south and southwest of Danville. Traffic for Raleigh and Greensboro would not pass through Danville ordinarily, and need not in any event, but these towns are in the vicinity of Danville, and are in competition with that city in much the same way that Danville competes with Lynchburg; and there are many instances in which traffic from New Orleans and from the West bears a higher rate to points which are strictly intermediate than to Danville.

The rates of the Southern Railway are apparently adjusted largely upon the "basing point" system, which so generally prevails in territory south of the Ohio and east of the Mississippi rivers. This system has been often referred to and commented upon by the Commission, and need not be gone into here. As is well understood, the central idea of that system is the higher intermediate rate. There is nothing in this case to show what the effect upon the revenues of the Southern road would be if the rule contended for by the complainants were applied to all this intermediate territory, and those rates reduced to the level of Lynchburg and Richmond. It is certain, however, that such an application of the 4th section would result in a most sweeping reduction of rates, and would very seriously impair the income of the Southern Railway unless the volume of traffic was very materially increased; it might even go to the length stated by the Traffic Manager of that company, of entirely eliminating the profits accruing from the transaction of business in that territory. * * * * * * *

Conclusions

* * * * * * * *

As stated in the *St. Cloud Case*,[1] the question for this Commission is one of fact arising upon the whole situation. We are to consider the interest of the producing market, the consuming market and the carriers, and upon the whole to determine whether there is such a dissimilarity of circumstances and conditions as justifies the rates in question. In the case before us we have nothing to do with the market of production, for, so far as the testimony shows, there is no question as to what market should supply Lynchburg, Danville and the surrounding localities, nor what market should receive the products of these localities. It is simply a question of the avenues by which supplies shall be transported to and products carried from this territory, or, in other words, of competition between carriers serving the same markets.

We have held in complaints under the 4th section, that a case for the complainant was made out by the mere showing of the higher rate to the intermediate point, and that the defendant was thereupon required to justify these rates. In the present

[1] *Vide*, p. 297, *supra*.

instance the complainant has gone further, and has shown in the first instance the injurious effects which these discriminations inflict upon Danville. We may follow the same order, and inquire first whether Danville is actually injured, and to what extent, by the adjustment of rates which is complained of.

The testimony establishes as a matter of fact that the burden thereby imposed upon the complainants is a most serious one. The facts in this connection have been already stated and need not be repeated here.... The case appeals to us more strongly, perhaps, for the reason that Danville is a larger community than usually prefers complaints of this sort. It cannot be said to be a little village which has no right to expect to do business, for it is a city which in the past has done business and whose people desire to continue it. The complainants have clearly established the injurious effects which result to them from the obnoxious rates.

It does not follow from this alone that the rates in question are unjustifiable. Deserted warehouses and depreciated values are always sad objects to contemplate, but they often occur in the development of society; and if the avenues of commerce have so changed as to dry up the prosperity of this particular locality, the Interstate Commerce Law cannot grant relief, for that law, as has been often said, was not intended to hamper, but to promote, trade and commerce. We turn, therefore, to the justification of the defendant, for the purpose of ascertaining whether the hardship which is inflicted upon these complainants is, under all the circumstances, a reasonable one. As stated by the defendant that justification is this: Owing to competitive conditions the Baltimore rate from almost all directions is an extremely low one. When the Chesapeake & Ohio Railway was completed from Cincinnati to Norfolk the management of that property determined to put Richmond and Norfolk upon an equality with Baltimore. Subsequently, by the acquisition of the Richmond & Allegheny Railroad, Lynchburg came to be on the main line, and was given the benefit of the same rate. When the Norfolk & Western Railway was constructed to Lynchburg and Norfolk it found in effect and adopted this system of rate making. The Southern came last of all into the field of competition. It simply accepted the rates which it already found in effect at Lynchburg, Richmond and Norfolk. Its rate to Danville is a reasonable one. The rate to Lynchburg is unreasonably low, but yields to the Southern Company something above the actual cost of movement. By handling this traffic through Danville the rate to Danville is not changed. Danville is not therefore injured, and the Southern Railway is to an extent benefited.

The facts have been already stated in our findings of fact. The Baltimore rate is an extremely low one. The Chesapeake & Ohio did determine to put Richmond, Lynchburg and Norfolk upon the same basis with Baltimore. The Norfolk & Western did adopt the same policy. The Southern Railway did enter this competitive field last, and did at the outset meet the rates which it found in effect by the Chesapeake & Ohio and the Norfolk & Western. It is not true that the Baltimore rate has during all the time since the completion of the Chesapeake & Ohio determined the Richmond rate. Upon the contrary, the Baltimore and the Norfolk rate have mutually affected each other. Competition has at times forced down the Norfolk rate below that of Baltimore, and at times *vice versa*. The resulting rate has always been a low one as compared with other rates. It cannot be found as a fact that the Southern Railway has simply accepted the rates named by its competitors.

The argument urged by the defendant is not new. It is the theory upon which every traffic manager justifies in every case the making of the lower rate to the more distant point. If proof of the facts upon which that deduction rests were a sufficient justification, there are few, if any, violations of the 4th section which could not be justified.

That argument omits, however, one most important factor, namely, the interest of the public. This, as well as the interest of the carrier, must be considered. The Southern road insists in this case that Danville would not be benefited if it should withdraw from Richmond, Lynchburg and Norfolk business. But this cannot be affirmed. The desire to transact business at the more distant point is a continual inducement to the Southern road to obtain an equitable adjustment of rates between the intermediate and the more distant point. If the Southern can only do business at Lynchburg by procuring a just relation of rates between Lynchburg and Danville, it becomes for the interest of the Southern road to secure that adjustment of rates, and it will use all its enormous power to that end. To-day the Southern Railway constructs its Danville tariffs with reference to its own interest alone. An order requiring a proper relation of rates between Danville and Lynchburg as the condition of transacting business at Lynchburg compels that company to consider the interest of Danville as well as its own. * *

In considering this case it may be well to refer separately to the rates from each direction involved, and first the rates from New York.

The transportation from New York to Norfolk is the same whether traffic is destined to Lynchburg or Danville. The distance from Norfolk to Danville is 205 miles by the Atlantic & Danville Railway, which is the direct line. For the year ending June 30, 1899, that road was operated by an independent company, and during that year its gross receipts were $2083.97 per mile, and its operating expenses 71.11 per cent of its gross earnings. . . .

As a part of the Southern system that line will undoubtedly carry much more traffic from Norfolk to Danville than it did as an independent line. Still, it can hardly be said that the above divisions afford an excessive return for the service rendered. Whether the entire rate from New York be considered, or the rail division from Norfolk to Danville, the present rate can hardly be said to be extravagantly high; neither is it extravagantly low.

There are three lines of railway by which this traffic can reach the city of Danville: The Atlantic & Danville, from Norfolk, the Richmond & Danville from Richmond, and the Lynchburg & Danville from Lynchburg. Previous to the acquisition of the Atlantic & Danville by the Southern, that company, as we understand the testimony, carried traffic from Norfolk to Danville by a fourth route, which was from Norfolk to Greensboro,

270 miles, and from Greensboro to Danville, 48 miles. If these routes were all independent lines, and all competing bona fide without agreement among themselves, as to the Danville rate, we think the effect must be, and ought to be, to give Danville a rate not much above that of Lynchburg.

As we have already seen, the direct line from Norfolk to Lynchburg is by the Norfolk & Western, and the distance, 204 miles, is almost identical with the short line distance to Danville. Lynchburg is upon the main line of both the Norfolk & Western and the Chesapeake & Ohio, whose location is such, and the volume of whose traffic is such, that they can perhaps afford to carry freight at a lower price than the Danville lines. On the whole we are impressed that legitimate competitive conditions would entitle Lynchburg to a somewhat lower rate than Danville on traffic from the North.

We turn now to rates from New Orleans. It has been seen that the Norfolk & Western, the Chesapeake & Ohio, and the Southern all carry this traffic into Lynchburg. Such traffic generally leaves New Orleans by either the Illinois Central, the Queen & Crescent, or the Louisville & Nashville. There are, however, numerous intermediate routes over which such traffic may pass. All traffic delivered by the Southern necessarily passes through Danville and 66 miles beyond to Lynchburg. The shortest line from New Orleans to Lynchburg is *via* the Louisville & Nashville to Montgomery, the Atlanta & West Point to Atlanta and the Southern to Lynchburg, distance 971 miles. The distance by this line to Danville is 905 miles. The shortest line by the Norfolk & Western, of which the Southern is not a part, is from New Orleans to Norton, Va., *via* the Louisville & Nashville, and from Norton to Lynchburg *via* the Norfolk & Western, the distance here being 1265 miles. The shortest route by the Chesapeake & Ohio is 1326 miles, being from New Orleans over the Illinois Central to Louisville, and from there by the Chesapeake & Ohio. As will be seen by referring to the findings of fact there are several routes by which the distance is less than 1265 miles, in all of which the Southern is an important link.

Taking now, for the purposes of comparison, the short line *via* the Southern, the short line *via* the Norfolk & Western, and the short line *via* the Chesapeake & Ohio, we find that sugar in car loads is carried from New Orleans to Lynchburg at the following rates per ton per mile:

via the Southern 6.59 mills;
via the Norfolk & Western 4.91 mills;
via the Chesapeake & Ohio 4.82 mills.

Upon the same traffic to Danville the Southern receives 9.49 mills.

Ordinarily the initial carrier makes the rate. In this case the Louisville & Nashville, Queen & Crescent, and Illinois Central, being the initial carriers, are without doubt largely responsible for the rate to Lynchburg, while the Southern, being the only carrier which enters Danville, can control the rate to that point. In fixing the rate the initial carrier would consult its own interest by obtaining as long a haul as possible. By the Norfolk & Western route, above referred to, the Louisville & Nashville obtains a haul of 1003 miles from New Orleans to Norton, while the Norfolk & Western has a haul of only 262 miles. Other things being equal, the Louisville & Nashville would carry New Orleans traffic for Lynchburg by this route. These competitive conditions, this bidding for business *via* the different lines entering Lynchburg, have undoubtedly tended to force down the Lynchburg rate.

While we are hardly prepared to say upon the testimony in this case that the rate from New Orleans to Danville upon sugar, molasses, coffee and rice is unreasonable when considered in and of itself, we are strongly of impression that it may be. We certainly do not find that it is reasonable, and in view of the rates in which the Southern road participates by various routes, and the rates which its competitors make upon this same traffic by other lines, those rates must be grossly unreasonable.

So far as the testimony shows, and so far as we have any understanding of the matter, here is no competition of contending markets. With respect to this traffic from New Orleans,

Lynchburg is upon no great thoroughfare which in its struggle for competitive business beyond gives to it an unduly low rate. There is nothing except the mere competition between several different lines of railway, and yet that competition has brought it about that merchandise is carried for the inhabitants and merchants of Lynchburg at an average rate per ton per mile of just about one half what the Southern receives for the same service when rendered for the inhabitants and merchants of Danville, but 66 miles distant, and that, too, although the Southern carries this traffic through Danville under exactly the same physical conditions for Lynchburg as when it is destined for Danville itself. We very much question whether in serving these two competitive localities competition between carriers should be allowed to have any such unreasonable and unjust effect as this.

Rates from the West to Danville and Lynchburg exhibit some peculiar features. It will be remembered that, treating the Cincinnati, New Orleans & Texas Pacific as a part of the Southern system, both the Chesapeake & Ohio and the Southern reach Louisville and Nashville over their own lines. The Norfolk & Western reaches both these points by its connections. These three lines, therefore, are competitors for traffic between Cincinnati and Louisville on the west, and Lynchburg and Danville on the east. By the Southern route traffic passes through Danville to Lynchburg; by the two other routes it passes through Lynchburg to Danville.

By referring to the findings of fact it will be seen that the distance by the Southern to Danville is considerably greater than by either the Norfolk & Western, or the Chesapeake & Ohio to Lynchburg. It will also be remembered that both the Norfolk & Western and the Chesapeake & Ohio transact a large through business both for export and domestic consumption *via* Lynchburg, and that Lynchburg takes the same rate which is granted to all this competitive business. An examination of the rates themselves in effect from Cincinnati and Louisville to Danville and Lynchburg, respectively, shows that there is no very extravagant difference in favor of Lynchburg upon class rates. The widest difference seems to be made upon grain and flour. We hardly think it can be said that the rates from these points to Danville are in the main unreasonably high when considered of themselves, if it is possible to measure a rate by any such standard.

Traffic from Chicago, St. Louis and other points similarly situated comes, or may come, to these three lines at either Cincinnati or Louisville, and the rate through either one of those points must determine the rate through all other points. The distance from points beyond Louisville and Cincinnati by these competitive lines is the same respectively as from those two cities, and the cost of movement is substantially the same whether the traffic originates at Louisville or Cincinnati, or whether it comes to these lines at those points. We might naturally expect, therefore, that the same difference in rate to Lynchburg and Danville would obtain in the case of traffic from beyond as in case of traffic which originates at Louisville or Cincinnati. Such is not, however, the fact. Traffic originating at Chicago, St. Louis, and all corresponding territory takes a much lower rate proportionately to Lynchburg than does Cincinnati and Louisville traffic. Thus, the first-class rate from Cincinnati is to Lynchburg 62 cents, to Danville 68 cents, a difference of but 6 cents per hundred pounds. From St. Louis the same class rate is to Lynchburg 84 cents, to Danville $1.06, a difference of 22 cents per hundred pounds. From Chicago the first-class rate to Lynchburg is 72 cents, while the corresponding rate to Danville is $1.08, a difference of 36 cents against Danville. In case of those commodities which are most consumed the difference is even more marked. Thus, the flour rate from Cincinnati to Lynchburg is 16 cents, and to Danville 22 cents per hundred, a difference of 6 cents; while from Chicago it is 19 cents to Lynchburg, and 34 cents to Danville, a difference of 15 cents. Since Danville desires to purchase largely in the markets of St. Louis, Chicago, and corresponding territory, it follows that these rates are the ones in which that community is particularly interested.

The reason for this discrimination has been fully stated in the findings of fact. It arises out of the rule that Lynchburg shall take the Baltimore rate. The Danville rate is in all cases made by adding the local rate from Chicago to the Ohio river to the Cincinnati or Louisville rate from the Ohio river, while the Lynchburg rate is determined by the Baltimore rate from the locality in question. On traffic from Chicago to Lynchburg the carrier from Chicago to the Ohio river receives 23 cents, and the carrier from the Ohio river to Lynchburg 49 cents. On the same traffic destined to Danville the carrier north of the Ohio river receives 40 cents, while the carrier from that river to Danville receives 68 cents. If the traffic, whether originating at Cincinnati or Louisville, reaches Danville *via* Lynchburg, the Southern exacts its full local rate of 36 cents. The divisions above stated are those of the first-class rate, but other rates are divided upon the same basis. Broadly stated, carriers from Chicago and St. Louis prorate upon business to all points on the Norfolk & Western Railroad. To all points in territory south of the Norfolk & Western Railroad there is no prorating, but each carrier receives the sum of its locals to and from the Ohio river. * * * * * * * *

This system of rate making into Southern territory by adding together the sums of the locals to and from the Ohio river is not before us as a general scheme in this case. We are only considering it with reference to the city of Danville, and with reference to that city we hold it to be utterly unreasonable. Danville is situated but 66 miles south of Lynchburg. It is in competition with Lynchburg. Now, these carriers have no right to put in effect a system of rates which prohibits the city of Danville from transacting business in competition with the city of Lynchburg. Whether or not they may make their rates into Southern territory in this manner is something about which we express no opinion, but if they desire to do that they must so adjust their rates in passing from Norfolk & Western to Southern territory as not to annihilate the city of Danville. They have no right to put that locality between the upper and nether millstone of these two schemes of rate making. Rates to Danville must be adjusted with relation to rates to competitive localities like Lynchburg, and the carriers from the point of origin to destination should prorate in these rates if they participate in either Lynchburg or Danville business.

Lynchburg is situated but 66 miles from Danville. Danville rates from most western territory and from New Orleans base upon Lynchburg; that is, they are made by adding to the Lynchburg rate the Southern local rate from Lynchburg to Danville. We do not think that the rate to Danville upon this through business from New Orleans or from the West ought to be constructed upon that basis. Whatever competitive conditions may be at Lynchburg, Danville to some extent should enjoy the benefit of those competitive conditions by reason of its proximity, for by reason of that same proximity it is thrown into competition with Lynchburg.

This traffic is in no sense local traffic, but is in every sense through traffic. There is no loading at Lynchburg, no billing at Lynchburg, no soliciting of traffic at Lynchburg. It is in fact a through shipment, and to some extent Danville should enjoy the benefit of that fact. We do not mean that the Southern Railway may not exact from the Norfolk & Western or the Chesapeake & Ohio a division upon this business when it moves by way of Lynchburg, which is equal to its full local rate. Perhaps it may do that in the protection of its own line. About that we are called upon to express, and we do express, no opinion. What we say is that in determining the Danville rate, the Southern Railway, which dominates that situation, must recognize the fact that this business is through business upon which Lynchburg, a competitor of Danville, enjoys a low through rate, and upon which Danville itself is entitled to a through rate.

If the various railroad properties leading from Danville north to the line of the Norfolk & Western and Chesapeake & Ohio were operated to-day by their original builders there would be three independent avenues by which these northern roads could obtain access to the city of Danville. These lines, however, have all been absorbed by one corporation. That corporation controls every line leading to the city of Danville, with the unimportant exception of the Danville & Western, and by virtue of that fact it is able to exact, as it does, its full local rate from Lynchburg to Danville.

As already remarked, the Southern Railway is the consolidation of numerous independent railroad properties. It has become through this process of growth a great railroad system embracing to-day a mileage of more than 6000 miles. In this operation properties which were worthless have been put together to form a valuable whole. The physical condition of those properties has been enormously improved. The facilities afforded to their patrons have been increased. The whole territory involved must be benefited by this amalgamation, so far as its physical service is concerned.

This enterprise is a perfectly legitimate one. The men who have conceived and executed it are entitled to a fair return upon the money which has been actually invested in it. They are entitled, in addition, to a reasonable profit upon the ability to conceive and execute a project of this sort. They have no right to exact a return upon an extravagant capitalization, but whatever has honestly and in good faith and reasonably gone into this enterprise should be protected.

On the other hand, the people in this territory are entitled to protection. The Southern Railway, by virtue of the fact that it has obtained possession of and now controls the avenues of communication by rail between the city of Danville and the outside world, has no right to deprive that community of the competitive advantages which the enterprise of its citizens in one way or another had secured, and upon the strength of which business conditions have grown up. It must recognize the geographical position and the commercial importance of the city of Danville.

We fully realize the serious consequences to the Southern Railway of any reduction in its Danville rate, or in corresponding rates to other points. Such reduction means a deduction from its net revenues. As applied to the volume of business handled at Danville alone, such reduction must be very considerable, — it cannot from the testimony in this case be determined just how considerable.

Upon the other hand we think that as an offset to this the Southern would obtain some additional revenue by virtue of the increased amount of business at Danville. The ability to do business at that point depends largely upon the freight rate. The amount of traffic handled in and out of Danville is determined by the volume of business transacted there, — by the prosperity of the community. Whether the Southern Railway shall reduce its rates to the city of Danville with the hope of thereby stimulating an additional flow of traffic is purely a question of policy with which this Commission has ordinarily nothing to do ; but when we are commanded to consider the interests of all parties, we must consider what the probable effect of our order will be upon the carrier interested. In this view we are bound to inquire what effect it will have upon the volume of traffic, and the consequent increase or decrease of revenue. Any development at Lynchburg is necessarily shared by the Southern with the Norfolk & Western and the Chesapeake & Ohio, whereas any corresponding development at Danville belongs to the Southern Railway Company alone. We feel that a reduction in the Danville rate might ultimately be for the advantage of this defendant.

Under our original interpretation of the 4th section the duty of this Commission in determining whether that section had been violated was a comparatively simple one. We were confined to inquiring whether competition between carriers not subject to the Act to Regulate Commerce influenced or controlled the rate at the more distant point. If it did, that created the dissimilar circumstances and conditions. Now, however, we are bidden to examine the whole situation, and to determine whether, taking all things into account, the conditions which surround that situation justify the charging of the higher rate at the intermediate point. It is impossible to apply to the solution of that question any definite rule. Each case has to be considered upon its own peculiar facts. It is difficult in every case to determine what ought to be done in justice to the public and to the carrier, and it is even more difficult to state the reasons for that determination. We have given this question the best attention we could. It is an extremely perplexing one, but it must be decided, and, without attempting to state the reasons more fully than has been already done, our conclusion is this :

We think that under all the circumstances and conditions the rate to Lynchburg may properly be somewhat lower than the rate to Danville. We do not think that the present difference in rates is justifiable; or, in other words, we do not think that the circumstances and conditions justify the rates now in force. It is our opinion that rates from northern and eastern cities to Danville and rates from New Orleans upon the commodities mentioned in the complaint to Danville should not exceed those to Lynchburg by more than 10 per cent, and that rates between Danville and the West should not exceed those between Lynchburg and the West by more than 15 per cent. This also applies to the rate on tobacco from Danville to Louisville. It may well be called outrageous to impose upon the chief industry of Danville a rate from Danville to Louisville 15 cents above the rate from Lynchburg to Louisville, when the difference in rates upon that class of merchandise in the reverse direction is only $2\frac{1}{2}$ cents. * * * * * * *

[No order was issued by the Commission at its first hearing; but ten months later, in November, 1900, after a rehearing of the case, a new opinion was rendered, concluding as follows. — ED.]

The Southern Railway shows that in the year 1899 it earned nothing upon its $120,000,000 of common stock, and urges that any order of this Commission which depletes the revenues of that company deprives the owners of this stock of their property without due process of law.

This common stock was issued as a part of a reorganization scheme under which the Southern Railway Company came into existence. It does not appear that the persons to whom this stock was originally issued ever paid one dollar in actual value for it. It simply appears that the stock is outstanding. This is not enough. Something more is needed when a claim of this kind is set up than the mere fact of the existence and amount of capitalization. It does not rest in the whim of a reorganization committee in Wall Street to impose a perpetual tax upon that whole southern country. In the year 1899 the Southern Railway earned net about 4 per cent on $40,000 a mile of the mileage of its entire system. That system extends, as a rule, through sparsely populated territories; no difficult and expensive engineering feats were involved in its construction, nor has it in proportion to its extent many expensive terminals. It will hardly be claimed that the cost of reproducing that property in its present state would equal $40,000 a mile.

The Southern Railway is of great benefit to the territory which it serves, and the money invested in that enterprise is entitled to the most careful protection; but the property of the citizens of Danville is just as sacred as are the securities of that company. No order should be made by this Commission which will deprive it of a dollar in revenue to which it is justly entitled, but we find nothing in its financial condition, as shown by the testimony, to prohibit a change of rates which will reduce to a limited extent its receipts.

This is not a question of revenue altogether. It is a question, to an extent, of right and wrong. The beggar upon the street has no right to steal merely because he is hungry; nor has the Southern Railway a right to do an unlawful act simply because it needs revenue. The state of its revenues has a bearing upon the lawfulness of the act, but is not conclusive.

Railway managers are prone to assume that, in the adjustment of their rates, only the interest of their own properties must be considered. Mr. Culp was asked what weight he gave to the interest of the city of Danville, to its proximity to Lynchburg, to the fact that it was a competitor of Lynchburg, and his reply in effect was, none. This is neither just nor lawful. Railways are public servants and subject to public control. In the exercise of that control the public has enacted that they shall not unduly discriminate in favor of one locality against another, and that they shall not charge more for the short than for the long haul under similar circumstances and conditions. The Supreme Court has declared that in determining what are similar circumstances and conditions, and what is undue discrimination, reference must be had to the interest of all parties, not merely the railway. After considering all the circumstances and conditions in the present case we have sustained the complaint of the city of Danville, and have indicated in a general way those changes in rates which should be made. If upon an actual trial, in good faith, the effect of those changes upon the revenue of the Southern Railway should prove to be more serious than anticipated, we might modify the opinion already expressed, but there is nothing in the testimony presented upon this motion for rehearing which leads us to do so now, and the motion is denied.

No order will be made until December 31, 1900. If the Southern Railway signifies by that time its disposition to endeavor to make this readjustment, such further time will be allowed as may be reasonably necessary. Otherwise an order will then issue in the premises.

* * * * * * * *

XVII

TRANSCONTINENTAL FREIGHT RATES

The St. Louis Business Men's League Case[1]

Prouty, *Commissioner:*

The Business Men's League of St. Louis, the complainant in this proceeding, is an incorporated body whose membership represents some two thousand persons, firms and corporations engaged in business in St. Louis and that vicinity. The complaint is that the defendant carriers unjustly discriminate by their tariff rates against St. Louis and other jobbing houses of the middle west, and it is alleged that this discrimination is effected in the following ways:

1. By making a lower rate to Pacific Coast terminals than to points upon the coast which are farther east, and through which traffic must pass in reaching the terminal points.

2. By making a blanket rate from all territory east of the Missouri river to Pacific Coast destinations.

3. By undue and unreasonable differences between car-load and less than car-load rates, by an unjust system of varied commodity rates, and by unreasonably refusing to permit shipment of mixed car loads. * * * * *

The complaint puts in issue the system of rate making between the territory east of the Missouri river and Pacific Coast points; and in order to understand the questions raised it is necessary to state briefly what that system is. Only west-bound rates are involved.

Certain points upon the Pacific Coast, of which Los Angeles, San Francisco and Portland may be taken as illustrative

[1] Decided November 17, 1902. Interstate Commerce Reports, Vol. IX, pp. 318–372. In editing, the issues concerning mixed car loads as well as details of cost of less than car-load service have been omitted for simplification. These matters as well as transcontinental rates in general are discussed in Ripley's Railroads: Rates and Regulation. (Index.)

examples, are designated as "Pacific Coast terminals," and rates to these points are known as "terminal rates." There are "terminal class rates," the western classification being used. There are also "terminal commodity rates," and the great bulk of the traffic moves under such latter rates, over two thousand articles being named. Both class and commodity terminal rates are the same from a given eastern point to all Pacific Coast terminals.

Stations upon the direct line by which traffic from the east reaches a terminal are called "intermediate" points. Rates to such points are made by adding to the terminal rate the local rate from the terminal back to such intermediate point, whether the rate in question be class or commodity. Thus, Reno, Nevada, is upon the main line of the Central Pacific, 155 miles east of Sacramento, California, a terminal. The terminal rate on zinc slab from Chicago to Sacramento is, C. L. (Car Load) $.80 ; L. C. L. (Less than Car Load) $1.10. The local rate from Sacramento to Reno is C. L. $.78, L. C. L. $.87, making the rate from Chicago to Reno, C. L. $1.58, L. C. L. $1.98.

Class rates are named to intermediate points which serve as maxima to those points ; *i.e.*, when the intermediate rate is less than the terminal plus the local back, the lower rate prevails. As an illustration of this we may take the rate on sheet zinc from Chicago to Reno. The terminal rate is higher than on zinc slab, being C. L. $1.25 and L. C. L. $1.75. Adding the local back from Sacramento we have a rate of C. L. $2.03 ; L. C. L. $2.62. But sheet zinc in less than car loads under the western classification is 4th class, and in car loads 5th class ; the intermediate class rates from Chicago to Reno are 4th class, $2.10 and 5th class $1.85. These rates apply as maxima, and therefore the rate on sheet zinc from Chicago to Reno is C. L. $1.85 and L. C. L. $2.10. The rate on zinc slab, which takes the same classification as sheet zinc, but a lower terminal rate, is made by the combination, while that on sheet zinc is limited by the intermediate class rate. There are also a few intermediate commodity rates which apply as maxima, and have the same effect in establishing the point to which the combination of the terminal and local back will apply.

It will be seen that under this system of rate making the rate upon the Pacific Coast increases as we proceed farther east, or as the distance decreases, until limited by the intermediate class or commodity rate. Rates are uniformly higher at the nearer intermediate point through which the traffic passes than at the more distant terminal. . . .

The complaint also attacked the method of rate making from territory east of the Missouri river to the Pacific Coast, and this point was earnestly pressed by the complainants. At the present time these rates are made upon what is known as the blanket system; that is, rates from all that territory are the same. The first-class rate for instance from St. Louis to San Francisco is $3 per hundred pounds and the same rate obtains from New York. . . . Commodity rates follow the same rule, and in general it may be stated that . . . all common points east of the Missouri river take the same rate to Pacific Coast terminals, and to those points which base upon Pacific Coast terminals. This so-called blanket system of rate making is vigorously attacked by the complainants, who insist that what are termed "graded" rates should obtain; that is, that the rate should increase toward the Atlantic seaboard; and as one reason for this, it is asserted that such graded rates were until recently in effect.

There is no means of determining exactly what these rates were previous to 1887, when carriers were first required by law to publish and file their tariffs. An examination of the first transcontinental tariff filed with the Commission shows that graded rates were then in effect. By that tariff the first-class rate was, from the Missouri river $4, from the Mississippi $4.50, from Chicago points $4.70; while east of Chicago rates were apparently made by combination upon Chicago. This tariff seems to have been in the nature of an experiment, and very frequent changes were made between that date and January 1, 1889, when a tariff was put into effect which continued substantially the same, so far at least as these gradations were concerned, down to 1894. By this tariff the following differentials or grades were made: from the Missouri to the Mississippi 20 cents; from the Mississippi to Chicago 20 cents; from

Chicago to Cincinnati 5 cents; from Cincinnati to Pittsburg 5 cents; and from Pittsburg to New York 20 cents. Under West-bound Tariff No. T 1, effective April 11, 1893, which continued in effect until the rate war of 1894, the first-class rate was as follows: from the Missouri River $3; from the Mississippi $3.20; from Chicago $3.40; from Cincinnati $3.45; from Pittsburg $3.50, and from New York $3.70. The same principle was applied to commodity rates. . . . Previous to 1894 the principle of graded rates was uniformly recognized in transcontinental tariffs.

In the beginning of that year, owing to conditions which will be hereafter detailed,[1] a transcontinental rate war occurred which lasted actively for two years, and the effects of which continued for some time afterwards. One of the first results of this disturbance was to abolish the graded rate; first as far east as Chicago, and later all the way to the Atlantic coast. Under the tariff of June 25, 1898, which is said to have restored transcontinental rates to a normal condition, this blanket system was retained.

The contention of the complainants in this respect is in favor of the middle west as against the Atlantic seaboard. Since St. Louis is more than one thousand miles nearer San Francisco than New York its business interests insist that it ought to be given the advantage of that difference in distance. The defendants justify the present tariff upon the ground of water competition, and the facts bearing upon that issue will be stated later. No particular industry is complaining. The testimony tended to show and we find that since 1894, when graded rates were first abolished and the blanket system put in effect, the middle west has been steadily gaining in its sales upon the Pacific Coast in comparison with the Atlantic seaboard. Pacific Coast jobbers now buy much more extensively in the middle west than they did five or ten years ago. Middle west jobbers sell more upon the Pacific Coast than they did formerly. It was said that at least 60 per cent of the goods consumed upon the Pacific Coast, which originate in the east, came from points

[1] P. 443, *infra*.

west of Buffalo and Pittsburg. This gain of the middle west in Pacific Coast business seems to be due mainly to the increase of manufacturing in that section, and in a measure to the fact that middle west jobbers and manufacturers have worked Pacific Coast territory with more vigor and persistence than their eastern competitors. It will be observed, moreover, in the subsequent statement of the case, that freight rates from 1894 to 1898 were such as to stimulate business from the middle west; and it should be still further noted that while the terminal rate is blanketed from the Missouri river, the "intermediate" class rates in all cases, and intermediate commodity rates in many instances, are still graded. The first-class intermediate rate to California points under the present tariff is: from the Missouri river $3.50, from the Mississippi $3.70, from Chicago $3.90; while from points east of Chicago the rate seems to be made by a combination upon Chicago. The effect of this is to give the Missouri river an advantage over the Mississippi and Chicago in all territory covered by the intermediate rate, and to virtually prohibit business from points east of Chicago in that territory.

The most serious complaint is addressed to the alleged discrimination against eastern jobbers in favor of Pacific Coast jobbers. By eastern jobbers are now meant all those located east of the Missouri river, although it does not appear that any considerable business is transacted by jobbing houses east of Chicago. The tariff complained of is that of June 25, 1898, and the above discrimination is alleged to be effected by making too wide a difference between car loads and less than car loads, and by applying a scheme of varied commodity rates which prevents the shipping of different articles of a similar character in the same package, and the combining of similar articles in car loads.

It is very difficult to state in a comprehensive way the extent of the difference in rates applicable to car-load and less than car-load shipments. The western classification places many articles in the 4th class when shipped in less than car loads, and in the 5th class when shipped in car loads. The difference between 4th and 5th class rates is 30 cents from the Missouri river and 25 cents from the Mississippi river and points east. It has already been stated that the great bulk of transcontinental traffic moves upon commodity rates. An examination of the west-bound commodity tariff shows that 2219 articles so move, of which 922 have both car-load and less than car-load rates; 835 take the same rate both car-load and less than car-load, while 462 are provided with car-load rates only. Of the 922 articles taking both car-load and less than car-load rates, the differential is in very many instances 50 cents per 100 pounds. There are 152 instances in which that difference is less and 29 in which it is greater than 50 cents. In case of the 462 articles which take only a car-load commodity rate, any less than car-load movement is under the class rate, and this produces a differential which is very much greater, being in some instances more than $3.00, in almost no instance less than $1.00 per 100 pounds, and making a less than car-load rate, which is in almost every instance more than double the car-load rate. It was said by several witnesses for the complainants that the differential would average 50 cents per 100 pounds. This was probably intended to refer to the traffic in which the witness was interested, and it seems probable that, as applied to the transportation involved in this proceeding, that may be a fair average. . . .

It is much more important to understand the manner in which these differentials discriminate against the eastern wholesaler, and the extent of that discrimination.

The great bulk of manufactured articles consumed upon the Pacific Coast is produced in the east. Whether these commodities are wholesaled by the Pacific Coast jobber or by the middle west jobber the shipment is ordinarily in car loads from the factory to the warehouse of the jobber and in less than car loads from thence to the retailer. Of rail shipments from eastern factories by Pacific Coast jobbers at least 90 per cent goes in car-load lots and a considerable portion of the balance are emergency orders which require quick delivery. Upon the other hand, testimony showed that the eastern jobber could distribute to the retailer in car loads only to a very limited extent. When it is remembered that the warehouse of the Pacific Coast jobber is located at a terminal point, and that the rate from the east to the intermediate point is made by adding the local from this terminal point back to the intermediate point, it will be seen that the wholesaler upon the Pacific Coast has the advantage of the wholesaler in the east by the difference between the car-load and less than car-load rate. This advantage is important just in proportion as the value of the goods per hundred pounds, or more properly the margin of profit per hundred pounds, is greater or less.

A concrete illustration will make this clear, and for that purpose we may take bar iron. The rate on this commodity from the east to Pacific Coast terminals is C. L. 75 cents, L. C. L. $1.25. Assume now some intermediate point to which the local rate from the terminal is 50 cents L. C. L. The Pacific Coast jobber pays in freight upon a hundred pounds of iron delivered to the retailer at that point 75 cents to his warehouse and 50 cents local, in all, $1.25 ; while his eastern competitor pays on the L. C. L. shipment from his warehouse $1.75. This gives the Pacific Coast jobber a clear advantage of 50 cents in the freight rate at all points which base upon the terminal point. The testimony of the complainants tended to show, nor was it denied by the defendants, that the profit to the jobber in the handling of bar iron is less than 50 cents per hundred pounds. Unless, therefore, there be some compensating advantage to the eastern jobber he is by this differential prohibited from wholesaling this commodity to retailers upon the Pacific Coast when his shipment from the east is in less than car loads. * *

What is true of bar iron is also true of most classes of heavy hardware, so called, which include most kinds of manufactured iron in its simpler forms, as sheet iron, corrugated iron, nails, pipe, horseshoes and in general any form of hardware where the cost of manufacture has not added very materially to the price of the raw material. It also appeared that the same thing was true of some of the more bulky articles among drugs and medicines, paints and oils, stationary supplies, wagon material, plumbers' supplies and some other lines, with respect to which the differential often exceeded and generally approximated the profit per hundred pounds to the wholesaler. The testimony of retailers upon the Pacific Coast was to the effect that after the putting in of the tariff of June 25, 1898, they were unable to buy many of the heavier articles from eastern jobbers. We think it appears, and we find, that with respect to many of the more bulky articles above named the differential is prohibitive against the eastern wholesaler.

While, however, this is true of many heavier articles, it is not true of the greater number of commodities in which the eastern wholesaler deals. In case of the higher priced commodities the profit per hundred pounds is much greater than the differential. When the tariff complained of took effect the Simmons Hardware Company determined to equalize the disadvantage which its customers incurred by making a freight allowance of 50 cents per hundred pounds. At first this allowance was paid upon all articles, but it soon became evident that there were certain articles which, including the freight allowance, were handled at actual loss, and that company very soon ceased to pay freight allowances upon these commodities. The vice president testified that these commodities were the fifteen following: Shot, bar lead, grindstones, nails, wire, rope, anvils, sheet zinc, sheet steel, horseshoes, sheet iron, staples, wire staples, small chains. Except so far as these articles can be shipped in car loads, either straight or combined, they cannot be wholesaled from the east upon the Pacific Coast. It was claimed that these heavier articles were usually staple commodities, and that the inability to handle them was a serious handicap upon the eastern jobber, since the retailer preferred to patronize that concern which could supply all his wants. * * * * * * *

The jobbing business of the Pacific Coast is transacted under peculiar conditions. As already said, the supplies of the jobber are almost entirely drawn from the east and middle west. Jobbing houses are situated mainly upon the coast, and these supplies are therefore taken to the coast and from thence sent back into the interior. Owing to the method by which rates are made, it necessarily follows that the territory to which the coast jobber can distribute is limited. It has been seen that the "intermediate" rate limits the territory within which the rate to intermediate points is made by building up upon the terminal rate, and it is evident that as soon as this limit is passed going towards the east the Pacific Coast jobber is at a disadvantage in the freight rate. This limit is not the same with respect to all commodities. In case of sheet zinc, as we have already seen, it is but 155 miles, while in some few instances the combination extends back from the coast a thousand miles, possibly farther. Nor does the line of demarcation so fixed exactly correspond with the actual business limit, since the jobber can only operate in territory accessible to most of the articles in which he deals. The distance towards the east which is open to the jobber upon the Pacific Coast varies somewhat in different lines of merchandise, but generally speaking it is about the 115th meridian, some three or four hundred miles from the coast. It was claimed by the defendants, and not seriously denied by the complainants, that east of this line the territory was exclusively occupied by the eastern wholesaler, except in case of some few articles originating upon the Pacific Coast.

This scheme of rate making also limits the territory of the individual jobber upon the Pacific Coast north and south as well as east. Rates from eastern originating points are the same to all terminals. Rates to interior points are made by adding the local rate to the nearest terminal. It follows therefore that the jobber located at some terminal point like San Francisco, as he goes north or south, very soon enters the territory of some other terminal point, like Portland or Los Angeles, in which his local rate is greater than that of his competitor located at such terminal. The effect is to draw a series of circles with each terminal point as a center within the circumference of which the jobber located at the terminal point has the advantage of all others.

Not only does this confine the territory within which a particular Pacific Coast jobber can compete upon even terms with some other Pacific Coast jobber, but it also limits the territory north and south within which the Pacific Coast jobber has the advantage of his eastern competitor. Less than car-load rates from the east are the same to interior points no matter upon what terminal a particular point may base, and it soon happens, therefore, that the less than car-load rate to such point is lower than the rate arrived at by combining the car-load rate to the terminal point and the local rate from that point. Take San Francisco as an example. Nominally, rates to San Francisco are the same as to other Pacific Coast terminals. Owing to its superior shipping facilities as a seaport it probably enjoys some actual advantage in the matter of the rate. When, however, the jobber attempts to distribute from San Francisco, he finds all around him terminal points through which he must operate, Marysville distant upon the north 142 miles, Sacramento upon the east 90 miles, Stockton to the southeast 103 miles and San José to the south 50 miles. Now, the rate to almost any interior point outside this cordon of terminals is made by adding the local from these points, while the San Francisco jobber must pay the local from San Francisco itself. This operates to materially decrease the advantage which the San Francisco wholesaler would otherwise possess. But still further, if he attempts to go farther north he very soon reaches territory where the rate bases upon Portland and where his combined car-load and less than car-load is higher than the less than car-load rate from St. Louis. So if he attempts to proceed south he speedily comes to a point where the rate bases upon Los Angeles and where the combined rate is in favor of the middle west jobber. Canned goods were frequently referred to in the testimony. Taking this commodity as an illustration, we find that the car-load rate to San Francisco plus the local rate to Ashland, Ore., a distance of 431 miles, is $2.08, while the direct L. C. L. rate from the Missouri river, basing on Portland, is $2.00. At Mojave, California, 382 miles southeast, the combined car-load and less than car-load rate of the San Francisco jobber is $1.81, as against a direct L. C. L. rate from the Missouri river of $1.99.

These illustrations serve to show how, while this scheme of rate making favors the Pacific Coast jobber as a class, it limits the territory of the individual Pacific Coast jobber both as against his competitor upon the coast and as against his competitor in the east. While it appears that San Francisco jobbers do business over the whole Pacific Coast, it is done at a serious disadvantage beyond the limits of a comparatively narrow sphere; indeed, one witness in behalf of the complainants expressed the opinion that the territory of the wholesaler upon the coast was so narrow that there was really no excuse for his existence.

The territory of jobbers east of the Missouri is of course limited against one another. It is not material here to discuss the extent of that limitation, since we are considering the competition between eastern jobbers as a whole and those upon the Pacific Coast. The fact that the rate from the warehouse of every wholesaler in the middle west to the store of each retailer upon the coast is the same, gives him an advantage over the individual Pacific Coast jobber outside the immediate "sphere" of the latter, which in a measure offsets the decided advantage of the Pacific Coast jobber within that sphere.

The effect of thus circumscribing the territory of the Pacific Coast jobber is to render the volume of his business comparatively small. That of all the houses with which he competes in the east is much more extensive. The two concerns most prominent in the prosecution of this proceeding were the Simmons Hardware Company of St. Louis and Hibbard, Spencer, Bartlett & Co. of Chicago; of which the former does business in all portions of the United States except New England, while the representative of the latter testified that the operation of his house was only limited by the confines of the earth. Jobbers upon the Pacific Coast earnestly insisted that these great establishments were not dependent upon that territory for any considerable part of their business, and that they used it as surplus territory in which they could afford to operate at a very small margin of profit. It also appeared that owing to the distance at which these houses upon the Pacific Coast were located from their base of supply, the amount of stock carried was very large in proportion to the volume of business done; and that the expense of transacting that business was greater than in the east.

Certain articles are produced upon the Pacific Coast, and certain others are imported from Europe and from eastern Asia, while still others manufactured in the eastern portion of the United States are sold at a delivered price. With respect to all these the Pacific Coast jobber has the advantage of his eastern rival. But it did not at all definitely appear what the extent of that advantage might be. We are inclined to think that if the Pacific Coast jobber had no advantage in the freight rate at which he could bring his merchandise from points of production and distribute it to points of consumption, he would find it extremely difficult to hold his own.

The principal contention of the Pacific Coast jobbers is that their location entitles them to such an advantage. The controlling factor in that location is the possibility of bringing in goods from the Atlantic seaboard and foreign countries by water. The effect of water competition is also the defense largely relied upon by the carriers in justification of their tariffs, and the facts in reference to it as applicable to each may be stated together.

Several of the jobbing houses whose representatives testified in this proceeding were established at Sacramento and San Francisco a half century ago. At that time the only means available for the transportation of merchandise from the Atlantic seaboard to their warehouses was by sailing vessel around Cape Horn, or through the Straits of Magellan. In 1854 the Panama railroad was constructed. By this route freight passes from New York to Colon by ship, from Colon to Panama, a distance of fifty miles, by rail, and from Panama to San Francisco by water. Upon this route steamers have been used instead of sailing vessels, the distance is much shorter, the time much quicker, the certainty of arrival much greater, and generally the advantages offered are much superior to those by sail around South America. It has from the first transacted a considerable amount of business between the two coasts.

The first transcontinental line of railroad was the Central Pacific in connection with the Union Pacific, and was opened for business in 1869. This line at once began to compete for transcontinental freight, with no great amount of success at first. It succeeded in carrying a portion of the higher class merchandise, but the great bulk of all commodities continued to move by water or by the Panama route. It was estimated that as late as 1878 not over 25 per cent of the total tonnage moved into California by rail. In that year, for the purpose of obtaining a larger share of this traffic, the rail line inaugurated what was known as the special contract system involving a contract between the railway and each individual shipper, by which the merchant agreed to patronize the railway exclusively, in consideration whereof the railway made certain special rates of freight. . . . This system was not popular at the outset, but before long every important jobbing house in San Francisco, with one exception, had made a contract of this kind. The effect was to very much increase the rail tonnage. It seems probable . . . that in 1884 when this plan finally went out of vogue, the percentage of rail tonnage had risen from 25 per cent to between 60 and 75 per cent.

In 1881 the Atchison, Topeka & Santa Fé Railway was built to a connection with the Southern Pacific at Deming, and in 1882 the Texas & Pacific connected with the same line at El Paso. In 1883 the Southern Pacific route from New Orleans was opened, and the same year saw the completion of the Rio Grande Western and the extension of the Santa Fé to Mojave. In the northwest the Northern Pacific was opened for traffic that year, and the completion of the Oregon Short Line the following year gave the Union Pacific an entrance into Portland. The multiplication of these transcontinental routes produced a corresponding diversity of interest, . . . the contract system was abandoned because the various lines could not agree among themselves upon the division of business and the maintenance of rates. To obviate this embarrassment the Transcontinental Association was organized, having for its purpose a pooling distribution of transcontinental traffic, or earnings, and the fixing and maintaining of transcontinental tariffs. * *

When the Central Pacific and Union Pacific began business as the first transcontinental railway line they found in the

Panama route their most troublesome competitor. For the purpose of controlling this competition these two lines and their connections in 1871 entered into a contract with the Pacific Mail Steamship Company, which then did the ocean carrying by the Panama route both from New York to Colon and from Panama to San Francisco, by which the railways leased and paid for the entire space in the steamships of the Pacific Mail Company which was devoted to California business. Under this contract the steamship company disposed of this space according to the direction of the railways, naming such rates, making such regulations and generally so conducting with respect to traffic as they directed. The policy of the railways was to offset the Panama route against the clipper ships. This contract was taken over by the Transcontinental Association when it was formed, and it continued in effect with some slight interruptions from 1871 until December 31, 1892. . . .

Previous to this time there had been in force a contract between the Pacific Mail Steamship Company and the Panama Railroad Company under which the steamship company acquired the exclusive use of the Panama railway for business moving between the Atlantic and Pacific Coasts. That contract expired about this same time, and the Pacific Mail declined to renew it upon the original terms in view of the expiration of its own contract with the transcontinental railways. In consequence the Panama Railroad Company put on a line of steamers of its own between New York and Colon known as the Columbia Steamship Company. Meantime the merchants of San Francisco had become dissatisfied with the treatment which they were receiving from the railways. They knew of the existence of contracts between the transcontinental lines and the Panama route, and regarded the whole arrangement in the light of a monopoly which extorted unreasonable rates and imposed unreasonable conditions. Learning that the contract between the Panama Railroad and the Pacific Mail was about to expire they proposed to put on a line of steamships between San Francisco and Panama, thus making, in connection with the Panama Railroad and its own steamships, an independent line from New York to San Francisco. In the execution of this plan the North American Navigation Company was organized by the merchants of San Francisco.

This route began operations in the year 1893, and attempted from the first to maintain a differential upon traffic moving between the Atlantic and Pacific Coasts which would deprive the railroads of a considerable share of the business previously handled by them. The result was a most bitter and reckless rate war during which there was an utter demoralization of rates and rate conditions. The San Francisco jobbers were upon the side of the ocean, and not only were rates abnormally reduced, but differentials were abolished, the right to ship in mixed car loads was extended, every inducement was held out to the jobber of the middle west to invade the territory of the Pacific Coast. The North American Navigation Company only operated about one year, but its vessels were taken over by the Panama Company and the competition itself continued in full force until the end of the year 1895.

This episode had been an expensive one for all parties concerned. It is in testimony that the merchants had put into the North American Navigation Company $350,000, which was entirely lost; and their indirect loss must have been greater still. They had seen their territory diminish, their profits grow less, their business decrease under the competition which had been fostered by rail rates from the east. The situation was not more satisfactory to the railways for they had sacrificed millions of dollars in revenue and were still receiving what they regarded as abnormally low rates. Both parties were therefore anxious for some sort of an accommodation. Representatives of the transcontinental lines upon the coast were instructed to mollify as far as possible Pacific Coast shippers and the shippers in their turn seem to have been anxious to meet this advance. In 1897 a communication was addressed to the railways by the jobbing interests upon the Pacific Coast stating in substance that rates ought to be readjusted in the interest of the coast jobber; that more rigid inspection rules should be enforced preventing their competitors in the middle west from obtaining fraudulent rates; and intimating that if this was done they would not object to an advance in rates and would find it for their interest largely to place shipments with railroads. . . . The result of this conference was the tariff of June 25, 1898, which is attacked in this proceeding.

The jobbers of the middle west vehemently insisted that in this tariff they had not received proper consideration, and a subsequent meeting was held at St. Paul in May, 1899, at which the matter was again gone into by the parties in interest, with the result that the Great Northern and the Northern Pacific companies modified in certain essential respects the tariff of the previous June by a supplement taking effect May 1, 1899, and known in this case as the St. Paul Supplement. This supplement reduced in some instances the differentials between car loads and less than car loads, and modified the varied commodity rates in the hardware schedule, and perhaps in some others.

The complainants insist that the tariff of June 25, 1898, was the result of an agreement between the railways and the jobbers of the Pacific Coast that tariffs should be adjusted in their favor, and that they in consideration would patronize the rail instead of the water; and that the effect of that agreement has been to largely destroy effective competition by water.

From 1871 until January 1, 1893, the Panama route was absolutely controlled with respect to Pacific Coast business in the United States by transcontinental lines, and there was during that period no competition with that line. For some years afterwards that competition was extremely active. It appears that finally the Pacific Mail became the steamer part of the line from Panama to San Francisco, while the Columbia Steamship Company continued to form the link between New York and Colon. To-day the agent of the Panama Company in New York makes the west-bound rates while the agent of the Pacific Mail at San Francisco controls the east-bound shipments. The tariffs west-bound are based upon the corresponding tariffs of the rail lines, being 20 per cent less on car loads and 30 per cent less on less than car loads. This apparently gives that route substantially the full capacity of its steamers in traffic. . . . While the testimony in this case fails to show any contract or understanding through which competition by the Panama route is limited it can hardly be said that at the present time that line affords much actual competition between the coasts.

With respect to competition by the all ocean route the matter has all along stood entirely otherwise. At first this was the only means of transportation for merchandise. As late as 1878 probably 75 per cent of the entire tonnage came in by sail. In 1884 this percentage had very much fallen, but still equaled 25 per cent. Since then there has been a further decline, the testimony showing that for the last ten years not more than 10 to 15 per cent has arrived in this way. But there is nothing in the case to show that any agreement has ever subsisted between rail lines and the route around South America as to any division of traffic, or any establishment of rates.

The principal witness as to the present state of water competition by all ocean routes was Mr. Jackson, representative of Flint, Dearborn & Co., of New York, managers of the principal line of clipper ships between the Atlantic and Pacific Coasts. . . . From his testimony it appeared that during the year 1898 there were shipped from New York to California, mainly San Francisco, by sailing vessels about 34,000 tons, and from Philadelphia about 6000 tons. Substantially the same tonnage had been forwarded the previous year, 1897. It also appeared that some other vessels were engaged in the same business between Philadelphia and San Francisco, and perhaps between New York and Pacific Coast points. Formerly the tonnage carried by these lines had been much greater than it was in those years. For some years previous to 1890 it had varied from 50,000 to 100,000 tons per annum. The rate war which broke out in 1894 diverted the tonnage from sail to rail, and the effect of this was continued after the close of those rate disturbances by the Spanish war, which rendered rates of insurance high and ships scarce. The outlook for the future was, however, said to be more promising.

Mr. Jackson . . . was also the treasurer of the American-Hawaiian Steamship Company, a corporation organized for the purpose of owning and operating a line of steamers between New York, San Francisco and Hawaii *via* the Straits of Magellan. He first testified in November, 1899, and at that time this company had placed orders for four steamers of 8500 tons each to be used in this service. It was said that these steamships would carry, beside the necessary coal, 7500 tons of freight, and would make the run from New York to San Francisco in about 60 days. It was expected that each steamer would make two trips per year, thus affording a capacity of 60,000 tons west-bound which it was believed could easily be obtained.

Subsequently, in December, 1900, Mr. Jackson again testified, and then stated that two of the steamers above referred to had already been delivered and put into service; that the two others referred to in his former testimony would soon be ready for delivery, and that his company had within the year contracted for three larger steamers for this same service with a capacity of 15,000 tons each. He stated that this would give a total carrying capacity west-bound of about 126,000 tons per annum. . . .

Almost every article which moves from the east to the Pacific Coast has been at times actually carried by ocean. A list of the articles transported during the year 1898 was introduced and it embraced nearly every article of merchandise. The territory from which this route draws its freight is mostly that in the immediate vicinity of New York. Shipments have been taken from as far west as Chicago, and even St. Louis, but this is of rare occurrence. The great bulk of its traffic is from points east of Buffalo and Pittsburg.

In the making of rates by ocean no distinction as such is observed between car-load and less than car-load lots. Mr. Jackson testified that about three fourths of the tonnage forwarded by him was in lots exceeding 30,000 pounds and one fourth in lots less than that figure; the range of the smaller lots being from 1000 to 20,000 pounds. While there is no less than car-load rate as such the amount charged per hundred pounds for smaller quantities is greater than that charged for larger quantities, the difference being from 10 to 30 cents per hundred pounds. Everything depends, however, upon the quantity offered for shipment and the state of the ship's contracts for the freight. Large quantities are often taken at very low figures. We are inclined to think that the ordinary difference made by water between car loads and less than car loads, while not a fixed sum, is considerably less than the difference prescribed by the tariff of June 25, 1898, upon rail shipments.

The witness objected to stating the exact rates at which merchandise had been carried by his line, but did give some illustrative examples; among others the following, in connection with which the rail rate is also given:

	Water Rate	Rail Rate	
		L. C. L.	C. L.
Bar iron	30 to 35¢	$1.25	$ .75
Grindstones	32½¢	1.90	.75
Soil pipe	35 to 40¢	1.90	.75
Radiators	40 to 45¢	2.20	1.30
Hardwood lumber . .	40 to 42¢	1.25	.75

It must be remembered that a water rate of a certain number of cents per hundred pounds is by no means equivalent in value to the shipper to a rail rate of the same amount. Several things must be taken into account in determining the relative desirability of the two rates. The item of marine insurance is important, and Mr. Jackson stated that this was by his sailing vessels about 1½ per cent of the value of the commodity; the time occupied in transit and the consequent loss upon the investment is an item of consequence, the ordinary run from San Francisco being in the vicinity of 135 days. In addition to this is the liability to damage by salt water in case of many articles as well as the delay and uncertainty incident upon that means of transportation. No witness was prepared to state what rate by ocean was equivalent to a rate of $1 by rail; indeed the witnesses seemed to agree that it would be impossible to answer that question definitely since its answer must depend upon the commodity transported. One witness said that after everything had been taken into account he would still pay the railways on most commodities a rate 5 per cent higher than that by water.

A portion of the disadvantages attending transportation by water will be largely obviated through the use of steamers in place of sailing vessels. As just stated the ordinary time by sail from New York to San Francisco is estimated at 135 days, but the time actually consumed often greatly exceeds this, sometimes being as much as a whole year. This uncertainty as to date of arrival has been a serious objection to that method of carriage. The steamer is expected to make the run around South America in 60 days, and its arrival can probably be counted upon with more exactness than arrivals by rail. The item of insurance will also be much less with steamers than with sailing vessels as will the loss on the investment during the period of transit. It was said that with a canal across the Isthmus of Panama the trip from New York by the steamers now ordered could be made in about 20 days, and that doubtless if such a canal were constructed faster steamers would be put on which would make the trip in from 15 to 16 days. * *

The carrier must meet this water competition mainly with the car-load rate. Ninety per cent of the merchandise brought from the east to the Pacific Coast by Pacific Coast jobbers comes in car-load lots. The less than car-load shipments are often in the nature of emergency orders requiring quick delivery and not therefore susceptible of ocean carriage. * * *

Conclusions

The complaint in this case attacks the system of rate making in vogue upon the Pacific Coast. What that system is appears in the findings of fact, and is well understood by all persons having an elementary knowledge of the situation. The rate from an eastern point like St. Louis is lowest to the so-called "terminal" upon the coast. Going east from the terminal point the rate increases until limited by the so-called "intermediate" rate. This produces a higher rate at the intermediate point through which the traffic passes to the terminal point and compels the St. Louis merchant, although nearer in distance, to pay more for the transportation of his merchandise. He insists that his rate to the nearer station ought to be no higher than to the more distant point. * * * * * *

The complaint also attacks the scheme of transcontinental rate making in force east of the Missouri river as applied to westbound rates. That system differs radically from the method followed upon the Pacific Coast. While upon the Pacific Coast the rate is lowest to the terminal at the ocean and increases toward the interior, in the east the rate from the seaboard does not increase as we proceed inland, but remains the same. This produces what is known as the blanket system of rates. The first-class rate from New York to San Francisco is $3 and the same rate applies from St. Louis. Commodity rates follow the same rule so that generally speaking rates both class and commodity to Pacific Coast terminals and points basing upon such terminals are the same from all points east of the Missouri river. This St. Louis declares to be unjust; being one thousand miles nearer San Francisco than New York it insists that it should be given the benefit of that advantage in distance.

The higher rate to the interior point in California is justified by the carriers upon the ground of water competition, the theory being this: Water competition between New York and San Francisco establishes a cheaper rate than could reasonably be exacted from the rail carrier. Merchandise at New York can be taken by water to San Francisco at the low water rate and thence carried by rail to an interior point for the water rate from New York to San Francisco plus the local rate from San Francisco to the interior point. If the rail carrier engages in this business it must meet the rate thus established by water at San Francisco, and by water and rail at the interior point. It is claimed that the carrier may at his election meet this competition and make its rates accordingly. It may therefore charge to the interior point a rate higher than the terminal rate by the local back, until a point is reached at which the rate so formed is more than a reasonable rate. This right upon the part of the carrier may perhaps be subject to certain qualifications and limitations, but generally speaking this is the theory upon which certain rates upon the Pacific Coast, which have been declared not in violation of the Act to Regulate Commerce, are constructed.

Now in theory the converse of this proposition would be true when applied to the point of origin in the east. Water transportation fixes the rate from New York to San Francisco. Pittsburg is four hundred miles west of New York. A commodity can move from Pittsburg to San Francisco in two ways; it may go directly by rail, or it may go by rail from Pittsburg to New York and from thence to San Francisco by ship. If it goes by rail and ocean manifestly the rate should be higher from Pittsburg than from New York, although Pittsburg is nearer San Francisco, since carriage by that route involves the rail haul from Pittsburg to New York. Applying this principle of water competition in the east exactly as it has been applied upon the Pacific Coast, rates to terminal points from the east would be lowest from the Atlantic seaboard and would gradually increase toward the interior until some point was reached at which the rate so constructed equaled a reasonable rate by the direct rail route. If that theory of rate making which has been sanctioned by the Courts and by the Commission in some cases were applied to this territory east of the Missouri river the rate from St. Louis to San Francisco would be, not lower than that from New York, as the complainants insist, but higher, unless the direct rail rate from St. Louis to San Francisco ought reasonably to be less than the rate established from New York by water competition.

That the same system is not in force in both the east and the west is due to differing conditions in those sections. Upon the Pacific Coast the great cities and the strong commercial interests are located at the seaboard. There are no interior towns of sufficient strength to insist upon a change of this policy, and apparently there never can be so long as the present system continues in force. In the east this is otherwise. Formerly manufacturing was mainly done upon the Atlantic seaboard, but to-day great cities have grown up and great commercial enterprises have developed in the middle west, and these demand an entrance to the markets of the Pacific Coast in tones which cannot be disregarded.

Still more important is the situation of the carriers themselves. Those lines which distribute upon the Pacific Coast control the adjustment of rates into that section, and their interests are united to maintain the present system. Indeed it is declared that to reduce intermediate rates to a level with terminal rates would bankrupt these lines, and it certainly would have a most serious effect upon their revenues. In the east we find many important systems beginning at the Missouri river or in the middle west. It is for the interest of these systems that traffic should originate at the eastern termini of their respective lines. Not only do they obtain more for the transportation of traffic so originating than they obtain from their division upon traffic originating farther east, but they also build up the industries of that locality and therefore remove these from the sphere of water competition. Moreover the traffic which the eastern connections of the transcontinental lines carry farther east is insignificant in amount and in revenue returned in comparison with the whole amount of their traffic. From these various causes it has transpired that the low rate which water competition establishes from New York has been extended to all points east of the Missouri river.

The Commission in a very recent case has examined and passed upon this same question. *Kindel et al.* v. *Atchison, Topeka & Santa Fé Railway Co. et al.*, 8 I. C. C. Rep. 608.

In that case the city of Denver alleged that by virtue of its location it was entitled to a lower rate to Pacific Coast terminals than the rate from points on the Missouri river and east. When the complaint was brought most rates were higher from Denver than from the Missouri river. The only fact upon which Denver based that claim was its location; being one thousand miles nearer San Francisco than Chicago, and nearly two thousand miles nearer San Francisco than New York, it insisted that it was entitled to a better rate. The Commission held that this did not necessarily follow; that while Denver was nearer in geographical miles it was not of necessity nearer in transportation units. The actual cost of transporting merchandise from New York to San Francisco by water was probably materially less than the cost of carrying it by rail from Denver to San Francisco. We said that if these carriers extended the low water rate of New York west to the Missouri river they must carry it still farther to Denver, but that we could not affirm upon the mere score of distance that the rate from Denver should be lower. We are satisfied with the disposition of that question in that case, and it must control the case before us.

To avoid any misapprehension it should be said that we . . . do not decide in this case that circumstances and conditions might not be such as to require a lower rate from the nearer point. If in this case the industries of St. Louis and the middle west showed that they were, by this adjustment of tariffs, excluded from the markets of the Pacific Coast their complaint might merit different consideration. But such is not the fact; on the contrary it appears that in recent years under the influence of this rate the industries, both manufacturing and jobbing, of the middle west have made steady gains upon the Pacific Coast. To-day, of all commodities transported into that territory which originate east of the Missouri it is estimated that more than 60 per cent is from points west of Buffalo and Pittsburg. The only grounds upon which the complainants rest in support of this contention are the greater proximity of the middle west, and the fact that these graded rates were formerly in effect; neither of which entitle them to the relief asked for.

It should also be observed that nothing in this decision would in any way interfere with the right of the transcontinental lines to put in effect, if they saw fit, such a system of graded rates as the complainants ask for. Carriers may or may not at their option meet the low water rate from New York. It is for the manifest interest of those lines beginning at Chicago and points west to maintain lower rates from there than from the seaboard, and if in the future such rates are established they will not be in violation of the Act to Regulate Commerce.

That branch of the complaint most discussed both in testimony and upon the argument was the alleged discrimination by the tariff of June 25, 1898, against the jobber of the middle west in favor of the jobber upon the Pacific Coast. This discrimination is accomplished, according to the complainants, by too wide a differential between car loads and less than car loads, by the application of improper varied commodity rates and by the refusal to permit shipment in mixed car loads. Of these three things the differential was by far the most prominent.

The statement of facts shows that most traffic from the east to the Pacific Coast moves upon commodity rates. Of these rates nearly one half name for the same commodity a car-load and less than car-load rate; about one third apply in any quantity, making no distinction between car loads and less than car loads, while the remaining one sixth apply to car loads only, leaving the less than car-load shipments to move under the class rate. The differential between car loads and less than car loads is all the way from nothing to $1.50 per hundred pounds, perhaps in instances even greater. Many of the differentials are exactly 50 cents; the complaint alleges that this is the average differential and the case finds that this is approximately true. Are these differentials in violation of the Act to Regulate Commerce?

In determining this the first inquiry is, by what standard shall the propriety of a differential between car loads and less than car loads be estimated? The complainants urged that the differential was justified largely by difference in expense of handling traffic at terminals, and that this difference when ascertained ought to constitute the difference between car loads and less than car loads; that the differentials thus arrived at would be approximately a fixed quantity, not varying materially with the rate or with the distance. This proposition can hardly be assented to. It really assumes that the proper differential is determined by the difference in the cost of handling the two kinds of traffic. But it appears from the statement of fact that this difference in expense is not confined to terminal points. It costs appreciably more to haul less than car-load business than car-load. If, therefore, the reason for the standard suggested by the complainants is a valid one, the differential ought to increase with the distance, and therefore ordinarily with the rate. * * * * * * * *

In order to understand the claim of the defendants it is necessary to have clearly in mind the entire situation. Traffic transported from the east to the Pacific Coast at the present time is controlled either by jobbers in the middle west or by jobbers upon the Pacific Coast. The middle west jobbers send their merchandise almost entirely in less than car-load lots. In the very nature of the case that freight is not subject to ocean competition, and the carrier may safely disregard such competition in the making of these less than car-load rates which apply to that transportation.

The Pacific Coast jobber upon the other hand brings his supplies from the east to his warehouse almost entirely in large lots. It is found that 90 per cent of his entire rail traffic moves in car loads. Of the remaining 10 per cent a considerable part is in the nature of emergency orders, which require quick delivery and which could not therefore be transported by water. In order to obtain the business of the Pacific Coast jobber it is necessary that the rail carrier make an attractive car-load rate, the less than car-load being of comparatively little importance. There is a certain amount of less than car-load traffic which can and does move by water, as the statement of actual movements by clipper ship and the tariffs of the Panama route show; but broadly speaking the less than car-load business is, from its point of origin, not subject to water competition; the car-load freight is that for which the rail carrier mainly contends with the ocean; hence water competition tends to produce a wide difference between the car-load and less than car-load.

There is still another reason. The fact that business originating in the middle west almost of necessity moves by rail, immediately suggests the thought that it would be for the ultimate interest of those lines which begin in the middle west to make such rates as would enable all business to be done by that section. Up to the present time two causes have prevented this. First, it has been in the interest of certain lines, notably the Southern Pacific, that traffic should move from the Atlantic seaboard, and second, the Pacific Coast jobber has objected to being extinguished. His warehouse is by the sea, and if the rail line makes a rate which will not permit him to bring traffic by rail and do business against his eastern competitor he must and he will turn to the ocean for relief. This may be disastrous to him; it proved to be so when tried; but it is even more disastrous to the railway. For the purpose therefore of maintaining peace, and at the same time obtaining a large part of the business of the Pacific Coast jobber, the railroad aims to maintain a differential which will enable that jobber to do business.

We have next to consider the interest of the wholesaler upon the coast and in the middle west, and it is really the conflicting claims of these parties which lie at the bottom of this controversy. The jobber upon the Pacific Coast insists that he rests under certain disadvantages in comparison with his eastern rival which render it extremely difficult for him to maintain himself without some advantage in the freight rate, and that his natural advantage of location entitles him to this preference. The alleged disadvantages have been fully stated in the findings of fact. They mainly spring from the limited territory to which his operations are necessarily confined. Owing to the adjustment of freight rates he cannot operate in any event more than about three hundred miles to the east, and the same distance north or south brings him to a point where both his eastern rival and his local competitor have an advantage in the rate. The field which is open to him is narrow, estimated in square miles, and even narrower when estimated by the population which he can reach. From this it results that the volume of his sales is small and the expense of transacting business large in proportion; still further his location and the manner in which he obtains his supplies force him to carry a disproportionately large stock. The Pacific Coast jobber finds it extremely difficult to maintain himself against his eastern rival without some advantage in the transportation charge, and we have seen that his location upon the seaboard by opening two avenues of communication gives him a certain advantage in this respect.

Most of the limitations under which the jobber upon the Pacific Coast works do not attach to the jobber in the middle west who is competing upon the Pacific Coast. His territory is extensive and the volume of his sales large. He goes east to New England, south to the Gulf of Mexico, north to the Dominion line, west 1700 miles, and whether he does or does not cover this narrow strip west of the 115th meridian in no way affects his general prosperity or his continued existence. This is true not of every jobber in the middle west but of those great houses in whose interest this complaint is prosecuted.

The controversy has been conducted by the railways and the two sets of wholesalers already referred to, but it must not be decided with reference to their necessities or desires alone. There is another interest seldom represented upon these hearings, but always to be considered by this Commission, and that is the consumer. No adjustment of rates made in the interest of carriers or of wholesalers should be permitted if it antagonizes unduly the public welfare. Considering the question before us as an economic problem two things should be secured. First, these commodities should be brought to the consumer at the least possible expense. Second, in both transportation and distribution unfettered competition should be maintained, thereby securing to the consumer the benefits to which he is entitled.

The greater part of the supplies consumed upon the Pacific Coast originate twenty-five hundred miles from the point of consumption, and these supplies should be transported that twenty-five hundred miles in the cheapest manner. Waste is always expensive; if the railways are required to carry this merchandise in an extravagant manner that extravagance is finally borne by the public. We have seen that the actual cost of handling this traffic in less than car loads is 50 per cent greater than the cost of handling car loads. It seems probable, therefore, that the cheapest way in which these supplies can be taken across the continent and distributed to the consumer is by transporting them in solid car loads from the factory to the warehouse upon the Pacific Coast and thence distributing to the retailer in less than car loads, although the effect of this may be somewhat diminished by the back haul from the wholesaler to the interior point which is not performed to the same extent where goods are sent across the continent in less than car-load shipments directly to the store of the retailer. It would in our opinion be unfortunate from an economic standpoint to establish a condition which would require distribution entirely or mainly in less than car-load lots from the middle west.

It is urged however that this tariff in effect stifles competition, thereby increasing the price to the consumer. It is alleged that this is done in two ways, first, by discouraging water competition and thereby permitting the maintenance of too high a rate, second, by restricting the market in which the retailer can buy, thus increasing the price to him and his customer.

The rate war of 1894 originated in the desire of the merchants of San Francisco to obtain a lower freight rate. The means which they employed was ocean transportation, and in that contest the jobber of the Pacific Coast was upon the side of the ocean. As a matter of retaliation rail lines gave to the eastern jobber every facility for entering Pacific Coast territory. Not only was the general level of rates reduced but differentials were abolished and the privilege of mixing shipments increased.

The result as has been noted in the statement of facts was disastrous to both parties. The San Francisco jobber lost in territory and in profits; the railways suffered severely in the diminution of revenues. At the expiration of three years both parties were anxious for relief and were seeking some ground of compromise. This was the genesis of the meetings at Del Monte and Milwaukee, and it was to effectuate this purpose that the tariff of June 25, 1898, was promulgated. The railway desired to retain its business at higher rates; the jobber upon the coast desired to retain his territory and increase his profits. There can be no doubt that the railways understood that the jobbers would patronize their lines at the higher rate, and that the jobbers had given them so to understand. There was no definite agreement of this sort, nothing like that involved in the old special contract system. It was rather a result growing out of the mutual interest of both parties.

The practical interpretation of this understanding has been to enable the railways to retain just about the same proportion of traffic at materially better rates. The tonnage brought from the Atlantic to the Pacific Coast since June 25, 1898, has not differed greatly from that of two or three years before. It ought perhaps to have increased, for the Spanish war had dealt this traffic a severe blow both by increasing the rates of insurance and by decreasing the supply of ships, and with the close of that war this traffic might be expected to recover. Clearly it is likely to do so in the future. The tonnage moving during the present year will probably greatly surpass that of the last six or seven years and within two years to come will be greater than at any time since 1880. We find a disposition upon the part of the coast jobbers to patronize the ocean whenever a rate is offered which is decidedly advantageous. It must be remembered that the effect of the rate war of 1894 was to depress ocean as well as rail rates.

Rail lines could not probably increase their car-load rates, and if we were to order a reduction of these differentials that would result in a reduction of the less than car-load rate. Another result would be to compel the coast jobber to seek cheaper means of transportation which might finally lead to a further reduction of the car-load rate and to the same disturbances which have previously occurred. We have already said that the reasonableness of the less than car-load rates considered by themselves is not questioned. Ought we then to order this reduction? If the effect of the present tariff, owing to any understanding between the rail lines and the coast jobbers, was to extinguish or seriously cripple ocean competition it would be our plain duty to interfere; but in fact this competition seems to be in a prosperous state. If the effect were to maintain a scale of rates unreasonably high, our duty would be equally plain; but there is no suggestion that this is true of the present terminal rates. We are not unmindful of the fact that a reduction in the terminal rate works a corresponding reduction at all points which base upon that rate; nor do we overlook the fact, although there is no mention of it in this case, that the earnings of transcontinental lines indicate that some reduction in their rates might properly be made; but we are of the opinion that if any such reduction is to take place it should be in the high and discriminating intermediate rate rather than in the already extremely low terminal charge. Competition is not healthy when it becomes destructive to the competing parties. It was said upon the argument that this present adjustment provided a state of "equilibrium" under which both the rail and the water, the east and the west could fairly compete. So far as the testimony shows we are inclined to think that this is true of competition by water.

It is said that this tariff is unlawful because it excludes the jobber of the middle west from this territory, gives to the wholesaler upon the Pacific Coast a monopoly, restricts the market in which the retailer can buy and thereby enhances the price to the consumer. The territory of the Pacific Coast jobber is extremely limited, and he is inclined to insist that he should be left in the peaceable possession of that territory; that the jobber of the middle west whose territory extends a thousand miles to the east and seventeen hundred miles to the west ought not to covet the narrow strip which lies beyond the 115th meridian. We do not accede altogether to this view. The adjustment of rates upon the Pacific Coast is such that it confines the local jobber to certain spheres making them almost omnipotent within those spheres; and for this reason competition from the east, which under this same adjustment of rates, tends to diffuse itself over the whole coast, is important. If there be no controlling reason to the contrary, rates should be so adjusted as to permit the operation of the wholesaler from the middle west throughout all this territory. * * * *

Viewing the case in this broad sense we find that these differentials are not abnormal when compared with others in different parts of this country at the present time; that they are not greater than those in effect under the west-bound transcontinental tariff of 1893, and not greatly disproportionate to the actual difference in cost of service. Considering them with respect to their bearing upon the parties immediately interested, namely, the carriers and the two classes of jobbers, we find that they conserve the interests of the carrier, that they give to the jobber upon the Pacific Coast a measure of advantage to which he is perhaps entitled by his location, and which he must probably have if he is to continue to exist, while they permit the jobber of the middle west to transact a considerable amount of business in this territory at a reasonable profit. Viewed as an economic problem, the tariff fosters that method of distribution which is probably the cheapest upon the coast, and at the same time permits reasonable competition and thereby secures to the customer the full benefits of such competition. This situation is in some sense the outgrowth of past experience. It is satisfactory to most interests upon the Pacific Coast, and we are not disposed to find fault with the adjustment of rates as a whole.

While, however, we cannot condemn this tariff as a whole upon the grounds put forward by the complainants, we are of the opinion that many of its details are in violation of law. Over four hundred commodity rates apply to car loads only, leaving the movement of these commodities in less than car loads to be governed by the class rate. This produces a differential which even under the peculiar circumstances of this traffic is in many cases excessive, provided there be any commercial reason for a corresponding less than car-load rate. In some instances there is none. Coal, for example, moves usually in car loads and takes a low commodity rate. What little movement occurs in less than car-load lots is not competitive with car-load shipments, and may well be governed by the class rate, although the difference between the two would otherwise be undue. Many similar instances will readily occur, but we are impressed from an inspection of these schedules that there are still many other instances in which the difference is altogether too great.

It is impossible to fix any standard by which these differentials shall be determined, for the reason that circumstances often render the application of a greater differential proper in one case than in another. This record finds that many of the commodity rates show a differential of 50 cents per 100 pounds, and it is said that this may be termed the average differential; it further finds that the cost of handling this less than car-load traffic exceeds the cost of handling car-load traffic by about 50 per cent. We are inclined to think that a differential which is at once more than 50 cents per 100 pounds and more than 50 per cent of the car-load rate is *prima facie* excessive. We do not mean that every differential may lawfully equal this, nor yet that every differential which exceeds this is unlawful, but that a differential exceeding this requires special justification.

* * * * * * * * *

FIFER, *Commissioner*, dissenting:

I concur in the opinion to the extent of deeming it inadvisable to attempt, without further investigation, a settlement of the great questions involved in this continental situation.

The undisputed facts involve three propositions: the postage stamp or blanket rate for the whole eastern territory from the Atlantic Coast to the Missouri river; the wide difference between the car-load and less than car-load rate on west-bound traffic, and, the system common to all, the western mountain territory of making the rates from the east to any intermediate point by adding to the through rate to any Pacific Coast terminal the local rate back to the intermediate point.

Concerning the first, while it may be conceded that the so-called blanket rate is too firmly established, and has proved in too many instances of a great utility and profit to both the road and its patrons to warrant me in denouncing it, yet I am firmly of opinion that, carried to the extent of above a thousand miles, as in this instance, on practically all the schedules, is such an exaggeration of the system as to work serious injustice to the jobbers of the middle west by robbing them of the natural advantages of geographical location to which they are as much entitled as are points located upon the Atlantic Coast, which for that very reason are favored by rates that are denied to those situated farther west.

For this reason it seems to me the only solution of the problem which will be fair to all parties is the graded rate, perhaps not in the proportions formerly in force; but that, at least, recognizes the advantage of proximity to the western market which

Pittsburg enjoys over New York, Chicago over Pittsburg, and the Missouri river over Chicago.

There seems to me to be just ground for protest against the differentials between car-load and less than car-load rates. These differences have been within a comparatively late period so much increased as to lead to the inference, inevitable to me, that they have been established with deliberate intention to discourage less than car-load shipments. To what extent these differentials should be modified, if at all, must depend upon a wider inquiry and deeper investigation than we have been able to accomplish at this stage of the present case.

The system of rate making which establishes rates for intermediate points by a combination of the through rate to the coast terminal point and the local rate back to destination has much in its favor, as water competition is held to justify even unreasonably low through rates, and as the freight thus favored is secured by the railroads by a rate which is to prevent its carriage by water — all freight, in theory, is treated as if it reached the coast by water and takes its place thereafter as local freight east — instead of through freight west.

But there comes a situation and a locality when this theory of rate making must break down of its own weight, and with a blanket rate from the east reaching to the Missouri river, the short middle west haul, say from the Missouri river to Ogden, is out of all proportion to the haul from the Missouri river to New York, from New York to San Francisco by water and back by rail to Ogden. Upon its face such a condition carries suspicion, and it requires some explanation to justify a situation where a haul practically a thousand miles shorter at each end is higher than the through rate. Just how far the combination through rate with the local back may extend under these circumstances will depend upon where it meets a reasonable rate from the east, and on that question in this case the evidence is incomplete; we having developed only enough to bring me to fear that the schedules in force are discriminating and unjust.

The opinion finds that the Pacific Coast jobber carries his business not farther east than the 115th meridian, or about 300 miles from the coast, and I am inclined to believe that the evidence fairly sustains that finding. But an examination of the tariffs on file in the office of the Commission shows that the zone of their operations may be much wider, the combination rate basing on Pacific Coast terminals extending as far east as 800 or more miles in numerous instances.

For many articles of hardware, such as axes and other edged tools, picks and mattocks, bar, rod and sheet iron and steel, billets, blooms, ingots and scrap iron, the combination rate extends east on the Southern Pacific Railroad (Ogden line) to various points from Millis, Wyo., 828 miles east of Sacramento, to Cheyenne, Wyo., 1239 miles east of Sacramento, except on picks and mattocks, on which the combination rate equals the intermediate rate at Rye Patch, Nev., 273 miles east of Sacramento. On the Southern Pacific (El Paso line) the combination rate extends east to various points from Strauss, N.M., 797 miles east of Los Angeles, to San Elizario, Tex., 833 miles east of Los Angeles, except on picks and mattocks on which the combination rate equals the intermediate rate at Montezuma, Ariz., 400 miles east of Los Angeles. On the Great Northern line the combination rate extends east to various points from Troy, Mont., 579 miles east of Portland, on picks and mattocks, to Wagner, Mont., 1042 miles east of Portland, on billets, blooms, etc. On the Northern Pacific the combination rate tends east to various points from Noxon, Mont., 662 miles east of Portland, on picks and mattocks, to Central Park, Mont., 1009 miles east of Portland, on billets, blooms, etc. On the Santa Fé System the combination rate extends east to various points from Amboy, Cal., 226 miles east of Los Angeles, on picks and mattocks, to Albuquerque, N.M., 889 miles east of Los Angeles, on billets, blooms, etc.

Thus it will be seen that while the business of the coast jobber may, through his own volition or methods of transacting business, be confined to territory lying west of the 115th meridian, there is nothing in existing tariffs that would in any way so limit his field of operations. So far as these rates are concerned, he can apparently do business as profitably as far east as the points named as he can in the territory lying between the 115th meridian and the Pacific Coast. It should be noted that the differences between the car-load and less than car-load rates complained of in this case serve, under this method of making rates to the intermediate point, to greatly enlarge the Pacific Coast jobber's sphere of operations, and that he will sooner or later take full advantage of the opportunity thus afforded is to be expected.

It seems to me necessary that in the further investigation to which the opinion in this case tends, the feature of reasonable rates for the whole so-called western mountain territory should be made a main issue that the inquiry may develop whether or not the zone of combination rates should not be narrowed to points nearer the coast, and thus remove not only a burden on our commerce but an apparent discrimination that invites criticism, even if justifiable.

The Nevada Railroad Commission Case[1]

Lane, *Commissioner:*

The highest main-line rates to be found in the United States are those from eastern points to stations in Nevada. For carrying a carload of first-class traffic containing 20,000 pounds from Omaha to Reno the Union Pacific-Southern Pacific line charges $858. If a like carload is carried 154 miles further, to Sacramento, the charge is but $600. The first-class rate to the more distant point, Sacramento, is $3 per 100 pounds, and to the nearer point, Reno, $4.29 per 100 pounds. If a like carload of freight originates at Denver, 500 miles west of Omaha, the same rates to Reno and Sacramento apply; and if the freight originates at Boston, 1700 miles east of Omaha, the rates are the same. This interesting rate condition arises out of two simple facts: (1) The whole of the United States from Colorado common points to the Atlantic seaboard, barring a few of the southeastern

[1] Decided June 6, 1910. 19 Interstate Commerce Commission Report, 238. Transcontinental rates are discussed in Ripley's Railroads: Rates and Regulation, pp. 395, 610.

states, is one wide group or zone from which practically uniform rates to Pacific coast water points are made, and (2) the rates to Reno are based upon these blanket rates to coast cities, and amount to the sum of the rates to the coast plus the local rates back to point of destination.

This great zone, extending from the Rocky Mountains to the Atlantic, a distance of over 2000 miles, from which practically uniform rates are made to Pacific coast terminal cities, is probably without parallel in the railroad world, excepting for a similar eastward blanket extended to Pacific coast producing points. The zone in which the same rates apply on California citrus fruits, for instance, extends from Salt Lake City on the west to Portland, Me. It is manifest that the transcontinental railroads have made a near approximation to the postage-stamp system of rate making. Their policy has been to give to all eastern producing markets an opportunity to sell to the terminal cities upon a parity as to transportation charges and to give to Pacific coast producing points access to all eastern markets upon a like basis. To the great basin lying between the Rocky Mountains and the Sierra Nevadas the carriers have in a limited degree extended this same policy by making rates into Nevada base on the coast cities, and thus, the carriers say, they give to this territory the advantage of its proximity to the Pacific seaboard; that the rates to the latter are made low because of water competition between the Atlantic and Pacific ports — lower than would be justified were Sacramento and San Francisco not upon the water — and that Nevada rates would be still higher but for its nearness to the Pacific coast.

The State of Nevada, through its railroad commission, now comes asking that Nevada points be given the same rates as are now given to Pacific coast terminals, urging that these coast rates are not unreasonably low in themselves, and are not the product of any real water competition.

The complaint originally filed in this case made the Southern Pacific the sole defendant; the reasonableness of the rates from the east to Nevada were not attacked, excepting in so far as they are based on the rates to further western points, and include a back-haul charge. As the complaint then stood the petition was that this Commission should hold it to be unreasonable for the Southern Pacific, delivering freight at Reno and other points in Nevada, to charge for a back haul which is not in fact given, and that we should adjudge the rates to Sacramento to be reasonable as applied to the intermediate points. Later the complaint was amended by adding carriers east of Ogden forming a single through route from the Atlantic coast. So that the petition of Nevada now is that from all points upon this through route reasonable rates shall be fixed which shall not exceed those now applicable on shipments from such points to the more distant coast terminals. It is suggested by the complainant that we bring in other carriers as defendants, so that the entire eastern territory may be covered by our order. This we think unnecessary, assuming, as we do, that the conclusions here reached as to a through route from the east to the west will be adopted and established by other lines similarly situated.

Construction of Nevada Rates

To reach a clear understanding of the basis upon which Nevada rates in general are now fixed, it is necessary to bear primarily in mind the fact before referred to, that the carriers of the country have united in establishing a zone 2000 miles in width from which rates are practically uniform to what are known as "coast terminals." There are 152 of these coast terminals, 97 of which are in California. They are points more or less arbitrarily established by the carriers, but which are either upon inlets from the ocean or rivers running to such inlets, or are but slightly removed from such water points. The most prominent coast terminals are Seattle, Tacoma, Portland, Sacramento, San Jose, Stockton, Oakland, San Francisco, Los Angeles, and San Diego. To these coast terminals are extended what are known as "terminal rates" on westbound transcontinental traffic. These rates apply either from all of eastern defined territory or from separate groups therein. The shaded portion of the accompanying map indicates eastern defined territory and the groups into which it is divided. These groups are lettered from A to J. A is limited to New York City piers, and has to do only with shipments by steamship *via* Gulf ports; B covers New England territory; C, New York territory and the middle states, with New York City as the principal point; D, Chicago and adjacent territory; E, the Mississippi river, with St. Louis as the principal city; F, the Missouri river; G, Kansas; H, Oklahoma; I, Texas; and J, Colorado, with Denver as its central point.

Class rates. Coming, then, to the construction of the Nevada class rates, we find that the carriers have employed three methods of construction during the past two years. Prior to January 1, 1909, there existed a body of what were known as intermediate class rates to Reno from certain designated eastern points. These rates were, on first class —

From Chicago-Milwaukee common points	$3.90
From Mississippi river common points	3.70
From Missouri river common points	3.50
From Colorado common points	3.00

An alternative clause gave Reno the right to the combination rate based on Sacramento whenever that should be lower. This indefinite method of stating rates the Commission condemned in a general ruling. The tariffs were then changed so as to cancel the alternative clause and the intermediate class rates and thus to make all Nevada rates base on Sacramento. This was the situation when the case was heard. Later, however, in June of last year, a third plan was adopted, and that now obtains, viz., to divide Nevada into two zones with Humboldt as the dividing point. Points west of Humboldt take the Sacramento combination. Points east of Humboldt take generally the Ogden combination. It is unnecessary herein to trace the history and the effect of these various changes in the method of rate basing. We shall deal with the rates to all Nevada points as joint rates. And inasmuch as rates on all ten classes were quoted by the carriers' tariffs from all eastern defined territory to coast terminals and therefore by combination to interior points, at the time when this proceeding was brought, we shall consider that our jurisdiction extends to the installation of such rates to all of such territory.

To ascertain the rate upon a shipment from New York to Reno one looks in vain for any one tariff in which such rate is to be found. By examination of the tariff of the Transcontinental Freight Bureau, to which the Southern Pacific Company is a party, this note is discovered:

Rates to intermediate points

When no specific rate is named to an intermediate point shown in Transcontinental Freight Bureau Circular No. 16–C (I. C. C. No. 864), supplements thereto, or reissues thereof, rate to such an intermediate point will be made by adding to the rate shown to the point designated herein as "Terminal," which is nearest destination of shipment, the local rate from nearest terminal point to destination.

Turning to Transcontinental Freight Bureau Circular No. 16–C (the issue at the date at which this complaint was brought), we find Reno named as an intermediate point, and that the nearest terminal to Reno is Sacramento, 154 miles west of Reno. We find, then, by returning to the Transcontinental Freight Bureau west-bound tariff, the rate applicable upon the shipment to Sacramento. Then, having ascertained this from a tariff to which all of the carriers from New York to Sacramento are parties, we must next find the local rate from Sacramento to the destination of the freight, which is east of Sacramento. This local rate, Sacramento to Reno, we find in a tariff to which the Southern Pacific Company alone is a party. Thus we have, through a maze of tariffs, at length discovered the rate from New York to Reno, which is made up of a joint through rate to Sacramento and a local rate of the Southern Pacific Company alone from Sacramento back to Reno.

The all-rail class rates, in cents, per 100 pounds from eastern defined territory to coast terminals were, when this case was brought, as follows:

	Classes									
	1	2	3	4	5	A	B	C	D	E
Groups B, C, D, E, F, G, H, and I	$3.00	$2.60	$2.20	$1.90	$1.65	$1.60	$1.25	$1.00	$1.00	$0.95
Group J :	3.00	2.60	2.00	1.75	1.60	1.40	1.20	.95	.85	.80

An examination of present tariffs will show that from New England and New York territories (Groups B and C) no class rates below fourth class are now extended. Prior to January 1, 1909, however, and at the time this complaint was brought, rates were given for the full 10 classes from these groups, and such rates upon the $3 scale are now given to coast terminals from Group A, the freight being carried from the New York City piers to New Orleans and Galveston by ocean carriers and thence by rail. It will also be seen that from Group J slightly lower rates are made on all classes below second class than are made from other groups. With these exceptions, however, the rates are uniform throughout the whole eastern defined territory as to classified freight.

The local rates on classes from Sacramento to Reno are as follows:

Class	1	2	3	4	5	A	B	C	D	E
Rate	129	112	102	87	78	78	24	23.5	25.5	25.5

The result of the combination on Sacramento is therefore to produce the following rates to Reno:

From Groups B, C, D, E, F, G, H, and I:

Class	1	2	3	4	5	A	B	C	D	E
Rate	429	373	322	277	243	238	159	133½	125½	120½

From Group J:

Class	1	2	3	4	5	A	B	C	D	E
Rate	429	373	302	262	238	218	154	128½	110½	105½

Rates to points east of Humboldt, such as Winnemucca and Elko, under the present method of making rates on the Ogden combination, vary as the rate from point of origin to Ogden.

The effect of this change in method of making rates may be illustrated briefly by the statement that the first-class rate to Reno from Chicago prior to January 1, 1909, was \$3.90, whereas it is now \$4.29; from Missouri river \$3.50, and now \$4.29. To Elko, on the other hand, the first-class rate from Chicago is now \$4.27, as against a previous rate of \$4.72½, when the rate based on Sacramento.

For many years the class rates to interior points, such as Reno, were no higher than to the terminals. On April 11, 1893, the practice of maintaining lower terminal rates was instituted. The first line of figures in the table below shows the Reno rates when this case was brought; the second line, the rates in 1892; and the third line, the difference, or the amount by which the rates have been increased.

To Reno from	Classes									
	1	2	3	4	5	A	B	C	D	E
Missouri river common points	429	373	322	277	243	238	159	133½	125½	120½
1892 rates	350	300	250	200	175	175	155	125	110	100
Difference	79	73	72	77	68	63	4	8½	15½	20½
Mississippi river common points	429	373	322	277	243	238	159	133½	125½	120½
1892 rates	370	320	260	205	180	182	163	130	115	105
Difference	59	53	62	72	63	56	...	3½	10½	15½
Chicago common points	429	373	322	277	243	238	159	133½	125½	120½
1892 rates	390	340	270	210	185	190	170	135	120	110
Difference	39	33	52	67	58	48	...	...	5½	10½

Commodity rates. While there are many hundred commodity rates extended to coast terminals, there are but few given to intermediate points. On the following articles the commodity rates are the same to Utah and Nevada points as to Pacific coast terminals from Groups D, E, F, G, H, I, and J of eastern defined territory, which include all points from Chicago west:

Apples; bananas; beer, in wood; bones; broom corn; butter, butterine, oleomargarine, eggs, cheese, and dressed poultry; cars, street; barley, corn, rye, oats, and speltz, c. l. and l. c. l.; bran and shorts, c. l. and l. c. l.; brewer's grits, brewer's meal, corn meal, corn chop or chop feed, chopped corn, cracked corn, and hominy; buckwheat, c. l. and l. c. l.; wheat, c. l. and l. c. l.; cooperage, cranberries; fertilizers, n. o. s.; household goods, c. l. and l. c. l.; live stock; machinery, mining; mineral-water bottles, returning; oil cake and oil-cake meal; onions; onion sets, l. c. l.; packing-house products; pineapples; plaster, building; poultry, alive; railway equipment; and staves and headings.

As to all but two or three of these commodities, the rates are the same to Reno as to Sacramento from Chicago. That is to say, the blanket rate made from all eastern defined territory to coast terminals on these commodities is applied from Chicago to Reno. There are a few other commodities upon which commodity rates are given to Reno which are somewhat higher than the rates from Chicago to Sacramento, viz., automobiles, buggies, carriages, wagons, vehicles, and coal, coke, and guano from certain far western points. From an examination of the tariffs it appears that the transcontinental commodity rates — rates from eastern defined territory to the coast terminals — are at the present time higher than they were ten years ago by a very considerable percentage and this regardless of the fact that the base of supplies has been constantly moving westward, thereby narrowing the distance between point of production and consumption.

Volume of Nevada Traffic

Nevada is colloquially known as the "Sage Brush State," and from the car window it presents the spectacle of an almost uninterrupted waste. Railroad men speak of it as a "bridge" — unproductive territory across which freight must be carried to reach points of consumption. The figures of the Southern Pacific demonstrate, however, that while Nevada traffic may at one time have been negligible such is no longer the case.

Some time before this proceeding was brought the Southern Pacific Company, which is the lessee of the Central Pacific running from Ogden west into California, brought suit in the United States circuit court for the district of Nevada attacking certain rate schedules upon state traffic established by the state commission. In support of its case the Southern Pacific Company filed an affidavit made by Mr. C. B. Seger, auditor of the Southern Pacific Company, showing the earnings of the Central Pacific on business wholly within the state, on business passing through the state, on business originating in and passing out of the state, and on business originating outside and having its destination in the state, for the fiscal year ending June 30, 1907. Mr. Seger said by way of explaining his figures:

The freight earnings accruing to and made by said Southern Pacific Company in Nevada, being the revenue itself, without reference to its disposition under any lease, agreement, or otherwise, are derived for the said fiscal year 1907 from through and local business, understanding by local business such as is strictly intrastate in character, picked up and laid down within the limits of the State of Nevada, and understanding by through business such as is interstate in character. Further differentiating, said interstate business consists, first, of business originating outside and coming into the state; second, of business originating in and passing out of the state; and, third, of business originating outside the state, having destination beyond the state, and, in relation to the state itself, simply passing through the state. The freight earnings for said fiscal year, and pertaining to the said business as above classified, are set forth under the appropriate heads, and are, in fact, as follows:

	Revenue	Percentage of Total
Intrastate	$159,791.40	0.02
Originating outside and coming into the state	1,683,687.69	.20
Originating in and passing out of the state	831,802.96	.10
	2,675,282.05	.32
Passing through the state	5,578,282.28	.68
Sum total	$8,253,564.33	1.00

Surprising as these figures are they apparently do not fully set forth the extent of Nevada business at this time, as is shown by an exhibit filed by the Southern Pacific Company in the present case, giving the business west of Ogden for the single month of February, 1909, which may be epitomized thus:

	Revenue	Percentage of Total	Tonnage	Percentage of Total
Intrastate	$29,001.00	0.03	4,715	0.04
Into and out of Nevada and Utah west of Ogden . . .	314,379.65	.38	64,367	.50
	343,380.65	.41	69,182	.54
Passing through the state . . .	495,128.37	.59	60,271	.46
Total for month of February, 1909	$838,509.02	1.00	130,453	1.00

Another most interesting showing is made by the Seger affidavit as to passenger business on the Southern Pacific in the State of Nevada for the year 1907, the figures given being these:

	Revenue	Percentage
Intrastate	$286,235.65	10
Originating outside and coming into the state . .	357,511.55	13
Originating in and passing out of the state . . .	267,582.85	9
		— 22
		— 32
Passing through the state	1,962,915.33	68
Sum total	$2,874,245.38	100

The statement for the month of February, 1909, referred to above, sets forth very clearly not only the volume of business going into and out of Nevada and the earnings of the Southern Pacific thereon, but also gives a specific analysis of the sources of the traffic, showing the volume which comes into Nevada from the east and that which comes from California. Under "Question 2" below will be found a statement of the freight received at Nevada and Utah points from points west of Calvada, which is a station directly on the California-Nevada state line. This table, however, should not mislead; a considerable percentage of the traffic from California is traffic of eastern origin reshipped from California to Nevada. The table also includes coal and other commodities of very large tonnage (approximately one-half of the total in weight) coming from points west of eastern defined territory.

Territorial Movement	Total	
	Tons	Southern Pacific Earnings
Gross total tonnage and earnings of the Southern Pacific Co. for the month of February, 1909 . .	913,302	$3,422,529.00
Question No. 1		
Freight *via* Ogden to California	37,886	320,220.55
Freight *via* Ogden from California	22,385	174,907.82
	60,271	$495,128.37
Question No. 2		
Freight *via* Ogden to points in Nevada and Utah . .	17,485	66,284.88
Freight received at Nevada and Utah points from points west of Calvada	16,823	144,965.00
Freight *via* Ogden from points in Nevada and Utah	18,381	33,462.77
Freight forwarded from points in Nevada and Utah to points west of Calvada	11,678	69,667.00
	64,367	$314,379.65
Question No. 3A		
Freight received in California, San Francisco and north, from all points in California, including interchange with connecting lines in California . . .	189,827	$365,168.00
Question No. 3B		
Freight picked up and laid down in Nevada and Utah and freight moving between Nevada and Utah —		
Nevada to Nevada	4,046	21,839.00
Utah to Utah	144	948.00
Utah to Nevada	499	5,122.00
Nevada to Utah	26	1,092.00
	4,715	$29,001.00

There was a time, doubtless, when Nevada traffic, save to the mines on its westernmost border, was but trifling. At present, however, it has a traffic, both freight and passenger, which is far too considerable to be overlooked under the rule *de minimis.* And it is to be remembered that the figures given apply to but one road, whereas a second is in operation across the state to the south, and a third is beginning operations on the north.

Sources of Eastern Traffic

It is interesting in this connection to regard the point of origin of this eastern freight. The railroad commission of Nevada had access to the billing of all shipments reaching Reno, and from these compiled a series of statements which appear to show that the great body of Nevada traffic which comes directly from the east *via* Ogden originates west of the Indiana-Illinois state line.

From one exhibit it appears that of the 1,063,687 pounds of less-than-carload shipments originating in eastern defined territory and delivered at Reno during the months of January, February, March, and April, 1908, only 10 per cent originated at the Atlantic coast cities of New York, Boston, and Philadelphia, and only 25 per cent in Connecticut, District of Columbia, Maine, Maryland, Massachusetts, New Jersey, New York, Pennsylvania, and Virginia. This exhibit further shows that on the traffic moved the charges were $32,719.30; that if terminal rates had been applied charges would have been $21,956.24; and that the difference is $10,748.07. In other words, the charges on these shipments to Reno were 48.3 per cent higher than would have been the charges on the same shipments had they been carried over the mountains to Sacramento.

Another exhibit shows that of 21,000,000 pounds of carload freight, earning $278,000, moved from eastern defined territory into Reno, 9,500,000 pounds, earning $120,000, moved in at rates no higher than terminals. It further shows that only 4,500,000 pounds of the 21,000,000 originated east of Chicago. This exhibit shows, aside from the products carried to Reno at terminal rates, that the charges were, for the year 1908, $157,824.94; that the terminal charge would have been $99,679.90; and the difference, $58,524.40. In other words, the charges on carload shipments to Reno were 59 per cent higher than the charges on the same shipments would have been had they been carried to Sacramento.

Commissioner Thurtell estimated from the figures at his hand that the total receipts under present rates upon business brought into Reno *via* Ogden for the year 1908 amounted to

$454,343.69 and under terminal rates the revenue would have been $363,865.23, a reduction of $90,478.46. The statement also shows that the revenue to the Southern Pacific from this business was $268,516.40 and would have been under terminal rates $178,037.94, a reduction of $90,478.46, or about 33 per cent. Expressed in revenue the Southern Pacific on the haul from Ogden to Reno earned $11.51 per ton, while if terminal rates had been charged its earnings would have been $7.63 per ton.

On the whole, the figures given in this case, which are the most authoritative thus far presented to the Commission with reference to the sources of westbound transcontinental traffic, indicate that less than 25 per cent of the traffic into Reno from the east originates east of Chicago, while 75 per cent originates between Chicago and Denver. In other words, the needs of the people on the west coast may be and are in great part supplied from sources nearer home than the Atlantic seaboard.

The manufacturing center of the country has moved westward and rates from the Atlantic seaboard that were once necessary are now almost unused. It may be historically the fact, as the carriers assert, that the transcontinental blanket rates given to the Pacific coast cities were put in to meet water competition from the Atlantic coast points, and that these rates were extended westward from the Atlantic as matter of grace to western manufacturers and producers; to-day, however, it might well be said that this blanket is extended not westward, but eastward, so as to give the eastern manufacturer or jobber some opportunity to reach the far western markets.

Water Competition

As we have seen, the rates are higher on almost all commodities from eastern producing points to Reno than on these same commodities to Sacramento, the more distant point. Without explanation this constitutes a violation of the long-and-short-haul clause of the act. The carriers justify the lower rates to the more distant point upon the ground of water competition. They say that the rates charged to Reno and other Nevada cities are reasonable in themselves measured by the cost of the service to the carrier or the value of the service to the shipper, and that rates to the coast cities measured by these standards are too low to be considered reasonable and would not be in effect but for the force of water competition. The Nevada commission, on the other hand, contends that while some commerce does move from the Atlantic seaboard by water, the volume is so small that it is not influential in determining the present rate to the coast terminals; that the coast rate itself is reasonable, and therefore that the application of a higher rate to an intermediate point can not be justified. The making of higher intermediate rates, they strongly urge, is a matter of railway policy and not of railway necessity, in that the railways wish to develop the coast cities as jobbing centers to the exclusion of interior points; that the revenues of the carriers would not be seriously impaired were this policy abrogated and as low rates given to the intermountain country as are now extended to the coast cities.

It is no reflection upon the traffic manager of a railroad to say that he bases his rates upon some line of policy. He deals directly, and in most cases exclusively, with the producer or the jobber. His concern is to keep these patrons satisfied and at the same time bring to his railroad the greatest possible revenue. This is what he means by saying that he charges what the traffic will bear. He regards as reasonable whatever rate will make for the best interest of his road, and in determining this he adopts a line of policy which affects either favorably or unfavorably the industrial growth of the communities which the carrier serves. The restrictions of the act to regulate commerce are governmental limitations placed upon the unlimited and arbitrary discretion of traffic officials. While the latter may adopt policies which they regard as most favorable to their roads, such policies must be restricted by the inhibitions of the law which this Commission must enforce. The policy of making Reno rates base upon those extended to the more distant point may not be justified upon the ground that Reno traffic will bear that imposition, but may be justified by conditions obtaining at the more distant point which the carrier may meet without offense to any provision of the act.

And this brings directly to our consideration the question of water competition at Sacramento and other coast terminals. It is, of course, a physical fact that commerce may be carried by water from the eastern seaboard to the Pacific coast. It is admitted by all, and substantiated by the evidence in this case, that some commerce does actually so move. An estimate has been made by complainant that approximately 3,000,000 tons of transcontinental traffic reaches the coast terminals during each year by rail, while the highest figure given as the volume of traffic reaching those points by water from the eastern seaboard is under 10 per cent of the rail movement. The fact, however, that it moves in large or small quantities does not of itself sustain the contention that the present rates from eastern defined territory to coast terminals are so low as not to make a reasonable return to the carrier for the service performed. A movement of traffic may be affected by water competition at a more distant point and yet a rate made up of the combination of the rate by water plus the rate back be unreasonable and unjust. Nevada, Utah, Arizona, and Idaho are nearer to the Pacific coast than to the Atlantic, but this does not of itself justify charging them overland rail rates which will give them none of the advantages arising out of their shorter distance to an eastern base of supplies. Nor does it follow that a rate to a point on the seaboard is lower than would be justified if that point were not so situated. In short, it is not sufficient to state that the terminal points are situated on the water to excuse the imposition of higher rates at intermediate points.

There has been little difficulty experienced from time to time by the rail carriers in raising rates to the Pacific coast; the only live water competitor on the Pacific to-day is a line which bases its rates on the rail tariffs, and the rates of both the rail and the water lines change simultaneously. Ways can be found, and have been found, by which the presence of the ocean as a controlling, or even greatly meddlesome, factor in the fixing of railroad rates can be nullified. There is no doubt but that rail rates have been influenced at times to all the Pacific ports by water carriers, and of course there is the possibility that at any time this water competition may become seriously aggressive and potent. The United States is not a maritime nation at present, and her great coast line on the Pacific side is served in great part by such water carriers as the railroads permit to live.

While, therefore, physical conditions at the coast are dissimilar to those at interior points the rates to the coast are not necessarily less than in fairness the traffic should carry. The water carriers between the Atlantic and the Pacific coasts at present charge rates from 25 to 40 per cent less than their railroad rivals. To get this business the water carrier at the eastern port reaches inland and absorbs a rail rate of 20 cents upon commodities which carry more than a 50-cent water rate to the Pacific coast. The American-Hawaiian Steamship Company then transports the freight by water to the Tehuantepec road, where it is transshipped across the Isthmus, and being loaded again is carried to a Pacific coast port and there reshipped either by rail or water to certain designated points of destination inland from the port. In such a movement there is involved a rail haul of 400 or 500 miles, at least six, and possibly more, separate handlings of each parcel of freight, and a haul by water of fully 5000 miles. Freight moving *via* Panama is subject to even heavier conditions. It is insisted by the Nevada commission that water competition of this character is not sufficiently aggressive or formidable to compel the railroads to make any other rates to the coast terminals than those which from reasons of policy they are at present making. The suggestion is not without pertinence that if four different transportation services, three by rail and two by water, involving at least six handlings of the freight and a total haul of 5500 miles, can be furnished profitably at from 60 to 75 per cent of the rail rate, the compensation to the rail carrier for an all-rail haul of 2500 miles, with no handling and but two terminal charges, should produce ample revenue to the rail carrier.

There are many interesting developments in this and other transcontinental cases touching this matter of competition by water. For instance, the lowest rate does not in all cases apply to and from the seacoast points. There are many commodities upon which the rates from Chicago and Kansas City to Sacramento and San Francisco are less than they are from New York. And yet it is said to be the competition from New York that produces the low rate. In no case is the rail rate from New York less than is the rate from other portions of eastern defined territory, while of course in all cases New York is nearer the source of the competing force, the ocean. This is accounted for by the carriers on the ground that by taking the same, or a lower, rate from the interior points to the coast terminals the rail carrier avoids the longer rail haul, the points of origin and destination being nearer together. This is an application of what the carriers term "market competition," but it is not a strong argument to sustain the theory of water competition.

As usually applied by carriers market competition results in the hauling of commodities produced at places distant from the point of consumption to compete with the same commodities from points nearer to the point of consumption. In this case, however, market competition is said to be the controlling factor which justifies a rate from an interior point less distant from destination. Thus we have a $3 rate from New York to Sacramento to meet water competition, and a $3 rate from Kansas City to meet market competition. We also have a $4.29 rate from Kansas City and from New York, to Reno, as a reasonable rate because of water competition from New York to Sacramento.

We do not regard the divisions of rates as in any wise conclusive as to the reasonableness of rates between certain points, but such divisions are sometimes of significance. In the present case we find that if 100 pounds of freight is shipped from Boston, or New York, or Chicago, or St. Louis, or Omaha to Sacramento on the $3 rate, and another 100 pounds of the same kind of freight is shipped from the same points to Reno on the same day, the carriers east of Ogden receive precisely the same earnings upon both shipments; but the Southern Pacific, west of Ogden, receives far more upon the Reno shipment than on the Sacramento shipment. This is illustrated in the following table:

From—	To—	Rate	Earnings east of Ogden	Earnings of Southern Pacific Company (west of Ogden)
		Cents	Cents	Cents
Group B, Boston	Sacramento	300	211.3	88.7
	Reno	429	211.3	217.7
Group C, New York	Sacramento	300	211.3	88.7
	Reno	429	211.3	217.7
Group D, including Chicago, etc.	Sacramento	300	181.9	118.1
	Reno	429	181.0	248.0
Group E, including Mississippi river	Sacramento	300	174.5	125.5
	Reno	429	174.5	254.5
Group F, including Missouri river	Sacramento	300	159.3	140.7
	Reno	429	159.3	269.7

Neither at the hearings nor in the argument did the carriers east of Ogden contend that their divisions of these rates were unreasonable. The Southern Pacific, however, the carrier which makes the last 700 miles of a 3100-mile haul, strenuously insists that its rates to the more distant points are compelled by water competition for the purpose of defending higher rates to intermediate points; while the carriers performing 2400 miles of that service appear to regard the rate as entirely reasonable. The line from New York to Sacramento and Reno constitutes a through route and in law the carriers engaging therein constitute one line. If the Sacramento rate is less than a reasonable rate and the result of competition then it would seem fair to assume that all of the carriers engaging in the transportation so consider it and would accordingly demand a lesser division than the division they would be justified in requiring out of the higher rate to the intermediate point. The fact remains, however, that for the 2400-mile haul from New York to Ogden the New York Central, the Lake Shore, the North Western, and the Union Pacific secure the same revenue out of the $3 rate to Sacramento that they do out of the $4.29 rate to Reno. This is graphically illustrated by the following diagram showing the division of the rate:

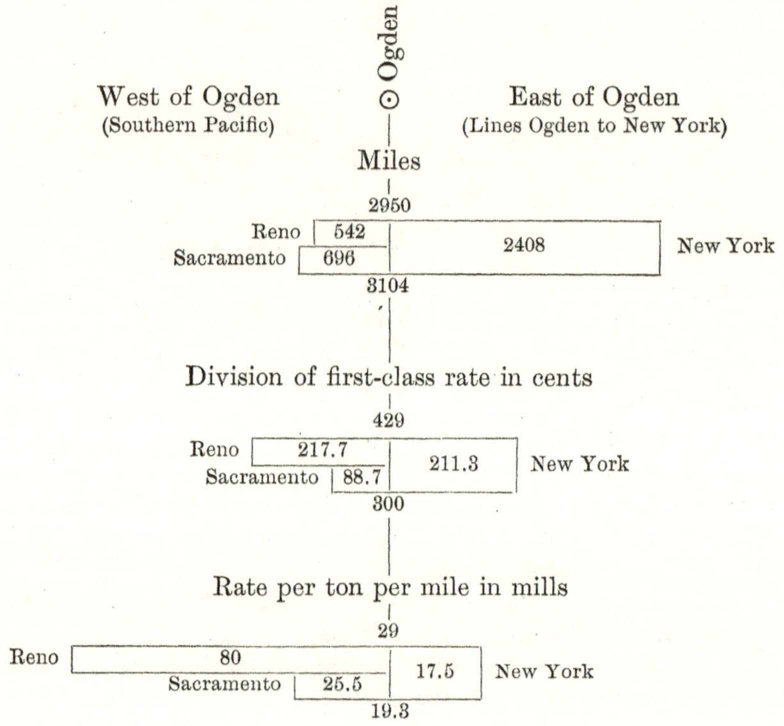

Productive Freight Territory

We have gone extensively into an investigation of the conditions surrounding this traffic and in anywise governing the basis upon which the rates to Nevada from the east should be governed. What has been said herein gives little more than a suggestion of the extent of the inquiry which has been made. We have, for instance, had reports made upon the financial condition of the carriers involved, and their ability to meet any reduction which the Commission might direct without serious impairment of their revenues, an interesting fact in this connection being this: During the past two years the operating revenues of the Southern Pacific Company's Pacific system have increased $8,000,000 while its operating expenses have decreased $5,000,000, thus producing an increased operating income of over $12,000,000, or a net increase of about $2000 per mile of road.

There appears in the record a compilation from the statistics of this Commission for the years 1898–1907 in which it is shown that in these ten years the carriers in the Pacific coast territory doubled their freight tonnage, which rose from 18,000,000 to 35,000,000 tons; almost doubled their gross revenue; their receipts per mile increased over 70 per cent; their receipts per ton per mile increased from 1.07 to 1.25, or about 20 per cent; while the relation of expenses to earnings remained practically constant at 62.50 per cent. These figures are for all the roads in the Pacific territory. But if we take the Central Pacific alone we find it third in the list of Pacific coast roads in tons carried and the highest of all in freight earnings per mile ($13,453 per mile in 1907). While it is one of three railroads in the West carrying over a million tons of freight per mile of road — the average for the United States — the earnings of the Central Pacific per mile are 65 per cent greater than the average for the United States and 100 per cent greater than the average of the roads west of Chicago.

Conclusions

The time has come, in our opinion, when the carriers west of the Rocky Mountains must treat the intermountain country upon a different basis from that which has hitherto obtained.

Nevada asks that she be given rates as low as those given to Sacramento. The full extent of this petition can not be granted. In making rates to Reno from a territory broader than the whole of continental Europe we have necessarily given consideration to existing rates to other intermediate points and to points upon the Pacific.

We are of opinion that the class rates to Reno, Winnemucca, and Elko, and other points in Nevada upon the main line of the Southern Pacific Company, from stations on the lines of the defendants between New York and Denver and other Colorado common points are unreasonable and unjust and that for the future no higher rates than those set forth below should be charged to Reno and points east thereof to, but not including, Winnemucca:

From —	Classes									
	1	2	3	4	5	A	B	C	D	E
Denver and other points in Group J[a]	$2.10	$1.82	$1.54	$1.33	$1.12	$1.12	$0.87	$0.70	$0.66	$0.60
Grand Island and other points in Group G[a]	2.30	2.00	1.68	1.45	1.22	1.22	.96	.76	.73	.65
Omaha and other points in Group F[a]	2.50	2.17	1.83	1.58	1.33	1.33	1.04	.83	.79	.71
Clinton and other points in Group E[a]	2.80	2.42	2.03	1.71	1.43	1.46	1.14	.91	.86	.78
Chicago and other points in Group D[a]	2.90	2.51	2.09	1.75	1.47	1.50	1.18	.94	.89	.80
Toledo and other Cincinnati-Detroit common points[b]	3.05	2.63	2.19	1.81	1.52	1.56	1.23	.98	.92	.83
Buffalo and other Pittsburg-Buffalo common points[b]	3.20	2.76	2.29	1.87	1.57	1.62	1.28	1.03	.96	.86
New York and common points[b]	3.50	3.01	2.49	2.00	1.67	1.75	1.38	1.11	1.03	.93

[a] As designated in Transcontinental Freight Bureau Westbound Tariff 1-K, I.C.C. No. 920.
[b] As designated in Nor. Pac. No. 23,500, I.C.C. No. 3295.

And that for the future no higher rates than those set forth below should be charged to Winnemucca and points east thereof to the Nevada-Utah state line:

From —	Classes									
	1	2	3	4	5	A	B	C	D	E
Denver and other points in Group J[a]	$2.00	$1.72	$1.46	$1.26	$1.06	$1.06	$0.83	$0.67	$0.63	$0.57
Grand Island and other points in Group G[a]	2.19	1.90	1.60	1.38	1.16	1.16	.91	.72	.69	.62
Omaha and other points in Group F[a]	2.38	2.06	1.74	1.50	1.26	1.26	.99	.79	.75	.67
Clinton and other points in Group E[a]	2.66	2.30	1.93	1.62	1.36	1.39	1.08	.86	.82	.74
Chicago and other points in Group D[a]	2.75	2.38	1.99	1.66	1.40	1.43	1.07	.89	.85	.76
Toledo and other Cincinnati-Detroit common points[b]	2.90	2.50	2.08	1.72	1.44	1.48	1.17	.93	.87	.79
Buffalo and other Pittsburg-Buffalo common points[b]	3.04	2.62	2.18	1.78	1.49	1.44	1.22	.98	.91	.82
New York and common points[b]	3.33	2.86	2.37	1.90	1.59	1.66	1.31	1.05	.98	.88

[a] As designated in Transcontinental Freight Bureau Westbound Tariff 1-K, I.C.C. No. 920.
[b] As designated in Nor. Pac. No. 23,500, I.C.C. No. 3295.

In directing the carriers to establish these class rates we have taken into consideration the fact that the general policy of the carriers is to make commodity rates somewhat lower than class rates on commodities, the movement of which is regarded as necessary to the development of mercantile interests and industries. There are at present, as we have seen, a considerable number of such commodity rates into Reno, but these are entirely insufficient to meet the needs of Nevada if she is to become in any way an independent business community. There is no foundation in the record in this case for the establishment of such commodity rates. The theory upon which the case was presented eliminated all other considerations excepting the claim that all rates extended to Sacramento were reasonable as to Reno and other Nevada points. The Nevada petition was tantamount to a request that under our legal authority to establish reasonable rates we should fix the same rate from Denver as from Boston. We do not so construe our authority as to permit this Commission to make rates upon such a basis. Without doubt the commodity rates made to the coast terminals are reasonable from a great portion of eastern defined territory, but a governmental authority may not exercise the latitude in fixing a rate blanket which the carriers themselves have here exercised.

In the *Spokane case*, 19 I. C. C. Rep. 162, some 600 commodity rates had been established voluntarily by the carriers, and the petition in that case was for the reduction of those rates to a reasonable figure. The carriers had made a special series of zones across the continent to meet the exigencies of the Spokane situation. In the case before us, however, no such favorable condition is presented. We have neither a schedule of commodity rates with which to deal as to which specific complaint is made, nor have the carriers so divided the continent into groups of originating territory, save in the sense that the transcontinental groups to the coast terminals, which are entirely different from those found in the *Spokane case*, *supra*, furnish a foundation for present combination rates to western Nevada.

In view of this situation we shall make no order as to commodity rates in this case at the present time, but shall direct the carriers to make a record of all shipments into Nevada from eastern defined territory during the months of July, August, and September, 1910, or during such other representative months as may be determined upon by the Commission after conference with the carriers, and furnish the Commission with a statement showing as to each shipment the following facts:

(1) The commodity; (2) the weight, carload or less than carload; (3) point of origin and the transcontinental territorial group in which the same is situated; (4) rate that would be applied under the tariffs in effect July 1, 1910; (5) the gross charges thereunder; (6) the rate applicable under the order made in this case; (7) the gross charges thereunder; (8) the rate that would be applied were the movement to Sacramento; (9) the gross charges thereunder.

The complainant will be ordered in this case, on or before October 1, 1910, to furnish to the Commission and to the defendant Southern Pacific Company a list of commodities upon which commodity rates are desired, together with an outline of the various territories or groups from which commodity rates should apply.

We are of the opinion that justice can not be done to Nevada unless Nevada points are put on a practical parity with points in eastern Washington and eastern Oregon, and a further hearing will, in due course, be held after the data here requested have been furnished by carriers and complainant.

XVIII

EXPORT AND DOMESTIC GRAIN RATES

Atlantic and Gulf Competition[1]

Prouty, *Commissioner:*

The purpose of this proceeding was the investigation of export rates upon grain and grain products. . . . The matters embraced were:

First. Relative domestic and export rates.

Second. Relative rates on grain and grain products for export.

Third. Publication of export tariffs upon grain and grain products.[2]

I

A domestic rate applies to traffic which is being transported for use in this country; an export rate to traffic which is on its way to some foreign country. * * * *

An examination of the tariffs filed with the Commission since 1887 shows that until recently the published rates upon domestic and export traffic have ordinarily been the same. Taking Chicago as an example, no export rate appears until October 1, 1896. Upon that date, the domestic rate on corn being 20 cents to New York, an export rate of 15 cents was made which expired October 31, 1896. January 20, 1897, the domestic rate still being 20 cents, a 15-cent export rate was again put in and remained effective until September 6, 1897. No other export rate appears until February 1, 1899, when an export rate of 18½ cents upon wheat and 16 cents upon corn was published, the domestic rates being 20 cents and 17½ cents, respectively. April 17th this rate was reduced to 12 cents upon both wheat

[1] Decided August 7, 1899. Interstate Commerce Reports, Vol. VIII, pp. 214–276. The English practice is suggestively described at p. 754, *infra*. At p. 404 of Ripley's Railroads: Rates and Regulation the larger aspects of both import and export rates are discussed.

[2] This part of the case is omitted. — Ed.

and corn, a domestic rate of 17 cents upon each commodity being made effective the following day.

From Minneapolis to the Atlantic seaboard the published rates upon all kinds of grain and the products of grain have been uniformly the same, that is, wheat, corn, and flour have always taken an identical rate. December 28, 1889, the domestic rate being 32½ cents, an export rate of 30½ cents was published which expired February 4, 1890. In one or two other instances export rates were in effect for short periods, but it was not until the present year that this became the rule. January 2, 1899, an export rate of 25 cents was made effective upon flour, the domestic rate upon grain and flour being 27½ cents. This same export rate was, January 4, 1899, extended to grain and other grain products as well as flour. February 7th this rate was raised 1 cent to 26 cents. April 18th the domestic rate was reduced to 24½ cents, and the export rate to 23 cents.

From the Mississippi river to New York no export rate is found until October 1, 1896, when a rate of 17 cents on corn was put in against a domestic rate of 25 cents. This export rate expired October 31, 1896. January 20, 1897, the domestic rate still being 23 cents, an export rate of 15 cents was applied to corn which remained in effect until September 6, 1897. February 1, 1899, a rate of 13½ cents upon corn was made effective, the domestic rate being 20½ cents. April 15th an export rate of 12 cents was made upon both wheat and corn, the domestic rate upon grain and grain products being established April 18th at 19½ cents. Both domestic and export rates to other Atlantic cities are a certain differential above or below the New York rate, so that the history of the export rate to New York indicates its history to the entire Atlantic seaboard.

It would appear that export rates have been in effect to the Gulf ports for a longer time than to the North Atlantic ports. April 28, 1890, an export rate of 28 cents on corn from Kansas City to Galveston was established, the domestic rate being 48 cents, and this rate continued in effect until December 28, 1895. The domestic rate during that period fluctuated from 48 to 27 cents. December 28, 1895, an export rate of 27 cents was made upon corn against a domestic rate of 36 cents. July 21, 1896, this was reduced to 16 cents, and July 31 to 13 cents, the domestic rate being 35 cents. An export rate of 28 cents upon oats was made between these points July 20, 1891. The first export rate upon wheat was made February 16, 1896, and was 31 cents. From this time on the export wheat rate fluctuated, the lowest being 12 cents August 17, 1896. At the time of the hearing the rate on all kinds of grain for export was 10 cents. The domestic rate since June 5, 1896, has been 37 cents on wheat and 35 cents on corn. * * * *

It will be seen that lower rates upon export than upon domestic grain have for a considerable time prevailed through the Gulf ports, but that until quite recently no substantial difference has been made through North Atlantic ports, except in the case of Boston and Portland, which have taken the New York export rate, and of Montreal, which takes an export rate 1 cent below New York. The question now before us is whether these lower export rates are an unjust discrimination against consumers at points bearing the higher domestic rate, and so in violation of the 3d section of the Act to Regulate Commerce. This must depend upon the conditions under which export and domestic grain moves, and those conditions arise both at home and abroad.

Directing our attention first to wheat, and considering the world as a whole, we find that certain countries produce more wheat than they consume, while certain other countries consume more than they produce. The principal nations in the former class are the United States, the Dominion of Canada, Argentina, Russia, India, and Uruguay. * * * *

The United States always produces more wheat than it uses for domestic consumption, but the amount of this surplus differs greatly from year to year. The following table gives the amount of wheat exported from the different wheat-exporting countries averaged in periods of five years for the time indicated:

Countries	1881-1885	1886-1890	1891-1895
United States	122,157,043	115,788,774	171,731,480
Other countries	115,690,816	134,484,937	179,646,922

The above table shows the exports from the United States of both wheat and flour reduced to bushels, and also from other countries, although the amount of flour exported from the United States is relatively much larger than it is from any other wheat-exporting nation. The exact statistics are not at hand to show exportations from other countries since 1895, but it sufficiently appears from the above statement what the relative position of the United States is as a wheat-exporting nation.

It is not material to state the wheat-consuming countries nor the amounts consumed by each. The United Kingdom and the European continent are the principal ones. It is sufficient to observe that all these principal grain markets are in direct communication with all wheat-producing countries. In Liverpool or Antwerp, American wheat comes into direct competition with foreign wheat from all these sources, and must be sold in competition with such wheat. It was said in testimony that the quality of American wheat was superior to that produced anywhere else, except in the Canadian Northwest, that this wheat was largely used by foreign millers to mix with inferior foreign grades, and that this sometimes created a demand for this particular quality of wheat which made the price higher than that of different grades of foreign wheat; but on the whole it must be true that the price of our American product is determined in these markets under the law of supply and demand in competition with all other wheat-producing nations. American wheat does not make the price abroad, although it may be the greatest single factor in the making of that price. To just what extent it does so operate must manifestly depend upon the amount available from different sources.

If the price of wheat in the foreign market is fixed by conditions outside the United States, that price of necessity determines the sum which can be realized in the foreign market for our American product. The cost of laying this wheat down in the foreign market is made up of two factors: the price paid the farmer who raises it, and the cost of transporting the grain from the grain fields to the foreign market. If the cost of transportation remains at all times the same, the price paid the farmer must vary with the price abroad, and a reduction in the cost of transportation would benefit the farmer by exactly the amount of the reduction. It was said by those familiar with the business that the price at which our surplus can be sold determines the market price of the entire product. It seems plain that this must be true to a large extent. We are inclined to think, therefore, that there might be, and at times probably are, market conditions abroad which require the making of a low export rate for the purpose of disposing of our surplus product, and that without such rate the surplus product could not be moved, resulting in a demoralization in price to the wheat producer. In that event the consumer would get the benefit of the low price which the producer is compelled to take, but it will hardly be claimed that, taking the people as a whole, such fluctuations in price are desirable.

Market conditions in case of corn are somewhat different than with wheat. In the sale of its corn in foreign markets the United States has no serious competitor. Argentina exports corn in limited quantities, and considerable appears to come from southeastern Europe, but, taken altogether, the amount is insignificant in comparison with that furnished by the United States. The corn market of Chicago fixes the price throughout the world. In an indirect fashion corn comes into competition with wheat both abroad and in the United States. Wheat and corn are both capable of sustaining life, and the comparative expense at which either article can be procured tends in a degree to determine the amount of its consumption. The same is true of other grains. It requires, however, a considerable difference in expense to overcome individual prejudices and habits in favor of a particular article of food. The opinion of exporters examined upon the hearing was that it would require a very substantial advance or reduction in the freight rate to materially influence the export of corn. We very much doubt whether market conditions abroad require a low export corn rate, or whether such low rates produce a material effect in the movement of our surplus corn crop. It is undoubtedly true that exporters in the United States are often enabled to make sales by some concession in the freight rate which they could not otherwise make, but in the making of those sales they are probably competing with some other dealer in the United States who is exporting his corn by some different route. The lower rate is required, not to meet competition from other countries, but competition between transportation companies in this country.

While, however, we are of the opinion that low export rates, especially upon wheat, might be justified and required by market conditions abroad, we are not of the opinion that the particular rates under consideration are due directly or indirectly to such conditions. Many grain exporters were examined in the course of this investigation, many railroad men were asked to state the reasons for the wide difference between the export and domestic rate, and no one of them suggested that this had been brought about by conditions abroad. It was the universal opinion of grain dealers and the unanimous admission of railroad representatives that these rates were entirely due to competition between railways in America.

Grain which is grown east of the Rocky Mountains can ordinarily be exported either through the Atlantic ports or through the Gulf ports. The principal North Atlantic ports are Montreal, Portland, Boston, New York, Philadelphia, Baltimore, Norfolk, and Newport News, and the principal Gulf ports, Galveston and New Orleans. Grain grown to the west of the Rocky Mountains passes out through the Pacific ports. * * *

The Pacific ports are not included in this investigation. Most of the grain exported through other ports is raised between a line drawn north and south through Chicago and the Rocky Mountains. All this territory is nearer in miles to the Gulf ports than the Atlantic ports. Owing to the geographical lines upon which our railway systems have been developed, export grain, until within a comparatively few years, has moved almost entirely through the Atlantic ports. These grain fields were first reached by roads from the East. Those roads have been strong and well equipped and have been able to control the greater part of this business. Within recent years, however, the lines leading to the South have become potential competitors for this traffic. Their physical condition has been greatly improved, expensive terminals have been constructed at New Orleans, and are being constructed at Galveston. Great sums have been expended by the government in improving the water approaches of these ports, until they now admit vessels of the largest tonnage. These railways, being in position to handle the traffic, and having a most important advantage in point of distance, now insist that a portion of the business belongs to them. The Illinois Central Railroad with its easy grades and unexcelled terminal facilities contends that the grain grown upon its own line, at least, should be exported by it. Lines leading south from Kansas City strenuously claim that grain should pass by their routes to the seaboard rather than go twice the distance to the Atlantic ports. Kansas City is distant from Galveston about 800 miles and from New York about 1400 miles. The whole country tributary to Kansas City, in which enormous quantities of wheat and corn are raised, is therefore much nearer the Gulf ports than the Atlantic ports. Testimony in this case showed that the grain exported through Galveston during the last two or three years had been hauled an average distance of from 700 to 1000 miles, while had it passed out by the Atlantic ports it must have been carried from 1400 to 1600 miles.

Plainly, this grain will pass out through that port by which it can reach its foreign destination most cheaply. The margin of profit in handling grain has been and is extremely small, and a slight difference in the freight rate, not more than one eighth to one fourth cent per bushel, determines the route which it will take. The ocean rate varies greatly from the same port, often fluctuating from day to day. It also varies between the different ports. The Gulf ports insist that they are under a very substantial and permanent disadvantage as compared with all the Atlantic ports, and especially Boston and New York, in that there are no regular lines of steamships from Galveston to foreign ports, and comparatively few from New Orleans. The volume of imports through these ports is extremely small, so that vessels coming there for cargoes must come mainly in ballast. From this and many other circumstances it results that the average of ocean rates from the Gulf ports to foreign markets is higher than from the North Atlantic ports. Upon this proposition the evidence in this case, and the evidence taken before the Commission in previous cases, leaves no question; but when the attempt is made to go a step further, and to determine what in cents per bushel, or per hundred pounds, represents the disadvantage attaching to the exportation of grain through these ports as compared with North Atlantic ports the problem is an exceedingly difficult one, and indeed one to which an exact answer is impossible. What is true of the Gulf ports as compared with the North Atlantic ports is true in a less degree of the North Atlantic ports in comparison with each other. Now the total rate must be the same by all the ports, and therefore the inland rate to the Gulf ports must be less than the corresponding inland rate to the North Atlantic ports, but just how much it is exceedingly difficult to say. From all this we conclude that competition between railways for a considerable portion of this export grain is most severe, both by reason of the number of competitors and the peculiar conditions under which the competition proceeds.

The first low export rates from the Mississippi river and Chicago were, by the admission of all parties, made to divert traffic from the Gulf ports to the eastern lines. It will be remembered that export rates were in effect from Kansas City to Galveston and New Orleans previous to this much lower than the ordinary domestic rates.

While Gulf competition was the cause of the low export rates from the Mississippi river to the Atlantic seaboard beginning October 1, 1896, that competition is not answerable for the extremely low rates which prevail at the present time, these being due to competition between carriers to different North Atlantic ports.

For many years previous to February 1, 1899, certain agreed differentials had existed in the rates from interior western points to the North Atlantic ports of export. On export traffic Boston and New York have taken the same rate, Philadelphia a rate 2 cents, and Baltimore, Norfolk and Newport News 3 cents per hundred pounds below New York. The lines leading to New York have long insisted that these differentials were too high as against that port, and in the month of January, 1899, an agreement was made by which they were to be reduced one half, leaving the rate to Philadelphia 1 cent and to Baltimore, Norfolk and Newport News 1½ cents per hundred pounds lower than to New York. Rates from St. Louis and Mississippi river crossings as far north as East Dubuque are the same. There was either in effect or in contemplation at the time of the making of the above agreement an export rate on corn from the Mississippi river of 15 cents to New York, 13 cents to Philadelphia and 12 cents to Baltimore, Norfolk and Newport News. The lines leading from St. Louis to Baltimore, Norfolk and Newport News insisted that the rate of 12 cents to these latter ports could not be advanced by reason of competition with the Gulf lines. It was therefore determined that the new differentials should be adjusted by reducing the rate to New York and Philadelphia. Accordingly, beginning February 1st, the rates were from the Mississippi river to New York 13½ cents, to Philadelphia 12½ cents, and to Baltimore, Norfolk and Newport News 12 cents.

Lines leading to the three latter points had always insisted that the original differentials did not unduly prefer those ports, and that under the modified differentials those ports would not obtain a fair share of the traffic. Some of these lines claimed that it was a part of the original arrangement by which the differentials were modified, that if an actual trial of the new differentials showed that lines leading to these ports did not obtain a fair share of the business the old differentials should be restored. These lines further insisted that the actual showing for the months of February and March demonstrated the correctness of their contention, and they accordingly published from St. Louis to these ports a rate of 10½ cents, being 3 cents below the New York rate. Thereupon lines leading to New York immediately met this by an export rate of 12 cents, thereby leaving the differential against that city at 1½ cents. In answer to this one line leading from St. Louis to Newport News published a rate of 9 cents upon corn, thus reëstablishing the 3-cent differential. Here the matter rested at the time of the hearing, this rate not having been met by either the Baltimore or New York lines.

Since the hearing other rates have been put in effect which will be stated hereafter.

It will be seen, therefore, that the first export rate from the Mississippi river was made to meet Gulf competition, and that subsequent reductions have been brought about entirely by competition between rail carriers leading to the North Atlantic ports. The recent low export rates to the Gulf have been made to meet these low rates east.

There seems to be certain territory from which it is conceded that grain ought to be exported by way of the Atlantic seaboard, and no attempt is made to divert it to the south. There may also be some regions from which eastern lines are willing to admit that grain ought to be exported through the Gulf, although if such regions do in fact exist their location was not very clearly developed upon this hearing. It is not our province to divide up this traffic nor apportion this territory; nor, if it were, is there evidence in this case which would enable us to do so. It is evident, and we find, that there is a large area from which this export business may properly be said to be competitive as between different ports, and that such competition does actually exist in a most intense degree; first, between the Gulf and the North Atlantic seaboard; secondly, as between different North Atlantic ports. This competition has produced the present export rates.

While, however, competition between rail carriers was responsible in the first instance for the present lower export rates, there is another factor which must have a most important bearing upon the maintenance of these rates. We refer to water competition.

Chicago is the most important grain market of the United States. The price of grain in that market probably controls the price throughout this country at least. Of all the corn which is sent from the West to the Atlantic seaboard the greater part passes through Chicago, or a Chicago junction. Of wheat the greater bulk seems to center at Duluth rather than Chicago, although Chicago handles large quantities.

Now it is possible to transport grain from Chicago to either Montreal or New York entirely by water. The same steamer which loads at a Chicago elevator can pass by way of the Great

Lakes, the St. Lawrence river and the Canadian canals to the side of the ocean steamship at Montreal. Grain carried by lake from Chicago to Buffalo can there be loaded into a canal boat and taken through the Erie canal and the Hudson river to the ship side in New York harbor. It did not appear very definitely what the rate per hundred pounds by water from Chicago to Montreal was, but the testimony leaves the impression that it is between 8 and 9 cents per hundred pounds. Neither did it appear exactly what the all water rate was from Chicago to New York. . . .

We have already seen that export corn, being at Chicago, and export wheat, being at Duluth, will reach the foreign port by the cheapest route. Unless, therefore, the rail carrier makes substantially the same route on this grain to New York as is made by water lines the traffic will of necessity move by water, and not by rail. Otherwise stated, no grain can be exported from Chicago through New York by rail unless the rail rate is practically the same as the water rate. There may be circumstances under which the rail carrier can obtain a slightly higher rate, but the testimony shows, and the necessary conclusion from the undisputed facts is, that no considerable difference can be made in favor of rail transportation.

There was no testimony to show what the ocean rate from Montreal to the foreign destination was, but it did appear in this case, and has appeared in several previous cases, that the ocean rate from New York is lower than from any other port except Boston. It must follow, therefore, that all grain at Chicago, or which can be brought to Chicago, will be exported through the port of New York unless carriers leading from Chicago to the other ports make a rate as low or indeed lower than is made to New York. The same remark applies to interior points. Peoria, St. Louis and the lines leading from these cities claim the right to participate in this export grain traffic, but this they cannot do unless the rates from such interior points to the port of export bear a certain relation to the Chicago rate, for the grain can reach either Chicago or these points. A reduction in the Chicago export rate necessarily forces a reduction in the export rate from these interior points to the Atlantic seaboard; but we have already seen that the rate to the Atlantic seaboard and the rate to the Gulf must correspond if any business is to move through the Gulf. Hence the inevitable conclusion that the water rate from Chicago to New York and from Chicago to Montreal determines the export rate through all the ports of the United States to a large extent while that rate is available. Whatever has been said in reference to Chicago applies equally to Duluth, the lake rate from there being but a trifle higher than from Chicago.

Not only is water competition a controlling factor in theory, but in volume as well. The testimony upon this hearing was that nearly all the wheat which reached Duluth went from there by water. It appeared that in the year 1898, 127,000,000 bushels of corn passed through Chicago, and of this amount 97,000,000 bushels left that port by water. It was in evidence that one exporter during the year 1898 had sent 14,000,000 bushels of grain all water through the port of Montreal. Competition which actually carries such enormous quantities of traffic must be controlling in its effect.

It should be observed that these lake rates only apply during the period of navigation, which is ordinarily from the middle of April to the middle of December. During some five months in the year grain cannot be transported from Chicago by lake, but the effect of this water competition is not entirely confined to the period of navigation. Considerable quantities are accumulated during the closed season at different ports of export, as well as at Buffalo and other lake ports, to be sent forward after navigation closes. Upon the contrary, the elevators at Chicago, which are estimated to contain about 50,000,000 bushels, are emptied during the season of navigation, but as soon as navigation closes they begin to fill up with grain which is stored there in anticipation of the opening of the next season. Considerable quantities are also stored in vessels lying at Chicago and Duluth during the winter months. While, therefore, there is during nearly half the year no actual lake transportation, the water route in a degree controls even then the rail rate; it limits to an extent at all times the amount which the rail carrier can obtain from this traffic.

Water rates from Chicago to Montreal and New York apply to both export and domestic traffic, and no distinction appears to be made between the two kinds of traffic in case of the lake and rail rate.

A pertinent inquiry in all investigations of this sort is, Who is injured? In the present case, Whom does this difference between export and domestic rates harm? There are four different classes involved: the producer, the carrier, the domestic consumer and the foreign consumer. Many witnesses expressed the opinion that the producer had the benefit of the low rate. These statements were, however, merely expressions of opinion. No witness was able to say that the putting in of these rates had produced any actual effect upon the general market price of wheat and corn, and for the obvious reason that the elements which determine the market price of these commodities are so complex and so various and the prices themselves so fluctuate that it would be impossible to observe the connection if it existed. Whatever fact is found in reference to this must probably be by inference from other facts.

It appears plain that if the price of grain were absolutely fixed by the foreign market the American farmer would receive the entire benefit of the low rate. If grain cannot be sold for more than a certain price, and if that price is less than the market price in this country plus the established rate, then either the rate or the price in this country must be shrunk or the grain cannot find a foreign market. Upon the other hand, if the price of grain in the foreign market is determined by the American market, then the foreigner has the benefit of the low rate. The price which the American farmer receives is fixed by his home market, and the exporter can sell in the foreign country for that price plus the rate. When the rate is reduced, the price in the foreign market is correspondingly reduced. As an actual fact it is doubtless true that the price of grain, certainly wheat, abroad is fixed neither by the foreign nor by the American supply alone, but by the one acting upon the other.

Undoubtedly the American market has more to do with the price abroad at some times than at others, but it must always have something to do with that price, and the state of the foreign market must always act to some extent upon the American market. It is probable, therefore, that the producer and the foreign consumer obtain in varying degrees the benefit of the low export rate upon wheat. In view of the almost unanimous testimony that market conditions abroad have not required the recent low export rate, and that the volume of exports has not been stimulated by those rates, we are inclined to think that from these particular reductions in rate the American producer has derived no special benefit. The carrier has lost and the foreign consumer has gained.

There was no claim in this case that the present domestic rates were too high. If the American consumer suffers from the low export rate it must be from the necessary consequences which result from such an adjustment of rates. We cannot find specifically from the testimony in this case that the American consumer in the East is injured.

Whatever injurious effect is capable of being perceived is much more likely to result between different sections in the West, and arises, not from the principle of the lower export rate, but from the application of that rate.

Nearly all these low export rates are what are termed proportional rates. They do not apply to traffic originating at the point from which they are made effective, but only to traffic which has already paid the local rate up to that point. The 12-cent rate from the Mississippi river to New York cannot be used for the transportation of grain grown upon the east bank of that river, but only applies to grain grown to the west, and which has already been transported from some point farther west up to that river. It is evident that the application of this rate to the Mississippi, without the putting in of corresponding rates at points east, must have affected the price of grain grown west of that river as compared with the price of that grown east. The export rate from Chicago and from the Mississippi river is nominally the same. If it were actually the same, wheat would be worth exactly as much at the Mississippi as it is at Chicago for export. The testimony tended to show that the putting in of this low proportional rate did actually increase the price of grain at the Mississippi river in comparison with the Chicago price. * * * * * *

It may happen and in many cases does happen, that, by the application of these so-called proportional rates, grain from the more distant point obtains transportation to Chicago or to the Gulf at a less rate than grain from the intermediate fields through which the transportation passes. We held in the investigation as to these export rates last April that this created, as against such intermediate points, an undue preference. *In the Matter of Export Rates from Points East and West of the Mississippi River*, 8 I. C. C. Rep. 185. We now repeat that finding.

* * * * * * * *

The carriers insist that while now, for the first time, a systematic difference is made in the published tariff between export and domestic rates, there has in fact always been such a difference in the actual rate. It is undoubtedly true that as to competitive traffic the published rate has been largely departed from in the past. This export traffic is highly competitive. It moves in large lots and is handled by comparatively few individuals. The idea has been more or less prevalent that the provisions of the Act to Regulate Commerce did not refer to export traffic. For these and other reasons export business has been peculiarly open to the manipulation of rates.

The testimony of representatives of carriers familiar with rates actually paid was to the effect that there had been in the past as wide a difference between the published rate and the actual rate upon export business as exists to-day in the published tariffs. We have no doubt that there has been in the past a difference between the published and actual rates. This difference has existed in the case of both export and domestic traffic. It has probably been greater in the case of export business, but how great we cannot definitely find.

Carriers also claim that they are justified in making a lower rate on export than on domestic business by the fact that the cost of service is less to them. This export business moves in large lots, often in train loads, from a single point of origin to a single destination. Large cars can be used and these cars can be loaded to their full capacity. For these and other reasons they urge that the cost of handling this traffic is less than in case of domestic. We are inclined to think that there may be some difference in the cost of service, but we cannot from any testimony in this case express an opinion as to the amount of such difference. * * * * * *

II

The second branch of this case refers to the relative rates upon grain and the products of grain. While the order instituting the investigation includes the products of both corn and wheat, the manufacturers of corn products did not appear and were not heard, nor were any complaints received from that class until after the close of this hearing. The only product of grain which was fully represented upon the hearing was flour. It seems, moreover, that flour is the only grain product which is exported in very large quantities, and that is the only subject accordingly to which this discussion will be directed.

From the time the Act to Regulate Commerce took effect until February 1, 1899, railway carriers have, with the exception of a short period in 1891, published the same rate upon export wheat and flour. Different rates upon these commodities have been made in certain parts of the United States, but those rates have never been applied to export traffic. February 1, 1899, carriers leading to the Atlantic seaboard published an export rate upon wheat from Chicago to New York of 18½ cents. The domestic rate was then 20 cents and the rate upon flour was the same. These rates were not changed, and the rate upon export flour was thus 1½ cents per hundred pounds higher than the rate upon export wheat. Subsequently the rate upon wheat was further reduced to 12 cents, the domestic rate upon wheat and the rate upon flour being established at 17 cents. Generally speaking the rate upon both domestic and export flour is the same as the rate upon domestic wheat, so that the difference between export wheat and export flour is represented by the difference between domestic wheat and export wheat. These rates have already been given, and need not be repeated here.

The statement that no distinction is made between domestic and export flour is subject to one most important exception. Flour from Minneapolis, the largest milling center in the United States, when for export takes a rate $1\frac{1}{2}$ cents per hundred pounds below the corresponding domestic rate by both rail and lake and rail routes, and this same difference obtains in the case of certain other milling points in the Northwest whose rates are governed by the Minneapolis tariff. This distinction does not apply in the case of Milwaukee, nor at any point south of a line drawn through Milwaukee east and west. * * *

The milling interests of Minneapolis and other points which now enjoy an export rate did not appear upon this hearing, but practically all other sections of the country in which flour is ground for export were represented before us, protesting against the difference in rates upon export wheat and flour. These milling interests may be properly divided into the seaboard and the interior millers, and while the difference in rate, when actually paid, apparently affects both these classes in substantially the same way, their claims may be stated separately.

American millers compete in foreign markets with one another, but the testimony shows that their most serious competitor is the foreign miller. Most wheat purchased by wheat-consuming countries is exported before being ground. Russia and Canada grind a small amount of their surplus wheat, but the United States is the only nation which exports any very considerable amount of flour.

Considering the seaboard miller as compared with the English miller who grinds American wheat, both must derive their supply of the raw material from the same source. The American miller at New York pays the domestic rate, which is from the Mississippi river $19\frac{1}{2}$ cents per hundred pounds, while the English miller transports his wheat from the same point to New York at the rate of 12 cents per hundred pounds. Clearly, therefore, the Englishman has an advantage by reason of this difference in freight rate over the American of $7\frac{1}{2}$ cents per hundred.

It also costs the American miller more to transport his product across the ocean than it does the English miller to transport his wheat; but this is a matter with which we are not concerned. Plainly the American miller at New York pays, if he pays the published domestic rate, 7½ cents per hundred pounds more than the Englishman in bringing his wheat to the seaboard, and is therefore placed at a disadvantage to just that amount.

While this must be so if the seaboard miller actually pays the published rail rate, it is not plain to us that at the present time he does pay that rate. During the period of navigation, practically all wheat moves to the east by lake and rail, and upon this traffic the rate is the same whether for export or domestic consumption. Apparently it costs the New York miller to-day exactly the same to get his wheat to New York that it costs the English miller. This would not be so during the period of closed navigation, since it seems that almost one half the grain actually received by the New York Central during the months of March and April last was billed and carried upon the domestic rate.

While the representatives of the seaboard millers stated that these rates seriously discriminated against them, their testimony did not show any considerable diminution in exports from these mills. The profit was said to be less both upon export and domestic flour than it had formerly been, but the relative amount which was exported continued to be about the same.

Chicago may be taken as a type of the interior milling situation, and to illustrate this situation we may select one Chicago mill. This mill had a capacity of about 1500 barrels a day. The wheat which it ground was entirely spring wheat and came from beyond the Mississippi river. In its export business it was in competition with the English miller who obtained his wheat from the same fields. The rate paid by the Chicago mill from the Mississippi river to Chicago was 5 cents per hundred pounds. That paid by the English miller upon the same wheat from the Mississippi river to Chicago was 1.8 cents per hundred pounds. From Chicago to New York the Chicago miller paid upon his manufactured product 17 cents while the English miller paid upon his raw product 10.2 cents, making a total difference in cost at New York against the Chicago miller of 10 cents per hundred pounds.

The Chicago miller could obtain the benefit of the through rate from the Mississippi river to New York under the milling-in-transit privilege by the payment of an added 1½ cents per hundred pounds, but he could not apply this to the export rate. The domestic rate from the Mississippi river to New York was 19½ cents per hundred pounds, which, with the added 1½ cents for the milling-in-transit privilege, makes a total through rate of 21 cents compared with a rate of 12 cents to the English miller. It is probable that the discrimination would be rather less against the American who was grinding winter wheat, but not materially less. A statement filed by the representatives of the Milwaukee millers shows by many illustrations drawn from actual rates a discrimination of from 4 to 11 cents per hundred pounds.

Considerable testimony was given as to the margin of profit in the manufacture of flour. This must of course vary at different times and under different conditions, but the testimony fairly showed that from 1 to 2 cents per hundred pounds was at the present time a fair profit, and as great a profit as had been realized recently upon export flour. The testimony upon the whole tended to show that the profit on flour sold abroad was rather less than that upon flour consumed at home. The primary object of the flouring mill is usually to grind for home consumption, the foreign market being resorted to as a means of disposing of that portion of the product which cannot be marketed at home.

Minneapolis and the northwest generally, where the lower export rate upon flour prevails, did not complain. The seaboard miller insisted that his margin of profit had been reduced by this discrimination, but the volume of business was apparently about the same. Upon the other hand, Milwaukee, Chicago, St. Louis and corresponding territory not only showed a diminution in profits, but a very marked decrease in the volume of export business. It was said by these millers that January 1st they were largely oversold for export, and that for this reason they sent abroad during the early months of the current year considerable quantities of flour, but that they were unable to sell at the present prices and were largely out of the export trade. It is our conclusion and finding that the adjustment of rates is largely responsible for this. The northwestern miller enjoys a relatively better export rate. The seaboard miller can buy his grain during a large portion of the year upon the same terms as the foreign miller. Against the interior miller all these causes combine with the effect that he must be largely or entirely driven from the export trade.

The carriers justify the difference in rates in part at least upon the ground of difference in the cost of service. It was urged by them that for several reasons the transportation of export wheat is more profitable at the same rate than the transportation of flour for export, and that there ought to be a difference, although some thought that the present difference was too wide. They urge that it is a universal rule that the manufactured product pays a higher rate than the raw material; that flour is much more valuable than wheat; that it is more liable to damage than wheat; that wheat moves in larger volume, so that not merely car loads, but whole train loads are embraced in one shipment; that the cars can be, and in fact are, loaded more heavily with wheat than with flour. It is also said that the rate includes a delivery over the ship side in case of flour, and at the ship side in case of wheat.

The millers deny most of the above allegations, and say that if the movement of wheat is in larger volume at times, that of flour is much steadier, and that it is for the interest of the carrier to build up industries which bring other traffic in turn.

It is undoubtedly true that the raw material commonly takes a lower rate than the manufactured product, and for this there is usually a substantial reason in the character of the two commodities; but this is not by any means a universal rule, and the uniform practice of carriers for years has been to make the same rate upon export wheat and flour.

Export flour is probably on the whole somewhat more valuable than wheat, although when it is remembered that the cheaper grades of flour are usually exported it is questionable whether the difference in value is material. * * * *

From all this we conclude that the actual cost of handling export flour somewhat exceeds that of handling wheat, but just how much cannot be determined with certainty. We do not think that the excess would be more than from 1 to 2 cents per hundred pounds.

The carriers also justify their rates upon the ground of water competition. It has already been seen that this species of competition between Chicago and the seaboard forces down the grain rate to a point much below the ordinary rail tariff. The same thing is true, although not to the same extent, of the transportation of flour. It is not only possible to carry flour from Chicago and Duluth to the Atlantic seaboard by all water routes, as well as by lake and rail routes, but considerable quantities of it are so transported. In 1898 nearly one fourth of all the flour leaving Chicago for the entire year went from that port by water. This for the most part is carried to some lake port like Buffalo, and from thence to the seaboard by rail, but it may be taken all water to Montreal or New York as in case of grain, and the possible rail route determines what the rail portion of the haul can exact in the case of flour, as it does in the case of grain.

When, however, the effect of this competition upon the rate is examined, we find that the lake or the lake and rail rate is not as low as the corresponding rate upon wheat. The reason seems to be that equal facilities do not exist for the carrying of flour by lake as for the carrying of grain. Boats which engage in this traffic upon the Great Lakes are either line boats or wild boats. Line boats ply between certain stated points like Buffalo and Chicago at frequent intervals, and are in all cases under the control of some railroad company in connection with which they are operated. Wild boats, on the other hand, ply between different points, sometimes starting from one port and sometimes from another. Line boats are equipped for the carriage of flour and other package freight, while wild boats as a rule are not. Flour is never carried by these wild boats, — at least such was the testimony, — but always goes by the regular lines. In consequence the rate upon flour can be better maintained than that upon wheat. The ruling rate by lake upon flour from Chicago to New

York in recent years has been from 11 to 15 cents as against a rate of from 8 to 10 cents upon wheat. The present lake and rail rate on flour is 14 cents per hundred pounds, and it was said that this rate was maintained. The present domestic rail rate is 17 cents, and under these rates the carriage of flour from Chicago for export was said to be pretty evenly divided between all rail and lake and rail. From this it would appear that the difference between all rail and lake and rail which can be secured in case of flour is somewhat greater than in case of wheat. The differential in favor of the lake lines in former years has usually been 5 cents per hundred pounds, instead of the present differential of 3 cents, and this was one ground of complaint by the millers. In the past the demoralization has been so general that the published rate has offered very little criterion of the actual rate. If the present differential were 5 cents in favor of lake lines the rate on lake and rail flour would be 12 cents, and the millers claim that the railroads take advantage of the fact that they control these regular lines to unduly raise the lake and rail rate on flour. There is probably something to this, since it appears that these regular lines which carry flour are all under the influence of railways leading from the lake ports to the Atlantic seaboard; but we think and find that lake competition fairly fixes the rate on flour at from 2 to 4 cents per hundred pounds above the wheat rate. Subject to this difference the effect of water competition upon export flour is exactly the same as upon export wheat, and that effect need not be restated here. * * * *

Conclusions

1. The first question presented for determination is, Does the Interstate Commerce Act, as a matter of law, prohibit the charging of an export and a domestic rate upon the same traffic to the same point? This question has recently been decided by the Commission in the negative in the case, *Kemble* v. *Boston & Albany R. Co.*, 8 I. C. C. Rep. 110. Since, however, the reasons upon which that decision rested have a certain bearing upon the questions of fact involved in this matter they may be briefly restated here. * * * * * * * *

January 29, 1891, a decision was announced in the case, *New York Bd. of Trade & Transportation* v. *Pennsylvania R. Co.*, 4 I. C. C. Rep. 447, 3 Inters. Com. Rep. 417, in which the matter of import rates was considered. The complaint was that carriers leading from New York to Chicago and the West were transporting freight which arrived from foreign destinations from New York to interior points at a less rate than was charged for the transportation of similar freight to the same interior points when such freight originated at New York. Many companies were made parties to this proceeding, and the case, in its original form, was intended to embrace practically all ports of entry upon the eastern seaboard and the Gulf. The conclusion reached was that the rate charged by the rail carrier from the port of entry to the inland destination must in all cases be the same upon merchandise originating at such port of entry as upon merchandise coming to that port from a foreign country. The Commission made this decision, however, not as question of fact, but as matter of law. Its holding was that the effect of the Act to Regulate Commerce extended no further than the boundaries of the United States; that the Commission had no power to consider conditions existing without the United States; that when traffic arrived at a port within the United States from a foreign country it was not proper to inquire from whence it came, but it must be treated in all respects as though it was domestic traffic originating at the port of entry.

The *Import Rate Case*, *Texas & P. R. Co.* v. *Interstate Commerce Commission*, 162 U. S. 197, 40 L. ed. 940, 5 Inters. Com. Rep. 405, was an attempt upon the part of the Commission to enforce its order in this last-named proceeding. The Texas & Pacific Railway Company, with its connections, was engaged in the transportation of merchandise from Liverpool, England, to San Francisco, Cal. This merchandise was taken upon a through rate, came by water from Liverpool to New Orleans, and by rail from New Orleans to San Francisco. This entire through rate was often much less than the rate on corresponding articles from New Orleans to San Francisco, and the division of the rail carrier was of course very much less than its domestic rate for a corresponding service. For example, one of the articles so transported was dry goods; the rate on dry goods by this line from Liverpool to San Francisco was 107 cents per hundred pounds, while the rate from New Orleans to San Francisco over the same rail line was 374 cents per hundred pounds. The defendants justified the rate from Liverpool upon the ground that water competition by various routes between Liverpool and San Francisco compelled them to charge this rate if they obtained any portion of the business.

The rule laid down by the Commission, and which was contended for by the Commission, in that case would have compelled the carrier to charge the same rate from New Orleans to San Francisco upon import as upon domestic merchandise, and would have excluded all consideration of conditions existing abroad. The Supreme Court refused to concur in this construction of the Interstate Commerce Act, holding that in case of imported traffic as well as of traffic originating within the United States the Commission should have reference to all conditions, whether at home or abroad, which bore upon the reasonableness of the rate adjustment. It held that the Act to Regulate Commerce did not prescribe a hard and fast rule which required that imported merchandise should be taken from the port of entry at the same rate which was applied to domestic merchandise originating at that point. The exact point decided was that carriers were not, as a matter of law, prohibited from participating in a through rate from a foreign destination to an interior point, of which the division received by the inland carrier was less than its rate for a similar service in the transportation of domestic merchandise between the same points. This decision must apply equally to export traffic, and upon its authority we are constrained to hold that, as matter of law, the Interstate Commerce Act does not prohibit a rail carrier from making a through rate from a point within the United States to a foreign destination, of which its division shall be less than the amount charged for the corresponding transportation of domestic merchandise to the port of export. * *

Carriers in some quarters seem to assume that the *Import Rate Case* above referred to in effect withdrew import and export traffic from the purview of this Commission. Such is not at all the result of that decision. It rather enlarged the power of this body over that species of traffic, for while it was held that there was no rule like that contended for by the Commission it was also held that conditions abroad as well as at home should be considered, and that the interests of all classes, and not of a single class, should be taken into account. It is still a question of fact whether rates upon export or import traffic, as well as those upon domestic traffic, are in contravention of the provisions of the Act to Regulate Commerce.

The question for our consideration is therefore one of fact, and seems to be, upon this branch of the case, whether the present adjustment of export and domestic rates discriminates against the domestic consumer and in favor of the foreign consumer. What reason is there why the foreigner who eats our wheat should have it transported from the Mississippi river to New York for 12 cents a hundred pounds, while the American is obliged to pay 19½ cents for the same service?

The Supreme Court in the *Import Rate Case* has laid down the rule which should guide this Commission in the determination of that question. It is not every discrimination which is forbidden by the Act to Regulate Commerce, but only unjustifiable discriminations; and the court holds that in determining whether a discrimination is in fact unjustifiable the interests of all parties involved must be considered. The parties involved in this case are the producer of the grain, the domestic consumer and the inland carrier; we are not concerned with the foreign consumer. Now, taking all these classes together, is the discrimination against the seaboard consumer an unjust one?

The railways insist that it is a matter of no consequence to the eastern consumer what rate is charged the foreigner, provided the domestic rate is a reasonable one, and there is no pretense in this case that domestic rates are not sufficiently low. To this proposition we cannot fully assent. In the first place the foreigner is to an extent in competition with the American. Both are engaged in the production of articles sold in the same market, either abroad or in the United States. If the Englishman can procure the necessities of life cheaper than his American competitor, that gives him the advantage. A few cents per hundred pounds in the price of his flour would not be, of itself, a matter of great consequence, but the same sort of a preference applied to all articles which enter into his daily support, as well as to the product of his labor, may determine whether he or the American can manufacture for our own market even.

Again, railway rates are in amount interdependent the one upon the other. The railway is entitled to earn a fair return upon its investment. If the proposition is made to reduce the rate, one important factor in the determination of that question is the total amount of earnings. If the rate is too low upon one article, in the end other articles pay too high a rate. Unless there is some good reason for the distinction, the rate to the American ought not to be higher than to the foreigner. If our carriers, in the absence of any constraining reason, can transport corn from the Mississippi river to New York for 12 cents per hundred pounds for export, that of itself shows that a rate of 19½ cents to the domestic consumer is unreasonable. Conditions may justify the existence of a lower rate for export than for domestic use, but in the absence of such conditions we cannot concur in the idea that any permanent system of rates which renders a service for the foreigner at a less price than is paid by the American can be just to the American; nor would we permit the continuance of such a system if we had the power to prevent it. From the standpoint of the eastern consumer the difference in rate of itself creates a discrimination which is undue, unless justifiable in the interest of the producer or the carrier.

How stands the interest of the producer; in other words, to what extent is the western farmer benefited by these low export rates?

The United States produces every year a certain quantity of wheat. Of that quantity the greater part is consumed by our own people, but a very large surplus still remains which must be disposed of abroad. This surplus is sold to foreign countries in competition with wheat from other parts of the world, and it must be sold at the price obtainable in the foreign market. While at times that price may be practically fixed by the United States, and while at all times it is influenced by the price here, still it must be admitted that ordinarily the foreign market is not entirely determined by our own market.

It has already been said, in the findings of fact, that our wheat must be delivered abroad at the market price there. If the foreign price is less than our market price plus the ordinary cost of transportation, either the price here or the price of transportation must be reduced. Witnesses of experience in this respect gave it as their opinion that market conditions abroad frequently require a low rate in order to dispose of our surplus product; that the price of our surplus wheat establishes the market price in this country, and that, therefore, at times a low rate was of distinct benefit to the farmer, and indeed was necessary to prevent the demoralization of prices.

Conditions with reference to corn are apparently somewhat different. The corn market of the United States controls that of the world. The price at which our corn can be sold abroad has something to do with the amount which will be taken by foreign countries, but so does a lower price upon the eastern seaboard stimulate the consumption of corn. It is probable, and this was the testimony of exporters, that the difference in rate has little influence upon the volume of corn exportation.

Our conclusion is that a low export rate is sometimes necessary to dispose of our surplus wheat, and that in a much less degree it may promote the movement abroad of our surplus corn; that to the extent that it does operate to move our surplus grain it is of distinct benefit to the producer, and that his interest would outweigh that of the American consumer, and would justify a moderate difference in the rate. The price of the surplus within certain limits, seems to fix the price of the whole, and in the disorganization of prices from a glut in the market the producer loses more than the consumer gains. The ability to dispose of an actual surplus is a sort of safety valve which steadies the whole situation. It must be observed, too, that in applying this low rate to our surplus product the railway does precisely what the miller does and what every other manufacturer is likely to do. The foreigner can buy American flour and almost every article of American manufacture cheaper than the American can at the mill or the factory. It is equally apparent that whether market conditions abroad do justify the lower export rate is a very delicate question to deal with, and one which had better be left to the law of supply and demand so far as it can.

An examination of this question from the point of view of the eastern consumer and the western producer leads to the conclusion that the low export rate is an unjust discrimination against the former unless it is required to move our surplus grain, in which event it is within some limits proper; that this Commission ought not to interfere unless it clearly appears that the difference is unduly great, or that no conditions abroad require it.

In the present case those facts did clearly appear. It appeared beyond all question that the low export rate in force at the time of the hearing had not resulted from any market conditions abroad. The witnesses were almost unanimous in the opinion that these rates had not been required by such conditions, and that they did not stimulate the export of our grain. It was practically conceded by the carriers that the rates were abnormally low, and that they had resulted entirely from competition between rail carriers themselves. If this is true, then it seems plain that the American producer has derived no substantial benefit from these rates; that the American carrier has lost enormously by them, and that the foreigner alone has had the benefit of them. The discrimination against the eastern consumer is not justified unless there is something in the interests of the carrier which excuses it.

* * * * * * * *

The cause of these low export rates has been fully stated in the findings of fact. The carriers themselves with one voice affirm that they were entirely the result of competition between American railways, first between the eastern lines and the Gulf lines, afterward between the different eastern lines. Since January 1st export rates on grain have been reduced in many cases almost one half; at these reduced rates enormous quantities of traffic have moved; no market conditions abroad required these reductions, and the American producer has not been materially benefited by them; our railways have sacrificed millions of dollars without producing any real effect upon the flow of traffic, for the relative rate has remained about the same and the low rate has not increased the total volume. This depletion in revenue has been a donation to the foreigner.

It is impossible more strongly to emphasize the folly of this whole proceeding than by the mere statement of it; and yet in just what way does it violate the Act to Regulate Commerce? The purpose of that Act was to foster railway competition. The highest judicial authority has declared that competition between railways may be a reason for making a lower charge to the more distant point. We have found that this traffic is not only the legitimate subject of competition, but that the competition for it must be conducted under such circumstances as to render it peculiarly active and difficult to control. To agree upon these differentials to the different ports might be a criminal act. Apparently there is no method by which these questions can be settled except by a resort to such measures.

The real question is whether, in this warfare, domestic as well as export rates ought not to be reduced; whether the American as well as the foreigner ought not to have the benefit of this competition. We should be inclined to take this view of the matter, and to make some order which would at least limit the extent to which export might be lower than domestic rates, were it not for two circumstances.

First: Assuming that the basis of export and domestic rates ought to be the same, we think there may be cases where a difference may properly exist. Of this Boston is a good illustration.

The through rate from Chicago to Liverpool must be the same by all the ports. The ocean rate from Boston to Liverpool is the same as from New York; therefore, unless the inland rate from Chicago to Boston is the same as that from Chicago to New York export traffic will move through New York, not through Boston. These circumstances have induced the railways serving these two ports to agree for the last thirty years that the export rate to Boston and New York from the West might be the same. It is difficult to see how this agreement can, in its operation, be treated as unjust or as in violation of the Act to Regulate Commerce. This Commission has twice decided that the Boston domestic rate may properly be higher than the New York domestic rate. We must assume, therefore, that the domestic rates to these two sections are properly adjusted, and that no discrimination is made against New England by charging the higher rate. The rate to the foreigner is fixed by that through New York, and therefore the making of the same rate *via* Boston does not discriminate in his favor as against the New England consumer. The commercial interests of Boston do not complain of the export rate. Under these circumstances, why should not New England carriers be permitted to engage in this export traffic?

It may be that if these carriers could be compelled, by an order of this Commission, to make the same domestic and export rates they would as a consequence reduce the domestic rate rather than surrender the export traffic, and that consequently Boston and perhaps some other New England territory would obtain the benefit of a lower domestic rate. They might, upon the other hand, prefer to surrender the export business rather than reduce the domestic rate; but the question before us is not what the carriers could be compelled to do, but what should they in fairness be required to do.

What is true of the rate to Boston is equally true of the export rate to Portland and Montreal; it is perhaps even more true of export rates to the Gulf ports. Taking effect July 1, 1899, the local export rate on wheat from Kansas City to Galveston is 19 cents, the proportional export rate 15 cents, and the local domestic rate 37 cents. Through rates *via* Kansas City undoubtedly make the ordinary domestic rate from Kansas City somewhat less than 37 cents, but the relation is probably pretty well indicated by the local export rate compared with the local domestic rate. We have here a domestic rate almost twice as great as the export rate. Without expressing any opinion as to the propriety of as wide a difference, or as to the reasonableness of the domestic rate, it seems evident, or extremely probable, that these lines may with propriety in competition for this export business make a lower charge upon export than upon domestic traffic.

Now if an order were to be made that domestic and export rates should under all circumstances be the same, it might result, and probably would result, in either driving out of business those lines where two rates may with propriety exist, or at all events in unjustly depleting the revenues of those lines. It would give to those lines in whose tariffs the difference is least an undue advantage over other lines in this competitive struggle. Before making any order which would not work injustice in the premises, it would be necessary to determine in each case by how much the domestic rate might properly exceed the export rate, if at all, and compel the observance of this relation. To do this would require us to determine what the differentials between these ports should be, and what reasonable domestic rates to these ports should be, and we certainly cannot undertake to do this upon the testimony before us.

The second circumstance which deters us from attempting to interfere is the existence of water competition. These rates were made before the opening of navigation, and were not probably influenced by that element; but we must dispose of the case with some reference to conditions as they now exist, and water competition is at the present time a factor which cannot be ignored.

By referring to the findings of fact it will be seen that Chicago and Duluth are the two points through which the greatest quantity of wheat and corn passes on its way to the seaboard. From both these points communication with the seaboard can be had by water. The greater part of the grain which leaves these cities for the east moves by water, and it cannot be questioned that the water rate to New York determines the rail or the water and rail rate to that same point. This Commission has always held that water competition, if it in fact exists, is an important circumstance in determining what rates may be justly charged by the rail carrier. The reasons for that have often been stated, and need not be repeated here. The water carrier is not subject to the provisions of the Act to Regulate Commerce; it publishes no rates; it may change its rates from day to day or from hour to hour; it can carry certain commodities at a lower rate probably than can be profitably made by rail. We have therefore been inclined to hold that competition of this kind might be met by the rail carrier without in all cases a corresponding reduction at points not affected by such competition. There is no invariable rule of this sort, nor can it be said that interior and intermediate points ought not to receive any benefit from water competition, but neither can it be affirmed that the carrier should in no case be allowed to meet such competition except at the expense of its interior and intermediate territory. Such a requirement would often be unjust to the carrier and of no benefit to interior points.

In this case the export rate to New York is absolutely fixed by water competition, although, as we have seen, the low export rates were first fixed without reference to such competition. The export rate to New York of necessity fixes that rate through every other port. This being true we are not inclined to say, so far as the export rate is actually controlled by water competition, and while it is so controlled, that carriers must at all points reduce correspondingly their domestic rates. The rate from Chicago to New York is a base rate. Thousands of other rates are a percentage of, or a differential above or below, that rate. A change in that rate automatically works a change in all these other rates. If the carriers prefer to leave the New York domestic rate higher than the export rate by reason of these many dependent rates, we should hardly be justified in interfering unless some specific injustice in some particular case was called to our attention.

Of course no business actually moves during the period of navigation between Chicago and New York upon the domestic rail rate so long as that rate is materially higher than the water rate. Grain to New York can move by water at the same rate both for export and domestic consumption, and the two rates must be practically the same to that point. Furthermore, the New York domestic rate of necessity to an important degree influences other domestic rates upon the seaboard. The Philadelphia miller cannot pay 5 cents per hundred pounds above the New York miller. Carriers apparently meet this condition by lake and rail rates which are much lower than the domestic rail rate, and which apply to both domestic and export traffic as a rule. Under the operation of these tariffs most of the eastern seaboard has the benefit of the low export rate, but we assume that there is some substantial reason why carriers do not reduce all rail domestic rates accordingly.

An examination of the tariffs in effect at the time of the hearing, as well as those at present in effect, shows that the difference between export and domestic rates is the least through the ports of New York, Philadelphia, Baltimore, Norfolk and Newport News. The published rates both at present and in the past show that the relation between the domestic and export rate through these ports is about the same; if there were but one rate at New York there would probably be no occasion for but one through all these ports.

Our conclusion upon this branch of the case is that market conditions sometimes in case of wheat, seldom in case of corn, justify an export rate lower than the domestic through the port of New York; and that water competition may have the same effect. Ordinarily, during the period of closed navigation the export and domestic rate should be the same through that port, and the Atlantic ports above mentioned. Lower export rates may perhaps with propriety be made through other ports, thereby enabling lines leading to them to compete for this export business. Such an adjustment of rates would be to the advantage of the carrier, just to the American consumer, and equally so to the producer. With the opening of navigation water competition introduces a new element which may necessitate, in the fair interest of the carriers, two rates at New York and consequently at all other ports. The problem is primarily one for the carriers rather than this Commission, and we do not think at the present time any interference on our part would contribute to its solution. * * * * * * *

III

The element of direct injury which was absent in the first branch of this case is abundantly present in the second branch. The complaint is that discrimination in the freight rate exists against the milling industry in certain sections of the United States, and the miller makes oath that these freight rates have destroyed or are fast destroying his export business. We have found that this is in a measure true of Milwaukee, Chicago, St. Louis and corresponding territory in the middle west; in all this territory millers are being excluded from the export trade; and we have further found that this apparently results from the improper adjustment of freight rates. In part this improper adjustment consists in giving to certain sections better rates on flour in comparison with the complaining territory than have been previously enjoyed, and in part in creating an unreasonable difference in the rate upon wheat and flour. This being so, to what relief, if any, are the millers entitled? * *

The main complaint of the millers is directed to the difference in rates between export wheat and flour. The findings of fact fully state the case, and from them it clearly appears that a discrimination, and a most grievous one, does exist. It needs no argument to show that, when the entire margin of profit to the American miller in the grinding of export flour does not exceed from 1 to 3 cents per hundred pounds, a difference in the freight rate in favor of the English miller amounting to from 4 to 11 cents per hundred pounds is, other things being equal, prohibitive. The serious question is whether that discrimination is justifiable. * * * * * * *

The carriers insist that the difference in rate is justified first, by water competition, and secondly by additional cost of service.

Water competition certainly limits during the period of navigation, and to a degree before the opening and after the close of navigation, the rates upon wheat and flour. Both the published and actual water rate on wheat has been lower than upon flour; we have found from 2 to 4 cents lower.

This water competition for seven months of the year is not only possible but actual. Of all the traffic leaving Chicago by regular line boats during the period of navigation, 30 per cent is said to be flour and the balance grain and other commodities. It has already been said that water competition may to an extent be properly met by the rail rate. The water line does actually fix these relative rates on wheat and flour, and we think the carriers are justified by that competition in making, to a degree at least, the same difference which is thereby created. The millers urge with force that the rail carriers, by virtue of their control over the line boats by which alone flour is transported, unduly exaggerate the difference in rate between wheat and flour; but the fact still remains that water competition does create a substantial difference in those rates.

We have also found that to a limited extent the cost of service is greater in the transportation of export flour than in that of export wheat, and for this reason under the circumstances of this case we think that a slightly higher rate on flour than on wheat for export is justifiable. This is especially true in view of the fact that the flour rate includes the delivery on shipboard while the wheat rate does not. Th[illegible] Chicago to New York upon flour puts the flou[illegible] vessel, whereas to put export wheat on shipboard an additional charge of about 1⅛ cents per bushel is made. * * * * *

It should perhaps be noticed that, although the rate upon flour has been confessedly higher than upon wheat for many years, the exportation of flour has steadily increased, being 3,947,333 barrels in 1878 and 15,349,943 barrels in 1898. The increase for the last six years has not, however, been marked, and exportations since 1894 have actually declined, having been in that year 16,859,533 barrels.

This Commission is of the opinion that public policy and good railway policy alike require the same rate upon export wheat and flour. Such rates tend to develop both the industries of the United States and the traffic of the railways. We are not, however, here settling national or railroad policy. We are simply administering the Act to Regulate Commerce; and in view of all conditions as we find them, we do not feel that charging a somewhat higher rate on flour than on wheat for export is in violation of that statute. We do think that the published difference is too wide, and that the rate upon flour for export ought not to exceed that upon wheat by more than 2 cents per hundred pounds. * * * * * * *

XIX

FREIGHT CLASSIFICATION

The Hatters' Furs Case[1]

Prouty, *Commissioner:*

The complainant is engaged in the manufacture of hats under the title of the Pioneer Hat Works at Wabash, Indiana, and his complaint is that "hatters' furs" and "fur scraps and cuttings" are wrongly classified, the present classification of both these commodities being double first class, while he insists that hatters' furs should be classified as first class and fur scraps and cuttings as second class. . . .

Hatters' furs is a trade name applicable to the various kinds of fur used in the manufacture of hats. These furs, as sold to the manufacturer and presented for transportation, are sheared from the skin, and packed in paper bags containing three or five pounds each, which are then assembled in wooden cases, 100 bags to the case. The case thus weighs from three to five hundred pounds and is in size about 36″ x 36″ x 40″, containing some 30 cu. ft. * * * * * *

The complainant testified that rabbit fur was the sort mostly used by him in the manufacture of hats, although he used to some extent nutria, and that the value of the furs which he used was from $.40 to $2.50 per pound. The complainant makes a medium grade of fur hats. More of the higher priced furs would probably enter into the manufacture of hats of a higher grade. These furs, nutria and beaver, average in price as high as $6 per pound, and the price list show that the best grade of beaver has at times listed at $15 per pound; but it is fairly

[1] Decided November 21, 1901. Interstate Commerce Reports, Vol. IX, pp. 79–86.

inferable from the testimony that rabbit fur is the kind mainly used in the manufacture of fur hats of all grades, the more expensive sorts of fur being used only in comparatively small quantities. The testimony is not sufficiently definite to justify an exact finding, but we think it fairly appears, and find, that the average value of hatters' furs would be from $1 to $2 per pound, the great bulk of that commodity presented for transportation being within these limits.

The term fur scraps and cuttings seems to include the waste produced in working up fur pelts for various purposes. It embraces not only the waste from the preparation of hatters' furs but also the pieces which are left in the manufacture of fur garments. These fur scraps are purchased by fur brokers, by whom they are assorted into different grades and sold to different persons for various uses at widely different prices. The complainant testified that the fur scraps and cuttings used in the manufacture of hats were worth from 2½ to 40 cents per pound. The pieces of fur which would also be embraced under the same title are often worth much more than this, sometimes as high as $1.50 per pound.

It is extremely difficult to fix any fair average value, but we are inclined to think that the great bulk of fur scraps and cuttings offered for transportation could not exceed in value 50 cents per pound, and that the average would not equal this. Fur scraps and cuttings are transported in cases, bags or bales weighing from 450 to 500 pounds. The proportion between bulk and weight is about the same as with hatters' furs.

Manufactured hats are classified first class and the complainant insisted that this was a discrimination against the raw material.

Upon this point testimony was given by both parties as to comparative value and desirability from a traffic standpoint of the raw material and the finished product.

Hatters' furs are put through three processes in preparation for use in the manufacture of hats and shrink about two ounces in the pound. Fur scraps and cuttings pass through from twelve to eighteen processes and only from 10 to 33⅓ per cent in weight of usable fur is obtained. In the manufacture of the hat itself the average is still further shrunk.

Hats are shipped in cases weighing about sixty pounds to the case and are from two to three times more bulky than hatters' furs or fur scraps and cuttings. The complainant also insisted that they were much more valuable by the pound. This was denied by the defendants who claimed that the average value of all hats was less by the pound than the average value of hatters' furs.

Hats other than straw are sometimes made of other material besides fur, but the complainant testified that the proportion of fur hats to other hats would be fifty to one. Caps are made of cloth. The average value of fur hats per pound must greatly exceed the average value of the hatters' furs which enter into their construction, and without doubt this is true of all hats other than straw. It would be unprofitable to hazard a guess as to whether this might or might not be the case if straw hats were included.

The complainant further insisted that hatters' furs and fur scraps and cuttings were a more desirable kind of traffic than hats and caps for the reason that they were less liable to loss or damage in transit. From the very nature of the articles it is almost impossible that hatters' furs or fur scraps and cuttings should be stolen. They are not combustible and not easily injured by water or by jamming; and any injury from these causes would be confined to what was actually injured. Upon the contrary a hat is ready to wear and this is an inducement to abstract one from a case. Injury to a small part of a hat spoils the entire article. The complainant testified that in the whole course of his business he had never made a claim for damage to hatters' furs or fur scraps in transit while he had frequently had occasion to do so in case of hats.

The complainant is the only manufacturer of hats located in the West. All his competitors are upon the Atlantic seaboard in near proximity to New York. Most of these hatters' furs are imported and are distributed from the port of New York. The complainant claims that by reason of the higher rate upon raw material than upon the manufactured product he is placed at a disadvantage in comparison with the eastern manufacturer.

The market of the complainant is the whole United States west of Pittsburg and in all that territory he competes with the eastern manufacturer. The exact points in the East at which these competitors are located did not appear, and it is not therefore possible to make any exact comparison of rates; but generally speaking the rate from these eastern points is that of Boston or New York. There is considerable territory, like the Pacific Coast, to which rates upon hats are the same from the Atlantic seaboard as from Wabash, and in nearly all territory the sum of the rates, upon the same class, from New York to Wabash and from Wabash to the point of consumption is considerably greater than the rate from New York to the last-named destination.

Some question was raised as to the amount of complainant's shipments per year. Mr. Gill, Chairman of the Official Classification Committee, stated that a compilation of these shipments had been made and that they aggregated about 150,000 pounds per year. The rate from New York to Wabash is 72 cents, first class, and $1.44 double first class. If, therefore, the complainant is right in his contention as to what the correct classification should be he is damaged to the extent of something more than $1000 annually upon the statement of the defendants.

The complainant also urged that the classification in question created undue prejudice against his commodities as compared with dry goods, boots and shoes and many other articles classified as first class.

About 250 articles are classified as double first class by the Official Classification. Generally speaking, such articles offer some special reason for the classification, like unusual bulk, extraordinary risk, or something of that nature. An examination of the entire list fails to disclose a single commodity which affords as desirable traffic as the one under consideration, and in only three or four instances is there any approach to this. Something like 1500 articles are classified as first class. We have examined this list and our conclusion is that but very few of them are as desirable freight as hatters' furs and fur scraps and cuttings, and that none of them are more so.

No special reasons were shown why these two commodities should pay a higher rate than other similar commodities.

Conclusions

Upon these facts the complainant contends that the present classification of hatters' furs and fur scraps and cuttings is in violation of the Act to Regulate Commerce. His position is that in the forming of a classification a proper relation between different articles should be preserved and that when these articles under consideration are compared with others analogous from a transportation standpoint it appears that this present classification is too high.

To this the defendant replies that one commodity should not be compared with another unless the two are competitive; hatters' furs cannot therefore be tested by dry goods or boots and shoes. Mr. Gill, Chairman of the Official Classification Committee, speaking both as a witness and as counsel for the defendants, asserts that the main element in the determination of a classification is "value of service" or "what the traffic will bear."

There is undoubtedly much, we do not find it necessary to now inquire how much, truth in this contention of Mr. Gill; but it cannot be admitted that those are the only considerations to be observed. It has been repeatedly claimed by carriers and repeatedly held by the Commission that in the forming of a classification bulk, value, liability to damage, and similar elements affecting the desirability of the traffic should be considered, and that analogous articles should ordinarily be placed in the same class. *Warner* v. *New York C. & H. R. R. Co.*, 4 I. C. C. Rep. 32, 3 Inters. Com. Rep. 74; *Harvard Co.* v. *Pennsylvania Co.*, 4 I. C. C. Rep. 212, 3 Inters. Com. Rep. 257; *Page* v. *Delaware, L. & W. R. Co.*, 6 I. C. C. Rep. 548. Manifestly in determining what freight rates shall be borne by different commodities an attempt should be made to obtain a fair relation between those commodities, and a classification which utterly ignores all considerations of this kind or which utterly fails to give due weight to such considerations is unjust and unreasonable.

The present case falls within this rule. Here are two commodities, not bulky, offered for transportation in packages of convenient size, of not great value, and with practically no liability to loss or damage in transit. It has been found that hardly an article among all those in first class is so desirable traffic as they are, and still these commodities are classified as double first class. In our opinion this is unlawful. They should not be classified higher than first class. We should be inclined to say that fur scraps and cuttings must not be rated higher than second class were it not for the claim of the defendants that this would lead to fraud in the billing of furs as fur scraps.

There is another ground upon which the same conclusion must be reached. Mr. Gill himself admits that when two articles are competitive no preference should be shown in the freight rate. Hatters' fur, the raw material, does compete in a way with hats, the finished product, and we do not think that, under the circumstances of this case, the rate upon the raw material ought to be greater than that upon the finished product.

The complainant is located at Wabash, Ind., and is the only manufacturer of hats west of the Atlantic seaboard. Most of his competitors are in the immediate vicinity of New York from whence supplies of hatters' furs and fur scraps and cuttings are almost entirely drawn. For the purpose of noting the effect upon the complainant, let us assume that his competitor is located in New York itself.

The complainant pays upon his raw material double first class, and that raw material shrinks about one half in process of manufacture. His competitor pays upon the finished product first class or just one half the rate paid by the complainant upon the raw material. The item of freight, therefore, costs the complainant at his factory three or four times what it costs his competitor in laying down the same hat at that point.

The complainant sells exclusively in territory west of Pittsburg and the defendants urge that he has an advantage over his competitors in freights by reason of closer proximity to the market. But a moment's consideration will show that at points other than Wabash the discrimination is even greater than at the complainant's factory. In some at least of this competitive territory rates from the Atlantic seaboard and Wabash are the same, so that the complainant pays freight upon the raw material in addition to the same rate as the eastern manufacturer upon the finished hat. In none of this competitive territory probably is the rate from the east as great as the rate to Wabash plus the rate from Wabash to the point of consumption.

In determining the relative amounts paid upon the raw material and the finished product we have disregarded the weight of the cases. This is somewhat more in the case of hats than hatters' furs, but there is no definite testimony upon this point.

The defendants say that the complainant is the only person who is finding fault with this classification. Were this true, and without apparent reason, it would be no ground for denying him the relief to which he is entitled; but here the reason is sufficiently obvious since the discrimination is to the advantage of every other manufacturer as against the complainant.

Neither is this a case, as the defendants intimate, where the matter is of so slight consequence that it should not be inquired into nor redressed. The law has a maxim that it will not concern itself with trifles and this perhaps ought to be all the more true of traffic conditions where there can be no exact rule; but in the case before us the excess paid by the complainants according to the statement of the defendants amounts to $1000 a year, which can hardly be called a trifle to the complainant, however it might be with the defendants. We think the present adjustment between the raw material and the finished product is unjust and unduly prejudicial to the complainant and that this should be corrected. * * * * * * *

The fixing of a classification determines the relation of rates, not the rate itself. If we transfer these two commodities from double first class to first class, we do not thereby determine the rate under which they shall move in the future. The revenues of the defendants are not necessarily diminished since they may advance rates applicable to these classes. In *Danville* v. *Southern R. Co.*, 8 I. C. C. Rep. 409, the right of determining the relation in rates which should exist between two localities was exercised and the same principle must apply to the relation between two commodities. In that case it was said that the authority was not clear, but having exercised it then, and believing that a plain distinction exists between fixing a rate and determining a relation in rates, we shall continue to do so until the Supreme Court of the United States has held otherwise.

* * * * * * * *

XX

HOW THE STATES MAKE INTERSTATE RATES[1]

THE widespread efforts of state legislatures and railroad commissions within the past two years to reduce railroad rates have presented many interesting phases to public observation. The extent and severity of the proposed reductions, the novel expedients adopted to prevent or to make difficult a review of the state action in the federal courts, the resulting conflict of judicial authority and the recent decision of the Supreme Court of the United States holding these expedients unconstitutional have kept the movement constantly in the public mind. Out of the many questions which discussion of the situation has evolved none are more interesting or important than those relating to the effect of state-made rates upon rates for interstate transportation. It is the purpose of this article not to show that the rate-making power of the states should be diminished or destroyed, or that this object, if desirable, can or cannot be accomplished under the federal constitution, but merely to state and to illustrate the proposition that, in fact, the states *do* make interstate rates.

The great movements of traffic in this country are eastward and westward. The volume of the westward movement has always been high-class merchandise, — dry goods, wearing apparel, groceries, hardware, and like articles. Formerly this was all produced in the East or imported through Atlantic ports; it is only within recent years that the larger cities in the West have become manufacturing centers.

When the evolution of our rate fabric began New York, Boston, Philadelphia, and Baltimore were the bases of supply.

[1] By Robert Mather. A paper prepared for the American Academy of Political Science, and published in its *Annals*, 1908. By permission. Much of the matter and all the maps for this article were prepared by Mr. Theodore Brent, of the Traffic Department, Rock Island-Frisco Lines, Chicago.

Chicago, St. Louis, St. Paul, Omaha, and Kansas City owe their development as trade centers primarily to strategic location at the head of navigation, or at points where the trans-continental trails left the watercourses for the West, Northwest, and Southwest. They commenced as outfitting points for prospectors and settlers; their business was that of distributing through the new western country the articles of commerce manufactured in or imported through the East; and that still constitutes a large part of their trade.

When railroads found their way to Chicago and St. Louis their rates were fixed largely by the water competition which met them on their arrival. Gradually railroads were constructed westward from these points and, as they reached common territory, the force of competition began to be felt. Intense rivalry developed between the distributing houses of Chicago and St. Louis, and pressure was brought to bear upon the railroads, both East and West, to keep the rate fabric so adjusted that goods, stored in and distributed from either city, might be laid down at any of the Missouri river points at substantially the same freight cost. The class rates from New York to Chicago thus became the basis of measurement for all class rates. The St. Louis rate was a fixed per cent higher, approximating the difference in the cost of reaching that point by water. The rates between the Mississippi river and Chicago on the one hand and the Missouri river on the other were fixed not at what would be a reasonable rate for the distance, but at what it was necessary to maintain in order that St. Louis and the lines leading through St. Louis might compete with Chicago for the expanding business of Kansas City, Atchison, St. Joseph, and Omaha.

In the territory west of the Missouri river the same process has been repeated, and rates are maintained in such relation not only that Kansas City, St. Joseph, and Omaha may compete with each other, but that goods distributed from St. Louis and Chicago, as well as from the eastern cities, may be handled through either Kansas City, St. Joseph, or Omaha and laid down at the several consuming points at practically the same freight cost. In the Northwest this same competitive adjustment is maintained between Chicago, Duluth, Minneapolis, and St. Paul. In the Southwest, Chicago, St. Louis, and Kansas City must be kept on an even keel, and when Texas is reached, the whole adjustment is modified to meet the competition of coastwise steamers plying from New York to Galveston. To Colorado and Utah, the routes through all these gateways are kept in constant adjustment, and the rates so arranged that Denver and Pueblo are enabled to do a distributing business.

What is true of westbound merchandise is equally true of the movement to the East of the great staples raised in the West. The grain territory is so divided and rates are so made that grain may move freely to the Mississippi river, the Lakes, and the Gulf, through the great storage centers of Minneapolis, Duluth, Chicago, St. Louis, Omaha, and Kansas City. In like manner live-stock rates are so arranged that the traffic may move freely to the rival packing centers of Kansas City, St. Joseph, Omaha, St. Paul, Chicago, and St. Louis.

These rate relations are not the work of the traffic departments of the railroads. They do not exist by virtue of acts of legislatures or of orders of commissions. They are the resultants of the commercial growth of the country. Trade is established along these lines; industries and communities are founded on the basis of these adjustments, and their existence and prosperity depend upon the continuance of these rate relations. They are the controlling facts in all rate disputes — more stubborn than distance and as immovable as mountains.

There is hardly a rate on any article of commerce but feels the force of these competitive conditions. They absolutely dictate the traffic policy of the railroads operating in the territory affected by them. The carrier makes no rates that are not effectively molded by these conditions, and the rate-making power of the Interstate Commerce Commission itself cannot ignore them. The only rate-regulating body that makes rates without reference to these commercial conditions is the legislature or the railroad commission of a single state. Its field of operations includes but a fraction of the territory whose traffic is controlled by these conditions; contains but few of the larger distributing centers which compete for that traffic; and is usually circumscribed, either wholly or in part, by imaginary boundaries fixed without regard to factors which exercise controlling influence upon the trend of traffic and of rates. The influence of lakes, of rivers and canals, the competition of rival markets, the relation between manufacturer and dealer, and other like forces that, in the making of rates, confront the traffic officer of an interstate railroad and the Interstate Commerce Commission itself, enter but slightly, if at all, into the calculations of the state. In every case, in the exercise of its rate-making power, distance is the one factor given serious consideration; and the result of its labors is invariably the production of a distance tariff.

This state distance tariff, is, on its face, a simple and a harmless thing. The right of the state to make it and to change it at its will seems to be amply buttressed by the conceded principle of law that the power of Congress over interstate commerce leaves untouched the power of the states to regulate their purely internal commerce. And no simpler or less obnoxious method of exercising that power would seem possible than to prescribe the rates at which traffic shall move from point to point within the state.

But when the traffic officer of an interstate railroad comes to apply this state distance tariff, made for state use on purely local considerations, to the traffic that actually moves over his rails, he finds that he cannot confine its influence to traffic within the state, and that, against his will and without his action, it readjusts his rates into and out of and through the state, and determines his revenue on traffic that never traverses the borders of the state. This is illustrated by the action of the following states:

Missouri and Iowa

Missouri has a far-reaching control over interstate rates by reason of the situation of the state at the point of least distance between the Mississippi river — the basing line for rates from the East — and the Missouri river, the base line for rates to the West.

There are three factors which go to make up the rates from the East to the western territory, — whether or not they are published as through rates, — namely, the rate from the seaboard to the Mississippi river or Chicago; the rate from the latter base line to the Missouri river; and the rate west of the Missouri river. Reduce the rate between the Mississippi river and the Missouri river and you reduce the rates on all business either locally or through or beyond these base lines.

The first-class rate between the Mississippi and Missouri rivers practically determines the interstate rates on all classified articles moving between the East and West. It is at present 60 cents per 100 pounds, this being the figure fixed by the Missouri Railroad and Warehouse Commission as a reasonable maximum rate for the short-line haul of approximately 200 miles across the state from the Mississippi to the Missouri — the distance from Hannibal to St. Joseph being 196 miles, and from Hannibal to Kansas City, 199 miles. Note the chart.

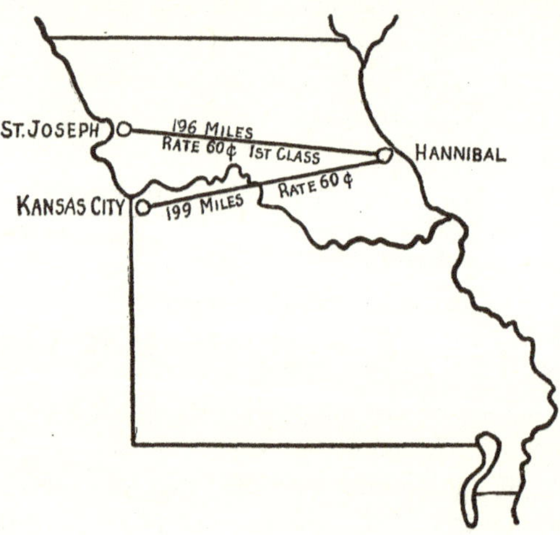

Though this rate is based on the distance of 200 miles, competitive conditions outside the state apply it at once to all hauls across the state, no matter what their distance. The short line from St. Louis to St. Joseph is 302 miles, and lines operating between those cities would be privileged, under the commission's maximum scale, to charge 74 cents, first class. The short line between St. Louis and Kansas City is 277 miles, for which distance the commission's scale is 71 cents, first class. But here considerations enter which are entirely outside the horizon of the Missouri commission. The rates from New York to Hannibal and St. Louis are the same. There are routes leading from New York to St. Joseph and Kansas City, through both Hannibal and St. Louis. Kansas City and St. Joseph compete in the same trade territory, and the rates to both points from New York must be kept the same through all gateways. Consequently the commission's maximum rate for the shortest distance becomes the rate between all four crossings.

Thus the element of distance even between points within the state is immediately modified by outside forces, controlling with the carriers, but which exerted no influence upon the commission when it fixed the nominal measure of the rates.

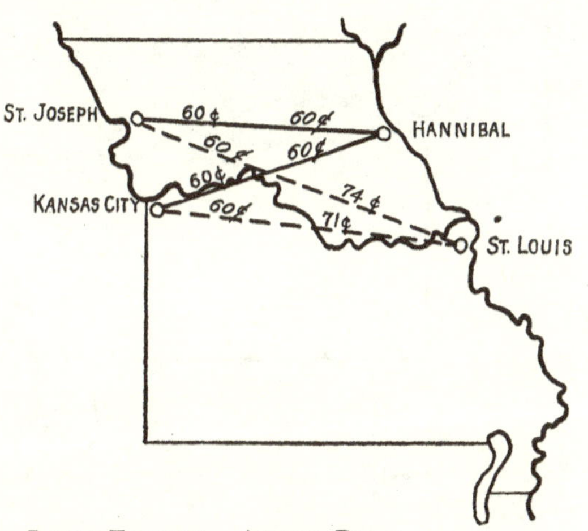

ITALIC FIGURES = ACTUAL RATES
ROMAN FIGURES = MISSOURI MAXIMUM RATES

Just north of Missouri lies the State of Iowa. To the untutored mind there would seem to be no reason why traffic of the same class should move within the State of Iowa for a less charge than within the State of Missouri. Yet the maximum charge under the Iowa distance tariff for hauling first-class merchandise 200 miles is 40 cents, as against 60 cents fixed by the Missouri tariff. The railroads in Iowa must haul the same class of merchandise 350 miles to be entitled to charge 60 cents; but, significantly enough, the 350 miles measure the distance in Iowa between the Mississippi and Missouri rivers, so that the rate between the two base lines is the same in both states. Should Missouri adopt the Iowa scale, the Missouri rate from the Mississippi river to the Missouri river, between all the points in Missouri that we have been considering, would, for the reasons already given, at once become 40 cents, regardless of distance.

The effect within the State of Missouri, however, is only the beginning. The rate between the Mississippi and Missouri rivers being, as previously explained, one of three factors of a through adjustment from points of production in the East; the rates from the East to all Mississippi river crossings being the same; there being competitive routes from the East to all Missouri river points passing through all of these Mississippi river crossings; and the merchants and manufacturers in the Mississippi river cities maintaining trade relations with all of the Missouri river cities and with the territory reached through them; it follows that the rate between Dubuque, Iowa, and Kansas City, Missouri, cannot be higher than the rate between Dubuque and Council Bluffs (both points within the state of Iowa); nor can the rate between St. Louis, Missouri, and Omaha, Nebraska, be higher than the rate between St. Louis and Kansas City or between St. Louis and St. Joseph (movements wholly within the State of Missouri).

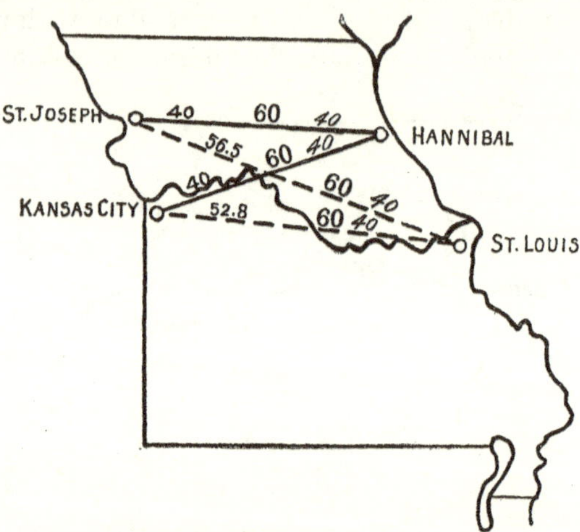

Small Roman Figures = Rates Permissible, based on Actual Mileage, Iowa Scale applied in Missouri.
Italic Figures = Rates Carriers would actually be forced to charge by Reason of Outside Forces.
Large Roman Figures = Present Rates

Thus from the act of the Missouri commission in reducing its distance tariff from 60 cents to 40 cents for 200 miles, the following results directly flow:

(*a*) The local *Missouri* rate from points on the Mississippi river to points on the Missouri river, regardless of mileage, is reduced from 60 cents to 40 cents;

(*b*) The local *Iowa* rate from points on the Mississippi river to points on the Missouri river (say Clinton to Council Bluffs, 350 miles) is reduced from 60 cents to 40 cents;

(*c*) The *interstate* rate from points on the Mississippi river in Missouri to points on the Missouri river in Iowa or Nebraska (say St. Louis to Council Bluffs or Omaha) is reduced;

(*d*) The *interstate* rate from points on the Missouri river in Missouri to points on the Mississippi river in Iowa (say Kansas City to Davenport) is reduced.

Not only this, but this Missouri commission rate for 200 miles fixes the maximum rate which the Missouri Pacific Railway may charge for its haul of 488 miles between St. Louis and Omaha, through Missouri, Kansas, and Nebraska; and in like manner the rate of the Illinois Central Railroad for its haul of 703 miles between the same points, through the States of Missouri, Illinois, and Iowa. See the map [p. 538].

Thus, within the territory inclosed by the Illinois Central, Missouri Pacific, and Rock Island as outlined on the map, any reduction made by the Missouri commission in the class rates for the 200-mile distance between Hannibal, Missouri, and Kansas City, Missouri, has the effect of bringing all rates to the level so fixed, not only between the crossings themselves but, with very slight exceptions, between all intermediate points.

This, again, is but a preliminary glimpse at the inevitable results of this action of the Missouri State Commission.

The first-class rate from Chicago to the Missouri river has for many years been 20 cents per 100 pounds higher than the rate from the Mississippi river. The competitive adjustment would require that there be no greater difference under the new scale. Indeed, the rates from the seaboard to Chicago and the Mississippi river remaining as at present, it is doubtful if Chicago and the routes through Chicago could compete should the present arbitrary difference be maintained under the reduced adjustment. The present rate of 80 cents, first class, from Chicago, is one-third higher than the rate from the Mississippi to the Missouri river. It is probable that not more than one-third greater would

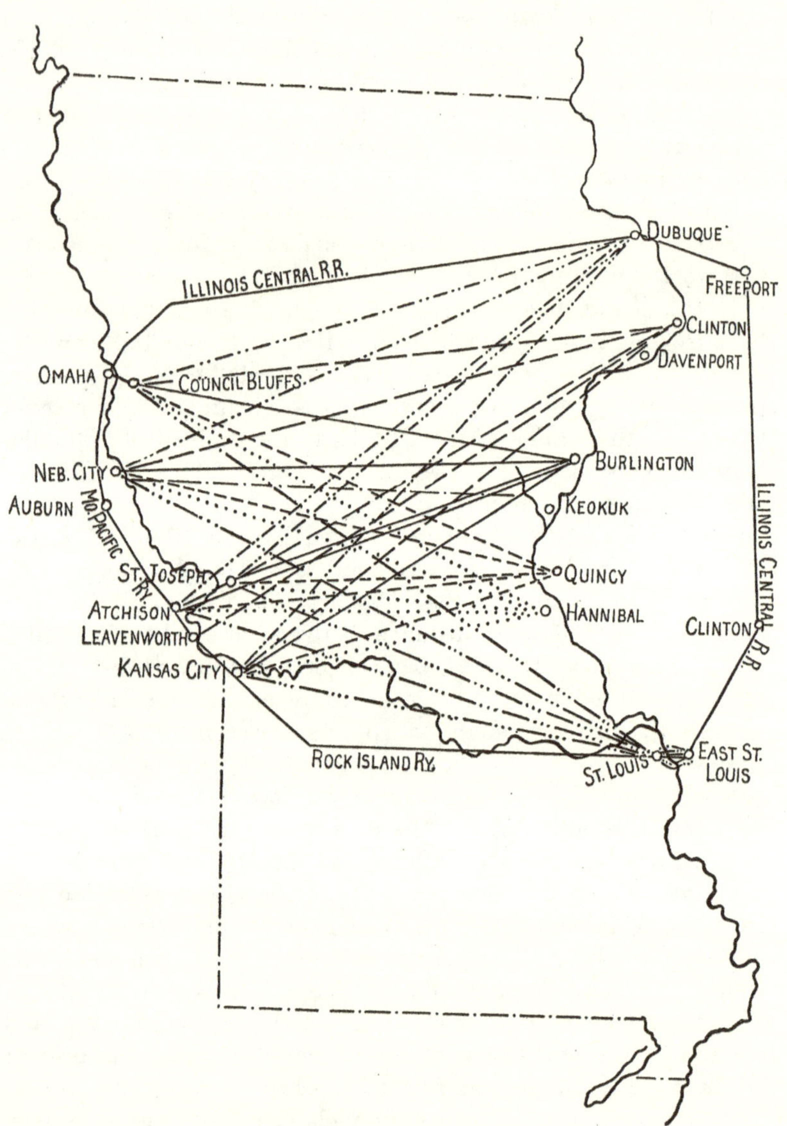
DUBUQUE
FREEPORT
ILLINOIS CENTRAL R.R.
CLINTON
DAVENPORT
OMAHA
COUNCIL BLUFFS
BURLINGTON
NEB. CITY
ILLINOIS CENTRAL R.R.
AUBURN
MO. PACIFIC RY.
KEOKUK
ST. JOSEPH
QUINCY
ATCHISON
HANNIBAL
LEAVENWORTH
CLINTON
KANSAS CITY
ROCK ISLAND RY.
ST. LOUIS
EAST ST. LOUIS

be practicable under the lowered scale, which would make the first-class rate from Chicago 54 cents per 100 pounds.

Peoria must be maintained at one half the difference between Chicago and the Mississippi river. Milwaukee must be kept on the same rate basis as Chicago. The rates from Minneapolis and St. Paul must be kept the same as Chicago to the Upper Missouri river crossings (Omaha, Council Bluffs, and Nebraska City), and 5 cents higher than Chicago to the lower crossings (St. Joseph, Atchison, Leavenworth, and Kansas City). Duluth takes fixed arbitraries above St. Paul. The intervening territory in Wisconsin, between Milwaukee and St. Paul, is built on arbitraries over either Chicago, Milwaukee, or St. Paul, and would call for readjustment accordingly. From Memphis, Tennessee, not higher than Chicago rates can be maintained to Lower Missouri river crossings, and to the upper crossings the first-class rate from Memphis cannot be more than two cents higher than Chicago. To Sioux City the rate from Chicago, St. Louis, and Peoria must be kept the same as from Chicago to Omaha. The first-class rate from Memphis to Sioux City is to-day 30 cents higher, and from Minneapolis and St. Paul 20 cents less, than from Chicago to Sioux City, and the same percentage relation must be maintained on the lower scale.

The immediate result, then, of the fixing by the Missouri commission of a maximum charge of 40 cents, first class, for the distance of 200 miles between Hannibal, Missouri, and Kansas City, Missouri, is to fix the rates for all routes shown on the map [p. 540] of what is termed Western Trunk Line territory.

The foregoing outline illustrates only the adjustment of first-class rates. In Western Classification territory there are five numbered and five lettered classes, and the other classes all bear a certain percentage relation to the first-class rates. This is true to the extent that any considerable reduction in the rate on first class involves necessary proportionate reductions in the rates on other classes, the severity of any such reduction lessening, of course, as the rates themselves grow less; but the rates on all classes must go down if one goes down, so that the same fixed relation between the classes may be maintained on the lower as on the higher basis.

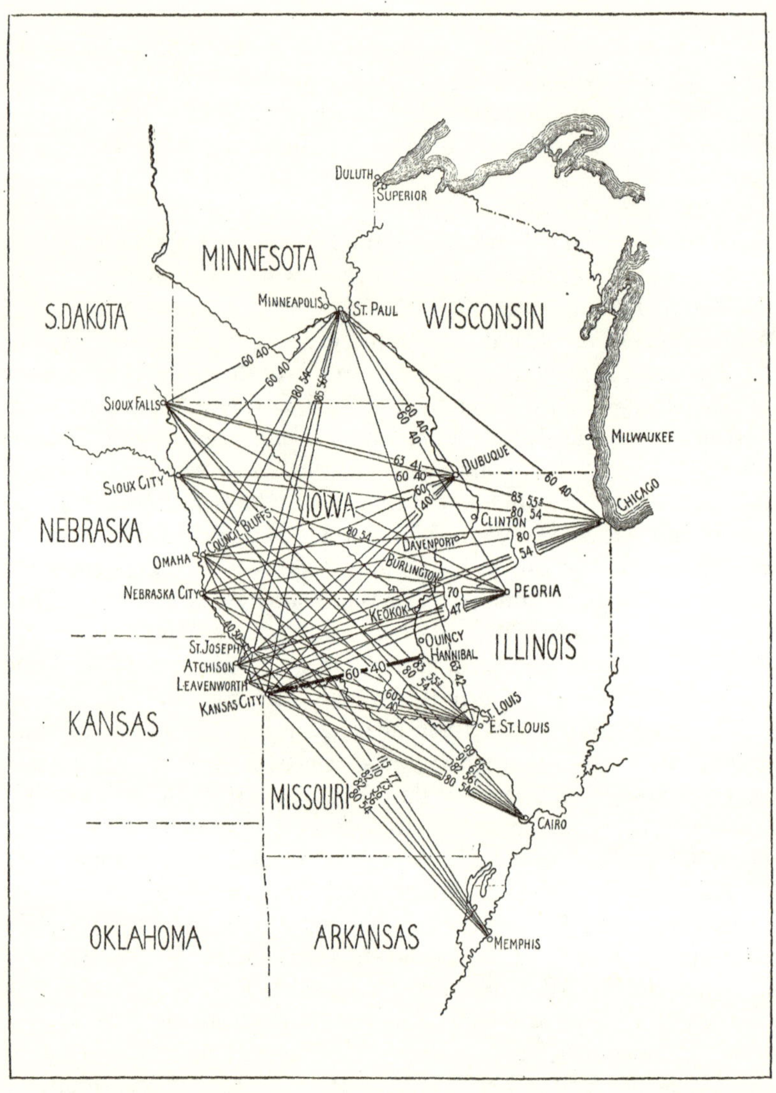

The broad line indicates the short-line distance of 199 miles across the state of Missouri between Hannibal and Kansas City which measures and controls all western rates.

Left-hand figures indicate present rates.

Right-hand figures indicate approximately the rates which would result were the Missouri commission to prescribe the Iowa scale as the maximum which may be charged in the State of Missouri.

Similarly, the outline only illustrates the change in the adjustment between the principal basing points in Western Trunk Line territory. But around these basing points are grouped all the adjacent cities and towns; so that an adjustment once reduced from Chicago, or Peoria, or the Mississippi river to the Upper or Lower Missouri river points, a corresponding reduction results from all points, both of origin and of destination, held common with these basing points. So the reductions become automatic, covering all interstate movements throughout the whole territory pictured in the outline.

The illustration thus far deals only with the change in rates on business which may be termed purely local to the territory immediately embraced in the illustration; that is, business which has both origin and destination within the territory. We have not yet touched upon that volume of eastern business to the Missouri river cities, to St. Paul and Duluth, and to the territory beyond as far west as the states of Utah, Idaho, and Montana, or to the southwest, including the State of Texas and territory of New Mexico. Yet the rates on this business are quite as vitally involved. The competitive adjustment between Chicago, Peoria, Memphis, the Mississippi river, and the head of the Lakes, as previously described, was originally evolved and has since been maintained in a measure to permit this merchandise to move freely by all routes to this trans-Missouri, northwestern and southwestern territory. Whenever the western factors of the through rates to this territory are reduced, the rates on such through business fall simultaneously with the rates on the local business.

Merchandise for this western territory moves from the East by every conceivable route. Every all-rail line and every conceivable combination of rail lines publish the rates. During lake navigation daily boats carry this merchandise to Chicago, Milwaukee, and the head of the Lakes. It is handled by steamer in connection with rail lines from every South Atlantic port from Norfolk to Jacksonville. There is a steamer load dispatched daily from New York and given to the rail lines at the port of Galveston, Texas. The rate fixed by the authority of the state of Missouri, between Hannibal and Kansas City, and based on purely local considerations, has its leveling effect upon the rates on every pound of this vast traffic. The next map shows the ultimate reach of the rate-making power of Missouri.

It is true that the illustration has proceeded thus far on the assumption that Missouri might make a reduction in its existing class rates, and not on the fact that such reduction has been made. But Iowa has precisely the same control over interstate adjustments that the illustration demonstrates Missouri to have, and as matter of fact east-and-west class rates are what they are to-day because Iowa some years ago prescribed 60 cents as the maximum charge, first class, for the haul within its borders between the Mississippi and the Missouri rivers. The Iowa distance tariff of 1887 actually measures to-day the revenues of the interstate railroads on all interstate freight passing into or out of or beyond that state.

Besides, Missouri has actually made radical reductions in other rates that illustrate as well the principle of our contention. The legislature of 1905 ordered drastic reductions of rates on grain, flour, lime, salt, cement, stucco, lumber, agricultural implements, furniture, wagons, and live stock, and the legislature of 1907 added stone, gravel, and other commodities. The rates have not been published, as the constitutionality of the legislation is in question before the courts; but if the state's right to order the reductions is finally established, the interstate rates on these bulk commodities, which constitute a large percentage of the carload tonnage of all western carriers, will come down with them.

The reductions which will result in rates on grain will illustrate. The short-line distance rate between the Missouri and Mississippi rivers will be reduced from 13 cents per 100 pounds, on wheat, and 12 cents per 100 pounds on corn and other grain, to 8½ cents per 100 pounds on all grain. The state's action also calls for a reduction of ½ cent per 100 pounds in the proportional rate on wheat between Kansas City and Hannibal. This proportional rate of 9 cents is the rate applied on all wheat coming from beyond the Missouri river, and, as in the case of the class rates, it is the pivotal rate in the whole adjustment. If the legislature's

is forced in the rate to Pensacola, Florida, Mobile, Alabama, New Orleans, Louisiana, and Port Arthur and Galveston, Texas, for export.

It has never been found feasible to carry local and proportional rates on the same basis, and there is therefore the probability of further reduction in the proportional basis. To what figure the proportional rate on wheat across Missouri might fall as the result of carrying a local rate of 8½ cents is, of course, problematical. The rates up to this time have always been maintained about four cents lower than the local rates. The accompanying chart only illustrates the direct reductions in the existing proportional rates.

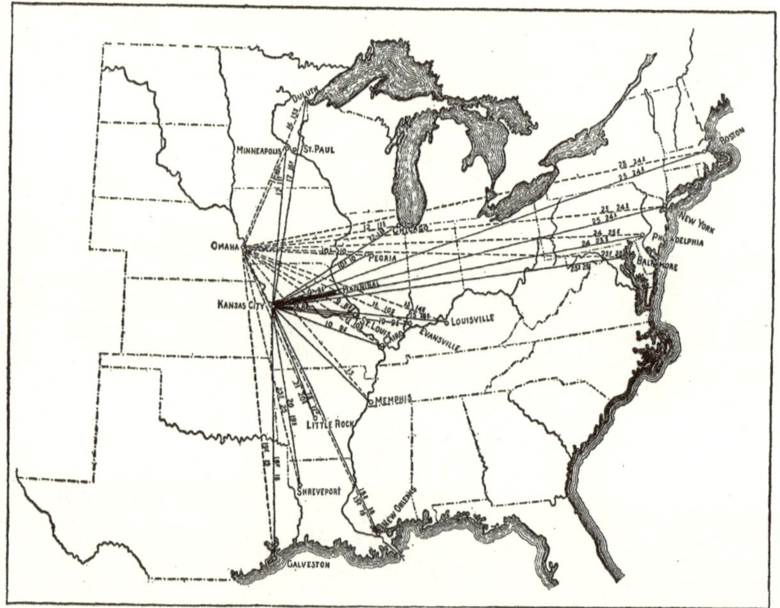

Reduction in the wheat and flour rate adjustment immediately resulting from reduction in the state mileage rates ordered by the Missouri legislature.

The broad line indicates the controlling distance of 199 miles between the Missouri and Mississippi river basing points.

LEFT-HAND FIGURES = PRESENT PROPORTIONAL RATES

RIGHT-HAND FIGURES = REDUCED RATES MADE NECESSARY BY REDUCTION IN RATE FROM KANSAS CITY TO HANNIBAL

KANSAS AND NEBRASKA

During the year 1907 the Railroad Commission of Kansas forced a reduction of 15 per cent in the existing rates on grain within the state. A reduction in grain rates always applies as well on flour, meal, and other grain products. The Nebraska Commission forced a 15 per cent reduction in state rates, not only on grain and grain products, but on live stock, coal, lumber and fruits, and vegetables.

Kansas and Nebraska do not consume a hundredth part of what they produce, and the great bulk of the commodities consumed within these states is produced outside of them. The freight destined from points of origin within either state and moving under the state's mileage rates to points of consumption within the state, is as nothing to that which moves to points beyond the state. That is to say, nearly all the traffic of both the states is interstate, and subject to the influence of the competitive interstate rate adjustments.

The products of Kansas and Nebraska find their primary markets (Kansas City, Kansas, and Omaha, Nebraska) on the Missouri river at the extreme eastern boundary of the state, and the state regulation fixes the rate at which the product is hauled from points of production to these primary markets, no matter what the ultimate destination of the product may be. As a result, the 15 per cent reductions in the grain rates required by both state commissions have called for a flat reduction of just that amount in all interstate rates, and a corresponding shrinkage in railroad revenues on practically all of the grain raised in both the states.

A contingent result is a horizontal reduction in the rates on Oklahoma grain. The Choctaw line of the Rock Island operates in Oklahoma under a charter which provides that its rates in that state must not be higher than they are in the states from which it enters Oklahoma. The line enters Oklahoma from Kansas, as well as from Arkansas, and the charter provision required an immediate adjustment of the Oklahoma rates on the Kansas scale. With the Oklahoma rates on the Kansas basis it was found impossible to maintain the adjustment formerly prevailing from points in southern Oklahoma to points in Texas, and a readjustment there was necessary. Similar reductions of the rates to Arkansas points will be required.

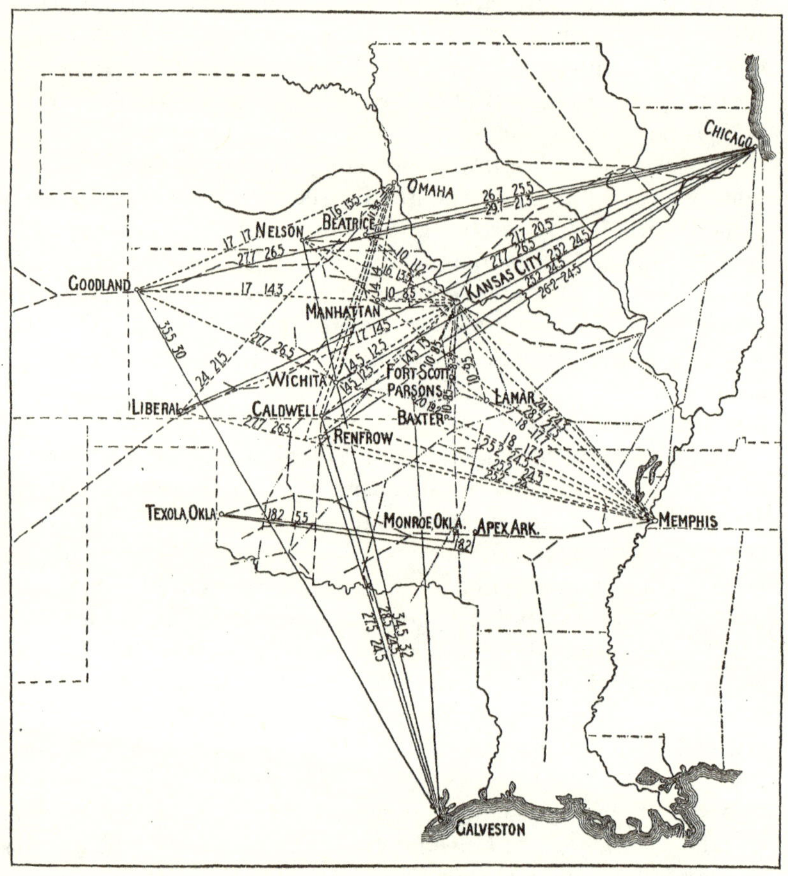

CHANGES IN WHEAT RATES[1]

Left-hand figures are former rates.
Right-hand figures are rates forced by Commission's reductions.

[1] Necessitated by the 15 per cent reduction ordered by the Kansas and Nebraska Commissions on their intrastate rates. Other grains and grain products are similarly affected. Every point is affected like the few here shown.

This situation clearly illustrates the interdependence of state and interstate rates. The chart on page 546 will give a partial illustration of the situation. It can, of course, picture the effect only at a few points. The reductions are general, affecting every point.

Texas

In Texas, state regulation of rates is deliberately designed to control the rates on interstate business both into and out of the state. There is, from the standpoint of the state, excellent reason for this policy; for, aside from its timber and a portion of its grain, little which Texas produces is consumed within the state, and the bulk of the food stuffs, wearing apparel, and manufactured articles which its citizens consume or use are imported from other states.

The State Commission has always conceived it to be to the state's interest to link its fortunes with the coastwise steamship lines rather than with the all-rail carriers reaching the state through its northern gateways. Consequently the Commission has made the port of Galveston the radiating point in its adjustment. The class rates from the eastern seaboard have always been made the exact combination of the steamship rates from New York, Boston, Philadelphia, and Baltimore to the port of Galveston, plus the Commission's local rates thence to every point in the state. This has forced the rail carriers to group all the producing territory west of seaboard territory, and to maintain a relative adjustment calculated to permit these territories to market their products in Texas in competition with the rates from the seaboard fixed for the rail carriers both in and outside the state by the Texas Commission and the steamship lines.

It necessarily follows that whenever the Texas Commission reduces a rate from Galveston the revenue of the state carrier on all Texas business originating at the Atlantic seaboard is lowered, and the interstate carriers are compelled to make corresponding reductions from every other basing point. The immediate effect of a reduction of 5 cents in the Commission's first-class rate from Galveston to Waco is outlined in the following chart.

Texas is above all a cotton-growing state. The wealth of its farming communities and the business of its cities is founded on the production and marketing of this staple. The revenues of the carriers within the state are largely dependent upon the movement of the cotton crop. Texas produces one quarter of

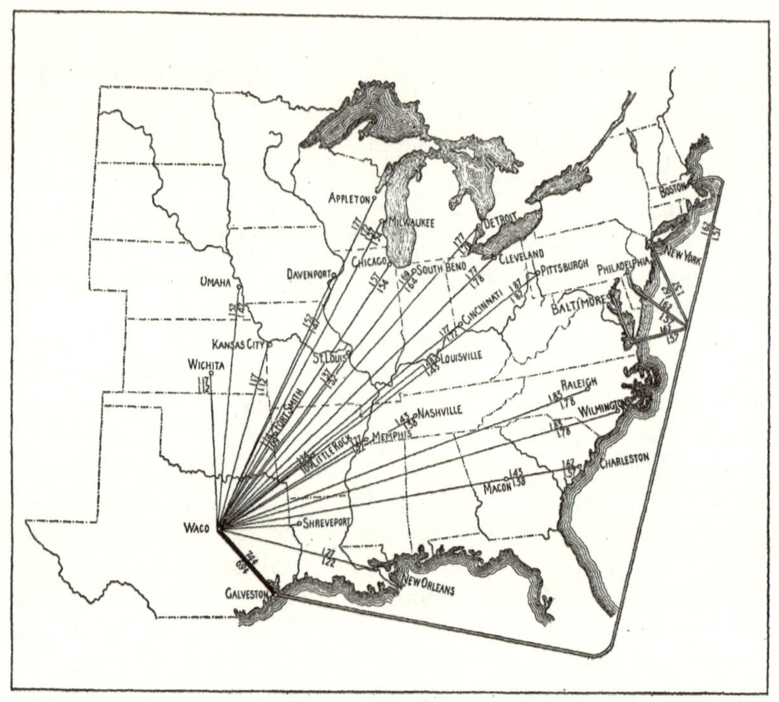

This chart shows the reduction in interstate rates which would follow a reduction of five cents in the Texas Railroad Commission's first-class rate from Galveston to Waco. (The rates shown apply only from the basing points. All other towns group around these and the reduction from all is the same as from the basing point.)

Upper Figures = Rates at Present in Effect

Lower Figures = Rates which would apply following the Above-Mentioned Reduction

all the cotton grown within the United States. It has, however, no cotton-spinning industry worthy the name. Probably 99 per cent of the cotton grown in the state is sent to New England and southeastern spinning points and to foreign countries. The revenues of the carriers on all this interstate and foreign cotton freight are absolutely dependent upon the rates fixed by the Railroad Commission of Texas to the port of Galveston.

Three years since, the Commission ordered a reduction in cotton rates of 5 cents per 100 pounds, or $1 per ton. The movement from Texas to interstate and foreign destinations in the fiscal year ending June 30, 1906, was a million and a half tons. The direct result to interstate carriers from this one act of the Commission has been an annual shrinkage in their revenues of something like a million and a half of dollars.

A cardinal principle in the three principal classification territories is that valuable commodities such as dry goods, notions, boots and shoes, hats, etc., shall take first-class rates, whether the goods are shipped in carloads or in less than carload quantities. There is no voluntary variation from this in any interstate adjustment. The principle has frequently been reviewed without disapproval by the Interstate Commerce Commission. The Texas Commission, however, has taken the opposite view, and in its state classification has fixed Class "A" basis on these commodities when shipped in carload quantities. This action on their part has no force or effect so far as concerns state traffic. None of these commodities are manufactured within the state, and no house in the state jobs them in carload quantities. The State Commission's action does, however, reduce the interstate rate on these commodities from New York to interior Texas towns 37 cents per 100 pounds in carload lots.

That the Texas Commission exercises its rate-making powers with deliberate intent to control the interstate rates for the benefit of its industries appears from the following illustration.

The Rock Island has a line running southwest from the State of Kansas, passing diagonally across the Panhandle of Texas into New Mexico and on to El Paso. There are large salt industries on this line at Hutchinson, Kansas, and in the year 1905 the Rock Island, being asked to establish a reasonable rate from Hutchinson into its Panhandle towns, published an average rate of 19½ cents. The average distance is about 300 miles. There are salt plants of considerable importance at Grand Saline, Salt

City and Colorado, Texas, and under the State Commission's orders, the Rock Island, in connection with other lines, had in effect an average rate of $20\frac{1}{2}$ cents per 100 pounds from these

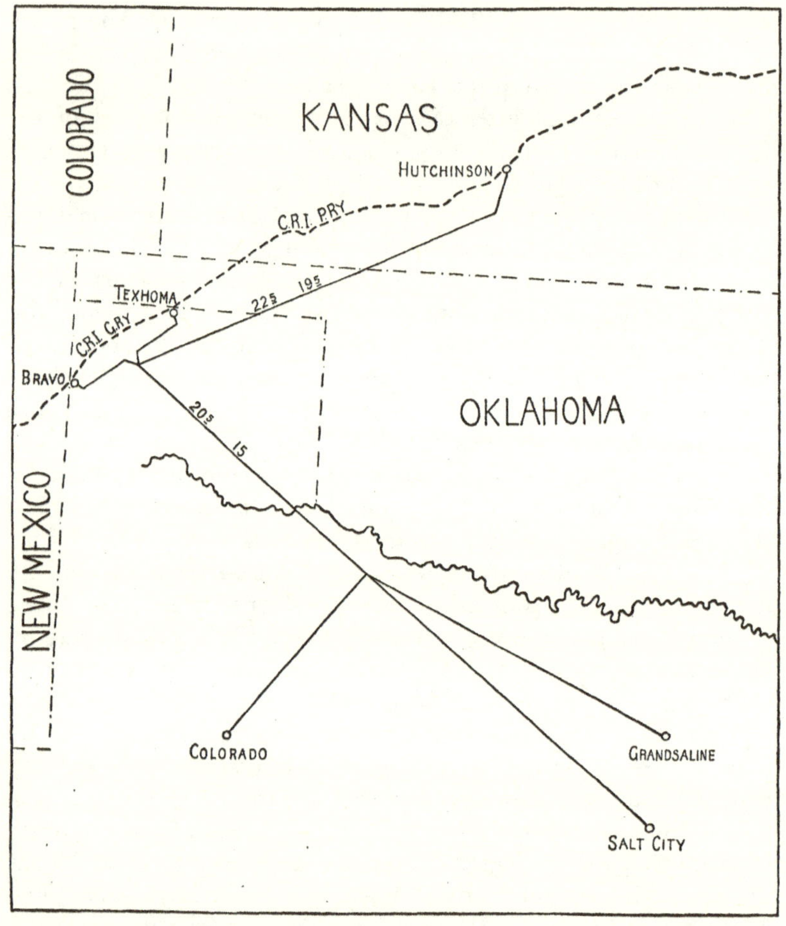

state salt plants to the Panhandle towns. The average haul to these points is from Grand Saline, 525 miles; from Colorado, 660; and Salt City, Texas, 690 miles. When the Rock Island's interstate rate came to the attention of the Texas Commission, it ordered the Rock Island's Texas line to nonconcur in the reduction, threatening that if the interstate rate were allowed to stay in, they would compel the state carriers to haul salt from these state plants to the Panhandle points for 15 cents per 100 pounds. Needless to say, the interstate rate was withdrawn, and it remains to-day at the Texas maximum rate of 22½ cents. The map on page 550 illustrates the situation.

Illinois

Recent reductions in class rates in Illinois have forced reductions of the interstate rates between St. Louis, Hannibal, Quincy, Keokuk, Davenport, and Dubuque, and will eventually force similar reductions in rates between intermediate local points either wholly interstate or wholly within other states than Illinois.

Arkansas

The Arkansas Commission has prescribed a full line of class and commodity rates which produce an effect on all the rates on merchandise brought into the state from points beyond, similar to the results of the Texas Commission's regulation of the rates in that state.

Minnesota

The Minnesota Commission has fixed a scale of class rates within the state which recently required the leveling down of all rates from Minneapolis, St. Paul, and Duluth to Iowa and Dakota points. It was with respect to this situation that Judge Lochren said in the case before him involving the validity of these rates:

> It would seem to be very difficult to avoid . . . the conclusion that these rates fixed in respect to Minnesota do necessarily and directly affect interstate commerce. . . . I have no doubt that Congress might very properly, under the constitutional provision giving it the entire power of control over interstate commerce, assume control of the avenues of interstate commerce, of the railroads which are engaged in interstate commerce, and of all rates which are collected by those railroads, whether within the states or without the states, because the matter of those rates would affect these avenues of interstate commerce, and might affect their ability to continue as avenues of interstate commerce.

And as to this argument, urged before the Supreme Court in the Minnesota rate case, recently decided, the opinion of Mr. Justice Peckham says:

> Still another Federal question is urged growing out of the assertion that the laws are, by their necessary effect, an interference with and a regulation of interstate commerce, the grounds for which assertion it is not now necessary to enlarge upon. The question is not, at any rate, frivolous.

XXI

THE NORTHERN SECURITIES COMPANY[1]

THE certificate of incorporation of the Northern Securities Company was signed by the three incorporators and acknowledged in the state of New Jersey on the twelfth of November, 1901. During the three days immediately following, resolutions were adopted by the newly organized company, authorizing the purchase of any shares that might be tendered to the company, under specified conditions and terms. Power to do so was expressly granted in the charter. "The objects for which the corporation is formed are: To acquire by purchase, subscription, or otherwise, and to hold as investment, any bonds or other securities or evidences of indebtedness. . . . To purchase, hold, sell, assign, transfer, mortgage, pledge, or otherwise dispose of, any bonds or other securities or evidences of indebtedness created or issued by any other corporation. . . . To purchase, hold, etc., shares of capital stock of any other corporation . . . and, while owner of such stock, to exercise all the rights, powers, and privileges of ownership, including the right to vote thereon. . . ." The nature of these powers, with respect to the signs of indebtedness of other corporations, has caused the company to be commonly described as a holding company.

This particular idea of a holding company antedates the Northern Securities Company by seven or eight years; and, in a larger sense, the principle involved in the holding company has found at least partial expression in the organization of railway companies for half a century. The voting trust may also be regarded as an antecedent of the modern holding company,

[1] From "A History of the Northern Securities Case," *Bulletin of the University of Wisconsin*, No. 142, July, 1906, pp. 225–241. Elaborate footnote references are omitted. The problems of railroad combination both economic and legal are discussed in Ripley's Railroads: Finance and Organization. — ED.

and the causes which have produced the one are analogous to those which have produced the other. The process of metamorphosis between the voting trust and the holding company does not appear to be either long or complex.

Both the remote and the immediate causes of the organization of the Northern Securities Company were partly personal and partly economic. They were personal in so far as the Securities Company was the outgrowth of a desire on the part of certain men to perpetuate a certain policy. They were economic in that the execution of certain large, almost empire-building plans could be promoted, in the estimation of its founders, by the company. The founders of the company, through years of effort, had become accustomed to associate their railway properties with a certain economic policy. And thus the personal and the economic causes of the organization of the company practically become merged into one, namely, the desire to insure uninterrupted progress in the building of a great system of transportation. The existence of other causes, like the desire to suppress competition, to inflate values, has been alleged. An examination of these will be taken up later.

The original idea of the Securities Company was that it should embrace the ownership of about one third of the Great Northern stock. A small number of the Great Northern stockholders, not to exceed eleven out of about 1800, felt that they were getting along in years. One of them was eighty-six, another eighty-two, and several of them past seventy years of age; and they desired to work together as they had done for more than twenty years. Some of these stockholders lived in foreign countries. Their powers and privileges had to be exercised by their legal representative. This might continue to work satisfactorily as long as the old circle of associates remained unbroken; but a number of them felt that a more permanent arrangement would be preferable. A close corporation, embracing six or eight men, was suggested, to which others objected because such an arrangement would violate the principle of equality which had always prevailed among Great Northern stockholders. As soon as the idea of exclusiveness had been abandoned and an inclusive organization decided upon, "the question came up: Why not put in the Northern Pacific? That is the way it occurred." This, in substance, is the manner in which President J. J. Hill summarizes what has been alluded to above as the "personal" element in the organization of the Securities Company. And to place at the head of the new company the guiding spirit and constructive genius of that group of men at once made the Securities Company doubly a matter of "moral control," of "fortification," and of "strength." In the words of a colleague, who is familiar with the territory through which the Great Northern railway runs, that road is "regarded as a personality. People know that there is some one whom they can see and talk to. If other means fail, they know they can go to see 'Jim' Hill about it, and he will give them a fair hearing." From the threefold point of view of public policy, of personality, and of business, the actual course of the organization represents the best that could have been done.

The desire to secure a permanent basis for the interchange of commodities between great producing sections of the United States and of the Orient may be characterized as the largest economic cause of the organization of the Securities Company. The Great Northern and the Northern Pacific railways had lived in comparative peace with each other for twenty years. Both had maintained joint rates with other roads like the Burlington. The Burlington taps the principal live-stock markets, important cotton, coal and mineral areas of the United States. The unified control and management of these three great systems of railways — Great Northern, Northern Pacific, and Burlington — makes it possible to secure a sufficient variety and quantity of freight to make systematic back loading a certainty. Back loading, together with a steady flow of freight large enough to insure the economical utilization of motive power and car capacity, results in a general economy of operation which makes rates that would bankrupt numerous other roads remunerative to the systems embraced in the Securities Company. Such a flow of freight had been developed on the basis of joint rate agreements with railways and agreements with steamship lines.

The value of the railway properties concerned, as well as the continued prosperity of the commercial and industrial interests served by them, depended largely upon the permanency and security of the arrangements which had begun to crystallize with the turn of the century, and to which the opening of the Orient promised to bring still greater returns. However, joint rates may be withdrawn at any time, and it was thought too hazardous to build up a great business "extending across the continent and even across the ocean on the basis that to-morrow the rate might be changed or the party with whom we were working to reach the different points of production or consumption had some other interest or some greater interest elsewhere. It was necessary in doing this that we should have some reasonable expectation that we could control the permanency of the rate and that we would be able to reach the markets. In other words, if the man producing lumber on the coast, or cattle on the ranches, or ore in the mines, could not find a market for it and if we could not take it to a market that would enable him to sell his stuff for a profit, he would have to stop producing it. That was the line we worked upon, and that was the reason we felt called upon to put ourselves in a position where we could control access to the markets." * * * * *

A glance at a railway map of the territory west of the Mississippi reveals the importance and strength of the Burlington system. West of the Missouri river it lies in the very lap of the Union Pacific, while east of that river it forms a great bridge, with its terminal pier in Chicago. The Northwestern, St. Paul and Burlington systems largely complement each other in the great manufacturing, agricultural and mineral regions of the greater northwest. In relation to the Great Northern and Northern Pacific, the Burlington is like the point and moldboard of a plow, the beam and handles of which are constituted by the former systems. The Burlington connects Chicago with St. Louis, Kansas City, Omaha, Denver, St. Paul and Minneapolis, and numerous smaller but important cities, which, taken collectively, represent the manufacture and sale of every staple commodity and the raw materials therefor.

An alliance with a system possessing the tactical and physical advantages of the Burlington could not be otherwise than a source of strength and profit to the party making such an alliance.

For many years the Great Northern and Northern Pacific had been contemplating direct connection with Chicago. The usual alternatives of the construction of a new line or the lease or purchase of an existing one, presented themselves. The former would result in unnecessary duplication and waste; the latter only was deemed expedient. The improved financial condition of the Northern Pacific and the dissolution of the voting trust planned for January 1, 1901, made the year 1900 propitious for the execution of the long-cherished plans for an eastward extension. At least five different lines were within the range of possibility. These were: the Wisconsin Central; Chicago & Northwestern; Chicago, Milwaukee & St. Paul; Chicago, Burlington & Quincy; and the Chicago Great Western. To what extent each of these great lines figured as possibilities in the minds of the Great Northern and Northern Pacific, and the relative degrees of desirability which were attached to each by them, does not appear in the testimony, although the statement may be positively made that more than two of these railways were made the subject of correspondence and probably, also, of tentative solicitation.

The preferences of J. J. Hill and J. P. Morgan, with respect to the particular line to be acquired as an eastward extension, do not appear to have coincided, when an extraneous factor appeared, which probably added the force of circumstances to Hill's preference. It appears that during the "fall of 1900 or early winter of 1901" the Union Pacific interests purchased in the market some $8,000,000 or $9,000,000 out of $108,000,000 or $109,000,000 of the Burlington stock. Much of the Burlington stock had been held for many years by people who had inherited it, and it was found impossible to secure control of the property through purchases in the open market. This episode in the stock-market hastened the completion of negotiations which probably had been begun before that time. The two northern transcontinental lines were not inclined to permit a rival interest to wrest from them this much-coveted property without leaving a single stone unturned. The testimony does not show a direct causal connection between the attempt of the Union Pacific interests to purchase the Burlington in the open market and the negotiations of Hill for the same property, although more than mere coincidence probably existed. Negotiations were opened by Hill with the executive committee of the board of directors of the Burlington system about Christmas, 1900, or January 1, 1901. Prior to this date no negotiations had taken place. "The actual negotiations commenced about or after the middle of January, 1901." Early in March, 1901, E. H. Harriman and Jacob H. Schiff, acting for themselves, or for the Union Pacific, or for interests friendly to the Union Pacific, requested to be allowed to join with the Great Northern and Northern Pacific in the purchase of the Burlington. This request was refused. At that time the Union Pacific interests no longer owned the eight or nine millions of Burlington stock which had been purchased during the preceding fall or winter, but they now desired to secure a half interest in the final purchase. A month later the Burlington sale was consummated. The two northern roads had made the offer which the Burlington directors had specified beforehand as satisfactory to Hill, and nearly all the Burlington shareholders accepted it. The Great Northern and Northern Pacific each received one half of the $108,000,000 of capital stock of the Burlington at $200 per share, payable in joint collateral four per cent, long-time bonds of the two companies, for the payment of which the acquired 96.79 per cent of the stock of the old Burlington Company was pledged as collateral security. These two companies had now become joint owners of all the Burlington stock, and, as such, they had the right thereafter to exercise all the rights and privileges of shareholders, including the right to elect the board of directors. The purchase of the Burlington stock by the two companies in equal parts, it was thought, would serve each of them as well as if it were the sole owner of such stock, while such a purchase might have been beyond the financial means of either company by itself. "The evidence is therefore uncontradicted and conclusive that the Great Northern and Northern Pacific companies each purchased an equal number of shares of the Burlington stock as the best means and for the sole purpose of reaching the best markets for the products of the territory along the lines, and of securing connections which would furnish the largest amount of traffic for their respective roads, increase the trade and interchange of commodities between the regions traversed by the Burlington lines and their connections and the regions traversed or reached by the Great Northern and Northern Pacific lines, and by their connecting lines of shipping on the Pacific Ocean, and as the best if not the only means of furnishing an indispensable supply of fuel for their own use and for the inhabitants of the country traversed by their lines. These connections and the interchange of traffic thereby secured were deemed to be and are indispensable to the maintenance of their business, local as well as interstate, and to the development of the country served by their respective lines, and of like advantage to the Burlington lines and the country served by them, and strengthen each company in its competition with European carriers, for the trade and commerce of the Orient."

During the very days when the Burlington transaction was being perfected, the men who had been refused what they regarded an equitable share in that purchase elaborated plans which were calculated to vanquish their enemies and elevate the Union Pacific interests to a position of supremacy in transcontinental traffic. These stirring events led a cosmopolitan editor to invent a parable of fishes in which the bass had swallowed the minnow, and the pike swallowed the bass. In this instance, however, the bass, armed with retirement fins, compelled the pike to spew him out.

The total outstanding capital stock of the Northern Pacific was $155,000,000 of which $80,000,000 was common and $75,000,000 preferred. During April and early in May, 1901, the Union Pacific interests acquired $78,000,000 of this stock, — $41,000,000 preferred and $37,000,000 common — with the view of controlling the Northern Pacific railway, with its half interest in the Burlington system. Such a movement appears to have been anticipated. "It was a common story at one time." Individuals representing the Great Northern and Northern Pacific interests, becoming apprehensive, increased their holdings in the Northern Pacific by purchasing about $15,000,000 of common stock in the market. Short selling of Northern Pacific stock and the scramble to cover, when it was discovered that only a limited supply was to be had, drove the price of Northern Pacific common stock up to about $1000 per share. This was the climax of a series of events which culminated in the stock-exchange crisis of May 9, 1901. "The markets of the world were convulsed, the equilibrium of the financial world shaken, and many speculative interests in a critical condition." On May 1, 1901, when the so-called "raid" upon Northern Pacific stock became known, J. J. Hill and his associates, who had been in possession of large blocks of Northern Pacific stock from the time of the reorganization of the company, were holding from $18,000,000 to $20,000,000, par value, of common stock; and J. P. Morgan & Co. were holding some $7,000,000 or $8,000,000. Together, May 1, 1901, these individuals lacked the dramatic $15,000,000 of common stock, which, when they had acquired it, gave them a majority of some $3,000,000 par value, of the $80,000,000 of common stock, when the "show down of hands" occurred after May 9. Although the Union Pacific interests represented by E. H. Harriman and Winslow S. Pearce, as trustees for the Oregon Short Line, held a majority of $1,000,000 of the total amount of stock, their majority lay in the preferred shares which could be retired on any 1st of January prior to 1917, — that is, before the present owners could get an opportunity of exercising the authority which was assumed to reside in them, and which would give them the coveted control. This is why the pike did not swallow the bass. To the country at large and to Wall Street these events appeared like a duel between giants, but one who appears to have been a leading participant in the duel, on the losing side, asserted that he never was in a contest, nor did he and his associates lose money.

According to the by-laws of the Northern Pacific Company, the annual election of its board of directors by the stockholders occurs in October, and under the distribution of stock existing after May 9, 1901, the Union Pacific interests could have controlled this election, and thus prevented the retirement of the preferred stock on January 1, 1902, which would legislate them out of control. Both the preferred and the common stock could vote under the conditions existing on May 9, 1901. A postponement of the annual meeting from October till after January 1, 1902, was frequently thought of and advised by counsel. It could have been done. This potential power of retiring the Northern Pacific preferred stock before the same could be voted, residing in the Northern Pacific Board of Directors, appears to have generated a conciliatory attitude on the part of the representatives of Union Pacific interests, and negotiations for the purchase of such shares were successfully carried through by J. P. Morgan & Co. Direct testimony admitting this causal connection does not exist, but the admitted facts make it appear highly probable. To be sure, the retirement of the preferred stock had been thought of long before, and the right to do so on any 1st of January between 1896 and 1917 was expressly reserved; yet up to 1901, when this plan was finally consummated, no plan had been devised for the retirement of that stock. The interested parties agreed not to wait until October, but to act at once, in order to establish permanent peace and "to show that there was no hostility." The detailed movements following the 9th of May do not appear clearly from the evidence, but the results of what took place are indicated in the bulletin published on June 1st. "It is officially announced that an understanding has been reached between the Northern Pacific and the Union Pacific interests, under which the composition of the Northern Pacific board will be left in the hands of J. P. Morgan. Certain names have already been suggested, not now to be made public, which will especially be recognized as representative of the common interests. It is asserted that complete and permanent harmony will result under the plan adopted between all interests involved." This "understanding" had been incorporated in the Arbitration Agreement of May 31, 1901, which the bulletin just quoted announced to the public, and which gave "every important interest its representative." In it the "vitality and vigor of the peace policy established between the railroads" found definite expression. It showed "that they were acting under what we know as a community of interest principle, and that we were not going to have that battle in Wall Street. There was not going to be people standing up there fighting each other." Had this battle in Wall Street been fought to the last ditch and the Union Pacific interests triumphed, the measure of the injury done to the Great Northern and Northern Pacific would have been destruction, in the judgment of those who are responsible for the administration of these properties, — destruction in the sense that the properties would have been incapacitated from doing what it was intended they should do and what they were quite able to do in building up a great interstate and Oriental traffic, unless they had all gone into a single combination. "With the Northern Pacific as a half owner in the shares of the Burlington and responsibility for one half of the purchase price of these shares, the transfers of the shares of the Northern Pacific or the control of the Northern Pacific to an interest that was adverse or an interest that had greater investments in other directions, the control being in the hands of companies whose interests would be injured by the growth and development of this country would, of course, put the Great Northern in a position where it would be almost helpless, because we would be, as it were, fenced out of the territory south which produces the tonnage we want to take west and which consumes the tonnage we want to bring east, and the Great Northern would be in a position where it would have to make a hard fight — either survive or perish, or else sell out to the other interests. The latter would be the most businesslike proceeding." With the view of preventing the possibility of future "raids" upon the Great Northern and Northern Pacific stock and of fortifying these two roads and their connections in their competitive struggle with "the Suez Canal and the high seas and the entire world," the idea of a permanent holding company was invented. It has been persistently denied that the desire to restrain competition among the constituent companies had anything to do with the organization of the Northern Securities Company. * * *

The organization of a holding company having been determined, it was necessary to decide upon the form and contents of a charter, or articles of incorporation, and the state in which the incorporation should take place. The general nature of the contents of such a charter had been discussed practically as long as the idea of a holding company had been entertained by the men interested in the matter; namely, for something like seven or eight years. The specific nature of such a charter for this particular company was not made the object of study until after the Arbitration Agreement of May 31, 1901. About this time several men began an examination of the laws of a number of states for the purpose of discovering a suitable charter and of deciding upon the state in which the company should be incorporated. The decision with reference to the place of incorporation was not made until a few days before the company was actually incorporated. The general aim in searching for a charter and a state "was to have beyond any question the power to purchase, own and hold and dispose of corporate securities on a large scale." Between June and October several different sketches of articles of incorporation were made and submitted to seven or eight men. These men were scattered so that no formal meeting for the consideration of the articles was ever held. The sketch referred to left blank the name of the corporation, the name of the state in which it was to be incorporated, and the amount of the capital stock. "There was practically no change in the substance of it from the beginning." Among the earliest efforts was a search for a special charter granted by the territory of Minnesota prior to the adoption of the constitution of 1858. "A large number of special charters that were passed when Minnesota was a territory have been very much sought after and extensively used by railroads that have since been built, by financial institutions of various kinds and business corporations." The old enactments were glanced through with a view of seeing if there was anything that would meet the desires and purposes of the contemplated organization, because "under our constitution all charters antedating the admission of the state into the union became fixed legislative contracts." Such a special, territorial charter could, however, not be found; nor could a later charter suitable for the occasion be discovered. Hence, recourse was had to the general incorporation laws of Minnesota, New York, New Jersey, and probably also of West Virginia. The Minnesota statutes were regarded as too "new in that class of corporations. There are no large business corporations incorporated under the laws of the state of Minnesota; she never has had any. There has been no occasion to put powers that are given by her general statutes to such organizations under judicial question." Furthermore, her own citizens, it was asserted, go to other states for the incorporation of enterprises of any magnitude. Whether West Virginia was any more than mentioned in this connection does not appear. As between the statutes of New York and New Jersey, the choice fell upon the latter because they had been in force a good many years and were regarded as "thoroughly well settled." Those of New York, on the other hand, while they were quite similar to those of New Jersey, and "had evidently been passed with a view of enlarging her legislation to put it on a parity with New Jersey," were of very recent origin, and had not been construed by the courts. In this connection, reference may be made to a pamphlet entitled "Advantages of the General Corporation Act of New Jersey," published without reference to the Securities Company, in which the author of it points out that since 1846 the policy of New Jersey towards capital has been that of "liberality." The changes introduced in the law since then have made it "simpler, more liberal and less burdensome." Since 1896, when the law was again revised and codified, its salient features have been simplicity of organization and management, freedom from undue publicity in the private affairs of the company, and facility of dissolution.

The charter, which was finally taken out in the state of New Jersey, is in many respects similar to the charters of other great corporations. It has many points in common with the charters of the United States Steel Corporation, and the Standard Oil Company, except that the Northern Securities charter does not grant the omnibus powers conferred by the others. The Standard Oil Company and the United States Steel Corporation can engage in practically every conceivable kind of enterprise, while the Northern Securities charter limits the company to the acquisition of valuable paper held by domestic and foreign corporations, exercising the rights of property over the same, aiding corporations whose paper is thus held, and acquiring and holding the necessary real and personal property. The amount of the capital stock with which the corporation began business was thirty thousand dollars, while the total authorized capital stock of the corporation is four hundred million dollars. The customary officers and committees are provided for and the usual powers conferred upon them. A board of fifteen directors was elected, six of whom represented Northern Pacific interests; four, the Great Northern, not counting the president; three, the Union Pacific; and two, unclassified. The composition of the board on the community of interest plan was one of the points of attack subsequently pursued by the state and federal authorities. Such an arrangement had numerous precedents, however. Chauncey M. Depew is an officer or director of fifty-six transportation companies; W. K. Vanderbilt of fifty-one; Geo. J. Gould of thirty-five; E. V. Rossiter of thirty-one; E. H. Harriman of twenty-eight; Charles F. Cox of twenty-seven; D. S. Lamont of twenty-four; J. P. Morgan of twenty-three, and so on through a list of more than a hundred names.

Much testimony was elicited with respect to the capitalization and the ratio at which the Northern Pacific and Great Northern shares were exchanged for Northern Securities stock. It seems that the capitalization of $400,000,000 was fixed at that figure in order to cover approximately the combined capital stock of the Northern Pacific and Great Northern at an agreed price apparently based upon earning capacity. The par value of the outstanding capital stock of the Great Northern was $123,880,400 and that of the Northern Pacific amounted to $155,000,000. The Northern Securities Company purchased about seventy-six per cent of the former and ninety-six per cent of the latter, on the basis of $115 per share of $100 of Northern Pacific and $180 per share of $100 of the Great Northern. The purchase of the stock of the two railway companies by means of the shares of the Securities Company was effected by and through the stockholders as such. An offer to make the purchase was conveyed to the Great Northern stockholders in a circular letter. This circular called forth numerous inquiries, in response to which President Hill sent out a letter setting forth the purposes of the company and suggesting that "the offer of the Securities Company is one that Great Northern shareholders can accept with profit and advantage to themselves." It was the expressed wish of the leading stockholders of the Great Northern that all of them should be dealt with on a basis of absolute equality, irrespective of the amount of their holdings. This appears to have been done. In case of the Northern Pacific no circular letter appears to have been sent out to stockholders; nor were the same rules of equality applied to them, for the Union Pacific interests received a cash premium of $8,915,629 in the exchange of their Northern Pacific holdings on the agreed basis for $82,492,871 par value of the Northern Securities stock. It also seems that the promoters of the Northern Securities Company had an understanding with the holders of at least a majority of the common stock of the Northern Pacific Railway Company that they would exchange that stock for the stock of the Northern Securities Company as soon as organized; and also an agreement that the preferred stock of the Northern Pacific should be retired on the first day of January following.[1]

BALTHASAR H. MEYER

[1] Practically the full text of the decision of the United States Supreme Court, declaring the Northern Securities Company illegal, is reprinted in our Trusts, Pools, and Corporations, pp. 322–382. The corporation is now in process of dissolution. — ED.

XXII

THE DECISION ON THE UNION PACIFIC MERGER[1]

EVER since the decision in the Northern Securities case dissolving the merger of the Hill lines, it has seemed probable that an attempt would be made to break up the equally powerful Harriman system in the Southwest. It is true that the facts in the two instances were not altogether the same. The component parts of the Harriman lines were not competitors before their union in any such obvious way as the Great Northern and Northern Pacific had been, while the combination of the Union and Southern Pacific was not accomplished through a holding company formed for the purpose, but came about through a stock purchase by a genuine operating company. Doubtless for these reasons prosecution was postponed until less equivocal cases had been disposed of. The delay had the advantage, as matters turned out, of allowing a prior investigation by the Interstate Commerce Commission; so that the Government was enabled to incorporate in its record a large amount of evidence presented in January and February, 1907, without the expense of taking the testimony itself.[2]

The suit for dissolution under the Sherman law was finally brought by the United States before the Circuit Court for the District of Utah. The Government named as defendants the Union Pacific and its subsidiary companies, the Southern Pacific, the Santa Fé, the San Pedro, Los Angeles, and Salt Lake, the

[1] From the *Quarterly Journal of Economics*, Vol. XXVII, 1913, pp. 295–328. The legal aspects of combination and the financial history of the Harriman system will be outlined in Ripley's Railroads: Finance and Organization. (In preparation.)

[2] References, unless otherwise stated, are to the record submitted to the Supreme Court. The testimony and exhibits in the Merger case fill thirteen volumes and constitute an important addition to the source material on railroad transportation.

Northern Pacific, the Great Northern; certain individuals, — Edward H. Harriman, Jacob H. Schiff, Otto H. Kahn, James Stillman, Henry H. Rogers, Henry C. Frick, and William A. Clark; and the Farmers' Loan and Trust Company, the depositary of the San Pedro shares under the trust agreement of 1902. It asked decrees forbidding the Union Pacific, Oregon Short Line, and Oregon Railroad and Navigation Companies from voting shares of the other companies named in the petition, and also decrees enjoining these other companies from recognizing any shares which the Union Pacific and its subsidiaries might happen to hold. Briefs were filed by P. F. Dunne and N. H. Loomis for the Union Pacific and its subsidiaries and for the Southern Pacific. A separate brief was submitted for Mr. Frick, and a memorandum in behalf of Messrs. Stillman, Schiff, and Kahn. The Government's case was directed by Frank B. Kellogg and Cordenio A. Severance, with the Attorney General's assistance in the preparation of the brief. All of these gentlemen had been employed before in prosecutions under the Sherman law, and Messrs. Kellogg and Severance had tried the case against the Southern Pacific in the Circuit Court. Mr. Severance, however, bore the burden of examining and cross-examining witnesses in the case at bar, and was the best informed, as he was perhaps the ablest, of the Government counsel.

The original report of the Interstate Commerce Commission had dealt with the Harriman lines as a great combination of competing railroads.[1] The Circuit Court rendered its decision on June 24, 1911, and contrary to general expectation this proved unqualifiedly adverse to the Government's contentions. The case turned on the question of competition. Two judges ruled that the Union Pacific and the Southern Pacific were connecting and only incidentally competing lines.[2] Judge Hook filed a dissenting opinion. Appeal was taken to the Supreme Court in October of the same year.

The facts in the case seem reasonably clear. The so-called Harriman group of railroads in 1912 comprised a mileage of

[1] 12 I. C. C. Rep. 277.

[2] 188 Fed. Rep. 102.

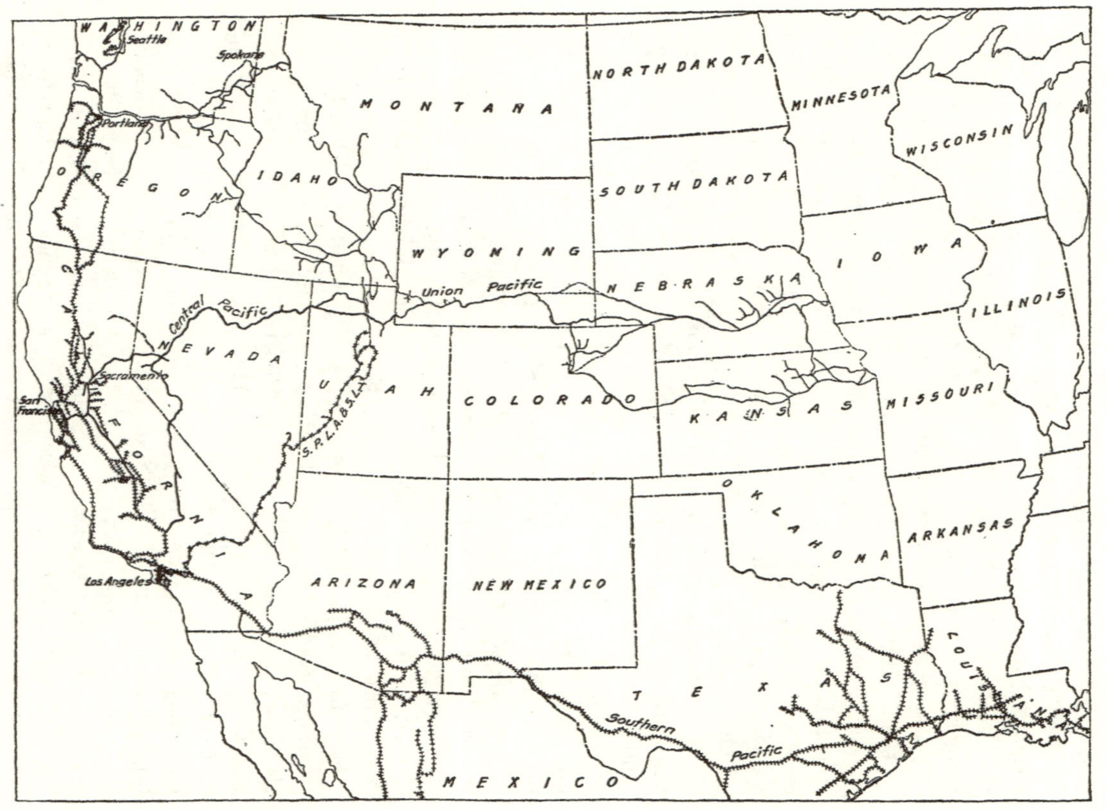

WASHINGTON
Seattle
Spokane
Portland
OREGON
IDAHO
MONTANA
NORTH DAKOTA
MINNESOTA
WISCONSIN
SOUTH DAKOTA
WYOMING
IOWA
NEBRASKA
Union Pacific
ILLINOIS
Central Pacific
NEVADA
Sacramento
San Francisco
UTAH
COLORADO
KANSAS
MISSOURI
S.P.L.A.&S.L.
CALIFORNIA
OKLAHOMA
ARKANSAS
Los Angeles
ARIZONA
NEW MEXICO
TEXAS
LOUISIANA
Southern Pacific
MEXICO

about 18,500 miles. It stretched from Omaha, Kansas City, and New Orleans on the east to Los Angeles, San Francisco, and Portland on the west, and by means of the Morgan Steamship Line it reached New York. In addition it owned a majority of stock in the Pacific Mail Steamship Company, which carries freight and passengers from the Pacific coast to the Orient and to Panama. Of the total mileage west of the Mississippi-Missouri river and south of the Northern Pacific Railroad the Harriman management controlled 19 per cent. Finally, through stock ownership in the Illinois Central, the Chicago and Alton, and other lines, and by contract with the San Pedro, Los Angeles, and Salt Lake, it possessed in varying degree influence over connecting and competing roads.

The different parts of the system were held together by a rather complex system of intercorporate stockholdings. The keystone of the structure was the Union Pacific Railroad, which held in its treasury all the stock of the Oregon Short Line, most of the stock of the St. Joseph and Grand Island, and considerable quantities of the shares of the Illinois Central and of the Chicago and Alton. The Oregon Short Line in its turn owned half of the stock of the San Pedro, Los Angeles, and Salt Lake, substantially all of the stock of the Oregon-Washington Railroad and Navigation Company, 46 per cent of the shares of the Southern Pacific Company, and interests in the Baltimore and Ohio, New York Central, Chicago and Northwestern, and other lines. The Southern Pacific Company, most important of all the Union Pacific subsidiaries, was a holding company, which owned substantially all the stock of the Central Pacific, the Southern Pacific Railroad, the Galveston, Harrisburg, and San Antonio and other roads in the Southwest, the Southern Pacific Railroad Company of Mexico, the Oregon and California, and other less important companies. The Southern Pacific Company also leased and operated the Central Pacific, the Southern Pacific Railroad, the Oregon and California, and the Southern Pacific Coast Railway. Including the Illinois Central the securities of the Harriman companies outstanding aggregated some $2,600,000,000, of which $1,650,000,000 were in the hands of the public.

Three periods may be segregated in the growth of the system.

The shares which the Union Pacific possessed in the capital of the Oregon Short Line, the holdings of the Short Line in the Oregon-Washington Railroad and Navigation Company, and the holdings of the Southern Pacific Company in the railroads of the Southwest and in the Central Pacific represented the normal growth of the Pacific railways which had been chartered in 1862 and 1864. The construction of the Short Line was undertaken by Union Pacific interests in order to secure a connection with the Pacific coast, and was financed in return for the stock of the company and a portion of its bonds. The Oregon Railway and Navigation Company [1] was purchased for the same reason, under the very nose of the Northern Pacific. In like manner, the parties which originally built the Central Pacific constructed additional track southward along the Californian coast, and then east through Arizona, New Mexico, and Texas. As a pure matter of convenience they organized different companies as they went along, and finally welded all together by means of stock control. It was in the second period that the control of the Salt Lake Company by the Union Pacific and Oregon Short Line was secured, and then also that the Union Pacific bought its holdings in the Southern Pacific. About the same time shares were purchased in the Northern Pacific which were later sold again. The third period began with the dissolution of the Northern Securities Company and represents the result of reinvestment of the sums secured from the sale of Northern Pacific and Great Northern stock. Among other securities certain shares in the Santa Fé were obtained. For the purposes in hand we have to deal mainly with the second group of purchases, as these, with the addition of the Santa Fé operation, were the basis of the Government suit. The characteristic feature of the earlier and later development was the acquisition of connecting lines; only in the middle period, if at all, was competition suppressed.

It is a matter of common knowledge that as late as 1901 the Union and Southern Pacific companies were entirely independent. Of the original builders of the Southern Pacific, Hopkins had

[1] Later expanded into the Oregon-Washington Railroad and Navigation Company.

died in 1878, Crocker in 1888, and Stanford in 1893; but until August, 1900, Mr. Collis P. Huntington, then holding $37\frac{1}{2}$ per cent of all the Southern Pacific stock outstanding, refused to compromise in any way his company's separate existence. The record shows that proposals were made to him. The Union Pacific, dependent on the Southern Pacific for direct connection with San Francisco, and fearful lest at Mr. Huntington's death his stock should fall into unfriendly hands, offered to purchase his shares, or failing this to conclude a permanent alliance. To this offer Mr. Huntington remained indifferent. Huntington died, however, in August, 1900, leaving his Southern Pacific stock to his widow and nephew in the proportion of two-thirds and one-third respectively; and both, as had been anticipated, proved willing to dispose of their holdings. Negotiations were carried to completion in February, 1901. 475,000 shares were purchased from the Huntingtons and from Edwin Hawley, the late financier's most intimate business associate, while enough was secured from other parties through Kuhn, Loeb and Company to make an aggregate of 677,700 shares, at an average price of 50.6146. Market quotations were then in the neighborhood of 45 per cent. On February 4, Kuhn, Loeb and Company engaged to deliver to the Union Pacific one month later 72,300 additional shares at the same price, plus 4 per cent interest from February 11, bringing the company's holdings up to 750,000 shares. This, in Mr. Harriman's opinion, was sufficient for control. A year or two later an attempt to force the Southern Pacific to pay in dividends earnings which its managers thought should be expended in improvements led the Union Pacific to acquire still another 150,000 shares. In January, 1910, purchases were renewed for the last time, in view of pending legislation in Congress which promised to make the possession of an absolute majority of Southern Pacific stock desirable; but these purchases ceased after 74,000 shares had been obtained, and 50,000 shares were subsequently sold. This concluded the episode. On June 30, 1911, the Union Pacific through the Oregon Short Line owned 1,266,500 shares of Southern Pacific common, or 46 per cent of all outstanding — sufficient to give undisputed control.

It was stoutly maintained by Mr. Kahn, of Kuhn, Loeb and Company, that the desire to control the Southern Pacific line from San Francisco to El Paso was not a motive in the transactions described. The necessity of buying the Sunset Route, he said, was considered an obstacle and a deterring feature. If a way could have been found to secure the Central Pacific alone, it would have been preferred at the time. The possible reduction of competition was not even considered at any of the meetings of the Executive Committee at which the subject was brought up. The same was true of the acquisition of the boat lines to the Orient, the business to Colorado and Utah points, and other minor phases.[1] Speaking of the Southern Pacific, Mr. Kahn declared:

> We knew it would require a great deal of money to be spent on it, we knew it added thousands of miles to the burden of administration and management. We were very anxious that the Union Pacific should receive as much of the administrative ability and of the railroad genius of Mr. Harriman as it was possible for him to give it, and we were rather disinclined to put upon him any more burden than was necessary to the best development of the Union Pacific; and therefore we, individually, felt that if the Southern Pacific could be separated, keeping only the Central Pacific and the north and south lines in California, and getting rid of the southern part of the Southern Pacific, we would be getting rid of a nuisance.[2]

Some plausibility was given to this contention by Mr. Gould's later admission that he had requested a half interest in the Southern Pacific purchase, and had told Mr. Harriman that if the Union Pacific did not take the stock he would take it himself for his roads.[3] At this time the Gould lines ended at Ogden, and the control by them of the Central Pacific would have been disastrous to Union Pacific interests. There was also talk of possible construction to Ogden by the Burlington or the Chicago and Northwestern. No proof of intent is now possible. One can only surmise that Mr. Harriman was unlikely to have overlooked the great extension of his power in the Southwest which acquisition of the Sunset Route was bound to bring, whatever might have been true of the bankers who were supporting him.

[1] Pp. 4713–4714 Kahn. [2] P. 4731 Kahn. [3] Pp. 4952–4957 Gould.

A few years after the Southern Pacific purchase, the San Pedro, Los Angeles, and Salt Lake was brought into the fold. This line runs from Salt Lake City southwesterly to Los Angeles, cutting three or four hundred miles from the route *via* Sacramento, and giving to the Union Pacific yet another independent outlet to the coast. It appears that the project had been originally planned by Union Pacific interests and over a million dollars spent; but that the plans had been interrupted by the Union Pacific bankruptcy and had not been resumed until 1898.[1] In that year the Oregon Short Line made a contract with a man named Eccles and his associates, who engaged to form a company and to build a railroad along the old grade for some seventy-five or eighty-five miles. Under this contract sixty-six miles were built,[2] when construction ceased. About 1900 the matter was taken up by parties in Los Angeles, and Senator Clark became interested.[3] Land for a terminal was applied for in Salt Lake City and support asked for on the ground that the new line would be independent of the Southern Pacific.[4] By June, 1901, the San Pedro Company had raised $2,501,600, had obtained in the neighborhood of one hundred acres of land in Los Angeles favorably situated for terminals, and through the Los Angeles Terminal Railway Company had acquired about three miles of water front on the Bay of San Pedro, California.[5] One hundred and ten miles of the proposed main line from Los Angeles toward Salt Lake had been surveyed, ninety miles located, and right of way for thirty miles secured.[6] These vigorous efforts led to renewed activity on the part of the Union Pacific system, although the original reasons for construction had lost force after its consolidation with the Southern Pacific lines. An option on the Eccles mileage (Utah and Pacific Company) was taken up, forty-two miles were built on towards Caliente, surveys were made towards Los Angeles, and litigation was begun with the Clark interests over the right of way through certain narrow passes through which both roads, if constructed, would have to run. It was from

1 P. 2435 Eccles.
2 Pp. 2435 *et seq.* Eccles.
3 Pp. 3282 *et seq.* Gibben.
4 P. 2460 Love.
5 Pp. 3278–3279 Clark.
6 P. 3280 Clark.

the beginning evident that two railroads through this district would not pay,[1] and the San Pedro Company came to terms. In July, 1902, the Clark people sold to the Harriman lines an undivided half interest in the enterprise and agreed to the trusteeing of all the stock for ten years. Directors were to be equally divided between the two parties and various traffic and other agreements effectually prevented independent action as to rates.

The abortive attempt to control the Northern Pacific in 1901 needs only a bare reference.[2] It had no result except to provide the Union Pacific abundantly with funds that could be used in future expansion. It should be remarked, however, that an interest in the Santa Fé was acquired in 1906, at a time of active rivalry between Santa Fé and Southern Pacific interests. The Santa Fé was then and still is the only road connecting San Francisco and Chicago by its own rails (except for a few miles in California where Southern Pacific tracks are used), and the only one of importance apart from the Harriman lines that penetrates the Southwest. In 1901 projects for Santa Fé extension in Arizona were under discussion. The company had just bought the stock and second mortgage bonds of the Santa Fé, Prescott, and Phoenix, a road running from Ash Fork on the Santa Fé main line south and southeast through Prescott to Phoenix. The county was not a rich one, but it had mineral possibilities, and expected a considerable agricultural development through irrigation. The president of the last-named company was one Frank Murphy, whom Mr. Morawetz, chairman of the executive committee of the Santa Fé, characterized as an enthusiastic son of Arizona.[3] Mr. Murphy was anxious that the Phoenix road should be extended south to Benson, where connection could be made with the El Paso and Southwestern and a direct and independent outlet secured to the Gulf over this road and the Texas and Pacific from El Paso. It is obvious that this was of great importance to the Santa Fé, Prescott, and Phoenix so long as it remained independent. To the Santa Fé

[1] P. 2569 Kearns.

[2] *Vide* Chapter XXI, *supra*, and Ripley, Railroads: Finance and Organization. — Ed.

[3] P. 1139 Morawetz.

it was less vital. Traffic which could be taken on Atchison rails clear to Chicago was scarce likely to be given to another road at Benson, and although part of the proposed road might have been used in a new low-grade route through Southern Arizona and New Mexico to Deming — a route parallel with the Santa Fé's existing line and about one hundred and fifty miles longer — the construction of this route was not immediately in prospect. For these reasons, and because the local business of the extension did not look attractive, Mr. Morawetz refused to undertake it.[1] Mr. Murphy promptly organized a new company, the Phoenix and Eastern, made surveys, secured rights of way, and negotiated for a trackage contract with the El Paso and Southwestern.[2] Seeing that the road was to be built, the Santa Fé decided that it had better build it itself, and arranged in 1902 for construction as far as Dudleyville, half-way.[3] Shortly after surveys were made for an eastern extension from Dudleyville toward the Santa Fé tracks at Deming, and a new road was incorporated to build through the Gila canyon.[4]

The construction south of Phoenix the Southern Pacific regarded as an invasion of its territory. Harriman graders occupied a canyon above the line of the Phoenix and Eastern and proceeded to blast down rocks upon their rival's right of way.[5] The next step was to ask the Santa Fé to sell to the Southern Pacific the constructed part of the Phoenix and Eastern, and to retire from the country in which it lay.[6] Mr. Morawetz was not unwilling to make the sale. He seized the opportunity, however, to secure certain advantages in northern California. In the summer of 1902, as he explained in his testimony, the Atchison had concluded that it would be desirable to extend its system north of San Francisco Bay. Negotiations were begun for the purchase of the stock of the California and Northwestern, but this stock was sold to Southern Pacific interests before the Atchison purchase was completed.[7] Thereupon the Atchison bought the stock of a short line running out of Eureka, about one hundred miles

[1] P. 1133 Morawetz.
[2] P. 1162 Douglas.
[3] P. 1133 Morawetz.
[4] P. 5069 Murphy.
[5] P. 1025 Murphy.
[6] P. 1134 Morawetz.
[7] P. 1134 Morawetz.

north of San Francisco. This railroad did a considerable passenger business and handled a good deal of lumber, but connected with San Francisco only by boat.[1] It was intended to build south to San Francisco,[2] but the construction would have been expensive, and the volume of business probably insufficient to support both a Southern Pacific and a Santa Fé line. The dispute in Arizona gave Mr. Morawetz the idea of attaching to his consent to sell the Phoenix and Eastern (at cost and interest) the conditions that Mr. Harriman sell him at the same time a half interest in the coast lines north of San Francisco Bay. Mr. Harriman at first refused,[3] but later agreed. As part of the same arrangement the Southern Pacific agreed to have built a low-grade line between Phoenix and Deming and the Santa Fé a line between Phoenix and Mojave — each company to have trackage rights over the other's road on mutually satisfactory terms upon request.[4]

It was while the relations between the Santa Fé and the Southern Pacific were thus subjects of dispute that Mr. Harriman informed Mr. Morawetz that he and some of his associates (Wm. Rockefeller, H. H. Rogers, Jas. Stillman, and Kuhn, Loeb and Company)[5] had purchased 300,000 shares of Atchison stock and desired representation on the Board of Directors. He called attention to the general desirability of establishing a better relationship between railroads, and offered Mr. Morawetz a place on the executive committee of the Southern Pacific; but stated that the stock referred to had been bought as a private investment. Mr. Morawetz declined to consider a change in the directorate until the differences between the Santa Fé and the Harriman lines should have been adjusted. By February, 1905, an agreement had been reached, and Messrs. Rogers and Frick were elected to the Atchison Board.[6] The bulk of the holdings of Mr. Harriman and his associates had been sold by the latter part of 1906, but by this time the Oregon Short Line had purchased 100,000 Atchison shares; and Rogers and Frick retained their positions. The stock owned by the Oregon Short Line was finally sold in 1909.[7]

[1] P. 509 Payson.
[2] P. 512 Payson.
[3] P. 1136 Morawetz.
[4] P. 974 Deming.
[5] P. 1105 Schiff.
[6] P. 1138 Morawetz.
[7] P. 4722 Kahn.

These were the bare facts on which the Government was to base its charge of violation of the law. They raised, it will be observed, three questions. (1) Was there competition between the companies named before the incidents occurred which were mentioned in the complaint? (2) Did these transactions do away with competition, assuming that it had existed? (3) If there had been competition, and it had ceased, was its suppression brought about by illegal means? Unless all three questions could be answered in the affirmative, the Government's case would fail. In the eyes of Mr. Wickersham and his associates the facts cited constituted cumulative evidence of a conspiracy to restrain and monopolize interstate and foreign commerce, carried through by competing railroads and by certain stockholders therein. On the other hand, the defendants interpreted the facts as isolated transactions, each justified by the special circumstances of the case, and totally devoid in intent and result of any semblance of restraint of trade or attempted monopoly.

In analyzing the evidence presented, we may first direct our attention to the matter which the Government offered as proof of the existence of competition between the Southern and the Union Pacific railroads, including with the latter the Oregon Short Line and Oregon Railroad and Navigation Companies. This evidence was vital, and was given more attention in briefs and testimony than any other portion of the case. The material was divided into seven parts:

1. Competition as to traffic between the Atlantic seaboard and the Pacific coast. The Government examined no less than seventy witnesses — shippers, Southern Pacific employees and ex-employees, and representatives of independent railroad lines. Among those who testified were Mr. Hawley, for nineteen years eastern agent of the Southern Pacific and after that a financier of prominence; Messrs. Stubbs, Spence, and Munroe of the traffic department of the Southern Pacific; Mr. Paul Morton, one time president of the Equitable Life Assurance Company, Mr. Jeffery, president of the Denver and Rio Grande, and Mr. Hannaford, in charge of traffic on the Northern Pacific. Substantially all of these witnesses testified that traffic from the

Atlantic seaboard could move to the Pacific coast either *via* the Morgan Steamship line to New Orleans and thence over the Sunset Route of the Southern Pacific to San Francisco, or *via* the trunk lines and their connections to Omaha, thence over the Union Pacific to Ogden and over the Central Pacific to the coast. Although the Southern Pacific was interested in both of these routes, yet it secured all the revenue from freight moving *via* the Sunset Route and only 30.1 per cent of the total revenue from freight delivered to it by the Union Pacific at Ogden. In consequence, it used its best efforts to influence freight to travel by the southern line. The Government showed by the evidence of shippers that freight was actually solicited in competition between the two Pacific companies. The Southern Pacific, it appeared, took traffic at New York rates from as far west as Buffalo and Pittsburg, not including those cities, and from as far south as Norfolk.[1] Not only this, but the Union Pacific was not altogether restricted to the route *via* Ogden. By diverting freight at Granger and sending it north to Portland over the Oregon Short Line and the Oregon Railroad and Navigation Company, it could affect the transcontinental rate in two ways. In the first place, it was physically possible for traffic to move from Portland to San Francisco by boat; and in the second place, a mere reduction in the rate to Portland compelled a cut to every Pacific terminal point in order to maintain these different cities in the same relative position for the distribution of eastern goods. As Mr. Stubbs expressed it: "Let the rate be cut on the Great Northern, and it goes down to the Gulf of California."[2]

Mention may also be made in this connection of the route *via* the Isthmus of Panama, in which the Southern Pacific had an interest by virtue of its control of a steamship line from San Francisco to Panama. The business was not large, but in so far as any moved this way it was in competition with the rail lines *via* Ogden.

2. Competition as to traffic between points in the interior of the country and the Pacific coast. Much the same was true of the traffic from points between Buffalo and Pittsburg and the

[1] P. 841 Hawley.

[2] P. 2005 Stubbs.

Mississippi river that held for the business from further east. It was plainly impracticable to send them through New York, but goods could move to the Gulf and thence *via* the Sunset Route to California, or they could go by way of Ogden. The Illinois Central was the most important road in this territory, and Mr. Fish, its president, testified that the Union Pacific and the Sunset Route competed for traffic originating anywhere in Illinois Central territory as actively as any two roads that were in the business.[1] Rates were the same either way, the competition being in service and solicitation.[2]

3. Competition as to traffic between the Atlantic seaboard and Colorado and Utah common points. A good many sheep wintered in the desert west of Salt Lake, and in the spring moved to the summer ranges in Idaho where they were sheared. The railroad near which the shearing took place secured the outbound wool, and for this reason the Union Pacific, Southern Pacific, and Rio Grande Western offered every attraction possible to influence the movement of the flocks. The Union Pacific, for instance, at one time paid a head tax which Wyoming levied on all sheep brought into that state.[3] The Oregon Short Line purchased salt on behalf of the sheep owners, carried it to Idaho, and only collected back the purchase price at the time the salt was delivered.[4] In the same way there was competition in respect to cattle and horses which wintered in southern Idaho and northern Nevada and moved east in the spring.[5] In return for the wool, cattle, hides, etc., shipped east, there were brought in shipments of miscellaneous merchandise, dry goods, machinery, and the like. When the Union Pacific handled the business it moved from New York to Norfolk or Newport News, thence by rail to Omaha and over the Union Pacific lines to destination. When the Southern Pacific took it, the freight went by Southern Pacific steamers to New Orleans or Galveston, and thence over railroads controlled by the company to Fort Worth, Texas, where it was given to connecting lines for delivery at destination. The rate was the same

[1] Pp. 1109–1110 Fish.
[2] P. 2189 Stubbs.
[3] P. 2391 Babcock.
[4] P. 2491 Love.
[5] P. 2661 McBride.

either way, but the rivalry between soliciting agencies was intense.[1]

4. Competition as to traffic between Portland and Utah and Colorado common points, including certain points in Nevada. Portland enjoys a fairly direct route over the Oregon Railroad and Navigation Company's tracks to Huntington, and from there over the Oregon Short Line to Granger, a few miles east of Ogden. The Southern Pacific runs south from Portland to Roseville, near Sacramento, and thence east through California, Nevada, and Utah to Ogden. The distance over the one route is 945.3 miles and over the other 1487.3. The Roseville route has nearly twice the rise and fall of the Huntington road, while the curvature also is greater. A calculation by Mr. Kruttschnitt estimated that the direct-line haul was equivalent to 3498 miles of straight level track, but that the haul *via* Roseville was equivalent to 6164 such miles.[2] The evidence nevertheless showed that some business, especially lumber, had moved the long way around before 1901. Traffic also had moved *via* the Oregon Short Line and Central Pacific to points as far west of Ogden as Wells, Nevada. How much all this amounted to was not clearly shown — at best it was probably not a great deal. After the consolidation of the Union Pacific and Southern Pacific in 1902 the Shasta Route took out its through rates with the Oregon Railroad and Navigation Company, and withdrew from the competition.

5. Competition as to traffic between San Francisco and Portland. Some of the business between these towns used the same Southern Pacific rails through Oregon and California that were traversed by business going to Utah and Nevada. About two-thirds of it, however, came by water.[3] Mr. Stubbs, traffic director of the Harriman lines, testified as follows:

> The steamship service between San Francisco and Portland is better than the rail service, with this single exception — that the rail service is daily while the steamship service is probably only once in five days. The points of delivery and taking at San Francisco and at Portland favor the steamship line. In the early opening of the Shasta Route, we had some

[1] Pp. 2358–2371 McCarthy.
[2] P. 4141 Kruttschnitt.
[3] Pp. 3953–3954 Stubbs.

ambition to load our trains north-bound, and made some attempts to get the business, but found that we absolutely could not take the business as against the steamship lines, but besides this, is the fact that there were outside competitors with the Oregon Railroad and Navigation; other steamship lines, and steam schooners, that made the rates not only unremunerative, but they were unstable; so, after several attempts to join in that business, we quit.[1]

The evidence showed clearly that for perhaps one and a half years after 1894, the railroad and steamship lines competed actively for the local coast-wise business, both freight and passenger. Rates fell to $1.00 a ton by water and $1.50 a ton by rail for the 653 miles between San Francisco and Portland.[2] Passenger fares were $2.50 and $5.00 on the boat,[3] and $5.00 and $10.00 by rail. The boat rate included meals and berth, for which the regular charge was $6.00, so that it was actually cheaper to pay fare than to ride on a pass. After the war was over a differential was put in of 6 cents a 100 pounds L.C.L. and 3 cents a 100 pounds C.L. between the steamers and the rail lines[4] — all this before 1901. Competition in service continued,[5] and large sums are still spent in advertising.[6]

6. Competition for traffic between San Francisco and points in Montana, Idaho, etc. Wine, dried fruit, sugar, beans, and other California products distributed from San Francisco could pass north to Portland and Seattle *via* the Shasta Route or by boat, and could go from there east over the Oregon Railroad and Navigation and Oregon Short Line, over the Great Northern, or over the Northern Pacific. Or it could go east from San Francisco by the Central Pacific to Ogden, and thence north over the Oregon Short Line into Montana and Idaho. The business was not large, but it was competed for actively.

7. Competition as to traffic between various ports in the Orient and points east of the Missouri river in the United States. The Southern Pacific Company bought a majority of the stock of the Pacific Mail in the fall of 1902,[7] and used the ships of that company for traffic from San Francisco to Yokohama,

[1] P. 3935 Stubbs.
[2] P. 2901 Connor.
[3] P. 2632 O'Reilly.
[4] P. 2666 Ward.
[5] Pp. 2757–2758 Hurlburt.
[6] P. 3980 Stubbs.
[7] P. 1666 Schwerin.

Kobe, Nagasaki, Shanghai, Hong Kong, and sometimes Amoy.[1] The greater part of the business moved *via* the Union and Central Pacific; some of it went west over the Sunset Route — in all, the rail lines west of the Missouri earned $63,382.86 on Oriental traffic moving through San Francisco in October, 1906.[2] On the other hand, the Oregon Railroad and Navigation Company owned all the stock of the Portland and Asiatic Company, running between Portland and substantially the same ports of call that the Pacific Mail reached in China and Japan. This company was the successor of three lines which in turn had failed to make the business through Portland pay,[3] and seems to have been established to assist the Oregon Railroad and Navigation in competition for the export business in grain and flour.[4] Ninety per cent of the traffic was westbound.[5] Of course the steamship company was eager for traffic, and competed in connection with the Oregon Railroad and Navigation, Oregon Short Line, and Union Pacific with the route formed by the Central Pacific and the Union Pacific, at least prior to 1901.

The voluminous evidence thus summarized showed that active competition had existed of almost every conceivable kind. There had been competition of parallel routes between the same termini, of parallel or roundabout routes between different termini, of roundabout routes entirely controlled by the competing lines, of routes in which the Union and Southern Pacific were links only in chains of connecting and independent roads, and finally there had been competition in cases where one competitor had to rely upon the other for a greater or less proportion of the haul.

There were certain considerations, nevertheless, which weakened the Government's case. Although the carriers had competed, yet counsel were able to show only in sporadic instances that rates had been cut. The most important through business which the Union Pacific had possessed had been the transcontinental traffic to and from the Pacific coast, and the connection with which it had interchanged most business was the Southern

[1] P. 1657 Schwerin.

[2] P. 1872 Stubbs, Exhibit 119.

[3] P. 4850 Campbell.

[4] P. 4851, *Ibid.*

[5] Pp. 4851–4852, *Ibid.*

Pacific. Now the Rio Grande Western reached as far west as Ogden, and it was at all times possible for the Southern Pacific to divert traffic this way. In consequence the Union Pacific had not dared to push competition very far. The Oregon Short Line and the Oregon Railroad and Navigation Company had remained practically unused for transcontinental business. Mr. Munroe, freight traffic manager of the Union Pacific, connected with the traffic department of that company since 1882, testified that the use of it would have been suicidal. Mr. Stubbs declared that in all his experience he had never known any business to be worked into or from California *via* the Portland gateway.[1] Even had the route been resorted to, movement by it would have been roundabout and difficult, and freight would have been necessarily distributed by the Southern Pacific from San Francisco. Restricted, therefore, to interchange with the Central Pacific at Ogden, the Union Pacific was unable to quote any through rates except with the consent of the very company which it was its interest to fight. Putting to one side the transcontinental business, the competitive traffic remaining was not large. Counsel for the carriers characterized it as incidental and insignificant, while the Government did not allege that the earnings on it exceeded three or four million dollars.

A somewhat different situation appears when we pass from the relations between the Southern Pacific and the Union Pacific to the evidence touching the other railroads named in the complaint. It was undisputed that the Santa Fé, Great Northern, and Northern Pacific had competed directly with the Central, Union, and Southern Pacific. But this was not the whole story. In the Salt Lake case there had been rivalry in construction rather than in operation. Mr. Clark had desired to build a railroad; the Union Pacific had threatened to parallel it. There was no rate-cutting, for there were no rates; but the pressure of imminent financial loss had been as strong as though a rate war had been well begun. *Mutatis mutandis*, the same was true of a part of the dealings between Mr. Harriman and the Santa Fé. The exchange of a right to buy a half interest in the

[1] P. 3906 Stubbs.

Northwestern Pacific for the privilege of buying a road in New Mexico had put an end to projects of building which would have involved considerable extension and great loss in profits. The position of the two parties to the suit in respect to these operations was confused. The Government was disposed to term them attempts at monopoly and to distinguish them on this ground from competition in rates or service. Counsel for the carriers referred to them as independent bargains which benefited the parties that made them and did not injure the public. It is difficult nevertheless to see why the negotiations in both the Santa Fé and the San Pedro cases were not forms of competition, bearing the same relation to rate conflicts that the strategy of a military campaign bears to the tactics of a battle. Nor is this disproved by the fact that the logical result of the conflict was consolidation; for this is true of any sort of competition whatsoever.

The second step in the Government's proof was the establishment of the fact that the consolidations which it charged had lessened competition. Mr. Wickersham had no difficulty in proving that the Union Pacific and Southern Pacific had consolidated the greater part of their soliciting agencies. The same officials were shown to be in general charge of traffic and operation on both roads. Business which formerly had been sought by the Sunset Route and the Harriman lines in competition was now routed so as to produce the most revenue for the system as a whole. So far as the San Pedro, Los Angeles, and Salt Lake Railroad was concerned, a traffic agreement had been entered into in 1902 which was a curiosity in railroad literature. The company had agreed to take no corporate action without the approval of Mr. Harriman. It was not to extend its lines north of the parallel of Salt Lake City; traffic was to be interchanged on a preferential basis with the Oregon Short Line and Union Pacific; the Salt Lake Company was to adopt Southern Pacific rates for its local traffic, and was to allow the Union Pacific and the Short Line to make through rates in both directions to and from points on its road.[1] In short, the Salt Lake road bound

[1] Pleadings, Exhibit A, pp. 24–27.

itself hand and foot. As for the Northern Pacific, the Northern Securities Company had been dissolved in 1905 and the old status of competition restored; but the Santa Fé was operating its lines in Northern California alternately with the Southern Pacific, and competitive construction in the Southwest had ceased. Besides this, an agreement had been entered into between the Southern Pacific and the Santa Fé dividing the citrus fruit traffic from Southern California, and another according to which cargoes from the Orient entering the port of San Francisco on steamships of the Pacific Mail were apportioned roughly in the proportion that the two railroads furnished outbound freight. Possibly because of this last-named arrangement, the Santa Fé had ceased to operate its line of steamships from San Diego.

The reply of the carriers on these points was technical. They urged, in the first place, quoting from *Whitwell* v. *Continental Tobacco Company*,[1] that "an attempt to monopolize a part of interstate commerce which promotes or but indirectly restricts competition therein, while its main purpose and chief effect are to increase the trade and foster the business of those who make it, was not intended to be made, and was not made, illegal by the second section." . . . The validity of this defense depended, of course, upon the acceptance of the assertion that only incidental restriction of competition had occurred,[2] and on proof that the merger of the Pacific railroads had, in fact, increased trade. Counsel put Mr. Kruttschnitt, chief operating official of the Harriman lines, on the stand, and drew from him a detailed and impressive list of the betterments and additions made since 1901, including the general statement that the Union and Southern Pacific together had spent $374,124,697.40 for these purposes in the eight years ending June 30, 1909. It was not a necessary conclusion that these expenditures had improved service or lowered rates; but the railroad officials testified positively that they had had such an effect, and the contrary was not satisfactorily established.

[1] 125 Fed. Rep. 458.

[2] Pp. 175 ff., Brief.

In the second place, the railroads maintained that, as a matter of law, ownership by one railroad of another's stock did not constitute control unless a clear majority were held. Control, said counsel, is a matter of *power*. A minority may direct the operation of a railroad because the majority has confidence in it; but this is lawful. The Southern Pacific stockholders had confidence in Mr. Harriman and his associates, but they could have superseded them at any time. The argument deserved and was given little weight. Unless courts are to shut their eyes to the facts in their interpretation of the law, they must recognize that under any ordinary circumstances less than a majority of the stock of a company will enable the holder to determine its policy. The indifference of a certain proportion of stockholders, the fact that the officers of the company alone have access to the stock list, the regularity with which a substantial number of proxies may be had for the asking, all work to the same result. This was, in fact, admitted by the defendants' own witnesses.

This left as a final step in the argument the charge that the Union Pacific had employed an illegal method in suppressing competition. The situation was not free from difficulty. The carriers maintained that the essential transaction complained of had been a purchase of stock. This, they contended, was a matter subject only to State legislation. The acquisition or disposition of property is not commercial intercourse.

> If any citizen should step into a broker's office on Broadway, New York, buy some stock in the Pennsylvania Railroad, pay for it, put the certificates in his pocket, and walk out, would he, or the broker, or the broker's principal, be engaged in commercial intercourse between nations and parts of nations? . . . Would a State corporation buying those certificates be in any different situation from an individual purchaser, if the State of its domicile had endowed it with corporate power to buy stock?[1]

But even though purchases of stock were subject to Federal law they would violate no provisions of the Sherman Act. A purchase or sale is not a contract in restraint of trade, — for a contract is executory, implying something yet to be done; while a sale is

[1] Brief, Dunne, pp. 219–220.

executed, completed when made and because it is made. Nor is a contract in restraint of trade necessarily unlawful. It must be undue, that is, not entered into with the legitimate purpose of reasonably forwarding personal interest and developing trade. The same may be said of an attempt to monopolize. Every act of competition tends to drive competitors out of business, but competition is legal, in the absence of fraud or duress. It follows that an individual may buy out a competitor, and then another competitor, and so on, and a corporation may do the same thing. "It is evident," said Mr. Dunne's brief, — "*fraudulent, intimidating, coercive, and other like wrongful and unlawful* methods apart — that here we touch a fundamental principle of the freedom to buy and sell, of the legal right of the individual in respect to his own property."[1]

The case, as thus made up, was docketed on the Supreme Court calendar on October 9, 1911, and on the same day a transcript of the record was filed. On the following day, a motion to advance was submitted to the court; the motion was granted on October 23, and the case was assigned for hearing. Arguments were heard on April 19, 22, and 23, and the decision was handed down on December 2, a year and three weeks after proceedings had been begun before the final court of appeal.[2]

The opinion of the Supreme Court was remarkable for its brevity, for the sweeping terms in which the law was laid down, and none the less for the exceptions in practice which it countenanced. As was to be expected, the main emphasis was laid upon the facts. Was there or was there not such competition between the parts of the Southern Pacific system that combination between them would tend to monopoly and thus be in violation of the law? "To compete," said the Court, "is to strive for something which another is actively seeking and wishes to gain." Did the Southern Pacific before 1901 strive for anything which the Union Pacific was actively seeking? To state the case in these terms was to compel the answer.

[1] Brief, p. 285.

[2] No. 446. October Term, 1912. *U. S.* v. *The U. P. R. R. Co.* et. al.

The Southern Pacific, through its agents, advertisements and literature had undertaken to obtain transportation for its "Sunset" or southern route across the continent while the Union Pacific had endeavored in the same territory to have freight shipped by way of its own and connecting lines, thus securing for itself about 1000 miles of the haul to the coast. . . .

Competition between two such systems consists not only in making rates, which, so far as the shipper was concerned, the proof shows were by agreement fixed at the same figure whichever route was used . . . but includes the character of the service rendered, the accommodation of the shipper in handling and caring for freight, and the prompt recognition and adjustment of the shipper's claims. Advantages in these respects were the subjects of representation and the basis of solicitation by many active, opposing agencies. The maintenance of these by the rival companies promoted their business and increased their revenues. The inducements to maintain these points of advantage — low rates, superiority of service and accommodation — did not remain the same in the hands of a single dominating and common ownership as it was when they were the subject of active promotion by competing owners whose success depended upon their accomplishment.

The Court replied to the suggestion that the traffic competed for was infinitesimal with the remark that though relatively small it amounted in the aggregate to many millions of dollars. To the argument that though physically able the Union Pacific had never dared to compete with the Southern Pacific because of its dependency upon the latter for direct connection with the Pacific coast, it answered, first, that it would have been detrimental to the Southern Pacific to have declined an arrangement for the carriage of freight received from the Union Pacific, and second, that the terms of the Pacific Railroad Acts of 1862 and 1864 forbade any discrimination in favor of the Denver and Rio Grande at Ogden.

Granted that substantial competition had existed before 1901 the conclusion that this competition had been restrained by the purchase on the part of the Union Pacific system of stock of the Southern Pacific Company, and that this restraint had been in violation of law followed unfailingly.

The consolidation of two great competing systems of railroads engaged in interstate commerce by a transfer to one of a dominating stock interest in the other created a combination which restrains interstate commerce within the meaning of the statute because, in destroying or greatly abridging the free operation of competition theretofore existing, it tends to higher rates. It directly tends to less activity in furnishing the public with prompt adjustment of the demands of patrons for losses. . . .

The contention that a consolidation by stock purchase was not subject to Federal regulation the court brushed aside.

Nor do we think it can make any difference that instead of resorting to a holding company, as was done in the Northern Securities case, the controlling interest in the stock of one corporation is transferred to the other. The domination and control, and the power to suppress competition, are acquired in the one case no less than in the other, and the resulting mischief, at which the statute was aimed, is equally effective whichever form is adopted.

On the other hand the Court dismissed the complaint against the Atchison, Topeka, and Santa Fé arising out of transactions in Arizona discussed in connection with the Government's case. It also refused to take action in the matter of the San Pedro, Los Angeles, and Salt Lake. The Circuit Court had not believed that the Salt Lake road was naturally competitive with the Union or Southern Pacific, and had been able to find in the agreement with the Union Pacific only a laudable purpose to adjust differences and to construct a line of railroad between two points which would serve their joint interests as well as those of the public. The Santa Fé matter had been thrown out on technical grounds. In neither case did the Supreme Court see fit to disturb the conclusion of the court below.

The only point of general interest in this decision is the Court's attitude toward the facts. The questions of law raised had been sufficiently covered in the Standard Oil and Tobacco decisions, and received merely brief, though emphatic re-assertion. It should be well understood now even by the legal profession that the ordinary property rights of the individual are limited by the Sherman Act, and cannot be pleaded as a defense against it. As the law stands, the only way of bringing about a material unification of interest between two railroads which are competing in interstate business appears to be the purchase by a natural person of control of each, and the importance of this is limited by the fact that individuals have but restricted means, and die in the end in spite of the best of care.

Several interesting observations, however, are suggested by the facts. This case is the first in which a thorough-going attempt has been made to trace the competitive relations between two great adjoining railroad systems. The result is likely to surprise the general public as it becomes known. Very little of the competition between the Union and the Southern Pacific systems, it appears, was the direct struggle between parallel roads so familiar in early railroad history. The record abundantly shows that the Southern Pacific dominated its connection at Ogden by its ability to divert eastbound traffic at that point to the Denver and Rio Grande. The Court's statement that the Pacific Railroad Acts obliged the Central Pacific to afford equal advantages and facilities as to "rates, time and transportation" to all connections at Ogden may be accepted as an authoritative though unexpected interpretation of the law; but it is too much to believe that the mere systematic diversion of unrouted traffic would not have involved a loss to the Union Pacific that no traffic manager would have suffered except under extraordinary circumstances. On the other hand, the more remote differences in interest appeared in practically every corner of the United States. It was shown that business from any point east of Omaha and New Orleans could make use of either the Union Pacific or the Southern Pacific, as the shipper desired, for stations in almost every state west of those cities. Nor was this the most striking fact brought out. Traffic from New York to Colorado moved *via* Southern Pacific steamers to New Orleans or Galveston, thence over railroads controlled by the Southern Pacific to Fort Worth, and from Fort Worth to destination it went over lines in which the Huntington carriers had no interest. Galveston is located very nearly on the meridian of Kansas City, and only that portion of the haul from New York by the southern route which lay west of Galveston, lay in any way parallel to it. Nevertheless, every single fraction of the southern route competed, in the sense in which the Supreme Court used the term, with every part of every other conceivable route which connected the two terminal points. For example, the

New York, Ontario, and Western operated between New York and Buffalo. It delivered business to the Wabash, which in turn gave it to the Union Pacific, or Rock Island, or Burlington, at Kansas City. It follows that the New York, Ontario, and Western was a competitor of the lines between Fort Worth and Denver, although distant from them 1250 miles as the crow flies and connected by no lines over which it had control. In the same way, the Atchison, Topeka, and Santa Fé, running north from Fort Worth, competed with the Old Dominion Steamship Company, plying between New York and Norfolk, and the Chicago and Northwestern between Chicago and Omaha competed with the Louisville and Nashville between River Junction and New Orleans. Where one railroad formed part of two routes, it could even be a competitor of itself, as the Pennsylvania from Pittsburg to Chicago and from Pittsburg to St. Louis.

In view of this very broad conception of the nature of competition in rates and service, it is curious that the Supreme Court failed to recognize the existence of the "financial" or "diplomatic" competition which has been continuously in existence between the western groups of roads, a competition no whit less important than that upon which the Court laid stress. This took such forms as the threat of new construction, the readiness to divert traffic in one section to secure favors in another, or the purchase of huge blocks of a competitor's securities as a demonstration of financial strength. It is not to be supposed, of course, that this sort of struggle is limited to western lines. Great railroads are like great nations, in that open warfare is the crudest weapon which they employ. The larger the company the more important the influence which it can exert in indirect ways. It takes a good deal of credulity to believe anything other than that the Clark interests undertook the construction of an independent railroad between Los Angeles and Salt Lake, which the Harriman people contrived to dominate in order to forestall competition which might have ensued. The story of the relations between the Santa Fé and the Southern Pacific likewise is full of illustrations of the larger kind of competition. Similar facts appear in the recent New Haven-Grand Trunk negotiations, or in the agreements between the Hill and Harriman lines in the Northwest. Indeed, the most serious objection to big business merely because it is big is to be found in the growth of the financial power of the single units. Sooner or later the courts will have to recognize the problem.

Another point of interest is suggested by the fact that this merger case is the first in which dissolution will provide evidence of the effect upon operating efficiency of the division of a great business into two or more parts. The information was not available in the case of the Standard Oil and American Tobacco companies because they were not public service corporations. It was not useful in the Northern Securities case because the units in that merger were not closely enough combined. But for the Harriman lines we shall have detailed sets of records, prepared on a uniform basis and open to all under the Interstate Commerce Law, and relating to a company which has made a more systematic attempt to secure the full economies of large-scale production than any other in the United States. Thus at the present time purchases for the whole system are made by the Director of Purchases, Mr. Thorne. Standards in construction and operation have been established after consideration and discussion by the officers from general superintendent up. The best brains in the accounting department have worked in harmony for improvements in method. By means of a car pool the Harriman equipment is utilized wherever the local demand is greatest. A carefully planned course of instruction offers to promising employees the best general railroad training in the country, while every effort is made by correspondence instruction to encourage thought and develop interest among subordinates. If the greater decentralization resulting from splitting the system in two compensates for the loss in efficiency in other ways, an important precedent will have been created. Some at least among the members of the organization itself expect this to be the result. A contrary opinion is indicated by a decline in the price of Union Pacific common stock, after the decision, of 19 points in ten days. It is, of course, to be remembered that many of the achievements of the old administration will be enjoyed as a legacy by the new; so that conclusions cannot safely be drawn until after the lapse of several years.

In conclusion, a word may be said about the nature of the decree. The Supreme Court had no decree of the lower court before it, since the Government suit had been dismissed by that tribunal. It confined itself, therefore, to general instructions to the Court below. These were in brief:

> The decree to be entered in the District Court shall provide an injunction against the right to vote the stock while in the ownership or control of the Union Pacific Company, or any corporation owned by it or while held by any corporation or person for the Union Pacific Company, and forbid any transfer or deposit thereof in such wise as to continue its control, and shall provide an injunction against the payment of dividends upon such stock while thus held, except to a receiver to be appointed by the District Court to collect and hold such dividends until disposed of by the decree of the Court.

Plans were to be presented to the District Court within three months, failing which the said Court should proceed by receivership and sale if necessary. Nothing in the Supreme Court's instructions was to be construed as preventing the Union Pacific from retaining the Central Pacific connection from Ogden to San Francisco, if desired. A later ruling has held that a distribution or sale of Southern Pacific shares now held by the Oregon Short Line to the stockholders of the Union Pacific will not satisfy the law. Arrangements for the purchase of the Central Pacific stock by the Union Pacific or one of its subsidiaries can readily be made, provided that the Central Pacific stock collateral bonds, secured by the stock of the same company, are paid off. With the Central Pacific would go the lines of ferries connecting Oakland with San Francisco. The Southern Pacific stock itself is pledged under the Oregon Short Line refunding 4's to the extent of $108,000,000; but under the terms of the mortgage, the company is entitled to withdraw any particular collateral on deposit at the rate at which bonds were originally issued against the same, provided that securities of railroads or car companies be substituted. The Union Pacific owned $244,073,200 of unpledged stock and bonds of companies within the system at the date of its last annual report, so the requirements of the indenture can be easily complied with.[1]

STUART DAGGETT

[1] The later history of the dissolution may be briefly outlined. A first plan to distribute the Union Pacific's entire holdings of 1,266,500 shares of Southern Pacific's common stock among its own shareholders *gratis* was vetoed by the Supreme Court on the very proper ground that it would leave control in exactly the same hands as before, except that such control would be exercised through the medium of private persons, — dominant stockholders of the Union Pacific. Farcical proceedings in apparent dissolution like those of the Standard Oil Company were thus forestalled. A second plan likewise came to grief through refusal of the California Railroad Commission to give its assent to essential details. This plan proposed: first, a sale of its Southern Pacific stock, under privileged conditions, to all shareholders *both* of the Union Pacific and Southern Pacific companies, except, of course, to the Union Pacific or the Oregon Short Line Company; and secondly, with funds thus acquired, an outright purchase by the Union Pacific from the Southern Pacific of the Central Pacific link. This would give the Union Pacific its long-desired access over its own rails to the coast — this having been the motive for taking over the Southern Pacific in first instance. But the California Commission insisted upon open and actual competition at all points.

A third plan was then evolved, quite different in principle. All the Southern Pacific shares were to be distributed *pro rata* among the Union Pacific stockholders, as by the first plan, but such disposition was to be coupled with disfranchisement for all purposes of control, of all holders of 1000 shares or over. A trustee was to issue certificates of interest upon deposit of all Southern Pacific shares held by the Union Pacific, which were to carry no voting rights while so held, and which should be exchangeable for actual Southern Pacific shares only on affidavit that the applicant for exchange held less than 1000 shares. This plan would exclude 368 other private shareholders from further increase of their holdings, and would thus appear to have been of doubtful legality.

The final plan adopted in July was entirely different in many ways. It aimed to dissolve another similar control by the Pennsylvania Railroad of a competing line, by substituting in each case control or at least a dominant interest in merely a connecting line. The Pennsylvania exchanged 212,737 preferred shares at $80 and 212,736 common shares at par of the Baltimore and Ohio Railroad with the Union Pacific system for its 382,924 shares of the Southern Pacific at par. This left the Union Pacific with a balance of 883,576 shares of Southern Pacific stock, which balance it was authorized by the court to distribute to the extent of 27 per cent of their then holdings among the other general shareholders of its own company. The expedient of issuance of certificates of interest by a trustee to be exchanged for actual stock upon affidavit that purchase was made in good faith on his own behalf independently of the Union Pacific interests, was borrowed from the preceding plan. The price of such privileged subscription was to be sufficiently favorable to insure the success of the distribution. This plan, it will be observed, differed from the first two in that it left the

Central Pacific link to the coast still in the hands of the Southern Pacific. But this feature, held by the outgoing administration as essential, was not emphasized by the new Democratic Attorney-General ; and as for the Union Pacific, it was deemed that a traffic alliance with the Central Pacific providing for a through route and most-favored treatment as to facilities for interchange — guaranteed in any event by the significant clause upon the subject in the Hepburn law of 1906 — would in some ways be preferable to ownership. It would be more elastic and would, moreover, as a detail of interstate commerce be free from interference by the railroad commissions of the states concerned. Such a traffic agreement would also insure to the Union Pacific a due share of eastbound business, which otherwise, had it purchased the Central Pacific, the Southern Pacific might choose to route entirely over its own long line. Thus, at this writing, the dissolution promised by 1916, — the ultimate time allowed by the judicial decree, — to be brought to a successful close. — Ed.

XXIII

REASONABLE RATES[1]

STATES may fix local rates for public service, but decisions of the United States Supreme Court have swept away the power of states to make their rates conclusive.

This result has been reached gradually through a line of decisions under the Fourteenth Amendment.

In the earliest cases of rate regulation under the amendment the court declined to review the reasonableness of rates fixed by states, holding this to be purely a legislative question. Later the court decided to review the extent of rate regulation, but held that rates which permitted some, though only a slight, return on the property devoted to a public service were legal. Finally a position has been reached where rates fixed by states are held invalid unless they permit as large profits as the court thinks the public service ought to yield. In this way the power to determine what are reasonable rates for public service has been transferred from state legislatures to the Supreme Court.

The first case in which the extent of state regulation of rates for public service was brought before the Supreme Court for review, after adoption of the Fourteenth Amendment, was *Munn* v. *Illinois*,[2] decided in 1876. This case involved the validity of an Illinois statute that fixed a maximum rate for storing grain in elevators at Chicago. Munn, having been convicted and fined in the state courts for violation of the statute, appealed to the United States courts on the ground that enforcement of the rate provided by the statute would take his property

[1] From the *Journal of Political Economy*, December, 1903, pp. 79–97. The same subject is much elaborated in *Publications of the American Economic Association*, 3d series, Vol. VII, 1906, pp. 24–82.

[2] 94 U. S. 113.

without due process of law and violate the Fourteenth Amendment. In the course of an opinion upholding the validity of the statute, Chief Justice Waite said, speaking for the court:

> It is insisted, however, that the owner of property is entitled to a reasonable compensation for its use, even though it be clothed with a public interest, and that what is reasonable is a judicial and not a legislative question.
>
> As has already been shown, the practice has been otherwise. In countries where the common law prevails, it has been customary from time immemorial for the legislature to declare what shall be reasonable compensation under such circumstances, or, perhaps more properly speaking, to fix a maximum beyond which any charge made would be unreasonable. . . . The controlling fact is the power to regulate at all. If that exists, the right to establish the maximum of charge, as one of the means of regulation, is implied.

From these statements it is perfectly clear that the question as to the right of those engaged in a public calling to have a judicial review of rates fixed by a legislature was squarely presented to the court in this case. It is equally clear that in the opinion of the court no such right existed.

Of the nine Supreme Court Justices, two, Field and Strong, dissented from the decision in *Munn* v. *Illinois*. The dissenting opinion was prepared by Justice Field and concurred in by Justice Strong. This dissent went on the broad ground that the storage of grain is not a public business or one for which a legislature has the power to fix rates. Nowhere in the dissenting opinion is it contended that in a public business where a legislature has the right to fix rates the amount or reasonableness of these rates can be reviewed by the court. On the contrary, Judge Field said in the course of his opinion:

> If it be admitted that the legislature has any control over the compensation, the extent of that compensation becomes a mere matter of legislative discretion. . . . The several instances mentioned by counsel in the argument, and by the court in its opinion, in which legislation has fixed the compensation which parties may receive for the use of their property and services, do not militate against the views I have expressed of the power of the state over the property of the citizen. They were mostly cases of public ferries, bridges, and turnpikes, of wharfingers, hackmen, and draymen, and of interest on money. In all these cases, except that of interest

on money, which I shall presently notice, there was some special privilege granted by the state or municipality; and no one, I suppose, has ever contended that the state had not a right to prescribe the conditions upon which such privilege should be enjoyed.

At the October term of the Supreme Court, in 1876, when the opinion in *Munn* v. *Illinois* was delivered, cases involving the validity of railway rates fixed by the legislatures of Iowa, Minnesota, and Wisconsin were also decided. Several of these cases involved the power of legislatures to fix conclusively the rates for public service under the Fourteenth Amendment, and in each case the court affirmed this power.

In *Chicago, Burlington & Quincy Railway Co.* v. *Iowa*,[1] maximum rates fixed for transportation by a statute of that state were contested on the ground, among others, that the rates fixed would take property of the railway without due process of law. Replying to this contention the court in an opinion upholding the statute said through Chief Justice Waite:

In the absence of any legislative regulation upon the subject, the courts must decide for it, as they do for private persons, when controversies arise, what is reasonable. But when the legislature steps in and prescribes a maximum of charge, it operates upon this corporation the same as it does upon individuals engaged in a similar business.

In other words, the court decided that due process of law was satisfied when rates for public service were fixed by the legislature.

The next case, *Peik* v. *Chicago & North-Western Railway Co.*,[2] was brought to restrain the enforcement of a law of Wisconsin that fixed maximum rates for passengers and freight. It was contended on the part of the railway security holders that the rates named in the statute would destroy the value of their securities, that the railway was entitled to collect reasonable compensation for its services, and that reasonable compensation was a question for the court and not for the legislature. Chief Justice Waite again delivered the opinion of the court, in which it was said, upholding the statute:

In *Munn* v. *Illinois*, *supra*, p. 113, and *Chicago, Burlington & Quincy Railroad Co.* v. *Iowa*, *supra*, p. 155, we decided that the state may limit the

[1] 94 U. S. 155. [2] 94 U. S. 164.

amount of charges by railroad companies for fares and freights, unless restrained by some contract in the charter, even though their income may have been pledged as security for the payment of obligations incurred upon the faith of the charter. So far this case is disposed of by those decisions. . . . As to the claim that the courts must decide what is reasonable, and not the legislature. This is not new to this case. It has been fully considered in *Munn* v. *Illinois.* Where property has been clothed with a public interest, the legislature may fix a limit to that which shall in law be reasonable for its use. This limit binds the courts as well as the people. If it has been improperly fixed, the legislature, not the courts, must be appealed to for the change.

In *Chicago, Milwaukee & St. Paul Railroad Co.* v. *Ackley*[1] the court said, speaking through Chief Justice Waite:

The only question presented by this record is whether a railroad company in Wisconsin can recover for the transportation of property more than the maximum fixed by the act of March 11, 1874, by showing that the amount charged was no more than a reasonable compensation for the services rendered. . . . But for goods actually carried, the limit of the recovery is that prescribed by the statute.

Two cases[2] involving railway rates under a statute of Minnesota followed those just considered, and the court in brief opinions stated that they were covered by the rulings already made.

In *Stone* v. *Wisconsin*,[3] which was decided in favor of a state statute fixing rates, the only question not covered by *Chicago, etc., Railway Co.* v. *Ackley*, according to the court, related to the construction of a certain charter.

Justices Field and Strong dissented in each of the above railway cases, but gave no opinion until *Stone* v. *Wisconsin* was reached, when Justice Field prepared an opinion in which Justice Strong concurred. In this opinion the dissent to this entire group of railway cases was put on the ground that the railway charters were contracts with the legislatures, which should protect the companies from state regulation of rates.

Besides Chief Justice Waite, the celebrated group of cases headed by *Munn* v. *Illinois* was supported by Justices Clifford, Hunt, Bradley, Swayne, Davis, and Miller. The assertion by these judges of the power of states to fix conclusive rates for

[1] 94 U. S. 179. [2] 94 U. S. 180. [3] 94 U. S. 181.

public service seems to have been as emphatic as any believer in local self-government could desire.

The doctrine of the Granger Cases, that a state may fix conclusive rates for local public service was reaffirmed in the case of *Ruggles* v. *Illinois*,[1] where the validity of a law of that state providing a maximum fare per mile on railways was called in question. In the course of its opinion sustaining the law the Supreme Court said:

> This implies that, in the absence of direct legislation on the subject, the power of the directors over the rates is subject only to the common-law limitation of reasonableness, for in the absence of a statute, or other appropriate indication of the legislative will, the common law forms part of the laws of the state to which the corporate by-laws must conform. But since, in the absence of some restraining contract, the state may establish a maximum of rates to be charged by railroad companies for the transportation of persons and property, it follows that, when a maximum is so established, that fixed by the directors must conform to its requirements, otherwise the by-laws will be repugnant to the laws.

Seven judges supported the majority opinion in this case, and two judges, Field and Harlan, delivered separate concurring opinions. Judge Harlan held that the charter of the railway in question was a contract that gave it the right to collect reasonable rates, but that the rates fixed by statute were not shown to be unreasonable. Judge Field held that the statutory rates had not been shown unreasonable, but did not state why he thought that they were bound to be reasonable.

By 1885 a fundamental change had taken place in the position of a portion of the court on the question of state power over rates for public service. This change was brought out by the case of *Stone* v. *Farmers' Loan & Trust Co.*,[2] where an effort was made to enjoin the enforcement of rates under a Mississippi statute. The court through Chief Justice Waite affirmed the power of the state to fix rates and upheld the statute, but added:

> From what has been said, it is not to be inferred that this power of limitation or regulation is itself without limit. This power to regulate is not a

[1] 108 U. S. 526. [2] 116 U. S. 307.

power to destroy, and limitation is not the equivalent of confiscation. Under pretense of regulating fares and freights, the state cannot require a railroad corporation to carry persons or property without reward; neither can it do that which in law amounts to a taking of private property for public use without just compensation, or without due process of law. What would have this effect we need not now say, because no tariff has yet been fixed by the commission, and the statute of Mississippi expressly provides "that in all trials of cases brought for a violation of any tariff of charges, as fixed by the commission, it may be shown in defense that such tariff so fixed is unjust."

Thus was the underlying principle of the Granger Cases as to reasonable rates brought in question. Unlimited power of regulation like that affirmed in those cases may certainly be used to destroy and did in fact destroy much of the value of railway securities under the Granger Acts. It was said of the United States Bank by Chief Justice Marshall in *M'Culloch* v. *State of Maryland*: [1]

That the power of taxing it by the states may be exercised so as to destroy it, is too obvious to be denied.

The tax imposed by Congress on note issues of state banks after the close of the Civil War in the exercise of its power to regulate the currency, and upheld in *Veazie Bank* v. *Fenno*,[2] certainly destroyed these issues completely. Of course, if the power to regulate is itself regulated by some other and higher power, the former may be held within any desired limits. The above quotation from the opinion in *Stone* v. *Farmers' Loan & Trust Co.*[3] must mean, therefore, an assertion by the court of its power to review rates fixed by a state. Even the Granger Cases never decided that a railway must continue in business against its will under rates fixed by a state; it was open to the railway to go out of business. Neither did the Granger Cases decide that the property used in a public service might be taken without due process of law, but rather that state regulation of rates for such service was due process of law. The power asserted by the court in the case under consideration must therefore relate to the review of the reasonableness or justice

[1] 4 Wheaton, 316. [2] 8 Wall. 533. [3] 116 U. S. 307.

of rates fixed by a state. This meaning is made clear by the statement that:

> What would have this effect we need not now say, because no tariff has yet been fixed by the commission. . . .

The opinion in the case under consideration was delivered by Chief Justice Waite who spoke in the Granger Cases, and was also supported by Justices Bradley, Miller, Woods, Matthews, and Gray, of whom Bradley and Miller took part in the Granger Cases. Justices Harlan and Field dissented, and Blatchford did not sit. The dissent of Harlan, J., went on the ground that the railway charters were contracts that permitted the companies to fix their own rates unless they were shown to be unreasonable.

In *Dow* v. *Beidelman*[1] a statute of Arkansas that fixed a maximum fare of three cents per mile on railroads in that state was upheld by a unanimous court. It was shown in this case that the rates fixed by statute, on the basis of the existing traffic, would yield a net yearly income of less than 1.5 per cent on the original cost of the road and only a little more than 2 per cent on the bonded debt. The evidence did not show, however, how much the then owners of the railway had paid for it. Justice Gray said in delivering the opinion of the court:

> Without any proof of the sum invested by the reorganized corporation or its trustees, the court has no means, if it would under any circumstances have the power, of determining that the rate of three cents a mile fixed by the legislature is unreasonable.

The dictum above quoted from *Stone* v. *Farmers' Loan & Trust Co.*,[2] as to limitations on the power of states to fix conclusive rates, was repeated with approval in the case under consideration.

In neither of these two cases was it open to members of the court who did not assent to this dictum, but who did agree with the decision, to dissent from the opinion, because the principle of the dictum was not acted on in either decision. The later of these two cases was decided by eight judges, Chief Justice Waite having died at Washington, March 23, 1888.

[1] 125 U. S. 680. [2] 116 U. S. 307.

In *Chicago, Milwaukee & St. Paul Railroad Co.* v. *Minnesota*,[1] the dicta put forth in previous cases that the reasonableness of rates fixed by a state is subject to review by the courts, was established by the force of a judicial decision. This case arose under a statute of Minnesota which authorized a commission to fix transportation rates. The commission reduced the rate for carrying milk between certain points from 3 cents to 2.5 cents per gallon, and the Minnesota courts refused to admit evidence offered by the railway that the latter rate was unreasonable, holding that under the statute the findings of the commission were conclusive. From this decision the railway appealed to the Federal court on the ground that the denial of a judicial hearing as to the reasonableness of the rates would deprive it of property without due process of law. Mr. Justice Blatchford delivered the opinion of the court, holding the Minnesota statute void because it made the rates fixed by the commission conclusive. In the course of this opinion the court said:

> The question of the reasonableness of a rate of charge for transportation by a railroad company, involving, as it does, the element of reasonableness, both as regards the company and as regards the public, is eminently a question for judicial investigation, requiring due process of law for its determination. If the company is deprived of the power of charging reasonable rates for the use of its property, and such deprivation takes place in the absence of an investigation by judicial machinery, it is deprived of the lawful use of its property, and thus, in substance and effect, of the property itself, without due process of law, and in violation of the Constitution of the United States; and in so far as it is thus deprived, while other persons are permitted to receive reasonable profits upon their invested capital, the company is deprived of the equal protection of the laws.

Dissent from some of the judges who decided the Granger Cases was now due. This dissent could not properly have been delivered in the earlier cases where the power of the court to review rates fixed by a state had been asserted, because those assertions were mere dicta and were not involved in the decisions of the cases where they occurred.

In the course of a long dissenting opinion, concurred in by Justices Gray and Lamar, Justice Bradley said:

[1] 134 U. S. 418.

I cannot agree to the decision of the court in this case. It practically overrules *Munn* v. *Illinois*, 94 U. S. 113, and the several railroad cases that were decided at the same time. The governing principle of those cases was that the regulation and settlement of the fares of railroads and other public accommodations is a legislative prerogative and not a judicial one. This is a principle which I regard as of great importance. When a railroad company is chartered, it is for the purpose of performing a duty which belongs to the state itself. It is chartered as an agent of the state for furnishing public accommodation. The state might build its railroads if it saw fit. It is its duty and its prerogative to provide means of intercommunication between one part of its territory and another. And this duty is devolved upon the legislative department. If the legislature commissions private parties, whether corporations or individuals, to perform this duty, it is its prerogative to fix the fares and freights which they may charge for their services. . . . But it is said that all charges should be reasonable, and that none but reasonable charges can be exacted; and it is urged that what is a reasonable charge is a judicial question. On the contrary, it is preëminently a legislative one, involving considerations of policy as well as of remuneration; and is usually determined by the legislature, by fixing a maximum of charges in the charter of the company, or afterwards, if its hands are not tied by contract. If this maximum is not exceeded, the courts cannot interfere. . . . Thus, the legislature either fixes the charges at rates which it deems reasonable, or merely declares that they shall be reasonable; and it is only in the latter case, where what is reasonable is left open, that the courts have jurisdiction of the subject. I repeat: when the legislature declares that the charges shall be reasonable, or, which is the same thing, allows the common-law rule to that effect to prevail, and leaves the matter there; then resort may be had to the courts to inquire judicially whether the charges are reasonable. Then, and not till then, is it a judicial question. But the legislature has the right, and it is its prerogative, if it chooses to exercise it, to declare what is reasonable.

This is just where I differ from the majority of the court. They say in effect, if not in terms, that the final tribunal of arbitrament is the judiciary; I say it is the legislature. I hold that it is a legislative question, not a judicial one, unless the legislature or the law (which is the same thing) has made it judicial, by prescribing the rule that the charges shall be reasonable, and leaving it there. It is always a delicate thing for the courts to make an issue with the legislative department of the government, and they should never do so if it is possible to avoid it. By the decision now made we declare, in effect, that the judiciary, and not the legislature, is the final arbiter in the regulation of fares and freights of railroads and the charges of other public accommodations. It is an assumption of authority on the part of the judiciary which, it seems to me, with all due deference to the judgment of my brethren, it has no right to make. . . . It is complained that the decisions of the board are final and without appeal. So are the decisions of the courts in matters within their jurisdiction. There must be a final tribunal somewhere for deciding every question in the world. Injustice may take place in all tribunals. All human institutions are imperfect — courts as well as commissions and legislatures. Whatever tribunal has jurisdiction, its decisions are final and conclusive unless an appeal is given therefrom. The important question always is, what is the lawful tribunal for the particular case? In my judgment, in the present case, the proper tribunal was the legislature, or the board of commissioners which it created for that purpose. . . . It may be that our legislatures are invested with too much power, open, as they are, to influences so dangerous to the interests of individuals, corporations, and society. But such is the constitution of our republican form of government; and we are bound to abide by it until it can be corrected in a legitimate way. If our legislatures become too arbitrary in the exercise of their powers, the people have always a remedy in their hands; they may at any time restrain them by constitutional limitations.

This strong dissent, in 1889, gives a glimpse of the conflict that had been going on in the Supreme Court since the decision of the Granger Cases, in 1876. As far as can be seen from the line of decisions noted, only two of the seven judges who decided those cases ever receded from the position there taken that the court could not review the reasonableness of rates fixed by a legislature. Of these two judges, Waite indicated his change of view by the dictum above quoted from *Stone* v. *Farmers' Loan & Trust Co.*, and Miller concurred in the majority decision of the Minnesota case just considered, by a separate opinion.

As new judges came on to the Supreme Bench, the support given by the court to the principles of the Granger Cases grew less. In *Chicago, etc., Railway Co.* v. *Minnesota*[1] the scales were turned and five justices — Fuller, Field, Harlan, Blatchford, and Brewer — supported the majority opinion. Of the nine judges who sat in the Granger Cases only Justices Field, Miller, and Bradley remained to take part in the case last decided, and of these three Justice Bradley alone adhered to the fundamental doctrine of the earlier decisions.

By *Chicago, etc., Railway Co.* v. *Minnesota*[2] the Granger Cases were in large measure overruled. Due process of law was no

[1] 134 U. S. 418. [2] 134 U. S. 418.

longer to be found in rates fixed by states, but in decisions of the court as to what was reasonable. Under this decision the states may exercise as much or as little control over rates as the court sees fit to permit. In *Munn* v. *Illinois*[1] the court said:

> The controlling fact is the power to regulate at all. If that exists, the right to establish the maximum of charge, as one of the means of regulation, is implied.

With equal force it may be said that assertion by the court of authority to review the reasonableness of rates fixed by legislatures opened the way for a great reduction in state powers. Since 1889, when the paramount authority of the court was established by a judicial decision, suits to invalidate rates fixed by legislatures have multiplied and decisions have borne with increasing severity on state powers.

In *Budd* v. *New York*, decided in 1892, the validity of a statute of that state was contested on the ground that rates fixed by it for elevating and storing grain were not within the state power to make and were unreasonable. Mr. Justice Blatchford in delivering the opinion of the court, supported the power of the state to regulate the business of storing grain and said:

> In the case before us, the records do not show that the charges fixed by the statute are unreasonable, or that property has been taken without due process of law, or that there has been any denial of the equal protection of the laws; even if under any circumstances we could determine that the maximum rate fixed by the legislature was unreasonable.

It was also said in this opinion, referring to *Chicago, etc., Railway Co.* v. *Minnesota:*

> What was said in the opinion in 134 U. S., as to the question of the reasonableness of the rate of charge being one for judicial investigation, had no reference to a case where the rates are prescribed directly by the legislature.

This statement was *obiter dicta*, pure and simple, as the rates in *Budd* v. *New York* were not shown to be unreasonable, was in direct conflict with the language of the Minnesota case and

[1] 94 U. S. 113.

no support for it can be found in later decisions. Moreover, the three dissenting judges in the Minnesota case certainly understood the decision there to apply to rates fixed directly by a legislature as well as to those fixed by a commission. It is to be noted that the Minnesota statute itself, as construed by the Supreme Court of that state, was declared invalid by the United States Supreme Court, and not merely the rates fixed under the statute. This statute evidently failed because it denied the right of the courts to investigate the reasonableness of rates fixed under it.

As to reasonable rates *Budd* v. *New York*[1] simply shows that their unreasonableness must be proved before the court will hold them void on that ground. Justices Brewer, Field, and Brown dissented in this case.

Brass v. *North Dakota*[2] involved the validity of a statute of that state that fixed rates for storing grain. The case turned on the power of the legislature to fix rates at all, rather than on the reasonableness of the rates actually fixed. The court upheld the statute, and said in its opinion, delivered by Justice Shiras:

> We are limited by this record to the questions whether the legislature of North Dakota in regulating by a general law the business and charges of public warehousemen engaged in elevating and storing grain for profit, denies to the plaintiff in error the equal protection of the laws or deprives him of his property without due process of law, and whether such statutory regulations amount to a regulation of commerce between the states.

Justices Brewer, Field, Jackson, and White dissented, leaving only Fuller, C. J., and Justices Harlan, Gray, Brown, and Shiras to decide the case.

In *Chicago & Grand Trunk Railway* v. *Wellman*,[3] decided a few months earlier than *Budd* v. *New York*, the court upheld a law of Michigan regulating railway rates, and said:

> The legislature has power to fix rates, and the extent of judicial interference is protection against unreasonable rates. . . . Surely before the courts are called upon to adjudge an act of the legislature fixing the maximum passenger rates for railroad companies to be unconstitutional, on the ground that its enforcement would prevent stockholders from receiving any

[1] 143 U. S. 517. [2] 153 U. S. 391. [3] 143 U. S. 339.

dividends on their investments, or the bondholders any interest on their loans, they should be fully advised as to what is done with the receipts and earnings of the company; for if so advised, it might clearly appear that a prudent and honest management would, within the rates prescribed, secure to the bondholders their interest, and to the stockholders reasonable dividends.

The opinion delivered by Justice Brewer in this case clearly upholds the doctrine of *Chicago, etc., Railway Co.* v. *Minnesota*, that the court has power to review the reasonableness of rates fixed by a legislature.

Reagan v. *Farmers' Loan & Trust Co.*[1] furnished another application of the same doctrine by restraining the railway commission of Texas from enforcing rates fixed under a statute of that state. The statute provided that rates fixed under it were to be deemed reasonable until finally found otherwise in a direct action, but enforcement of the rates fixed was enjoined before their reasonableness was determined by evidence, in spite of the language of the statute. In the opinion of the court, delivered by Justice Brewer, affirming the preliminary injunction and holding the rates unreasonable and void, it was said:

Is there anything which detracts from the force of the general allegation that these rates are unjust and unreasonable? This clearly appears. The cost of this railroad property was $40,000,000 ; it cannot be replaced to-day for less than $25,000,000. There are $15,000,000 of mortgage bonds outstanding against it, and nearly $10,000,000 of stock. These bonds and stock represent money invested in the construction of this road. The owners of the stock have never received a dollar's worth of dividends in return for their investment. The road was thrown into the hands of a receiver for default in payment of the interest on the bonds. The earnings for the last three years prior to the establishment of these rates were insufficient to pay the operating expenses and the interest on the bonds. In order to make good the deficiency in interest the stockholders have put their hands in their pockets and advanced over a million of dollars. The supplies for the road have been purchased at as cheap a rate as possible. The officers and employees have been paid no more than is necessary to secure men of the skill and knowledge requisite to suitable operation of the road. By the voluntary action of the company the rate in cents per ton per mile has decreased in ten years from 2.03 to 1.30. The actual reduction by virtue of this tariff in the receipts during the six or eight months that it has been

[1] 154 U. S. 362.

enforced amounts to over $150,000. Can it be that a tariff which under these circumstances has worked such results to the parties whose money built this road is other than unjust or unreasonable?

It may be suggested that the decision in this case rested on the provision of the Texas statute that suits might be brought to determine the reasonableness of rates fixed by the commission. This view cannot be maintained, however, because the statute expressly provided that rates so fixed should be deemed reasonable until finally found otherwise in an action brought by the dissatisfied party, and that in such actions "the burden of proof shall rest upon the plaintiff, who must show by clear and satisfactory evidence that the rates, regulations (etc.), complained of are unreasonable and unjust." The case in which the injunction restraining the commission from enforcing the rates in question was granted came up to the Supreme Court on demurrer by the commissioners and the Attorney-General to the complaint of the Trust Company, so that there was no hearing on the merits as the statute required. In deciding the case the court went on the broad ground that it had power to determine whether rates fixed by states were reasonable. This was shown by the statement in the course of the opinion

that no legislation of a State, as to the mode of proceeding in its own courts, can abridge or modify the powers existing in the Federal courts sitting as courts of equity.

And also that there could be

no doubt of their power and duty to inquire whether a body of rates prescribed by a legislature or a commission is unjust and unreasonable, and such as to work a practical destruction to rights of property, and if found so to be, to restrain its operation.

The court modified the force of its decision by the statement that

It is unnecessary to decide, and we do not wish to be understood as laying down as an absolute rule, that in every case a failure to produce some profit to those who have invested their money in the building of a road is conclusive that the tariff is unjust and unreasonable. . . . There may be circumstances which would justify such a tariff; there may have been extravagance and needless expenditure of money; there may be waste in the management of the road; enormous salaries, unjust discrimination as between individual shippers, resulting in general loss. The construction may have been at a time when material and labor were at the highest price, so that the actual cost far exceeds the present value; the road may have been unwisely built, in localities where there is no sufficient business to sustain a road. Doubtless, too, there are many other matters affecting the rights of the community in which the road is built as well as the rights of those who have built the road.

Evidently this case decides only that under the circumstances stated a road is entitled to earn interest on its bonds and something for its stockholders, besides paying necessary operating expenses. How much the return to stockholders may be is not decided. As no evidence was taken, it does not appear how the court knew that the failure of the road to earn "some profit" was not due to some of the "matters" named above.

In the case just considered and also in that of *St. Louis & San Francisco Railway* v. *Gill*,[1] decided during the same year, 1894, there was no dissent, but the entire court concurred in the opinion. These two cases present interesting comparisons, as the railway company in each sought protection from a law for the regulation of rates, and each alleged in its pleadings that the rates fixed for transportation would yield no profit on the invested capital, and each case was decided on demurrer.

The case of *St. Louis & Santa Fé Railway* v. *Gill* came up under a law of Arkansas, passed in 1887, that fixed a maximum rate of three cents per mile for the transportation of passengers on railroads of that state, and named a penalty of $300 payable to any passenger from whom an overcharge was exacted. Gill was charged five cents per mile and obtained a verdict in the state courts against the railway for the amount of the penalty. The railway took the case to the Supreme Court on the ground that the rate fixed by statute would result in a taking of its property without due process of law. Proof was offered for the railway that on the branch where Gill was charged five cents per mile the actual cost to the railway was 3.3 cents per mile

[1] 156 U. S. 649.

for each passenger carried; that this branch line had never earned more than 1 per cent annually above actual operating expenses on the capital stock that had been paid in cash and invested in this line. These offers of proof were not accepted, and the demurrer of Gill to the pleadings of the railway was sustained by the court in an opinion sustaining the validity of the rates fixed by the Arkansas law. The opinion, delivered by Justice Shiras, took occasion to assert the power claimed in previous cases, by saying:

> This court has declared, in several cases, that there is a remedy in the courts for relief against legislation establishing a tariff of rates which is so unreasonable as to practically destroy the value of property of companies engaged in the carrying business, and that especially may the courts of the United States treat such a question as a judicial one, and hold such acts of legislation to be in conflict with the Constitution of the United States, as depriving the companies of their property without due process of law, and as depriving them of the equal protection of the laws.

The line of railway on which Gill was charged five cents per mile, and to which the offers of proof seemed to refer, extended from the northern boundary of Arkansas to Fayetteville in that state, and had formerly been owned by a separate company. Referring to these circumstances the court said:

> In this state of facts we agree with the views of the supreme court of Arkansas, as disclosed in the opinion contained in the record, and which were to the effect that the correct test was as to the effect of the act on the defendant's entire line, and not upon that part which was formerly a part of one of the consolidating roads; the company cannot claim the right to earn a net profit from every mile, section, or other part into which the road might be divided.

Finally came the important statement that

> Even if the evidence could be understood as applicable to the entire line in Arkansas, there was no finding of the facts necessary to justify the courts in overthrowing the statutory rates as unreasonable, but that, on the contrary, the company's case depended on allegations admitted by the demurrer of a party who, in no adequate sense, represented the public.

This case seems to represent an effort of the court to stay the tendency of former decisions toward the destruction of state power in the regulation of rates. It is hard to see why the rates on a distinct line of railway should not be regulated according to the investment and expense of operation on that line, even though the line in question forms only a part of a large consolidated system.

The demurrer by a private litigant as a barrier to judicial annulment of rates fixed by legislatures did not stand the test of the next case on the subject that came before the court, namely, *Covington, etc., Turnpike Co.* v. *Sandford.*[1] By an act of the Kentucky legislature in 1890 the rate of toll that might be charged on the turnpike owned by the company just named was reduced. Sandford obtained an injunction in the state courts which required the turnpike company to charge no more than the statutory rate of toll. From this injunction the company sought relief in the Supreme Court on the ground that the reduction in rates would take its property without due process of law. In the decision of the Supreme Court, prepared by Justice Harlan, it was said that the answer of the company

> alleged that the receipt for the several preceding years had not admitted of dividends greater than 4 per cent on the par value of the company's stock; that the act of 1890 reduced the tolls 50 per cent below those allowed by the act of 1865; and that such reduction would so diminish the income of the company that it could not maintain its road, meet its ordinary expenses, and earn any dividends whatever for stockholders.
>
> These allegations were sufficiently full as to the facts necessary to be pleaded, and fairly raised for judicial determination the question — assuming the facts stated to be true — whether the act of 1890 was in derogation of the company's constitutional rights. It made a *prima facie* case of the invalidity of that statute.

This opinion reversed the action of the Kentucky courts which granted the injunction, though no evidence was before the court that the allegations of the company in its pleadings were true. Sandford acted in this case simply as a private person who wished to use the turnpike, and the admissions of his demurrer to the pleadings of the company were held sufficient ground on which to overturn the statute. The previous decision

[1] 164 U. S. 578.

in the Gill case that a statute cannot be held invalid on the demurrer of a private person was thus overruled. Admitting the statements in the pleadings of the company in this Sandford case to be true, the case simply follows the rule previously laid down that rates cannot be reduced to a point where they allow no return on the investment above operating expenses. This case, decided in 1896, was concurred in by the entire court. Though not required for the decision of the case, it was stated in the course of the opinion that

> It cannot be said that a corporation is entitled, as of right, and without reference to the interests of the public, to realize a given per cent upon its capital stock. When the question arises whether the legislature has exceeded its constitutional power in prescribing rates to be charged by a corporation controlling a public highway, stockholders are not the only persons whose rights or interests are to be considered. . . . If a corporation cannot maintain such a highway and earn dividends for stockholders, it is a misfortune for it and them which the constitution does not require to be remedied by imposing unjust burdens upon the public.

These dicta indicate that there might be instances due to unwise investments, or perhaps to competition, where a corporation would not be protected in a right to earn any return on its investment.

The next case to come before the court involving the reasonableness of rates fixed by state authority was that of *Smyth* v. *Ames*, decided in 1898.[1] A notable difference between this case and those that had preceded it lay in the fact that the decision of the court was based on evidence taken at the trial as to the investments and earnings of the railways involved, instead of on allegations or admissions of parties to the suit. The case arose under a Nebraska statute of 1893, that prescribed rates for the transporation of freight on railways in that state, by a prayer on the part of persons interested in these railways for an injunction to prevent enforcement of these rates. In a unanimous opinion, delivered by Justice Harlan, the court said:

> We hold, however, that the basis of all calculations as to the reasonableness of rates to be charged by a corporation maintaining a highway under

[1] 169 U. S. 466.

legislative sanction must be the fair value of the property being used by it for the convenience of the public. And in order to ascertain that value, the original cost of construction, the amount expended in permanent improvements, the amount and market value of its bonds and stock, the present as compared with the original cost of construction, the probable earning capacity of the property under particular rates prescribed by statute, and the sum required to meet operating expenses, are all matters for consideration, and are to be given such weight as may be just and right in such case.

We do not say that there may not be other matters to be regarded in estimating the value of the property. What the company is entitled to ask is a fair return upon the value of that which it employs for the public convenience. On the other hand, what the public is entitled to demand is that no more be exacted from it for the use of a public highway than the services rendered by it are reasonably worth. But even upon this basis, and determining the probable effect of the act of 1893 by ascertaining what could have been its effect if it had been in operation during the three years immediately preceding its passage, we perceive no ground on the record for reversing the decree of the circuit court. On the contrary, we are of opinion that as to most of the companies in question there would have been, under such rates as were established by the act of 1893, an actual loss in each of the years ending June 30, 1891, 1892, and 1893; and that, in the exceptional cases above stated, when two of the companies would have earned something above operating expenses, in particular years, the receipts or gains, above operating expenses, would have been too small to affect the general conclusion that the act, if enforced, would have deprived each of the railroad companies involved in these suits of the just compensation secured to them by the Constitution.

The injunction confirmed by the court in this case enjoined the Nebraska Board of Transportation and the Attorney-General of the state from taking any steps to enforce the rates fixed by the act of 1893. It should be noted that the court based its decision on the income that would have been derived from the local freight actually carried by the railways during the fiscal years of 1891, 1892, and 1893, ending June 30, at the rates prescribed by the act which took effect August 1, 1893. This takes no account of the fact that a decrease in rates may be followed by an increase in traffic, especially as to heavy farm produce which it may not pay to move at all if the freight is more than a very moderate figure.

The most important rule laid down by the case is that the basis of calculations as to reasonable rates of a corporation "must be the fair value of the property being used by it for the convenience of the public."

This statement with others in the opinion, appears to limit "fair value" to that of the physical property and to exclude franchise valuations. Unless the value of the physical property employed in a public service and the actual cost of performing that service are to be taken as the basis of rate calculations, the amount of rates would appear to depend mainly on the arbitrary opinion of the company or legislature making them. Though the majority of the railways in Nebraska could have made nothing on their investments under the rates prescribed by the act of 1893, as the court understood the evidence, yet the opinion states that two companies could have earned "something" above operating expenses. Reference to the evidence on which the court relied, and which was repeated in the opinion, shows that this something amounted to 1.99, 4.06, 6.84 and 10.63 per cent annually on the values of the railways. Unless the court thought that this rate of net earnings was so small as to amount to a taking of property without due process, it does not appear why the Nebraska act was unconstitutional as to the roads making this rate. According to dicta in the Sandford case above cited, an act might be constitutional as to some roads and unconstitutional as to the others.

A still later case in the Supreme Court, that of *Cotting* v. *Goddard*, decided in 1901, goes farther than any of the foregoing in its limitation of state powers. This case arose under a Kansas statute of 1897 that fixed charges for handling live stock at stock yards where more than a certain amount of business was done, and affected the yards at Kansas City. Petitions were filed asking that the Attorney-General of Kansas be restrained from enforcing the statute as to these yards, and, after hearings in which evidence was taken as to the value of the yards and the annual earnings, the injunction was granted. In the course of the unanimous opinion of the court, delivered by Justice Brewer, it was said:

If the rates prescribed by the Kansas statute for yarding and feeding stock had been in force during the year 1896, the income of the stock-yards company would have been reduced that year $300,651.77, leaving a net income of $289,916.96. This would have yielded a return of 5.3 per cent on the value of the property used for stock-yard purposes, as fixed by the master.

The actual net income of the company during 1896, as found by the master and the court below, was $590,558.73, and the value of its property in the stock yards was $5,388,003.25, so that its net income during that year amounted to nearly 11 per cent on its investment. After pointing out the liability of a person engaged in the operation of public stock yards to some legislative regulation, the court proceeded to define the limits of such regulation, and said:

> The question is not how much he makes out of his volume of business, but whether in each particular transaction the charge is an unreasonable exaction for the services rendered. He has a right to do business. He has a right to charge for each separate service that which is reasonable compensation therefor, and the legislature may not deny him such reasonable compensation, and may not interfere simply because out of the multitude of his transactions the amount of his profits is large.

These reasons for the decision of the court are negative in character. They tell us that it matters not that profits are large if rates are only reasonable. But what are reasonable rates? How are they to be determined if considerations as to investments and profits are put aside? If reasonable rates do not imply reasonable profits, where is the amount of charge to stop short of what the person receiving the service can be induced to pay?

A quarter of a century has transferred the test of reasonable rates from the opinions of state legislatures to the opinion of the Supreme Court. In the Granger Cases the court denied its right to interfere with local rates fixed by legislatures, even when these rates were so low as to destroy all profits. This doctrine, after various adverse dicta, was fully repudiated by the case of *Chicago, etc., Railway Co.* v. *Minnesota*, decided in 1889, thirteen years after the Granger Cases. From that date to 1896, when *Covington, etc.*, v. *Sandford* was decided, the court went no farther than to hold that legislative rates must afford some income above operating expenses. Another step was taken the following year, when the court held in *Smyth* v. *Ames* that rates which permitted a net profit of as much as 10.63 per cent on one road, but nothing on others, could not be enforced as to either.

Finally, in 1901 comes the decision, in *Cotting* v. *Goddard*, that rates which yield a profit of 10.9 per cent on the investment are not unreasonable, and that rates which would reduce this profit to 5.3 per cent are unconstitutional.

Alton D. Adams

XXIV

THE DOCTRINE OF JUDICIAL REVIEW[1]

WE are now to undertake an investigation of the influence which the doctrine of judicial review has exerted on our American system of railroad control, in order to discover whether it has strengthened or weakened the efficiency of that control. In this inquiry we shall consider, first, its effect on the state's power to reduce rates; second, its effect on the state's power to enforce the rates it has established; and third, its effect, as a resultant of the other two, upon the spirit and ideas of railroad commissions.

Before coming to these precise questions, however, we shall do well to reflect for a moment upon the spirit of the law which has shaped the doctrine of judicial review, and which directs its application; for it will serve to illumine our entire discussion of this subject to recall at the outset the general attitude of the law and of the courts in all cases which involve both public and private interests. The attitude of the courts is determined by the fact that they are charged with the duty of interpreting and applying a law in which the individualistic spirit of the age has been firmly crystallized. In our modern régime the *individual* is the central figure. His importance, his dignity, his sanctity, his rights, and his liberties are everywhere recognized. His use of a free ballot is supposed to guard civil rights and to shape aright the course of government; his pursuit of his individual self-interest is supposed to secure industrial justice and welfare; his freedom of conscience, of thought, of will, and of action is not to be lightly infringed. "All men are created free and equal," says our Declaration of Independence, "and are endowed

[1] From "Railroad Rate Control," by Harrison Standish Smalley, Ph.D., *Publications of the American Economic Association*, 3d series, Vol. VII, 1906, pp. 83–110.

by their Creator with certain inalienable rights. . . . *To secure these rights, governments are established among men.*" The only limitation upon them is that they shall not, in their exercise, encroach upon the equal rights of other individuals.

It is true that this is a theory which has been gradually losing its hold both upon the minds and upon the hearts of men. So pernicious have been some of its results, especially in the world of industry, that the inquiry now is whether it has not passed the zenith of its usefulness, and whether it is not now necessary to modify it by an assertion of the social duties and responsibilities of individuals, and accordingly, by the enactment of laws restricting the individual for the general good. In this inquiry different minds have pursued different courses, have gone different lengths, and have, of course, reached different conclusions. Socialists would have us abandon the theory of individualism entirely and substitute therefor a theory of social duty, to be applied by the state. Long since, more conservative minds suggested factory legislation. Some thirty years ago, the consensus of public opinion demanded regulation of railroads for the public good. To-day there is agitation for municipal ownership, trust regulation, and other limitations upon private enterprise. This view is not intended to be complete. Its purpose is merely to recall the fundamental theory upon which our society is based, and some of the modifications of it which have been urged by many from time to time.

But while observing the gradual departure from the theory of individualism in industrial economics we must always remember that the law under which we live grew up with the growth of the individualistic theory and has received its stamp. The history of the English law is a record of the successful struggle of the individual, first for recognition, and then for supremacy. Indeed our law is permeated, saturated, with the theory of individual rights. Two centuries ago English law had been shaped to that theory, while in our country it no less lies at the basis of our law; and its dignity has been recognized in the bills of rights of our state constitutions, and in most of the Amendments to the Federal Constitution. Such limitations as the state may impose on private rights are regarded as exceptions to the general rule, repugnant to the spirit and genius of the law, and therefore to be confined within strict bounds. Moreover — and this is a point of deep significance — for almost all purposes the law considers those artificial persons, corporations, as individuals entitled to the legal rights and privileges of natural persons.

This is the law which our courts are established to interpret and apply. "The primary duty of the courts," said Mr. Justice Brewer, in deciding *Railway Co.* v. *Dey*, "is the protection of the rights of persons and property."[1] And again, speaking for the Supreme Court in the Wellman case, he said, "the protection of vested rights of property is a supreme duty of the courts."[2] This duty, it must be admitted, has not been neglected. In railroad rate cases its demands have been faithfully obeyed.

Such being the character of the law in which our judges are trained, and such being the acknowledged duty of the courts in its application, it is but natural that the professional sympathies of judges should all be with the railroads. Not that the judges, as *men*, are callous to the abuses which for a third of a century have irritated the general public, sometimes beyond the point of endurance; but nevertheless, as *judges*, they must apply a law which is in thorough sympathy with private persons, their property and rights, and which knows almost nothing of the "public welfare" except as it is to be secured through the assertion and maintenance of individual rights. If it be true, as is sometimes stated, that judges are disposed to subordinate the public weal to individual advantage, it is because they have entered fully into the spirit of a system of law which allows no other course.

In the light of these general observations, let us proceed to inquire the effect of the doctrine of judicial review, as developed and applied under our legal system, and first to notice the manner in which it has affected the power of the states to reduce rates.

Low rates are not, of course, the only ideal of railroad regulation. Doubtless the most important thing is *proportion*, that

[1] 35 Federal Reports, 872. [2] 143 United States, 346.

is, a proper adjustment of rates as among the various commodities and the various localities. But given this adjustment, the lower rates are, the better. There can be no doubt that the public interest demands that, so long as the due proportion is not disturbed, rates shall be as low as possible. A commission, therefore, being charged with the duty of advancing the public welfare, must require reductions in railroad schedules which are too high to be in accord with the public interest. And the efficiency of a commission must depend in no small measure on its ability to accomplish the reductions which are demanded by considerations of public utility. Now how great is its ability in this regard?

Clearly, if its action in the matter of rates were final and binding upon the companies, its power of lowering rates would be absolute. There would be no obstacle to prevent it from meeting in the most complete manner the requirements of the industrial situation. We have seen, however, that its rates are subject to review by the courts, and the consequence of judicial review has been to seriously impair a commissioner's power to reduce rates. While it is impossible to measure with exactness the extent to which this power is impaired, it is possible to see that the limitation placed upon the commissions' activity in this particular is very great. And in order that this may clearly appear, let us consider at length three reasons why the doctrine of judicial review, as practically applied by the courts, stands in the way of public reduction of rates. These reasons may be stated as follows:

I. The doctrine fixes an improper limit beyond which reduction of rates cannot be carried.

II. The methods employed by the Supreme Court in determining the effect of rates on earnings are such as to make that effect seem more disastrous than is the fact.

III. The principles recognized by the Court in determining reasonableness of income are unduly favorable to the railroads, and afford no adequate protection to the interests of the public.

These propositions we shall take up in order.

I. The first limitation upon the state's power to reduce rates is found in that part of the doctrine of judicial review which requires that rates shall be high enough to permit the railroad company to secure reasonable earnings. A state cannot lower rates so as to reduce earnings below that point without making adequate compensation to the company for all earnings, below the point of reasonableness, which are so taken. For to take any part of a railroad's "fair returns" is to deprive of property, —an act which, under the Fourteenth Amendment, must be accompanied with proper reimbursement.

This phase of the doctrine of judicial review is certainly subject to criticism, and the criticism touches a point so vital as to call in question the entire doctrine. The vulnerable point is the distinction made between earnings above the point of reasonableness, and earnings below that point. In effect the Court declares that above that point earnings are not property; but below it they are property; for the state may freely appropriate earnings above that point without violating the constitutional provision protecting property, though to take any below that point is declared to be a violation of it. This distinction is ingenious, and in making it the Court has perhaps saved from annihilation the state's right of rate control, but whatever merit may be claimed for it on that account, it may be admitted that it is a distinction which is artificial and which cannot be supported by reason. For, if income from property is itself property at all, surely all income must be property. To divide income into two parts — "property" and "not-property" — giving one part the protection of the constitution, and leaving the other defenseless, is an extraordinary proceeding. No one has ever thought of making a similar division in the case of any other kind of property. If the state were condemning a person's lot, it would not divide the lot into two parts and say: "one of these parts is property, and for it you may have compensation; but the other is not property, and for it, therefore, no payment will be made." Such a proceeding is unheard of, even in the case of property belonging to a quasi-public corporation. It cannot be imagined that the state, in taking any such property, would divide it into two parts and say: "one of these parts is property, and for it compensation will be made, but no payment will be made for the other because it is not property, since you are a quasi-public corporation and, your property being devoted to a public use, a part of it has ceased to be property"! But the absurdity is more clearly seen when such a distinction is applied, not to real estate or equipment but to the income of railroads. Suppose the state were to seek in the treasury of a railroad company the earnings it had received from the operation of its road, and were to attempt to appropriate those earnings. There is not the least doubt that if the appropriation were permitted at all, the courts would require the state to reimburse the company for every cent of the earnings taken. The wildest stretch of the imagination cannot picture the courts saying to the state: "a part of these earnings are reasonable, and hence are property, and if you take them you must recompense the company; but the rest of the earnings are not property, because not reasonable, and you can have them for nothing." Yet this is just what the Supreme Court has said in regard to depriving a railroad of its income through the agency of low rates. The distinction is clearly without warrant and must be given a place among the pure fictions of the law.

It is evident from the absurdity of this distinction, which the Court has found it necessary to maintain in order to prevent judicial review from practically denying the established legislative power of rate control, that somewhere in the reasoning of the Court there is an error which is fundamental and which vitiates the whole process. That error, it is believed, consists in the actual, though not professed, transfer of rate regulation from the basis of the police power, where it has always been held to rest, to the basis of the eminent domain. While continuing to insist *in words* that rate control is an exercise of the police power, the Court has *in fact* treated it as if it were a phase of the power of eminent domain. The Court has apparently looked upon it as a means whereby the state may take property (in the form of income) for public use, and has consequently subjected it to the ordinary rules of eminent domain, requiring just compensation for property appropriated. It is because of this change of base that the Court has been driven to the dilemma of holding either that all income is property, which practically denies the ancient legislative right of control, or else that none of it is property, and hence that all of it is beyond constitutional protection, which the judicial mind is unwilling to concede. From this dilemma our jurists have extricated themselves by advancing the extraordinary idea that a part of income is property and a part is not. But they would have saved themselves from getting into the dilemma, and so would have spared themselves the necessity of resorting to this untenable fiction, had they actually continued to regard rate control in the light of their own repeated assertions, as a phase of the police power. For viewed as a part of the police power, rate regulation is, of course, not subject to the rules applying to the condemnation of property. It is the exercise of an entirely different sovereign power, subject to entirely different rules and restraints. If the court should really so regard it, there would be no question of appropriation or compensation to consider, no inquiry as to the effect of rates on earnings would have to be made, and hence no classification of income.

But, it may be objected, though rate regulation is a part of the police power, is it not true that in its exercise the income of the railroad may be decreased, which would amount to a deprivation of property, income being regarded as property? True; — from the control of rates many consequences may flow, and among other results, the income of a company may be reduced. But that is a consequence which also flows from other police regulations which the state may adopt. Railroad rate control is not peculiar in that regard. Yet no one thinks of subjecting other police regulations to the rules of eminent domain. Thus the legislature may pass laws requiring railroads to put in cattle guards at highway crossings, or to equip each passenger car with an ax, saw, and hammer, or with drinking water, or to substitute, within a given time, automatic couplers of a certain type for the couplers in use. Any of these requirements would necessitate an expenditure of money and consequently would reduce the net income of the company by increasing expenses while the improvements were being installed. In effect, if one wishes to think of it in this way, it amounts to an appropriation of property for a public purpose. A portion of the income, instead of being devoted to paying operating expenses, or interest on bonds, or dividends on stock, must be expended in a manner required for the benefit of the public. Thus income is affected just as truly — though in a somewhat different way — through these measures as through rate control. A railroad company may be deprived of income just as truly through police regulations requiring an expenditure of money for the public welfare as through those requiring a reduction in rates.

Nevertheless a railroad company is not permitted to object to ordinary police regulations on the ground that its "reasonable income" is threatened. A case can be imagined where a railroad could show that its existing income was no more than reasonable, and where the courts would so hold. In such a case to enforce a law requiring the installation of new couplers or other equipment would so increase the expenses of the company that the income would no longer be reasonable. Its existing income being just barely a reasonable one, to require expenditures from it for the public good would be in effect to deprive the company of a part of its reasonable income. But could the company demand compensation for the sum so taken? Of course not. In passing upon police regulations a court does not consider their incidental effect on earnings. It makes no difference whether the road can earn a reasonable income under them or not. A company in the last stages of insolvency is just as subject to them as the most prosperous of roads.[1]

[1] It should be noted that the validity of a police regulation is not a matter which is personal to certain individuals within the class affected, but rather is a quality of the regulation itself. A factory act applying to factories of a certain class is never valid as to some and void as to others. Its validity is determined on its own merits, irrespective of its financial effect on certain factories, and if it is held to be a valid exercise of the police power, it is binding on all the persons coming within its terms. Yet a general schedule of railroad rates may, under the present judicial doctrine, be held void as to one road but binding upon another, perhaps a competing line. This unfortunate consequence is, of course, a result of bringing into rate cases the rules of eminent domain, instead of judging rates on their merits, as a police measure designed to promote the public welfare.

In short the state is permitted through police regulation to appropriate earnings for the public benefit without any obligation, under the Constitution, to provide compensation. But the police power differs from eminent domain in that the appropriation of property is not direct, but is incidental and resultant. The direct and immediate effect of a police regulation is always the establishment of some condition or method or other regulation which the public safety or welfare or comfort demands. And its indirect or consequent effect on income is not regarded as a deprivation of property such as is contemplated in the law of eminent domain. There is no valid reason why an exception to this rule should be made in the case of that form of police regulation called rate control. It is a perfectly legitimate exercise of the police power and should certainly be treated in the same way as other police regulations, — at least it should not be subjected to more stringent restraints.

Two objections to this view of the case might conceivably be raised, neither of which, however, it is believed, is well taken. In the first place it may be said that there is a difference between rate control and other forms of police regulation, in that the latter are of real benefit to the company. The railroad is in possession of equipment which proves of decided advantage to it. For example, its automatic couplers and cattle guards decrease accidents, with their losses of property and subsequent damage suits, while passenger car equipment encourages patronage by the greater security and comfort offered to travelers. But two replies may be made to this objection. One is that public regulation of rates also is of advantage to the company. It does away with lawsuits to recover damages for overcharge, for a company is never guilty of extortion so long as it keeps within the maximum fixed by the state. Moreover, it tends to increase the popular favor in which the roads are held and to encourage traffic. The development of industry resulting from efficient public regulation is in itself of great advantage to the roads. But while this answer to the objection can be made, a better one, and one fully sufficient, is this: that the benefit which a police regulation confers on the road is *not* the reason why the courts do not subject the regulation to the law of eminent domain. The reason is simply that it is not an exercise of that power. The second possible objection is that a regulation of rates necessarily affects income ; but that in the case of other police laws the company may recoup whatever expense is involved, by raising its rates and so increasing its earnings. The reply to this objection is that a company is not able thus to manipulate its earnings. It is at many points subject to competition, and so is not, commercially speaking, free to raise its rates. And an increase of rates at any point might simply have the effect of decreasing traffic, so that earnings would be but slightly increased, if at all. Moreover, it may be that the state has prescribed rates and they are in force, so that the company is without legal power to raise its rates, and thus without the means wherewith even to try to recoup the expense forced upon it. Even here the attitude of the courts is just the same. A railroad cannot claim exemption from police regulations because it is unable to make up the expense through the manipulation of its rates.

We conclude, therefore, that since rate control is an exercise of the police power and not of the eminent domain, it should not be subjected to the law of eminent domain; that accordingly the test of its validity should not be, as is now held by the courts, its effect on the income of the company.

Does this mean that the legislative power of rate control is absolute and without limit? No. It simply means that the legislature is subject to the same limitations that it is in exercising other forms of the police power. In other words, the validity of rate control is to be determined just as the validity of other police regulations is determined. The same test that is applied to them should be applied to it. The question upon which the validity of a cattle-guard, or automatic-coupler, or drinking-water law hangs — or, for that matter, a factory act, or sanitary legislation, or an inspection law — is whether a sufficient public interest demands the law. Upon that same question should the validity of rate regulation depend. It should be a question of public welfare. And therefore just as a court sometimes sets aside a police law because its enactment is not justified by the public advantage to be secured through its operation, so rates made by public authority might be set aside on the same grounds. But this is vastly different from saying that their effect on earnings should be the conclusive test in determining their validity.[1]

If the view of the matter here suggested were to command acceptance, judicial review would be transformed. Instead of being what it now is, it would become a judicial investigation designed to apply to rate control the same test which is judicially applied to other police regulations. And beyond a doubt this would result in giving to legislatures and commissions much greater freedom of action in rate matters than they enjoy under the present doctrine. The full measure of their proper authority, of which they have been largely deprived by the courts, would be restored to them. And that it is their proper authority is made more evident by the following consideration. A state may, of course, and frequently does employ the police power to control private persons in matters of private concern. In such cases, as has been said, the regulation stands or falls according to whether the public interest, welfare, safety, health, morals, comfort, or, sometimes, even convenience, demand it. If that is the only limitation placed upon the legislature in its control of private persons in their management of private matters, surely no more stringent limitation should be placed on it in its regulation of the management of public business by quasi-public corporations. Indeed there is evidently much ground on which to contend that legislative authority should be even more extensive over public than over private business. It would certainly seem that the government should have more control over property devoted to public use than over property retained for purely private use. It is not an immoderate suggestion, therefore, that the authority in the first case should be barely equal with that in the second.

[1] Of course it is perfectly conceivable that the effect of rates on earnings might be *one* of the points considered by a court. It might be made a question whether the public interest demanded certain rates, if they reduced income so much that bare operating expenses could not be paid, for in that case the road might have to suspend operation. But even if the effect of rates were so considered, the limitation on legislative action would be decidedly different from what it is at the present time.

That a broader governmental power over rates would render more precarious the earnings from railroad properties is evident, but that, of course, is simply one of the hazards which one must contemplate in going beyond the boundaries of private enterprise, into the uncertain field of public activities. A forcible judicial expression of this idea may be found in the words of Mr. Justice Brewer, uttered *obiter*, in *Cotting* v. *Kansas City Stock Yards Company*.[1] In entering a public business, said he, a person "expresses his willingness to do the work of the state, aware that the state in the discharge of its public duties is not guided solely by a question of profit. It may rightfully determine that the particular service is of such importance to the public that it may be conducted at a pecuniary loss, having in view a larger general interest. At any rate, it does not perform its services with the single idea of profit. Its thought is the general public welfare. . . . Is there not force in the suggestion that as the state may do the work without profit, if he voluntarily undertakes to act for the state he must submit to a like determination as to the paramount interests of the public?"

In this connection it is instructive to notice that in other ways persons embarking in a public business must assume the risk of losing much or even all of their investments. Such dangers exist, — have been permitted by the courts to exist even since the adoption of the Fourteenth Amendment. Thus, it has been held that a state may grant a franchise to one railroad to parallel an already existing road. The value of the older property may be impaired by competition with the new road, yet it is held that the owners have no vested rights which can prevent its construction and operation. So also the value of a turnpike may be practically annihilated by the state through a franchise permitting a parallel railroad. Yet it has been held that the Fourteenth Amendment does not command just compensation in any sense which would require the state to compensate the turnpike company for the property so taken.[2] When

[1] 183 U. S. 93.

[2] For further illustrations, see Cooley's Principles of Constitutional Law, 3d ed., p. 370.

the public welfare demands more efficient means of transportation, the owners of existing roads must expect to suffer; and the courts, aside from declining to relieve them, have not even claimed that any one but the legislature should be the final judge of the public necessity of the new improvement. A power such as this is one which properly belongs to the state to enable it to deal with property devoted to a public use in a manner conducive to the welfare of the community, and one of which the state has been deprived, so far as rate regulation is concerned by the doctrine of judicial review.

We thus conclude the discussion of our first reason why the doctrine of judicial review has seriously impaired the legislative power to reduce rates. It has fixed a limit beyond which reduction cannot be carried, and that limit is an improper one. By basing rate regulation on eminent domain rather than on the police power, it has prevented the legislatures and commissions from exercising the authority that is their right, and has thus subjected them to a serious restraint.

II. But this is not the only reason why the judicial doctrine has impaired the power of the state to reduce rates. The present judicial limit on legislative action is, as we have seen, the point of "reasonable income." But while the Court has repeatedly declared that this is the proper limit, it has, nevertheless, adopted principles and methods in the trial of rate cases which do not permit a state to fix rates so as to reduce income even to the point of reasonableness. In other words, the Court employs principles and methods which unduly favor the railroad and unduly restrict the state; and thus the legislature cannot exercise even the limited authority which the Court has in general terms allowed it. Rates may be made which will not actually reduce the income below the point of reasonableness, yet the Court may hold that they will — so erroneous is the way in which it determines that point. In the further elucidation of this contention, let us consider the methods by which the Court determines the effect of rates on earnings. We shall see that those methods inevitably make that effect appear more favorable to the railroads than is really the case.

As we have already seen,[1] the Court begins with the rule that the effect of rates upon earnings shall be determined on the basis of *past* business. That is, the judicial estimate of earning capacity of the road under the new rates is arrived at on the assumption that the rates will neither increase nor decrease the traffic, but that the traffic will remain the same that it was for a period of time prior to the establishment of the rates.

Extraordinary as this assumption is, it is one which, as we have seen from our review of the cases, the courts have repeatedly recognized as legitimate. It need hardly be said that in this matter the courts have failed to take into consideration one of the most fundamental charactistics of the railroad business. For it is a matter of general knowledge that, usually, a reduction in rates results in an increase of business. At this stage of the railroad controversy no argument is needed to prove this contention, nothing beyond a mere appeal to those general facts of which all are cognizant. Curiously enough it was even admitted, with innocent frankness, by Mr. Carter, of counsel for the railroads in *Smyth* v. *Ames*. In arguing that there are sufficient protections against the danger of extortion, he said, "Moderate charges yield more profit by the greatly increased business they draw. A sound policy, perfectly well known to railroad managers, advises them that it is better to tempt and draw out a large traffic by low prices than to try to make a large profit on a small business."[2]

In spite of this universally accepted fact, however, the courts have definitely settled that the effect of lower rates may properly, for judicial purposes, be determined on the assumption that increase of business will not result from the decrease in rates. It must, of course, be admitted that compensating circumstances may occasionally prevent an increase in traffic, but such an occurrence is out of the ordinary. The rule remains that a reduction in rates, other conditions remaining the same, always tends to augment the volume of business. For the courts, then, to proceed upon the assumption which it does, is to unduly favor the railroads. It enables them to make a

[1] P. 58 of original monograph.

[2] 169 U. S. 506.

stronger case than they could were the correct assumption to be made. Upon this principle the judicial view must always be that rates will more seriously affect the earnings of the companies than would be true in nineteen cases out of twenty. As a matter of fact, to put the rates in operation might not reduce either gross or net earnings at all, or might reduce them but slightly. Yet, in contemplation of the courts, earnings would be diminished exactly in proportion to the reduction in the rates.

Of course it may be urged that this is the only definite test which the courts can apply; that to attempt to estimate the probable increase in traffic resulting from a decrease in rates would involve the courts in speculations in which they could never have the guidance of reliable principles.[1] Let this be granted as true; let it be conceded that the courts can find no other test. Nevertheless that fact does not make the test a good one, nor one adequate to the needs of rate cases, nor does it affect the fact that the test gives to the railroads an undue advantage as against the public.

No more favorable is the view which must be taken of the next step in the procedure of the Court. After declaring that the effect of rates upon earnings must be decided on the basis of past business, the Court goes on to hold that that effect must further be determined by applying to past earnings the percentage of reduction in the rates.[2]

If the effect of the new rates upon earnings were to be determined at all on the basis of past business, it would seem that the correct method of arriving at the result would be to apply freight rates to past tonnage, and passenger rates to past passenger traffic. This would give the maximum earnings which could be secured by the railroad under the new rates, on the condition, assumed by the courts, that traffic would continue

[1] It is said that it cannot be determined in advance what the effect of the reduction of rates will be. Oftentimes it increases business, and who can say that it will not in the present cases so increase the volume of business as to make it remunerative, even more than at present? But speculations as to the future are not guides for judicial actions; courts determine rights upon existing facts. — Mr. Justice Brewer in *Chicago, etc., Ry. Co.* v. *Dey*, 35 Fed. Rep. 881.

[2] P. 58 of original monograph.

unchanged. Instead of this method, however, the courts determine the percentage of reduction made by the new rates in the rates in force, and then assume that future earnings will equal past earnings reduced in the same proportion. For example: Suppose that past earnings were $1,000,000, and that the new rates are 80 per cent of the old rates. It is assumed by the courts that earning capacity under the new rates will be $800,000.

Now, here, again, is an assumption which gives the railroads a distinct advantage in suits involving rates. For the basis of the whole process is the reduction made by the new rates in the old schedules. Yet the old schedules, of course, contain only the *nominal* rates established by the railroad. As a matter of fact, in very many cases, the *actual* rates charged are lower than those named in the schedules. Discriminations, rebates, drawbacks, preferential advantages, all awarded, usually, under the veil of secrecy, are not yet, unfortunately, things of the past. The past earnings of the company, therefore, have been derived, not by charging the rates fixed in the schedules, but by charging rates which average considerably less than those scheduled. When the courts, then, compare the new rates with the old *nominal* ones, they discover a percentage of reduction greater than the percentage of reduction made by the new rates in the old *actual* ones. The assumption, therefore, that the earning capacity of the road will be reduced in proportion to the greater percentage, is clearly wrong. It makes the company's criminal practices a source of advantage to it, and of disadvantage to the public, in the trial of rate cases.

For example, let us make the same assumption, made above, that past earnings were $1,000,000, and that the new rates are 80 per cent of the old nominal rates. In such a case the courts hold that the maximum earning capacity of the road under the new rates will be $800,000.

Suppose that the nominal rate per mile was $.01; the new rate is, then, $.008. Now, it is evident, from the merest knowledge of railroad practices, that the earnings of $1,000,000 were not secured by charging an average of $.01 for each of 1,000,000 ton miles. As a matter of fact, the actual average rate charged was less then \$.01. It might have been \$.009, or \$.008, or \$.007, or even less. But in order to deal generously with the railroad, let us assume for the moment that it was as high as \$.009. Then, the earnings of \$1,000,000 were secured by charging \$.009 for each of 111,111,111 ton miles. The actual traffic, therefore, being 111,111,111 ton miles, to put in force a rate of \$.008 would give an earning capacity of \$888,888.88. This, indeed, is less than the former earnings, but, on the other hand, it is over \$88,000 greater than the earning capacity which the Court assumes the railroad would possess under an \$.008 rate.

Now let us alter our last assumption, and suppose that the actual average rate which earned the receipts of \$1,000,000 was low, say \$.007. Then the \$1,000,000 were earned by charging \$.007 for each of 142,857,142 ton miles. But to apply to that tonnage a rate of \$.008 would give an earning capacity of \$1,142,857. This is greater by \$142,857 than the old earnings, and is \$342,857 greater than the earning capacity reached by the processes of the Court.

Thus it appears that the earning capacity determined by the courts is always less than that which the railroad will actually possess under the new rates. Furthermore, it appears that the earning capacity of the road under the new rates, if it will abstain from discrimination, may even exceed the actual amount of earnings received under the old rates.

This practice of the courts, then, is always unfair to the new rates, since it makes out their effect upon earning capacity to be more disastrous than it will be, except in the purely hypothetical case of a road which has not deviated from its nominal rates. As an item in a test of reasonableness, it is, therefore, clearly inadequate, and unduly favorable to the railroads. Under this practice, the more flagrant a company's violations are of the laws against discriminations, the more complete is its immunity from public regulation of its rates. In any event, a railroad is able to make out before the Court a stronger case than it has in fact.

True, in the Reagan cases, it was laid down that a railroad's right to profitable compensation is limited, *inter alia*, when it has indulged in "unjust discriminations resulting in general loss."[1] Accordingly the way is opened for the state to attempt to prove the unjust discriminations of which the road has been guilty. But satisfactory evidence upon such matters is, of course, almost impossible to get; and even were it secured, it is not certain to what extent and in what way the courts would make use of it. So far as the question of the effect of rates upon earning capacity is concerned, no fair or correct result can be secured by the method now employed by the courts. As said above, if past business is to be the basis of the calculation at all, the correct method would seem to be the application of the new rates to past tonnage, or past passenger traffic. Without discussing this point farther, however, it is sufficient for our present purposes to note that the method now employed by the Court may often result in the suspension of rates which, while looking toward the public welfare, are not really calculated to impair the earning capacity of the railroads, to say nothing of reducing it to the point of "reasonable returns."

III. Beyond this, however, it may be urged that the judicial conception of "reasonable income" is not adequate. At least it may fairly be said that the principles which the Court has laid down as the controlling considerations in determining reasonableness of income have so far proven unduly favorable to the railroads, and have not, as yet, given proper expression to the interests of the public. Let us recall what these principles are. Briefly stated, the Court has held[2] that a railroad's earnings must be sufficient, in general, to pay all expenses including interest on bonds, and yield a reasonable dividend upon stock, but that the reasonableness of the dividend, and, indeed, a railroad's right to any dividend at all, is dependent upon a large number of considerations. These considerations, we have also seen, may be grouped into four classes — one pertaining to the base upon which the rate of profit shall be reckoned, the second to the management of the road, another to the rights of the public, and the fourth to the industrial condition of the community.[3] The enunciation of these limitations upon a railroad's right to

[1] P. 74 of original monograph. [2] *Ibid.*, p. 70. [3] *Ibid.*, p. 72.

compensation is a most interesting feature of rate cases. At first blush it might seem that they are admirably calculated to aid in restoring the proper balance between the public and private interests. Yet it cannot escape observation that almost all of them are simply *obiter dicta*, and investigation shows that the Court has often forgotten them, either in determining procedure or in deciding special cases.

A few instances of this kind will serve both to explain and to enforce the point. In the Reagan cases is laid down the doctrine that the failure of rates to yield profitable compensation is not conclusive of reasonableness when, *inter alia*, the railroad has indulged in unjust discriminations resulting in general loss. And yet, as has just been seen, the Court has employed a method of determining the effect of new rates, which enables a railroad to take refuge under the very shelter of its own discriminations, and from that safe retreat, protected by the strong bulwark of the law, to defy legislatures and commissions. Again, the Reagan cases also recognized a limitation when a road was unwisely built, in districts where there is not sufficient business to sustain a road. Yet such was the case with almost all, if not all, of the roads involved *in those very cases*. The International & Great Northern had never been able to pay the interest on its bonds, and had been in a receiver's hands for three years. Of two other roads the Court speaks as follows:

> The St. Louis Southwestern Railway Company is called by counsel for defendants, in their brief, "a reorganized bankrupt concern." It would seem to be a railroad *which was unwisely built, and one whose operating expenses have always exceeded its earnings*. Counsel says that "it is familiarly known as a 'teazer,' and, if it ever passes beyond this interesting but unprofitable stage, even its friends will be surprised." We are not advised and we can hardly be expected to take judicial notice of what is meant by the term "teazer," but *it is clearly disclosed by the record* that this was an unprofitable road. . . . The Tyler Southwestern Railway Company has a short road of ninety miles, and also appears to be a "reorganized bankrupt concern," and one whose road has been operated with constant loss.[1]

Here are cases which clearly, by the admission of the Court, come under the general limitation expressed in the body of the

[1] 154 U. S. 403.

opinion. Yet the limitation was entirely ignored. After making the statement quoted above, the Court continued, "it will not do to hold that, because the roads have been operating in the past at a loss to the owners, it is just and reasonable to so reduce the rates as to increase the amount of that loss." Here, then, one who has read, a few pages back in the opinion, the general rule laid down by the Court, finds the hopes aroused by it most rudely dashed.

Further evidence may be found of the Court's tendency to ignore the limitations upon a railroad's right to profitable rates. It is worth while mentioning that the Court in the Reagan cases specifically denied two claims which were allowed in general terms in later cases. The Covington case limits the railroad's right when competition of parallel lines so diminishes business as to make profitable rates exorbitant, and the last Minnesota case further limits that right when the industrial condition of the country is such that profitable rates would be exorbitant. Yet in the Reagan cases the Attorney-General showed that there were four lines in competition with the International & Great Northern, reducing its share of the traffic; alleged that there had recently been a commercial depression; and offered evidence to show that the price of products was so low that rates would have to be lower than those charged by the railroads in order to permit the farmers to market their produce with any profit. All this was not gladly received by the Court, as tending to support the rates which are "presumed to be reasonable." On the other hand it was summarily dismissed, and given no weight whatever in the case. We are accordingly left in grave doubt as to whether the Court meant much if anything by its later dicta in the Covington and the last Minnesota cases. At any rate, it is evident that the play of the Court's sympathy for individual as opposed to public rights, operates to seriously limit the limitations, as it were, which it has recognized upon the rights of the railroads. The view of the railroad industry which has been taken by the Court since the Granger cases requires the limitations to be stated; but the predilections of the judges create a tendency to disregard them. As statesmen, or publicists, the judges might recognize the full force and importance of those limitations; but as *lawyers or judges*, they almost inevitably forget them.

It is true that as yet the Court has not been put to a severe test, and consequently it is not clear to just what extent it will go. For, up to the present time, counsel for the states have shown comparatively slight disposition to urge upon the Court the limitations it has recognized, or to introduce evidence in such matters. The Court by its repeated declaration and affirmation of its dicta, has offered an opportunity the significance of which has apparently not been fully appreciated by the representatives of the public. But the treatment which those dicta have received in the cases where they have been urged, as we have just seen, forbids any very sanguine hope that they hold much promise of better things for public control.

But it is not only because the Court tends to ignore in special cases the rules it has laid down in general terms, that they are not available for the cause of the public welfare. A further reason is that many of the limitations upon the rights of the railroads are so vague in character, and involve considerations so difficult to establish, that the public can derive little advantage from them. One illustration of this fact is to be found in the limitation which is recognized to exist when the management of the road has not been prudent and honest. But how difficult must it always be for state officers to secure satisfactory evidence upon such a point! The secrecy which enshrouds many railroad operations and the possibility of manipulating accounts make difficult even the discovery of imprudence and dishonesty, to say nothing of securing evidence which will be satisfactory at law.

Again, the courts have, in general terms, given recognition to the rights of the public. In the Gill case the Court was hesitant to declare rates unreasonable when, among other things, the claims of the railroad were admitted in the demurrer of a party who in no adequate sense represented the public. In the Reagan cases it was said that the right of the road to compensation is limited, among other things, by "matters affecting the rights of the community in which the road is built."[1] And in the Covington and Smyth cases, it was stated that the rights of the public are not to be ignored, that rates must not be more than the services are worth to the public, that, in short, rates must be just to the public as well as to the railroad.[2] But what are the "rights of the community," or the "rights of the public," and how are they to be established? How is it to be determined what a railroad's services are worth to the public? How, indeed, is it to be discovered what rate is just to the public as well as to the railroad? And, when the interests of the public and of the railroad clash, which is to prevail? It need hardly be stated, in view of the preceding discussion, what the coloring is which must necessarily prevail in the Court's answers to these questions. The rights of the public are indeed difficult to establish. Generally speaking, the public has rights, which must not be invaded by the railroads. But specifically, what rights? To be exempt from the high rates necessary to compensate a railroad for losses due to its discriminations, or necessary to make profitable a road unwisely built, or necessary to sustain as many competing roads as may chance to divide the traffic? We have seen what answers the Court has given to these questions. The vague "rights" of the public have vanished with the appearance of a practical test.

But there is still another "limitation" upon the right of the railroad to compensation, namely, the industrial condition of the community, which is too vague and general to mean much in practice. Here again, it may be asked, how is the industrial condition of the community to be established at law, and just what "industrial condition" will justify a reduction of a road's earning capacity? Is it not inevitable that counsel for the state should find it difficult to secure satisfactory evidence in such a matter? The limitation is in general terms. In specific cases how much would it amount to? Probably not much. The only points ever argued by the states have, as we have already seen,[3] been summarily rejected by the Court.

[1] 154 U. S. 402.

[2] 164 U. S. 596–598; 169 U. S. 544–547. And see also 173 U. S. 754–756.

[3] P. 106 of original monograph.

The fact unfortunately seems to be that the euphonious generalities in which the Court has bound up the industrial welfare of the American commonwealths are more beautiful for contemplation than they are efficacious in use. To discover the practical meaning which is embodied in them, and to obtain recognition of it by the courts, is one of the difficult problems which now confronts the commissions, and one in the performance of which the attitude of the judiciary up to the present time gives little encouragement.

In these three ways, then — by placing an improper limitation on the legislative power to reduce earnings through regulation of rates, by employing erroneous methods in determining the effect of rates on earnings, and by setting up inadequate standards of reasonableness in earnings — has the Court practically destroyed the state's power of rate reduction. The doctrine of judicial review is therefore of great importance in the development of the railroad problem. But, more than that, it is of significance as a notable triumph achieved by the principle of individual interest over that of the public welfare. Under whatever constitutional pressure the courts may have been in announcing the doctrine, it is felt that it is a movement against the current of the times, and that it must result, in part, in deepening the conviction already growing in the minds of men, that the proper balance between the public and the private interests in industrial action has been much disturbed, and should be speedily restored.

HARRISON STANDISH SMALLEY

XXV

THE MINNESOTA RATE CASE, 1913[1]

Mr. Justice HUGHES delivered the opinion of the court:

These suits were brought by stockholders of the Northern Pacific Railway Company, the Great Northern Railway Company, and the Minneapolis & St. Louis Railroad Company, respectively, to restrain the enforcement of two orders of the Railroad & Warehouse Commission of the state of Minnesota, and two acts of the legislature of that state, prescribing maximum charges for transportation of freight and passengers, and to prevent the adoption or maintenance of these rates by the railroad companies. In addition to the companies, the attorney general of the state, the members of the Railroad & Warehouse Commission, and also, in the cases of the Northern Pacific and Great Northern Companies, certain representative shippers, were made defendants.

The orders and acts, which, by their terms related solely to charges for intrastate transportation, were as follows:

(1) The commission's order of September 6, 1906, effective November 15, 1906, fixing the maximum class rates for general merchandise.

(2) The act approved April 4, 1907, to take effect May 1, 1907, prescribing 2 cents a mile as the maximum fare for passengers, except for those under twelve years of age, for whom the maximum rate was to be 1 cent a mile. Laws of 1907, chap. 176.

(3) The act approved April 18, 1907, to take effect June 1, 1907, fixing maximum commodity rates for carload lots of specified weights. Laws of 1907, chap. 232.

[1] 33 Supreme Court Reporter, p. 729. The conflict of Federal and State authority is discussed in Ripley's Railroads: Rates and Regulation, chap. xx, leading up to this decision, not then rendered. The inter-related cases have been only in part decided, but follow the same general line of argument, differing only in detail.

(4) The commission's order of May 3, 1907, effective June 3, 1907, establishing maximum "in-rates" for designated commodities in carload lots from St. Paul, Minneapolis, Minnesota Transfer, and Duluth to certain distributing centers. No complaint is made of this order in the case of the Minneapolis & St. Louis Railroad Company.

In 1905, the legislature of Minnesota had adopted a joint resolution directing the commission "to undertake the work of securing a readjustment of the existing freight rates in this state, which will give a more uniform system of rates throughout the state, and a uniform scale of percentages which each class rate shall bear to the first class, the readjustment to secure a substantial reduction in the existing merchandise rates." Laws of 1905, chap. 350. Pursuant to this direction, the commission conducted a prolonged investigation. Public hearings were held extending over several months, in which the railroad companies took an active part, submitting a large amount of testimony with respect to the matters involved. The commission found the existing class rates for general merchandise to be unreasonable, and by the order of September 6, 1906, above-mentioned, established a new schedule of lower maximum rates. These rates were applied to the classes shown by the so-called "Western Classification" between stations in the state. This was a classification, by which articles were arranged in groups with reference to their general character, value, and the cost of transportation, and with modifications made from time to time, it had long been used by common carriers in the West and Northwest as a basis for rates, the commodities of each class taking the same rate under like conditions. In Minnesota, however, a large number of commodities, amounting to several hundred, had, by the intervention of the commission, been removed from this classification by the application of special rates, known as "commodity rates," or reduced in class so that the Western Classification in operation in that state was very materially different from that in general use as a basis of rates in other states.

The schedule of rates set forth in the order of September 6 was such that each rate for each class bore an exact relation to each other rate. The plan of the schedule was this: For first-class merchandise an allowance of 11.02 cents per cwt. was made for terminal charges, and, in addition, there was permitted a hauling charge of .98 of a cent for each 5 miles up to 200 miles, for each 10 miles over 200 miles up to 400 miles, and for each 20 miles over 400 miles up to 500 miles. For other classes, the rates were a fixed per centum of the corresponding rates for the first class. These rates were maximum terminal rates; that is, they related to transportation to or from certain important stations called terminal or distributing stations. Between stations neither of which is so designated, the rates of the schedule might be increased by 5 per centum.

The railway companies complied with this order and the class rates were put into effect on November 15, 1906.

The commission also had under consideration a reduction in the commodity rates, at which certain commodities such as grain, coal, lumber, and live stock were moved in carload lots. Because of the agitation with respect to these charges, the railroad companies voluntarily reduced their rates about 10 per cent on grain (September 1, 1906) and coal (October 22, 1906). The commission, however, on December 14, 1906, ordered a further reduction in the commodity rates. The railroad companies brought suit in the circuit court of the United States, and obtained a temporary injunction restraining the enforcement of this order. Thereupon the legislature passed the act above-mentioned, approved April 18, 1907, which established a new schedule of maximum commodity rates in all respects like that fixed by the commission, save that the reduction was not so great. The act grouped the various commodities which it embraced in several classes, for which different rates were prescribed. There was no fixed percentage relation between the classes, and no regular rate of progression of the various charges with increasing distance. In other respects the method of making the schedules was similar to that adopted in the order of September 6, 1906, the hauling charge decreasing as the mileage increases.

The remaining action with respect to freight rates was taken by the commission in the order of May 3, 1907, for the purpose of securing more favorable in-rates to a number of minor jobbing centers. It applied to certain commodities, such as groceries in carload lots, and was supplemental to the order of September 6, 1906, being intended to re-establish the relation which had previously existed between the in-rates to these distributing points and the general schedule of class rates.

The railroad companies obeyed this order of May 3, 1907, as they had that of September 6, 1906, and they also put into effect the passenger rate of 2 cents a mile. They were about to adopt the commodity rates fixed by the act of April 18, 1907, when these suits were brought and a temporary injunction restrained them from taking that course. The other rates, that is, the class rates, special in-rates, and the passenger rates were permitted to remain in force pending the suits.

The complainants assailed the acts and orders upon the grounds (1) that they amounted to an unconstitutional interference with interstate commerce, (2) that they were confiscatory, and (3) that the penalties imposed for their violation were so severe as to result in a denial of the equal protection of the laws and a deprivation of property without due process of law. The jurisdiction of the circuit court was sustained in *Ex parte* Young, 209 U. S. 123, 52 L. ed. 714, 13 L.R.A. (N.S.) 932, 28 Sup. Ct. Rep. 441, 14 Ann. Cas. 764, where it was also held that the penal provisions of the acts, operating to preclude a fair opportunity to test their validity, were unconstitutional on their face. The circuit court then referred the suits to a special master, who took the evidence and made an elaborate report sustaining the complainants' contentions. His findings were confirmed by the court, and decrees were entered accordingly, adjudging the acts and orders (with the exception, in the case of the Minneapolis & St. Louis Railroad Company, of the order of May 3, 1907) to be void, and permanently enjoining the enforcement of the prescribed rates, freight and passenger, and their adoption or maintenance by the railroad companies. 184 Fed. 765.

From these decrees, the attorney general of the state and the members of the Railroad & Warehouse Commission prosecute these appeals.

The penal provisions being separable . . . the question of the validity of the acts and orders fixing maximum rates is presented in two distinct aspects: (1) with respect to their effect on interstate commerce, and (2) as to their alleged confiscatory character.

First. As to interference with interstate commerce.

None of the acts and orders prescribes rates for goods or persons moving in interstate commerce. By their terms, they apply solely to commerce that is internal. Despite this obvious purport, it has been found below that the inevitable effect of the state's requirements for intrastate transportation was to impose a direct burden upon interstate commerce, and to create unjust discriminations between localities in Minnesota and those in adjoining states; and hence, that they must fall, as repugnant to the commerce clause and to the action of Congress under it. To support its conclusion, the circuit court presents an impressive array of facts drawn from the approved findings of the master. 184 Fed. 775–792. Without giving all the details they embrace, these findings may be summarized as follows:

I. The railroad property of each of the three companies constitutes a single system. On June 30, 1906, the Northern Pacific Railway Company (a Wisconsin corporation) operated 7,695 miles of track, of which 1,625 miles were in Minnesota. The Great Northern Railway Company (a Minnesota corporation) at the same time operated 8,528 miles of track, of which 2,779 miles were in Minnesota. Their lines extend westerly from Superior, Wisconsin, and Duluth, Minnesota, and from St. Paul and Minneapolis, through the states of Minnesota, North Dakota, Montana, Idaho, Washington, and Oregon, to the Pacific coast. The Minneapolis & St. Louis Railroad Company (also a Minnesota corporation) operated 1,028 miles of track running from St. Paul and Minneapolis westerly and southerly to points in South Dakota and Iowa. In the case of each company, the movement of interstate and local traffic takes place at the same time, on the same rails, with the same employees, and largely by means of the same trains and cars. There has never been a separation, and it is impracticable, in the exercise of fair economy, to make a separation, between the interstate and intrastate business in the case either of freight or of passengers. By far the larger part of the traffic is interstate. In the year 1906 the freight business of the Northern Pacific Company, local to Minnesota, was 2.67 per cent of its entire freight business, and 12.33 per cent of its freight business touching the state, and its passenger business local to the state was 5.79 per cent of its entire passenger business, and 67.21 per cent of its passenger business touching the state.

The conditions attending the transportation of passengers and freight are substantially the same for like distances within those portions of the states of Wisconsin, Minnesota, North Dakota, and South Dakota reached by the lines of these companies, whether the transportation is interstate or wholly intrastate. Prior to the acts and orders in question, the companies had maintained rates which were relatively fair, and not discriminatory as between interstate and intrastate business; and it is concluded that any substantial change in the basis of rates thus established, due only to the fact that the transportation was interstate or was local to a state, and any substantial difference in rates as between the two sorts of traffic, would constitute unjust discrimination in fact.

II. The state line of Minnesota on the east and west runs between cities which are in close proximity. Superior, Wisconsin, and Duluth, Minnesota, are side by side at the extremity of Lake Superior. Opposite one another, on the western boundary of the state, lie Grand Forks, North Dakota, and East Grand Forks, Minnesota; Fargo, North Dakota, and Moorhead, Minnesota; and Wahpeton, North Dakota, and Breckenridge, Minnesota. The cities in each pair ship and receive, to and from the same localities, the same kinds of freight. The railroad companies have always put each on a parity with the other in the matter of rates, and if there were a substantial difference it would cause serious injury to the commerce of the city having the higher rate. If the Northern Pacific Company failed to maintain as low rates on traffic in and out of Superior as on that to and from Duluth, its power to transact interstate business between Superior and points in Minnesota would be seriously impaired and the value of its property in Superior would be depreciated.

The maximum class rates fixed by the order of September 6, 1906, were from 20 per cent to 25 per cent lower than those theretofore maintained by the Northern Pacific and Great Northern Companies for transportation in Wisconsin, Minnesota, and North Dakota, whether such transportation was local to one of these states or was interstate between any two of them. When the Northern Pacific Company, pursuant to this order, installed the new intrastate rates, it reduced its interstate rates between Superior and points in Minnesota to an exact parity with its rates from Duluth. Reduction was also made in the rates between both Duluth and Superior and the above-mentioned points on the western boundary, so as to put the border cities in North Dakota on an equal basis with the neighboring cities in Minnesota. This reduction was substantial; and, had it not been made, the places adjoining the boundary, but outside the state, could not have competed with those within. Although the Northern Pacific Company thereby suffered a substantial loss in revenue from its interstate business, it had the choice of submitting to that loss or suffering substantial destruction of its interstate commerce to these border localities in articles covered by the orders. At the same time, the Great Northern Company made similar reductions, although, in its case, the transportation between Duluth and points in Minnesota was interstate, — its line passing through Wisconsin. The reason for these reductions was to preserve the relation in rates from Duluth which had always existed between localities on the Great Northern line and those similarly situated on the line of the Northern Pacific, and to meet the reduced rates on the latter.

III. Moorhead, Minnesota, Fargo and Bismarck, North Dakota, Billings and Butte, Montana, are so-called jobbing centers. Rates had always been accorded to them by the Northern Pacific Company which would allow them to compete with their nearest neighbors and with St. Paul, Minneapolis, and Duluth. The order of September 6, 1906, as supplemented by that of May 3, 1907, substantially reduced carload rates from the eastern terminals to Moorhead. This reduction would have given Moorhead an advantage in territory accessible to its jobbing industry not only as against Fargo, unless carload rates to Fargo were similarly reduced, but also as against Duluth, St. Paul, and Minneapolis unless less-than-carload rates from these places to points accessible to Moorhead, which included a considerable territory in North Dakota, were proportionately reduced. If Fargo were protected as against Moorhead, it would have an advantage over Bismarck in territory common to them both, and an advantage over the eastern terminals in territory common to them and to Fargo, unless carload rates from the eastern terminals to Bismarck and less-than-carload rates from those terminals to the territory accessible to Fargo were correspondingly reduced; and so on from distributing point to distributing point.

IV. Every rate comprehends two terminal charges, the initial and the final, and a haulage charge. It is declared to be a cardinal principle of rate-making that a rate for a longer distance should be proportionately smaller than one for a shorter distance; for even if the haulage charge in the former case were the same per mile, the rate per ton per mile should be less for the longer haul, as the terminal charges would be spread over a greater distance. A comparison disclosed that the rates established by the order of September 6, 1906, and maintained by the Northern Pacific Company between St. Paul and Moorhead, were in general substantially less than the proportion of the interstate rates maintained by the company to various points in North Dakota and Montana, based on the mileage in Minnesota as compared to that of the entire haul. Maintaining such a relation of rates involves, it is found, substantial and unjust discrimination in fact against the interstate localities.

V. After the installation by the Great Northern and Northern Pacific Companies of the rates prescribed by the order of September 6, 1906, it appeared that the sum of the local rates from St. Paul to Moorhead and from Moorhead to many points in North Dakota was less than the interstate rates theretofore maintained from St. Paul to these points. Both companies thereupon established rates from St. Paul to the North Dakota points as a rule no greater than the sum of the locals on Moorhead, but substantially lower in general than the interstate rates in force when the order took effect. Maintaining interstate rates from St. Paul to North Dakota localities substantially greater than the sum of the locals based on the state line would have caused unjust discrimination in fact. The actual reason for the reduction in the interstate rates was to prevent transhipment at Moorhead in order to take advantage of the lower sum of the locals, and to retain on its line traffic which might reach Moorhead over other lines by reason of competition, and, as to less-than-carload lots, to enable jobbers in the Twin Cities and Duluth to compete with those in Moorhead and Fargo in territory which otherwise the latter would have exclusively occupied by reason of their closer proximity.

VI. It is further held to be one of the fundamental dogmas of rate-making that the haulage charge per mile should not increase with increasing distance if the conditions be the same. Under the progressive decrease in the haulage charge within the state, provided by the order of September 6, 1906, 100 pounds of merchandise transported by the Northern Pacific from St. Paul to Moorhead, 248 miles, would have been hauled for 48 miles, at the rate of .98 cents per 10 miles, when Moorhead is reached. If the same haulage charge of .98 cents per 10 miles were applied for the remaining distance to Spokane, 1510 miles from St. Paul (which is said to be taken as a fair example merely to illustrate the principle), it would produce a rate from St. Paul to Spokane on first-class merchandise of $1.79 per cwt. The Interstate Commerce Commission in the Spokane rate case fixed the reasonable rate on first-class merchandise from St. Paul to Spokane of $2.50 per cwt. Maintaining this rate and the state schedule in Minnesota at the same time necessarily involves the raising of the per mile haulage charge after the Minnesota state line has been crossed, or the charge of a higher rate within Minnesota for its mileage proportion of long-haul interstate business than for business local to the state which is carried under the same conditions, and hence is found to result in unjust discrimination in fact against localities west of the Minnesota line.

VII. For more than twenty-five years the Northern Pacific Company has maintained an equal basis of rates on merchandise between its eastern and western terminals, respectively, and

Butte, Montana, and between its eastern and western terminals, respectively, and localities intermediate between them and Butte. Other railroads reaching Butte have, during the same time, maintained like rates to Butte from Sioux City, Omaha, St. Joseph and Kansas City on the east, and from San Francisco, Sacramento, and Los Angeles on the west. Butte has been as the hub of a wheel with spokes representing equal rates to these various cities. Industries, it is said, have been born and have grown in reliance upon this parity of rates. Intermediate points have had rates fixed in proportion to the Butte rates. Competition of markets and of carriers has brought this about. The Northern Pacific Company cannot maintain the state rates between its eastern terminals and Moorhead, and at the same time its interstate rates from its eastern terminals to Butte, without substantial discrimination in fact against Butte or localities intermediate between its eastern terminals and Butte. If it lowers its rates from its eastern terminals to Butte and intermediate stations to such an extent as to obviate this discrimination, it must, to preserve the relation which has always existed, lower to a like extent its rates from its western terminals to Butte and intermediate stations. Consequently, it is found that if the Northern Pacific Company maintains the commission-made rates between its eastern terminals and Moorhead, it must either substantially discriminate in fact, or destroy the general relation of rates which has existed for many years in the territory between the Missouri river and the Pacific coast.

VIII. Prior to the taking effect of the order of September 6, 1906, the Great Northern and Northern Pacific Companies had established joint through rates in connection with other carriers from all localities east or south of Minnesota to all points in Minnesota west of St. Paul and Minneapolis. After the rates prescribed by this order were installed, the sum of the locals on St. Paul from all localities south and east of Minnesota to points in Minnesota west of St. Paul and Minneapolis was substantially less than the then-existing interstate rates for the through haul to such western points. To avoid the resulting discrimination in favor of St. Paul, the companies withdrew the existing interstate rates, and established a new tariff no higher than the sum of the locals on St. Paul.

IX. Further illustrations are given of inequalities resulting from the reduced Minnesota rates as compared with rates for like transportation under similar conditions into adjoining states; as, for example, from Moorhead easterly to Minnesota points and westerly into North Dakota, and also of the effects produced in the application of the state rates by reason of the difference in the distances from St. Paul at which the state line is reached on similar hauls over different lines. As the schedule of September 6, 1906, prescribes a fixed relation between rates for different distances and different classes, the conclusion is that if the rule must be adhered to in Minnesota, it cannot be departed from substantially because of the intervention of a state line at one distance or another without involving unjust discrimination in fact.

It is found further that while, after the order of September 6, 1906, became effective, both the Great Northern and the Northern Pacific Companies reduced certain interstate rates, as already mentioned, the reduction was not to such extent as to remedy the discrimination resulting from the fact that in most cases the general basis of rates within Minnesota was substantially lower than that maintained in North Dakota or upon traffic crossing the state line.

X. The similarity in the conditions of interstate and intrastate transportation is found also with respect to the commodities for which rates were prescribed by the act of April 18, 1907 (chap. 232). The main lines and branches of the Northern Pacific and Great Northern Companies within Minnesota and North Dakota, with the exception of certain limited tracts, lie within grain fields, and grain is shipped in substantial quantities from nearly all stations in these fields to Duluth, Minneapolis, and Superior. Shipments of coal originate at the head of the Lakes, — that is, at Duluth or Superior, — and find their destination at all localities served by the companies in Minnesota and eastern North Dakota. Shipments of lumber originate at Duluth, Cloquet, Little Falls, and other places in Minnesota, and are destined to points throughout Minnesota and North Dakota. Shipments of live stock are made in Minnesota, South Dakota, and eastern Montana and go to South St. Paul or Chicago. So far as the conditions of transportation are concerned, it matters not, as to commodities moving eastwardly, whether the shipment is made in Montana, North Dakota, or Minnesota, or the transportation ends in Minnesota or in Wisconsin; and, as to commodities moving westwardly, whether the shipments are from Minnesota points or from Superior, or whether they find their destination in Minnesota or in North Dakota. The conclusion is that to maintain the commodity rates for transportation wholly within Minnesota simultaneously with the interstate rates now in force would involve unjust discrimination and would seriously impair the interstate business of the companies, to avoid which it would be necessary to reduce the basis of the interstate rates to a substantial parity with that prescribed by the state law. It is also stated that if the rates fixed by chapter 232 of the Laws of 1907 should become effective, the rate on shipments of wheat, with milling-in-transit privileges, from points in Minnesota *via* Minneapolis to Chicago, would be automatically reduced, and that unless all interstate rates between Minnesota points and Chicago *via* interior mill towns with similar privileges should be correspondingly reduced, Minneapolis would have a substantial advantage over such towns in its interstate rates.

XI. Prior to the act of 1907, fixing the rate of 2 cents a mile, the general basis of rates for passengers (of twelve years of age or over) between any two points on the Northern Pacific system had been for some years 3 cents a mile. After the new state rate had been installed, the sum of the locals between Moorhead and other Minnesota points and Moorhead and points westerly thereof was less than the then-existing through interstate rates. The passenger fare act took effect May 1, 1907, and in the first month thereafter the revenue for passengers on the Northern Pacific line between Moorhead and other Minnesota points increased 647 per cent over that of the corresponding month of the preceding year, while, eliminating Moorhead business, the revenue for passenger business within the state decreased 2 per cent. In

June, 1907, the second month, there were sold by the Northern Pacific Company, 4,037 tickets between St. Paul or Minneapolis, on the one hand, and Moorhead or East Grand Forks on the other, as compared with only 172 such tickets in the corresponding month of the year before; and in June, 1907, there were sold only 173 tickets between St. Paul or Minneapolis, and Grand Forks and Fargo, as compared with 984 such tickets in the corresponding month of the previous year. In May and June, 1906, only one cash full fare was collected on a train from Moorhead to St. Paul or Minneapolis. In those months in 1907 there were 1,168 cash full fares and 82 cash half fares so collected. Hence, it is said, the necessary, immediate, and direct effect of the law was to deprive the Northern Pacific Company of a substantial amount of its interstate passenger business through Moorhead.

Notwithstanding the facility with which interstate passengers could avoid the discrimination against them by making two contracts with the company, it is found that discrimination in fact still existed against the interstate passenger who, applying for a through ticket, did not know that the sum of the locals on Moorhead was less than the through rate, against the passenger with a trunk which he could not check through unless on a through ticket, and against a passenger who was compelled to use a sleeping car. The Northern Pacific Company shortly remedied this discrimination by reducing all its interstate fares for passenger transportation through Moorhead to an amount no greater than the sum of the locals over Moorhead. Before this reduction Wisconsin had fixed the maximum passenger fare at 2 cents a mile, and North Dakota at 2½ cents a mile. The rates thereafter established by the Northern Pacific Company between St. Paul, for example, and points in North Dakota and beyond, and by the Northern Pacific Company jointly with other companies for transportation between points easterly of Minnesota and points on the line of the Northern Pacific, were in general less than the previous rates by approximately 1 cent per mile for the mileage in Wisconsin and Minnesota, and by ½ cent per mile for the mileage in North Dakota. It is concluded that these reductions were compelled to avoid unjust discrimination, and in order that the companies might transact interstate passenger business freely and without impairment of volume.

There are added various hypothetical calculations of the losses which would have been sustained if the basis prescribed by the state acts and orders had been applied to the interstate business and to local business in other states. We shall have occasion later to refer to the actual results of the business of the railroad companies during the time that the rates fixed by the acts and orders (with the exception of the commodity rates) were in force, and to the effect upon revenue which the adoption of the commodity rates would have had.

The foregoing findings, as stated by the master, were made "without regard to the justness or otherwise in fact of the interstate rates so affected by such local rates." The determination of the reasonableness of the interstate rates was not deemed to be within the province of the court.

The appellants do not concede the correctness of the findings in their full scope, and insist upon qualifications. They deny that the evidence justified the finding that the companies had maintained "an equable, that is, relatively fair, basis of rates" prior to the acts and orders in question. The general or comprehensive system of interdependent and fairly related rates, each so equitably adjusted to the others that any local change must of necessity throw the whole out of balance, is declared to exist only in imagination, — to be a fiction constructed in disregard of the facts of rate-making, and without attention to the inconsistencies shown by the schedules which had been in force. The actual reductions in interstate rates, which followed upon the adoption of the state tariffs, were made, it is urged, in rates voluntarily established by the companies themselves which had not been declared to be reasonable by competent authority, and in any case furnish no standard by which the validity of the action of the state, in the control of its internal affairs, should be judged. The appellants say that the local rates in Minnesota were incongruous and unreasonable; that frequent changes in the interest of favored shippers had been made through the filing of temporary intrastate tariffs until the practice was stopped by a statute of 1905 (chap. 176), forbidding changes without the consent of the commission; that with respect to grain and live stock, the principal agricultural products of the state, the companies maintained an "inharmonious jumble of arbitrary rates"; and that the acts and orders in question were designed to correct inequalities in the intrastate tariffs, and to prescribe charges which, upon thorough investigation and after public hearings in which the companies participated, were found to be reasonable and were brought into suitable relation with each other by means of a scientific plan. And it is denied that unjust discrimination as against localities without the state can be predicated of the establishment of reasonable state rates.

It is also insisted that the prescribed intrastate freight rates were not in general lower than the existing interstate rates. Reference is made to the long-distance traffic, which, it is said, was moved within the state on proportionals of long-haul rates which were much below the local rates fixed by the state. It is pointed out that the master found, in passing upon the question whether the rates were confiscatory, that the gross revenue which was derived from the interstate freight business during the fiscal year ending June 30, 1908 (when all the rates in question were in force save the commodity rates), was greater per ton-mile than that derived in the same period from the interstate business within the state, being in the case of the Northern Pacific Company in the ratio of 1.4387 to 1, and in that of the Great Northern Company of 2.02894 to 1. The appellants also contest the validity of the argument based on a hypothetical extension beyond the state line of the "rate of progression" for additional distance which had been prescribed by the state solely with reference to internal traffic, and they submit illustrations of incongruities which they contend would be shown by a similar extension of the rate of progression disclosed by the former intrastate tariffs of the companies. Again, it is urged that the extent of the reductions attributable to the 2-cent fare law may not be estimated properly by a comparison with the former maximum rate of 3 cents a mile. Various rates had been in force less than the maximum allowed. For the six years prior to the 2-cent fare law the average rate per passenger per mile for intrastate transportation in Minnesota, on the Northern Pacific line, had ranged from 2.299 cents in 1901 to 2.435 cents in 1905, 2.406 cents in 1906, and 2.197 cents in 1907;[1] and during the same time the average rate per passenger per mile for interstate transportation in Minnesota varied from 2.075 cents in 1901, 2.027 cents in 1905, 1.949 cents in 1906, and 1.981 cents in 1907.[1] In the fiscal year ending June 30, 1908, with the 2-cent fare law in force the average rate per passenger per mile in Minnesota was 1.930 cents for intrastate and 1.928 cents for interstate carriage.

It is conceded, however, that the schedules fixed for intrastate transportation "necessarily disturbed the equilibrium theretofore existing between the rates on the two classes of business" (state and interstate) "on the boundary lines." This applies to the rates to and from the cities situated on opposite sides of the Red River of the North, the boundary between Minnesota and North Dakota, and to and from Duluth and Superior on the eastern boundary. The reduction of the state rates brought them below the level of the interstate rates in those instances in which formerly both had been maintained on a parity. So, also, whatever may be said as to the nonexistence of a general or comprehensive system of equitably adjusted rates, it is clear that there are competitive areas crossed by the state line of Minnesota, and that the state's requirements altered the existing relation between state and interstate rates as to places within these zones of competition, and not merely as to the cities on the boundary of the state.

The situation is not peculiar to Minnesota. The same question has been presented by the appeals, now before the court, which involve the validity of intrastate tariffs fixed by Missouri, Arkansas, Kentucky, and Oregon. Differences in particular facts appear, but they cannot be regarded as controlling. A scheme of state rates framed to avoid discrimination between localities within the state, and to provide an harmonious system for intrastate transportation throughout the state, naturally would embrace those places within the state which are on or near the state's

[1] The 2-cent fare law was in force for two months of the fiscal year ending June 30, 1907.

boundaries; and when these are included in a general reduction of intrastate rates, there is, of course, a change in the relation of rates as theretofore existing to points adjacent to, but across, the state line. Kansas City, Kansas, and Kansas City, Missouri; East St. Louis, Illinois, and St. Louis, Missouri; Omaha, Nebraska, and Council Bluffs, Iowa; Cincinnati, Ohio, and Covington and Newport, Kentucky; and many other places throughout the country which might be mentioned, present substantially the same conditions as those here appearing with respect to localities on the boundaries of Minnesota. It is also a matter of common knowledge that competition takes but little account of state lines, and in every part of the land competitive districts embrace points in different states.

With appreciation of the gravity of the controversy, the railroad commissioners of eight states[1] have filed their brief as *amici curiæ*, in support of the appeals, stating that, if the doctrine of the court below were accepted, the regulation by the states of rates for intrastate transportation would be practically destroyed. They say that "there is practically no movement of traffic between two towns within a state that does not come into competition with some interstate haul," and that "if the disturbance of the existing relation between competitive state and interstate rates is the correct criterion, no reduction can be made in state rates without interfering with interstate commerce." The governors of three states, pursuant to a resolution of a conference of the governors of all the states, have also presented, by leave of the court, their argument in defense of the position taken by Minnesota. They do not seek "to belittle the effect of the action of Minnesota on the business between the places" named in the findings, but they are convinced that if the principle announced by the circuit court is upheld, it can be made to apply by a showing of similar facts in virtually every state. Insisting that, under their reserved power, "the right of the states to regulate their own commerce is as clear and broad as that of Congress to regulate interstate commerce," they assail

[1] Nebraska, Iowa, Kansas, South Dakota, North Dakota, Oklahoma, Missouri, and Texas.

the decision below, not upon the ground that it incorrectly sets forth conditions in Minnesota and adjoining states, but for what they consider to be "its plain disregard of the provisions of the Federal Constitution, which establish the relations between the nation and the states." "The operation of these provisions," they maintain, "was not made to depend on geography or convenience or competition. They cannot apply in one state and not in another, according to circumstances as they may be found by the courts, because they are vital principles which constitute the very structure of our dual form of government."

The controversy thus arises from opposing conceptions of the fundamental law, and of the scope and effect of Federal legislation, rather than from differences with respect to the salient facts.

For the purpose of the present inquiry, the rates fixed by the state must be assumed to be reasonable rates so far as intrastate traffic is concerned; that is, they must be rates which the state in the exercise of its legislative judgment, could constitutionally fix for intrastate transportation separately considered. If the state rates are not of this character, — a question to be dealt with later, — they cannot be sustained in any event; but, assuming them to be otherwise valid, the decree below, with respect to the present branch of the case, rests upon two grounds: (1) That the action of the state imposes a direct burden upon interstate commerce; and (2) that it is in conflict with the provisions of the act to regulate commerce.

These grounds are distinct. If a state enactment imposes a *direct burden* upon interstate commerce, it must fall regardless of Federal legislation. The point of such an objection is not that Congress has acted, but that the state has directly restrained that which, in the absence of Federal regulation, should be free. If the acts of Minnesota constitute a direct burden upon interstate commerce, they would be invalid without regard to the exercise of Federal authority touching the interstate rates said to be affected. On the other hand, if the state, in the absence of Federal legislation, would have had the power to prescribe the rates here assailed, the question remains whether its action is void as being repugnant to the statute which Congress has enacted.

Prior to the passage of the act to regulate commerce, carriers fixed their interstate rates free from the actual exertion of Federal control; and under that act, as it stood until the amendment of June 29, 1906 [34 Stat. at L. 584, chap. 3591, U. S. Comp. Stat. Supp. 1911, p. 1288], the Interstate Commerce Commission had no power to prescribe interstate rates. *Interstate Commerce Commission* v. *Cincinnati, N. O. & T. P. R. Co.* 167 U. S. 479, 511, 42 L. ed. 243, 257, 17 Sup. Ct. Rep. 896.[1] The states, however, had long exercised the power to establish maximum rates for intrastate transportation. Was this power, apart from Federal action, subject to the limitation that the state could not fix intrastate rates, reasonable as such, generally throughout the state, but only as to such places and in such circumstances that the interstate business of the carriers would not be thereby affected? That is, was the state debarred from fixing reasonable rates on traffic, wholly internal, as to all state points so situated that, as a practical consequence, the carriers would have to reduce the rates they had made to competing points without the state, in order to maintain the volume of their interstate business, or to continue the parity of rates, or the relation between rates as it had previously existed? Was the state, in prescribing a general tariff of reasonable intrastate rates otherwise within its authority bound not to go below a minimum standard established by the interstate rates made by the carriers within competitive districts? If the state power, independently of Federal legislation, is thus limited, the inquiry need proceed no further. Otherwise it must be determined whether Congress has so acted as to create such a restriction upon the state authority theretofore existing.

(1) The general principles governing the exercise of state authority when interstate commerce is affected are well established. The power of Congress to regulate commerce among the several states is supreme and plenary. It is "complete in itself, may be exercised to its utmost extent, and acknowledges no limitations, other than are prescribed in the Constitution." *Gibbons* v. *Ogden*, 9 Wheat. 1, 196, 6 L. ed. 23, 70. The conviction of its necessity sprang from the disastrous experiences under the

[1] P. 187, *supra*, and Ripley's Railroads: Rates and Regulation.

Confederation, when the states vied in discriminatory measures against each other. In order to end these evils, the grant in the Constitution conferred upon Congress an authority at all times adequate to secure the freedom of interstate commercial intercourse from state control, and to provide effective regulation of that intercourse as the national interest may demand. The words "among the several states" distinguish between the commerce which concerns more states than one, and that commerce which is confined within one state and does not affect other states. "The genius and character of the whole government," said Chief Justice Marshall, "seems to be, that its action is to be applied to all the external concerns of the nation, and to those internal concerns which affect the states generally; but not to those which are completely within a particular state, which do not affect other states, and with which it is not necessary to interfere, for the purpose of executing some of the general powers of the government. The completely internal commerce of a state, then, may be considered as reserved for the state itself." *Id.* p. 195. This reservation to the states manifestly is only of that authority which is consistent with, and not opposed to, the grant to Congress. There is no room in our scheme of government for the assertion of state power in hostility to the authorized exercise of Federal power. The authority of Congress extends to every part of interstate commerce, and to every instrumentality or agency by which it is carried on; and the full control by Congress of the subjects committed to its regulation is not to be denied or thwarted by the commingling of interstate and intrastate operations. This is not to say that the nation may deal with the internal concerns of the state, as such, but that the execution by Congress of its constitutional power to regulate interstate commerce is not limited by the fact that intrastate transactions may have become so interwoven therewith that the effective government of the former incidentally controls the latter. This conclusion necessarily results from the supremacy of the national power within its appointed sphere. . . .

The grant in the Constitution of its own force, that is, without action by Congress, established the essential immunity of interstate commercial intercourse from the direct control of the states with respect to those subjects embraced within the grant which are of such a nature as to demand that, if regulated at all, their regulation should be prescribed by a single authority. It has repeatedly been declared by this court that as to those subjects which require a general system or uniformity of regulation, the power of Congress is exclusive. In other matters, admitting of diversity of treatment according to the special requirements of local conditions, the states may act within their respective jurisdictions until Congress sees fit to act; and, when Congress does act, the exercise of its authority overrides all conflicting state legislation. . . .

The principle which determines this classification underlies the doctrine that the states cannot, under any guise, impose direct burdens upon interstate commerce. For this is but to hold that the states are not permitted directly to regulate or restrain that which, from its nature, should be under the control of the one authority, and be free from restriction, save as it is governed in the manner that the national legislature constitutionally ordains.

Thus, the states cannot tax interstate commerce, either by laying the tax upon the business which constitutes such commerce or the privilege of engaging in it, or upon the receipts, as such, derived from it. . . .

They have no power to prohibit interstate trade in legitimate articles of commerce . . . or to discriminate against the products of other states . . . or to exclude from the limits of the state corporations or others engaged in interstate commerce, or to fetter by conditions their right to carry it on . . . or to prescribe the rates to be charged for transportation from one state to another, or to subject the operations of carriers in the course of such transportation to requirements that are unreasonable or pass beyond the bounds of suitable local protection. . . .

But within these limitations there necessarily remains to the states until Congress acts, a wide range for the permissible exercise of power appropriate to their territorial jurisdiction although interstate commerce may be affected. It extends to those matters of a local nature as to which it is impossible to derive from the constitutional grant an intention that they should go uncontrolled pending Federal intervention. Thus, there are certain subjects having the most obvious and direct relation to interstate commerce, which nevertheless, with the acquiescence of Congress, have been controlled by state legislation from the foundation of the government because of the necessity that they should not remain unregulated, and that their regulation should be adapted to varying local exigencies; hence, the absence of regulation by Congress in such matters has not imported that there should be no restriction, but rather that the states should continue to supply the needed rules until Congress should decide to supersede them. Further, it is competent for a state to govern its internal commerce, to provide local improvements, to create and regulate local facilities, to adopt protective measures of a reasonable character in the interest of the health, safety, morals, and welfare of its people, although interstate commerce may incidentally or indirectly be involved. Our system of government is a practical adjustment by which the national authority as conferred by the Constitution is maintained in its full scope without unnecessary loss of local efficiency. Where the subject is peculiarly one of local concern, and from its nature belongs to the class with which the state appropriately deals in making reasonable provision for local needs, it cannot be regarded as left to the unrestrained will of individuals because Congress has not acted, although it may have such a relation to interstate commerce as to be within the reach of the Federal power. In such case, Congress must be the judge of the necessity of Federal action. Its paramount authority always enables it to intervene at its discretion for the complete and effective government of that which has been committed to its care, and, for this purpose and to this extent, in response to a conviction of national need, to displace local laws by substituting laws of its own. The successful working of our constitutional system has thus been made possible.

The leading illustrations may be noted. Immediately upon the adoption of the Constitution, Congress recognized the propriety of local action with respect to pilotage, in view of the local necessities of navigation. . . . It was sixty years before provision for Federal license of pilots was made (act of August 30, 1852, chap. 106, 10 Stat. at L. 61), and even then port pilots were not included. . . .

A state is entitled to protect its coasts, to improve its harbors, bays, and streams, and to construct dams and bridges across navigable rivers within its limits, unless there is conflict with some act of Congress. Plainly, in the case of dams and bridges, interference with the accustomed right of navigation may result. But this exercise of the important power to provide local improvements has not been regarded as constituting such a direct burden upon intercourse or interchange of traffic as to be repugnant to the Federal authority in its dormant state. . . .

While the state may not impose a duty of tonnage . . . it may regulate wharfage charges and exact tolls for the use of artificial facilities provided under its authority. The subject is one under state control, where Congress has not acted, although the payment is required of those engaged in interstate or foreign commerce. . . .

Quarantine regulations are essential measures of protection which the states are free to adopt when they do not come into conflict with Federal action. In view of the need of conforming such measures to local conditions, Congress from the beginning has been content to leave the matter for the most part, notwithstanding its vast importance, to the states, and has repeatedly acquiesced in the enforcement of state laws. . . .

State inspection laws and statutes designed to safeguard the inhabitants of a state from fraud and imposition are valid when reasonable in their requirements, and not in conflict with Federal rules, although they may affect interstate commerce in their relation to articles prepared for export, or by including incidentally those brought into the state and held for sale in the original imported packages. . . .

* * * * * * * *

. . . It has also been held that the state has the power to forbid the consolidation of state railroad corporations with competing lines although both may be interstate carriers, and the prohibition may have a far-reaching effect upon interstate commerce. . . .

Again, it is manifest that when the legislation of the state is limited to internal commerce to such degree that it does not include even incidentally the subjects of interstate commerce, it is not rendered invalid because it may affect the latter commerce indirectly. In the intimacy of commercial relations, much that is done in the superintendence of local matters may have an indirect bearing upon interstate commerce. The development of local resources and the extension of local facilities may have a very important effect upon communities less favored, and to an appreciable degree alter the course of trade. The freedom of local trade may stimulate interstate commerce, while restrictive measures within the police power of the state, enacted exclusively with respect to internal business, as distinguished from interstate traffic, may in their reflex or indirect influence diminish the latter and reduce the volume of articles transported into or out of the state....

Within the state power, then, in the words of Chief Justice Marshall, is

> that immense mass of legislation which embraces everything within the territory of a state, not surrendered to the general government; all which can be most advantageously exercised by the states themselves. Inspection laws, quarantine laws, health laws of every description, as well as laws for regulating the internal commerce of a state, and those which respect turnpike roads, ferries, etc., are component parts of this mass. No direct general power over these objects is granted to Congress: and, consequently, they remain subject to state legislation. If the legislative power of the Union can reach them, it must be for national purposes; it must be where the power is expressly given for a special purpose, or is clearly incidental to some power which is expressly given. *Gibbons* v. *Ogden*, 9 Wheat. 203, 204, 6 L. ed. 71, 72.

And whenever, as to such matters, under these established principles, Congress may be entitled to act, by virtue of its power to secure the complete government of interstate commerce, the state power nevertheless continues until Congress does act and by its valid interposition limits the exercise of the local authority.

(2) These principles apply to the authority of the state to prescribe reasonable maximum rates for intrastate transportation.

State regulation of railroad rates began with railroad transportation. The railroads were chartered by the states, and from the outset, in many charters, maximum rates for freight or passengers, or both, were prescribed. Frequently — and this became the more general practice — the board of directors was permitted to fix charges in its discretion, — an authority which, in numerous instances, was made subject to a limitation upon the amount of net earnings. In several states maximum rates were also established, or the power to alter rates was expressly reserved, by general laws. In 1853, the state of New York fixed the maximum fare for way passengers on the railroads forming the line of the New York Central at 2 cents a mile (Laws of 1853, chap. 76, § 7), and this rate extending to Buffalo and Suspension Bridge, on the boundary of the state, has continued to the present day (Consol. Laws [N. Y.] chap. 49, § 57). As a rule the restrictions imposed by the early legislation were far from onerous, but they are significant in the assertion of the right of control. More potent than these provisions, in the actual effect upon railroad tariffs, was the state canal. It is a matter of common knowledge that the traffic on the trunk lines from the Atlantic seaboard to the West was developed in competition with the Erie canal, built, maintained, and regulated by the state of New York to promote its commerce.

The authority of the state to limit by legislation the charges of common carriers within its borders was not confined to the power to impose limitations in connection with grants of corporate privileges. In view of the nature of their business, they were held subject to legislative control as to the amount of their charges unless they were protected by their contract with the state. . . . The question was presented by acts of the legislatures of Illinois, Iowa, Wisconsin, and Minnesota, passed in the years 1871 and 1874, in response to a general movement for a reduction of rates. The section of the country in which the demand arose was to a large degree homogeneous and one in which the flow of commerce was only slightly concerned with state lines. But resort was had to the states for relief. In the Munn Case, the court had before it the statute of Illinois governing the grain warehouses in Chicago. Through these elevators, located with the river harbor on the one side and the railway tracks on the other, it was necessary, according to the course of trade, for the product of seven or eight states of the West to pass on its way to the states on the Atlantic coast. In addition to the denial of any legislative authority to limit charges it was urged that the act was repugnant to the exclusive power of Congress to regulate interstate commerce. The court answered that the business was carried on exclusively within the limits of the state of Illinois, that its regulation was a thing of domestic concern, and that "certainly, until Congress acts in reference to their interstate relations, the state may exercise all the powers of government over them, even though in so doing it may indirectly operate upon commerce outside its immediate jurisdiction." In the decision of the railroad cases, above cited, the same opinion was expressed. The language of the court, however, went further than to sustain the state law with respect to rates for purely intrastate carriage. Thus, the act of Wisconsin covered traffic which started within the state and was destined to points outside, and this was treated as being within the state power (*Peik* v. *Chicago & N. W. R. Co.* 94 U. S. 164, 177, 178, 24 L. ed. 97–99), a view which was later repudiated (*Wabash, St. L. & P. R. Co.* v. *Illinois*, 118 U. S. 557, 30 L. ed. 244, 1 Inters. Com. Rep. 31, 7 Sup. Ct. Rep. 4).

It became a frequent practice for the states to create commissions, as agencies of state supervision and regulation, and in many instances the rate-making power was conferred upon these bodies. A summary of such legislation is given in *Interstate Commerce Commission* v. *Cincinnati N. O. & T. P. R. Co.* 167 U. S. 479, 495, 496, 42 L. ed. 243, 251, 252, 17 Sup. Ct. Rep. 896. One of these state laws, that of Mississippi, passed in 1884, came under review in *Stone* v. *Farmers' Loan & Trust Co.* 116 U. S. 307, 29 L. ed. 636, 6 Sup. Ct. Rep. 334, 388, 1191. The suit was brought to enjoin the railroad commission from enforcing the statute against the Mobile & Ohio Railroad Company. It had been incorporated in the states of Alabama, Mississippi, Tennessee, and Kentucky, for the purpose of constructing a railroad from Mobile to some point near the mouth of the Ohio river, where it would connect with another railroad, thus forming a continuous line of interstate communication between the Gulf of Mexico and the Great Lakes. The commission as yet had not acted. Sustaining the state power to fix rates upon the traffic wholly internal, the court directed the dismissal of the bill. The state, said the court, "may beyond all question, by the settled rule of decision in this court, regulate freights and fares for business done exclusively within the state, and it would seem to be a matter of domestic concern to prevent the company from discriminating against persons and places in Mississippi." In the same case, it was declared that the power of regulation was not a power to confiscate ; and that under pretense of regulating fares and freights, the states could not "require a railroad corporation to carry persons or property without reward," or do that which in law amounted "to a taking of private property for public use without just compensation, or without due process of law." *Id.* p. 331.

In *Wabash St. L. & P. R. Co.* v. *Illinois*, *supra*, it was finally determined that the authority of the state did not extend to the regulation of charges for interstate transportation. There the state statute was aimed at discrimination. It was said to have been violated by the railroad company in the case of shipments from points within Illinois to the city of New York. The state court had construed the statute to be binding as to that part of the interstate haul which was within the state, although inoperative beyond the boundary. So applied, this court held the act to be invalid.

But no doubt was entertained of the state's authority to regulate rates for transportation that was wholly intrastate. And, in illustrating the extent of state power (118 U. S. p. 564), the court selected transportation across the state from Cairo to Chicago and from Chicago to Alton, all boundary points constituting important centers of commerce — the one on Lake Michigan, and the others at the confluence of the Mississippi and Ohio rivers, and of the Mississippi and Missouri rivers, respectively. After reviewing decisions holding state laws to be ineffective which imposed a direct burden upon interstate commerce . . . the court emphasized the distinction with respect to the operation of the statute upon domestic transactions, saying:

Of the justice or propriety of the principle which lies at the foundation of the Illinois statute it is not the province of this court to speak. As restricted to a transportation which begins and ends within the limits of the state, it may be very just and equitable, and it certainly is the province of the state legislature to determine that question. *Id.* p. 577.

The doctrine was thus fully established that the state could not prescribe interstate rates, but could fix reasonable intrastate rates throughout its territory. The extension of railroad facilities has been accompanied at every step by the assertion of this authority on the part of the states and its invariable recognition by this court. It has never been doubted that the state could, if it saw fit, build its own highways, canals and railroads. *Baltimore & O. R. Co.* v. *Maryland*, 21 Wall. 456, 470, 471, 22 L. ed. 678, 683, 684. It could build railroads traversing the entire state, and thus join its border cities and commercial centers by new highways of internal intercourse, to be always available upon reasonable terms. Such provision for local traffic might indeed alter relative advantages in competition, and, by virtue of economic forces, those engaged in interstate trade and transportation might find it necessary to make readjustments extending from market to market through a wide sphere of influence; but such action of the state would not for that reason be regarded as creating a direct restraint upon interstate commerce, and as thus transcending the state power. Similarly, the authority of the state to prescribe what shall be reasonable charges of common carriers for interstate transportation, unless it be limited by the exertion of the constitutional power of Congress, is state-wide. As a power appropriate to the territorial jurisdiction of the state, it is not confined to a part of the state, but extends throughout the state, — to its cities adjacent to its boundaries as well as to those in the interior of the state. To say that this power exists, but that it may be exercised only in prescribing rates that are on an equal or higher basis than those that are fixed by the carrier for interstate transportation, is to maintain the power in name while denying it in fact. It is to assert that the exercise of the legislative judgment in determining what shall be the carrier's charge for the intrastate service is itself subject to the carrier's will. But this state-wide authority controls the carrier, and is not controlled by it; and the idea that the power of the state to fix reasonable rates for its internal traffic is limited by the mere action of the carrier in laying an interstate rate to places across the state's border is foreign to our jurisprudence.

If this authority of the state be restricted, it must be by virtue of the paramount power of Congress over interstate commerce and its instruments; and, in view of the nature of the subject, a limitation may not be implied because of a dormant Federal power; that is, one which has not been exerted, but can only be found in the actual exercise of Federal control in such measure as to exclude this action by the state which otherwise would clearly be within its province.

(3) When Congress, in the year 1887, enacted the act to regulate commerce (24 Stat. at L. 379, chap. 104, U. S. Comp. Stat. Supp. 1911, p. 1284), it was acquainted with the course of the development of railroad transportation and with the exercise by the states of the rate-making power. An elaborate report had been made to the Senate by a committee authorized to investigate the subject of railroad regulation, in which the nature and extent of state legislation, including the commission plan, were fully reviewed (Senate Report 46, submitted January 6, 1886, 49th Congress, 1st session). And it was the fact that beyond the bounds of state control there lay a vast field of unregulated activity in the conduct of interstate transportation which was found to be the chief cause of the demand for Federal action.

Congress carefully defined the scope of its regulation, and expressly provided that it was not to extend to purely intrastate traffic. In the 1st section of the act to regulate commerce there was inserted the following proviso:

> Provided, however, That the provisions of this act shall not apply to the transportation of passengers or property, or to the receiving, delivering, storage, or handling of property, wholly within one state, and not shipped to or from a foreign country, from or to any state or territory as aforesaid.

When in the year 1906 (act of June 29, 1906, chap. 3591, 34 Stat. at L. 584, U. S. Comp. Stat. Supp. 1911, p. 1288), Congress amended the act so as to confer upon the Federal commission power to prescribe maximum interstate rates, the proviso in § 1 was reënacted. Again, in 1910, when the act was extended to embrace telegraph, telephone, and cable companies engaged in interstate business, the proviso was once more reënacted, with an additional clause so as to exclude intrastate messages from the operation of the statute. (Act of June 18, 1910, chap. 309, 36 Stat. at L. 545 [U. S. Comp. Stat. Supp. 1911, p. 1285].) The proviso in its present form reads:

> Provided, however, That the provisions of this act shall not apply to the transportation of passengers or property, or to the receiving, delivering, storage, or handling of property wholly within one state, and not shipped to or from a foreign country, from or to any state or territory as aforesaid, nor shall they apply to the transmission of messages by telephone, telegraph, or cable wholly within one state, and not transmitted to or from a foreign country, from or to any state or territory, as aforesaid.

There was thus excluded from the provisions of the act that transportation which was "wholly within one state," with the specified qualification where its subject was going to or coming from a foreign country.

It is urged, however, that the words of the proviso are susceptible of a construction which would permit the provisions of § 3 of the act, prohibiting carriers from giving an undue or unreasonable preference or advantage to any locality, to apply to unreasonable discrimination between localities in different states, as well when arising from an intrastate rate as compared with an interstate rate as when due to interstate rates exclusively. If it be assumed that the statute should be so construed (and it is not necessary now to decide the point), it would inevitably follow that the controlling principle governing the enforcement of the act should be applied to such cases as might thereby be brought within its purview; and the question whether the carrier, in such a case, was giving an undue or unreasonable preference or advantage to one locality as against another, or subjecting any locality to an undue or unreasonable prejudice or disadvantage, would be primarily for the investigation and determination of the Interstate Commerce Commission, and not for the courts. The dominating purpose of the statute was to secure conformity to the prescribed standards through the examination and appreciation of the complex facts of transportation by the body created for that purpose; and, as this court has repeatedly held, it would be destructive of the system of regulation defined by the statute if the court, without the preliminary action of the Commission, were to undertake to pass upon the administrative questions which the statute has primarily confided to it. . . . In the present case there has been no finding by the Interstate Commerce Commission of unjust discrimination violative of the act; and no action of that body is before us for review.

The question we have now before us, essentially, is whether, after the passage of the interstate commerce act, and its amendment, the state continued to possess the state-wide authority which it formerly enjoyed to prescribe reasonable rates for its exclusively internal traffic. That, as it plainly appears, was the nature of the action taken by Minnesota, and the attack, however phrased, upon the rates here involved as an interference with interstate commerce, is in substance a denial of that authority.

Having regard to the terms of the Federal statute, the familiar range of state action at the time it was enacted, the continued exercise of state authority in the same manner and to the same extent after its enactment, and the decisions of this court, recognizing and upholding this authority, we find no foundation for the proposition that the act to regulate commerce contemplated interference therewith.

Congress did not undertake to say that the intrastate rates of interstate carriers should be reasonable, or to invest its administrative agency with authority to determine their reasonableness. Neither by the original act nor by its amendment did Congress seek to establish a unified control over interstate and intrastate rates; it did not set up a standard for interstate rates, or prescribe, or authorize the commission to prescribe, either maximum or minimum rates for intrastate traffic. It cannot be supposed that Congress sought to accomplish by indirection that which it expressly disclaimed, or attempted to override the accustomed authority of the states without the provision of a substitute. On the contrary, the fixing of reasonable rates for intrastate transportation was left where it had been found; that is, with the states and the agencies created by the states to deal with that subject. *Missouri P. R. Co.* v. *Larabee Flour Mills Co.* 211 U. S. 612, 620, 621, 53 L. ed. 352, 359, 360, 29 Sup. Ct. Rep. 214.

How clear was the purpose not to occupy the field thus left to the exercise of state power is shown by the clause uniformly inserted in the numerous acts passed by Congress to authorize the construction of railways across the Indian territory. This clause, while fixing a maximum passenger rate, made the laws of an adjoining state (in some cases Arkansas, in others Texas, and in others Kansas) applicable to the freight rates to be charged within the territory; and while the right to regulate rates on the authorized line of railroad was reserved to Congress until a state government should be established, it was expressly provided that, when established, the state should be entitled to fix rates for intrastate transportation, — the right remaining with Congress to prescribe rates for such transportation as should be interstate. Within a month after the act to regulate commerce was enacted, two acts were passed by Congress for this purpose with respect to railways extending across the territory from the Texas to the Kansas boundary. The provision — in both cases in identical language, save that the one referred to the laws of Texas and the other to the laws of Kansas — was as follows (act of February 24, 1887, chap. 254, § 4, 24 Stat. at L. 420; act of March 2, 1887, chap. 319, § 4, 24 Stat. at L. 447):

Sec. 4. That said railroad company shall not charge the inhabitants of said territory a greater rate of freight than the rate authorized by the laws of the state of Texas for services or transportation of the same kind: Provided, That passenger rates on said railway shall not exceed three cents per mile. Congress hereby reserves the right to regulate the charges for freight and passengers on said railway, and messages on said telegraph and telephone lines, *until a state government or governments shall exist in said territory within the limits of which said railway, or a part thereof, shall be located; and then such state government or governments shall be authorized to fix and regulate the cost of transportation of persons and freights within their respective limits by said railway;* but Congress expressly reserves the right to fix and regulate at all times the cost of such transportation by said railway or said company whenever such transportation shall extend from one state into another, or shall extend into more than one state: Provided, however, That the rate of such transportation of passengers, local or interstate, shall not exceed the rate above expressed: And provided further, That said railway company shall carry the mail at such prices as Congress may by law provide; and until such rate is fixed by law, the Postmaster General may fix the rate of compensation.

The same provision is found in similar statutes passed in almost every year from 1884 to 1902, and relating to lines intended to serve as highways of interstate communication. When Oklahoma became a state, the laws of other states which were referred to in these various acts ceased to be operative within its limits, and by virtue of its statehood and with the direct sanction of Congress, it became authorized to prescribe reasonable maximum rates for intrastate transportation throughout its extent. . . .

The decisions of this court since the passage of the act to regulate commerce have uniformly recognized that it was competent for the state fix such rates, applicable throughout its territory. If it be said that, in the contests that have been waged over state laws during the past twenty-five years, the question of interference with interstate commerce by the establishment of state-wide rates for intrastate traffic has seldom been raised, this fact itself attests the common conception of the scope of state authority. And the decisions recognizing and defining the state power wholly refute the contention that the making of such rates either constitutes a direct burden upon the interstate commerce or is repugnant to the Federal statute.

In *Dow* v. *Beidelman*, 125 U. S. 680, 31 L. ed. 841, 2 Inters. Com. Rep. 56, 8 Sup. Ct. Rep. 1028, the statute of Arkansas, enacted in April, 1887, which established 3 cents a mile as the maximum fare for carrying passengers within the state on railroads over 75 miles in length, was sustained against the objection of the owners of the Memphis & Little Rock Railroad, who attacked the act as confiscatory and arbitrary in its classification. The same statute was again upheld in *St. Louis & S. F. R. Co.* v. *Gill*, 156 U. S. 649, 39 L. ed. 567, 15 Sup. Ct. Rep. 484. In *Chicago, M. & St. P. R. Co.* v. *Minnesota*, 134 U. S. 418, 33 L. ed. 970, 3 Inters. Com. Rep. 209, 10 Sup. Ct. Rep. 462, 702, the statute of that state (1887) creating a commission with power to prescribe intrastate rates was adjudged to be invalid, but this was upon the ground that the act as construed by the state court made the rates published by the commission final and conclusive, and precluded any judicial inqury whether they were reasonable. In *Chicago & G. T. R. Co.* v. *Wellman*, 143 U. S. 339, 36 L. ed. 176, 12 Sup. Ct. Rep. 400, the act of the legislature of Michigan (1889), fixing the maximum fare for passengers within the state at 2 cents a mile in the case of companies whose gross earnings exceeded $3,000 a mile, was unsuccessfully assailed as confiscatory, and no contention was advanced that such an act, operating throughout the state, was an unwarrantable interference with interstate commerce.

In *Reagan* v. *Farmers' Loan & Trust Co.* 154 U. S. 362, 38 L. ed. 1014, 4 Inters. Com. Rep. 560, 14 Sup. Ct. Rep. 1047, the trustee of a railroad mortgage attacked the statute of Texas (1891), which established a railroad commission with authority to regulate tariffs, and the order of the commission providing a schedule of classified rates for the transportation of goods within the state. The challenge was of the tariff as a whole, and the inquiry was whether the body of rates was unreasonable, and such as to work a practical destruction of rights of property. Viewed in this aspect, the court, upon the allegations admitted by demurrer, held the action of the commission to be beyond its constitutional power, and affirmed the decree of the circuit court, enjoining the rates. The decree, however, was reversed so far as it restrained the commission from discharging the duties imposed by the statute, and from proceeding to prescribe reasonable rates and regulations. A further question was presented in *Reagan* v. *Mercantile Trust Co.* 154 U. S. 413, 38 L. ed. 1028, 4 Inters. Com. Rep. 575, 14 Sup. Ct. Rep. 1060, in respect to the same statute and order as applied to the Texas & Pacific Railway Company, which had been organized under the laws of the United States (16 Stat. at L. 573, chap. 122), and operated its road not only within that state, but also for several hundred miles outside. It was insisted that this company was "not subject to the control of the state, even as to rates for transportation wholly within the state," the argument being that it was not within the state power to limit the Federal franchise to collect tolls. But the court held that the act of Congress did not go to the extent asserted, but left the company, as to its intrastate business, subject to state authority.

The effect of intrastate rates upon interstate rates was urged in *Smyth* v. *Ames*, 169 U. S. 466, 42 L. ed. 819, 18 Sup. Ct. Rep. 418, and in the cases decided therewith. These suits were brought by stockholders of the Union Pacific Railway Company, the Chicago & Northwestern Railroad Company, and the Chicago, Burlington & Quincy Railroad Company, to enjoin the enforcement of the act of the legislature of Nebraska, passed in 1893. This was a comprehensive statute, classifying the freight transported from any point in Nebraska to any other point in that state, and prescribing tables of maximum rates. The companies affected were interstate carriers engaged in a vast commerce, only a small portion of which was wholly local to the state. On the eastern boundary lay Omaha, a city of large importance in interstate trade, situated on the Missouri river, with Council Bluffs, in the state of Iowa, directly opposite. The point was distinctly made in the circuit court that the statute interfered with interstate commerce because, first, it established a classification of freights different from that which prevailed west of Chicago, and second, by reducing local rates it necessarily reduced rates on interstate business. Mr. Justice Brewer, who tried the cases, overruled these objections, holding that neither the convenience of the carriers nor the consequences of competition with respect to interstate rates could be pleaded "in restraint of the otherwise undeniable power of the state." *Ames* v. *Union P. R. Co.*, 64 Fed. 165, 171, 172. Having disposed of this contention, the court considered the question of the reasonableness of the rates, and reached the conclusion that they were invalid because they amounted to a deprivation of the carriers' rights of property. On appeal to this court, the counsel for the appellees directed attention to the conditions of transportation in Nebraska. It was argued that the local traffic was carried over the same tracks, in the same trains, and often in the same cars with the interstate traffic; that to separate the cost of carrying the one sort of traffic from that of the other was a "manifest impossibility"; and that it was a necessary consequence of existing conditions that, if Nebraska controlled the local rates, it, at the same time, controlled the interstate rates. But this contention was not sustained, and the affirmance of the decree was placed upon the distinct ground that the rates were confiscatory. It was ruled that the reasonableness of intrastate rates was to be determined by considering the intrastate business separately. In answer to the suggestion that the conditions of business might have changed for the better since the decrees, the court called attention to the proviso in the decrees intended to meet such a case, adding that if the circuit court found that conditions were such as to permit the application of the state rates without depriving the carriers of just compensation, it would "be its duty to discharge the injunction" and to make whatever order was necessary "to remove any obstruction placed by the decrees in these cases in the way of the enforcement of the statute." 169 U. S. 550; see *Smyth* v. *Ames*, 171 U. S. 361, 365, 43 L. ed. 197, 198, 18 Sup. Ct. Rep. 888.

In that one of the Smyth cases which was brought by the stockholders of the Union Pacific Railway Company, not only was the case presented of a trunk line crossing the state with a relatively small proportion of business local to Nebraska, but the company had been formed by a consolidation of several companies by authority of Congress, one of them being the Union Pacific Railroad Company, incorporated by the act of July 1, 1862, chap. 120, 12 Stat. at L. 489. By this act (§ 18, p. 497), it was expressly provided that Congress might reduce the rates of fare if unreasonable, and might fix the same by law whenever the net earnings of the entire road and telegraph should exceed a certain amount. But this language, while showing that Congress intended to reserve the power to prevent unreasonable exactions, was not deemed to be equivalent to a declaration that the states through which the road might be constructed should not regulate rates for intrastate transportation. The court said:

> It cannot be doubted that the making of rates for transportation by railroad corporations along public highways, between points wholly within the limits of a state, is a subject primarily within the control of that state. . . .

Congress not having exerted this power, we do not think that the national character of the corporation constructing the Union Pacific Railroad stands in the way of a state prescribing rates for transporting property on that road wholly between points within its territory. Until Congress, in the exercise either of the power specifically reserved by the 18th section of the act of 1862, or its power under the general reservation made of authority to add to, alter, amend, or repeal that act, prescribes rates to be charged by the railroad company, it remains with the states through which the road passes to fix rates for transportation beginning and ending within their respective limits. 169 U. S. 521, 522.

It is plain that had the intrastate rates, established by the comprehensive statute of Nebraska, not been found to be confiscatory, they would have been sustained in their application to all intrastate traffic notwithstanding the reserved power of Congress over the Union Pacific line, and despite the argument based upon the interdependence of interstate and intrastate rates.

The cases of *Louisville & N. R. Co.* v. *Kentucky*, 183 U. S. 503, 46 L. ed. 298, 22 Sup. Ct. Rep. 95, and *Louisville & N. R. Co.* v. *Eubank*, 184 U. S. 27, 46 L. ed. 416, 22 Sup. Ct. Rep. 277, concerned the validity of the long and short haul provision of the Constitution of Kentucky, adopted in 1891. In the first case, violation was charged with respect to the transportation of coal from Altamont to Lebanon, an intermediate station, as compared with charges for transportation from Altamont to Elizabethtown and Louisville, all places being within Kentucky. The difference in rate was justified by the company on the ground that at Louisville the coal hauled from Altamont came into competition with that brought down the Ohio river, and at Elizabethtown with western Kentucky coal brought there by the Illinois Central Railroad. The contention that the state provision operated as an interference with interstate commerce was presented and overruled, the court saying:

It is plain that the provision in question does not in terms embrace the case of interstate traffic. It is restricted in its regulation to those who own or operate a railroad within the state, and the long and short distances mentioned are evidently distances upon the railroad line within the state. The particular case before us is one involving only the transportation of coal from one point in the state of Kentucky to another by a corporation of that state. It may be that the enforcement of the state regulation forbidding discrimination in rates in the case of articles of a like kind, carried for different distances over the same line, may somewhat affect commerce generally; but we have frequently held that such a result is too remote and indirect to be regarded as an interference with interstate commerce; that the interference with the commercial power of the general government to be unlawful must be direct, and not the merely incidental effect of enforcing the police powers of a state. 183 U. S. 518, 519.

In the Eubank case, which had been argued before the first case was decided, it appeared that the state court had construed the same provision of the Kentucky Constitution as embracing a long haul from a place outside to one within the state (Nashville and Louisville), and a shorter haul on the same line and in the same direction between points within the state. The court held that, so construed, the provision was invalid, as being a regulation of interstate commerce, because it linked the interstate rate to the rate for the shorter haul, and thus the interstate charge was directly controlled by the state law. 184 U. S. 41, 43. The authority of the former decision upholding the state law, as applied to places all of which were within the state, was in no way impaired, and the court fully recognized the power of the state to prescribe maximum charges for intrastate traffic although carried over an interstate road to points on the state line. *Id.* 33, 42.

The case of *Minneapolis & St. L. R. Co.* v. *Minnesota*, 186 U. S. 257, 46 L. ed. 1151, 22 Sup. Ct. Rep. 900, involved shipments of hard coal in carload lots from Duluth, Minnesota, to points in the southern and western portion of that state. The Railroad & Warehouse Commission of Minnesota, in 1899, prescribed a joint rate to be observed by the St. Paul & Duluth Railroad Company, the Minneapolis & St. Louis Railroad Company, and other carriers. The state court directed the issue of a writ of mandamus to compel compliance with the order. It was objected that the act under which the order was made was unconstitutional so far as it assumed to establish joint through rates over the lines of independent connecting railroads, and to divide joint earnings, and that the tariff as fixed was not compensatory. This court affirmed the judgment. In *Alabama & V. R. Co.* v. *Mississippi R. Commission*, 203 U. S. 496, 51 L. ed.

289, 27 Sup. Ct. Rep. 163, the company made what it called a "rebilling rate" on grain shipped from Vicksburg to Meridian, Mississippi, which was applicable only in case of shipments received at Vicksburg over the Shreveport line. It gave, however, to such shippers an option for a specified time to send other grain from Vicksburg instead, and thus it was in fact a local rate. To end this discrimination, the state commission, in 1903, fixed the same rate for all grain products shipped from Vicksburg to Meridian. It was urged that the effect of the order would be to force the plaintiff to enter into joint through interstate tariffs and divisions with all lines reaching Vicksburg by rail or river, whether it desired such arrangements or not. The court sustained the order, holding that it was competent for the state to enforce equality as to local transportation, and that this equality could not be defeated "in respect to any local shipments by arrangements made with or to favor outside companies."

In *Northern P. R. Co.* v. *North Dakota*, 216 U. S. 579, 54 L. ed. 624, 30 Sup. Ct. Rep. 423, the attorney general of North Dakota charged the company with continuous violation of a law fixing rates for the carriage of coal within the state (North Dakota, Laws of 1907, chap. 51), and asked for an injunction. It appears by the record that in its return to the rule to show cause in the state court, the company alleged that the statute was void because repugnant to the commerce clause, and also that the rate fixed thereby was confiscatory. In support of the last contention the return set forth that the maximum rates for carrying coal which the company was allowed to charge under the act in question were greatly lower than the rates for similar service fixed by Minnesota for that state (reference being made to chapter 232 of the Laws of 1907, the commodity rate act now in question), and those fixed by the railroad commissions of Illinois and Iowa, respectively; and that the conditions existing in North Dakota made it impossible to transport coal at a less rate than in the states named. The contention that the act violated the interstate commerce clause was said by the supreme court of the state to be based upon the assumption that state regulation of local rates on interstate lines amounted to an interference with interstate commerce. In view of the decisions of this court, the last question was not considered open to debate. *State ex. rel. McCue* v. *Northern P. R. Co.* 19 N. D. 45, 55, 25 L.R.A. (N.S.) 1001, 120 N. W. 869. This ruling was not challenged by the argument for the plaintiff in error here, and the question as to interference with interstate commerce was treated as removed from the case by the holding of the state court that the rates applied only to transportation within the state. 216 U. S. 580.

To suppose, however, from a review of these decisions, that the exercise of this acknowledged power of the state may be permitted to create an irreconcilable conflict with the authority of the nation, or that, through an equipoise of powers, an effective control of interstate commerce is rendered impossible, is to overlook the dominant operation of the Constitution, which, creating a nation, equipped it with an authority, supreme and plenary, to control national commerce, and to prevent that control, exercised in the wisdom of Congress, from being obstructed or destroyed by any opposing action. But, as we said at the outset, our system of government is a practical adjustment by which the national authority, as conferred by the Constitution, is maintained in its full scope without unnecessary loss of local efficiency. It thus clearly appears that, under the established principles governing state action, the state of Minnesota did not transcend the limits of its authority in prescribing the rates here involved, assuming them to be reasonable intrastate rates. It exercised an authority appropriate to its territorial jurisdiction, and not opposed to any action thus far taken by Congress.

The interblending of operations in the conduct of interstate and local business by interstate carriers is strongly pressed upon our attention. It is urged that the same right of way, terminals, rails, bridges, and stations are provided for both classes of traffic; that the proportion of each sort of business varies from year to year, and, indeed, from day to-day; that no division of the plant, no apportionment of it between interstate and local traffic, can be made to-day, which will hold to-morrow; that terminals, facilities, and connections in one state aid the carrier's entire business, and are an element of value with respect to the whole property and the business in other states; that securities are issued against the entire line of the carrier and cannot be divided by states; that tariffs should be made with a view to all the traffic of the road, and should be fair as between through and short-haul business; and that, in substance, no regulation of rates can be just which does not take into consideration the whole field of the carrier's operations, irrespective of state lines. The force of these contentions is emphasized in these cases, and in others of like nature, by the extreme difficulty and intricacy of the calculations which must be made in the effort to establish a segregation of intrastate business for the purpose of determining the return to which the carrier is properly entitled therefrom.

But these considerations are for the practical judgment of Congress in determining the extent of the regulation necessary under existing conditions of transportation to conserve and promote the interests of interstate commerce. If the situation has become such, by reason of the interblending of the interstate and intrastate operations of interstate carriers, that adequate regulation of their interstate rates cannot be maintained without imposing requirements with respect to their intrastate rates which substantially affect the former, it is for Congress to determine, within the limits of its constitutional authority over interstate commerce and its instruments the measure of the regulation it should supply. It is the function of this court to interpret and apply the law already enacted, but not, under the guise of construction, to provide a more comprehensive scheme of regulation than Congress has decided upon. Nor, in the absence of Federal action, may we deny effect to the laws of the state enacted within the field which it is entitled to occupy until its authority is limited through the exertion by Congress of its paramount constitutional power.

Second. Are the state's acts and orders confiscatory?

The rate-making power is a legislative power and necessarily implies a range of legislative discretion. We do not sit as a board of revision to substitute our judgment for that of the legislature, or of the commission lawfully constituted by it, as to matters within the province of either. *San Diego Land & Town Co.* v. *Jasper*, 189 U. S. 439, 446, 47 L. ed. 892, 896, 23 Sup. Ct. Rep. 571. The case falls within a well-defined category. Here we have a general schedule of rates, involving the profitableness of the intrastate operations of the carrier, taken as a whole, and the inquiry is whether the state has overstepped the constitutional limit by making the rates so unreasonably low that the carriers are deprived of their property without due process of law, and denied the equal protection of the laws.

The property of the railroad corporation has been devoted to a public use. There is always the obligation springing from the nature of the business in which it is engaged — which private exigency may not be permitted to ignore — that there shall not be an exorbitant charge for the service rendered. But the state has not seen fit to undertake the service itself; and the private property embarked in it is not placed at the mercy of legislative caprice. It rests secure under the constitutional protection which extends not merely to the title, but to the right to receive just compensation for the service given to the public. . . .

In determining whether that right has been denied, each case must rest upon its special facts. But the general principles which are applicable in a case of this character have been set forth in the decisions.

(1) The basis of calculation is the "fair value of the property" used for the convenience of the public. . . . "What the company is entitled to demand, in order that it may have just compensation, is a fair return upon the reasonable value of the property at the time it is being used for the public."

(2) The ascertainment of that value is not controlled by artificial rules. It is not a matter of formulas, but there must be a reasonable judgment, having its basis in a proper consideration of all relevant facts. The scope of the inquiry was thus broadly described in *Smyth* v. *Ames* (169 U. S. 546, 547):

In order to ascertain that value, the original cost of construction, the amount expended in permanent improvements, the amount and market value of its bonds and stock, the present, as compared with the original, cost of construction, the probable earning capacity of the property under particular rates prescribed by statute, and the sum required to meet operating expenses, are all matters for consideration, and are to be given such weight as may be just and right in each case. We do not say that there may not be other matters to be regarded in estimating the value of the property. What the company is entitled to ask is a fair return upon the value of that which it employs for the public convenience. On the other hand, what the public is entitled to demand is that no more be exacted from it for the use of a public highway than the services rendered by it are reasonably worth.

(3) Where the business of the carrier is both interstate and intrastate, the question whether a scheme of maximum rates fixed by the state for intrastate transportation affords a fair return must be determined by considering separately the value of the property employed in the intrastate business and the compensation allowed in that business under the rates prescribed. This was also ruled in the Smyth Case (*id.* p. 541). The reason, as there stated, is that the state cannot justify unreasonably low rates for domestic transportation, considered alone, upon the ground that the carrier is earning large profits on its interstate business, and, on the other hand, the carrier cannot justify unreasonably high rates on domestic business because only in that way is it able to meet losses on its interstate business.

In the present cases the necessity of this segregation of the domestic business in determining values and results of operation was recognized by both parties. Voluminous testimony was taken before the master, and numerous exhibits containing data and calculations were submitted for the purpose of showing their respective estimates of the value of the entire property of the carriers in Minnesota, the amount of income and expense in that state, their theories of apportionment between the interstate and intrastate business, and their contentions as to the net return for intrastate transportation under the state rates. The multitude of facts which are involved makes it impossible here to present a comprehensive review, even in a summary way. We must be content with a statement of the salient points, and deal only with those matters which, after a careful consideration of the entire record, we regard as controlling our decision.

In each of the three cases (save in certain particulars with respect to that of the Minneapolis & St. Louis Railroad Company) the method adopted by the master was as follows:

The period taken for the purpose of testing the sufficiency of the rates was the fiscal year ending June 30, 1908. During this period, all the rates in question, freight and passenger, were actually in force, with the exception of the commodity rates prescribed by the act of April 18, 1907, which had been enjoined. The amount of the reduction in the intrastate revenue which would have been caused by the application of the commodity rates is shown.

The master found the present value of the entire property of the carrier, used in the public service in the state of Minnesota. This valuation was as of June 30, 1908, and was made on the basis of the cost of reproduction new. The master also made findings as to the original cost of construction, and as to the present value on the basis of cost of reproduction new, of the entire system of the carrier. The estimated value of the railroad property within the state was divided between the freight and passenger business upon the relation of the gross revenue derived from each. The part of the total value which was thus assigned to the freight business within the state was then divided between the interstate and intrastate freight business on the basis of gross revenue; and a similar division was made between the interstate and intrastate business of the property value assigned to the passenger department. In this way the master found the value of the property used in intrastate transportation, freight and passenger, upon which he computed the net return received by the carrier.

There was no substantial dispute as to the amount of the entire revenue assignable to the state or as to its division between interstate and intrastate business, as an examination of the transactions in which the revenue was obtained permitted the making of the requisite apportionments with reasonable certainty.

The master also ascertained the total expense incurred by the carrier within the state. This expense was first divided between freight and passenger business. Those items of cost which were directly incurred in each sort of business, and not common to both, were directly assigned; and such items were found to cover about 60 per cent of all expenses. The remaining items, those of common expense, were divided between the freight and passenger business upon the relation, as to most of them, of revenue train-miles, and as to the others, of revenue engine-miles.

Having thus ascertained the share of the expense within the state of the freight and passenger departments respectively, it remained to divide that share, in each case, between the interstate and intrastate business. This apportionment was made, in the case of freight expense, upon what was termed an "equated ton-mile basis"; and in the case of passenger expense upon an "equated passenger-mile basis." That is to say, the master concluded that the cost per ton mile of doing the intrastate freight business was at least two and one-half times the cost per ton mile of the interstate freight business, and hence he divided the total freight expense according to the relation of the interstate and intrastate ton miles after the latter had been increased two and one-half times. In the case of the passenger expense, he concluded that the cost per passenger-mile in the intrastate business was at least 15 per cent greater than that in the interstate business, and the total passenger expense was divided upon the relation of passenger-miles after increasing the intrastate passenger-miles 15 per cent.[1] By the use of equalizing factors,

[1] The method is illustrated from the following extract from the findings in the Northern Pacific Case:

EQUATED TON-MILE BASIS

Freight—On basis of 1 intrastate ton mile costing as much as 2.5 interstate ton miles	Actual	Equated	Proportion	Operating Exps.
Intrastate ton miles . . .	130,580,988 × 2.5 =	326,452,470 =	25.362%	$1,355,273.82
Interstate ton miles . . .	960,709,494 × 1.0 =	960,709,494 =	74.638%	3,988,444.43
	1,091,290,482	1,287,161,964 =	100.%	$5,343,718.25

EQUATED PASSENGER-MILE BASIS

Passenger—On basis of 100 intrastate passenger miles costing as much as 115 interstate passenger miles	Actual	Equated	Proportion	Operating Exps.
Intrastate passenger miles .	52,317,140 × 1.15 =	60,164,711 =	37.347%	$863,325.18
Interstate passenger miles .	100,931,180 × 1.00 =	100,931,180 =	62.653%	1,448,306.77
	153,248,320	161,095,891 =	100.%	$2,311,631.95

the same result was obtained upon what was called an "equated revenue basis." [1]

The net profits of the interstate and intrastate businesses, respectively, passenger and freight, were then found by deducting the apportioned share of expense from the apportioned share of revenue, and the rate per cent of the net profit upon the rate value assigned to each sort of business was computed. The master concluded that the returns from intrastate transportation were unreasonably low, and hence that the rates in question were confiscatory.

The validity of the result depends upon the estimates of the value of the property within the state and the apportionments both of value and of expense between interstate and intrastate operations.

[1] Equated Revenue Basis.—In the case of the Northern Pacific Company it was found that the relation of freight revenue per ton per mile derived from the intrastate business, as compared with the interstate business, was as 1.4387 is to 1.0000. The relation of cost per ton per mile in the intrastate business in proportion to revenue, to the cost per ton per mile in interstate business in proportion to revenue, was then found to be as 1.7377 is to 1.0000, as follows:

$$\frac{250}{100} \div \frac{1.4387}{1.0000} = \frac{1.7377}{1.0000}$$

The actual intrastate freight revenue was multiplied by 1.7377 to obtain the equated revenue, and thus the same percentages were obtained as on the equated ton-mile basis, as follows:

EQUATED REVENUE BASIS. FREIGHT

	Actual Revenue	Equated Revenue	
Intrastate	\$1,555,342.92 × 1.7377 =	\$2,702,719.39 =	25.362%
Interstate	7,953,734.41 × 1. =	7,953,734.41 =	74.638%
		\$10,656,453.80 =	100.%

The relation of revenue per passenger mile, intrastate and interstate, was found to be as 1.0092 is to 1.0000; and thus, the relation of cost per passenger mile in relation to revenue was as 1.1395 is to 1.0000. The division was then made as follows:

EQUATED REVENUE BASIS. PASSENGER

	Actual Revenue	Equated Revenue	
Intrastate	\$1,015,150.34 × 1.1395 =	\$1,156,763.81 =	37.347%
Interstate	1,940,718.17 × 1. =	1,940,718.17 =	62.653%
		\$3,097,481.98 =	100.%

It will be convenient to take up the three cases separately:

1. *Northern Pacific Railway Company.* The par value, April 30, 1908, of the stock of this company, was found to be $215,539,634.99, and of the bonds, $190,256,577.66; total, $405,796,392.65. (Included in this statement of capital stock is the sum of $60,539,634.99 received to April 30, 1908, upon subscriptions to new capital stock [$95,000,000] authorized by stockholders' resolution January 7, 1907.)

These securities and their value in the market rest upon the entire property of the company. They include assets of considerable value (for example, the stock of the Northwestern Improvement Company, owning extensive coal lands), which, however, do not form part of what may be called the operating property of the company, or that devoted to the public service, upon which the fair return is to be calculated (15 Inters. Com. Rep. 376, 397, 407). Referring to the market value of the securities, the master said: "Assets and property not devoted to public service have not been valued, and as they are a large element in stock valuation it follows that value of bonds and stocks is wholly unreliable and cannot be used in these cases as an element in determining the value of operating property, or as a basis for rate-making." In this view the master was undoubtedly right.

Much evidence was produced before the master for the purpose of showing the actual cost of construction and equipment of the entire railroad system from the beginning down to April 30, 1908. This, the master states, could be shown only by the corporate books and records; and in the early history of the original company these are somewhat obscure and uncertain, and, by reason of lapse of time, could not be verified by other proof. The total investment cost of the railroad system of the Northern Pacific thus shown was $369,252,755. This included certain items which the master held not to be properly allowable as a part of the cost, and after their deduction the cost was found to be $312,243,555. Of this investment cost, it appears from the evidence submitted by the company's comptroller that the sum of $128,184,985.82 was expended for construction and equipment, and for improvements and betterments, during the period from September 1, 1896, to April 30, 1908. The master found that the Minnesota track mileage is substantially 21 per cent of the track mileage of the whole system [1] and that if the cost were proportioned accordingly, the amount assignable to the state of the entire cost of construction and equipment, as stated, would be $65,571,462.

The master, however, and the court below, in confirming his findings, held that rates were not to be predicated upon the original investment.

Taking, as the basis, the cost of reproduction new, the master found the value of the entire railroad system or operating property of this company to be $452,666,489.[2] The value of that portion of the system which was in the state of Minnesota was separately found, on the same basis, to be $90,204,545. It was upon this estimate of the value of the property in the state, as apportioned between the interstate and intrastate business, that the master computed the rate of return.

The total net profits of the company for the fiscal year ending June 30, 1908, from its Minnesota business (interstate and intrastate), was found to be $5,431,514.56. This was equal to 6.021 per cent on the entire estimated value of the property. This showing of the results of the entire business at once directs attention to the importance of the methods adopted in making apportionments; but before considering these, the question is presented as to the soundness of the underlying estimate of value. May it be accepted as a basis for a finding that the rates are confiscatory?

[1] The master found that the total track mileage of the system was 7695.80 and that the track mileage in Minnesota was 1625.20. In both cases spurs, yards, and sidings were included. In Minnesota, as shown by the company's statement, the "passing, side, and industry tracks" amounted to 512.41 miles, leaving for the single track, and second and third main track, miles, a total of 1112.79 miles.

[2] This estimate did not include the interest of the Northern Pacific in the Spokane, Portland & Seattle Railroad which was under construction, or the Big Forks & International Falls Railway, or the Minnesota & International Railway, or in certain lines in Manitoba, under lease, which were found not to be part of the operating system.

Values. The items entering into the valuation are set forth in the margin.[1]

[1] Valuation — Northern Pacific:

1.	Lands for right of way, yards and terminals	$21,024,562
2.	Grading, clearing, and grubbing	12,331,541
3.	Protection work, rip-rap, retaining walls	374,091
4.	Tunnels	253,250
5.	Cross ties and switch ties	3,657,576
6.	Ballast	1,960,969
7.	Rails	5,645,307
8.	Track fastenings	727,228
9.	Switches, frogs, and railroad crossings	303,717
10.	Track laying and surfacing	1,600,591
11.	Bridges, trestles, and culverts	3,586,063
12.	Track and bridge tools	28,073
13.	Fences, cattle guards, and signs	471,609
14.	Stockyards and appurtenances	37,098
15.	Water stations	436,489
16.	Coal stations	120,039
17.	Stations, buildings, and fixtures	920,423
18.	Miscellaneous buildings	1,054,874
19.	Steam and electric power plants, gas plants	196,338
20.	General repair shops	1,162,934
21.	Shop machinery and tools	529,322
22.	Engine houses, turntables, and cinder pits	1,026,346
23.	Track scales	38,520
24.	Docks and wharves	768,306
25. 26.	Interlocking plants and other signal apparatus	114,430
27. 28.	Telegraph and telephone lines	285,145
28½.	General office furniture	73,654
29.	Solidification of roadbed. (Absorbed in above.)	
	Total 1 to 28	$58,728,685
30.	Engineering, superintendence, legal expenses, 4½ per cent 1 to 28	2,785,036
31.	Locomotives	3,454,040
32.	Passenger equipment	1,349,829
33.	Freight car equipment	7,519,722
34.	Miscellaneous equipment	372,477
35.	Marine equipment (none)	
	Total items 1 to 34	$74,209,789
36.	Freight on construction material — absorbed.	
37.	Contingencies, 5 per cent 1 to 34	3,710,479
38.	Stores and supplies in Minnesota	2,658,976
39.	Interest during construction, 4 per cent, 2½ years, items 1 to 36	7,420,957
40.	Interest in terminal properties, St. Paul depot, Duluth depot, Minnesota transfer	2,204,344
		$90,204,545

The first item is:

"Lands for right of way, yards, and terminals, $21,024,562."

This is for the bare land, without structures or improvements of any sort, as the entire cost of reproduction in building the road and erecting all the existing structures is covered in other items. The master states that the amount thus allowed for land is made up as follows:

Terminal properties, St. Paul appraisement of Read, Watson & Taylor, as modified by railroad company	$7,645,100.24
Add 5 per cent for the cost of acquisition and consequential damages	382,255.01
Property acquired after appraisement	328,725.69
Minneapolis appraisement of Elwood, Barney, and Ridgeway, as modified by railway company	4,027,616.17
Add 5 per cent for acquisition and consequential damages . .	201,380.80
Property acquired after appraisement	227,737.26
Duluth, appraisement of Stryker, Mendenhall, and Little . .	3,602,443.43
Add 25 per cent for railway value, cost of acquisition, and consequential damages	900,610.85
Total value of terminals	17,315,869.45
Lands outside of terminals	3,708,693.45
Grand total	21,024,562.90

The appellants insist that no more than $9,498,099.27 should have been allowed.

It is contended that the valuation was made upon a wrong theory; that it is a speculative estimate of "cost of reproduction"; that it is largely in excess of the market value of adjacent or similarly situated property; that it does not represent the present value, in any true sense, but constitutes a conjecture as to the amount which the railway company would have to pay to acquire its right of way, yards, and terminals, on an assumption, itself inadmissible, that, while the railroad did not exist, all other conditions, with respect to the agricultural and industrial development of the state, and the location, population, and activities of towns, villages, and cities, were as they now are.

We may first consider the basis for the finding with respect to the "lands outside terminals," — that is, the right of way and station grounds, etc., outside the three cities.

(a) *Lands outside terminals.* The complainants' witness was Mr. Cooper, the land commissioner of the company, who has charge of the land grants for its entire system, of its right of way and land purchases, and has had a wide experience in connection with land values along the lines of the railway. In the latter part of 1906, the state notified the company to report the value of its properties, requiring a statement in one column of the "market value," and in another column, of the "value for railway purposes." Mr. Cooper was instructed to prepare the valuation for this report. From the information he received in special inquiries, and his own knowledge, and following what he understood to be the instructions from the state, he set down under the heading of "market value," not the market value in the proper sense of that term, but what in his judgment it would cost the railroad company to acquire the land. This included an excess which he estimated the company would have to pay over the market value of contiguous and similar property if it were called upon to undertake such a reproduction of its right of way. It did not, however, embrace an allowance for payments which might have to be made for improvements that possibly might be found upon the property in such case, or for the consequential or severance damages which might possibly have to be met, or for the expense of acquisition. These supposed additional outlays he undertook to estimate. For this purpose he increased the "market value" as stated (in the case of agricultural lands generally multiplying it by three), and thus reached the amount set down as the "value for railway purposes." As it serves clearly to illustrate the theory upon which the land valuations were made, we make the following excerpts from Mr. Cooper's testimony:

The Master. When you speak of value, you mean cost of purchase?

Witness. Cost of purchase; we are using the word "value" somewhat wrongly, as we are talking along here. It is the cost of purchasing that property to-day.

* * * * * * * *

Witness. The word "value" does n't seem to me to fit this case, because all the time we are figuring on the cost of reproducing this property, and our instructions from the state use the word "reproduce." Now, if a railroad company could buy property at what is generally considered its value, the word "value" would fit in all right, but there is this excess which a railroad company has to pay beyond what is generally accepted as its value which increases the cost of reproducing a railroad property.

Q. And this excess which you now speak of is included in your market values as reported to the state and used in your testimony?

A. That is right. . . .

Q. . . . Well, now, does the term "market value" as you have used it in making this report to the state and in your testimony here have the same meaning, or is it used in the same sense with reference to the values you have fixed and reported to the state for properties on the right of way outside of the terminals and outside of the larger cities?

A. Oh, yes.

Q. As in the cities here?

A. Yes; the same rule was applied all through in the Minnesota valuations.

* * * * * * * *

Q. Therefore, your judgment as to the value of the railroad property is always that it is higher than the value of contiguous property?

A. Yes, yes, that is true. . . .

Q. So that, in every case, what you call the market value is the value of contiguous or similarly situated property, with an additional amount which a railroad company is ordinarily compelled to pay?

A. That is right. . . .

Q. You have put into the market value the excess which a railroad company pays for land?

A. That is correct.

Q. Then, when you multiply that by 3, you are multiplying by 3 one of the elements going to make up excessive cost to a railroad company?

A. That is right. . . .

Q. And you are unable to state how much upon the average you have added to the true or normal market value, to allow for the additional amount which the railroad company would have to pay upon the hypothesis that it is now compelled to purchase the land?

A. That is correct.

Q. And then having determined to your satisfaction at what figure or sum you would place the market value of this property to the railroad company, as you have described, you have added another sum for severance damage, cost of improvements unnecessary to the company, easements in abutting property, and general expenses?

A. That is correct.

Q. And you have determined that, in agricultural communities, this second addition is shown by the use of the multiple 3?

A. I think the multiple of 3 is too low, and I so testified in this case When you are going through a highly cultivated country I think the multiplier of 3 is not enough.

Q. But that is what you used for the purpose of the right of way value of land through the agricultural communities?

A. That is right, in this state.

Q. And in the cities, in the three large terminals, you have added to what you describe as the market value of the lands to the railroad company, ascertained as described by you already, the amount necessary to produce the difference shown in your testimony between the market value of the terminals and the right of way value?

A. That is right.

Q. And while you are able to show, and we can ascertain from an inspection of your testimony, the amount of the difference between the market value to the railroad company, as you have described, and the right of way value, and, in the rural communities or agricultural districts, the difference between the market value to you and the right of way value, there is nothing in any of your exhibits which will show, nor are you now prepared to state, the difference in what might be termed the normal, true, ordinary market value of the lands to the ordinary individual, and the sum which you have fixed as the market value to the railroad company if it were now compelled to purchase.

A. That is correct.

The "market value" of the lands (outside of the three cities) thus fixed and reported to the state was $2,008,491.50, and the increased amount estimated, in the manner stated, which was reported as the "value for railway purposes" was $4,944,924.60. The latter amount was submitted by the complainants in this case as the value of the lands. The master thought that the complainants' witness used too large a multiplier, and allowed 75 per cent of the amount thus claimed, or $3,708,693.45, stating that this was determined upon as the "fair reproduction value of the property." This allowance, it will be observed, was about $1,700,000 in excess of Mr. Cooper's estimate of "market value" as that term was used in making the report.

(b) *Terminal properties.* This term is used to designate the lands for the right of way, yards, and terminals in St. Paul, Minneapolis, and Duluth. The total original cost of these lands to the company (according to its statement based on the best information obtainable), including purchases to April 30, 1908, was $4,527,228.76. The master allowed as their value, apart from the improvements made by the company, which, as we have said, were embraced in the other items of reproduction cost, the sum of $17,315,869.45.

In preparing the valuation for the report to the state, Mr. Cooper employed real estate men in each of the cities to make an appraisement. He instructed them, as he testifies, "to make a conservative report of the cost of reproducing the properties owned by the company in each of their respective cities." They divided the property into districts and reported their estimate of units of value, as, for example, by the square foot. Mr. Cooper took these reports, discussed their valuations with the appraisers, and, aided by his own knowledge, formed an independent judgment, in no case increasing and in some instances (with respect to certain St. Paul and Minneapolis property) reducing the appraisers' values. He then set forth under the heading "market value," in the report to the state, as described in the testimony we have quoted, his estimate of what it would cost the company to purchase these lands, exclusive of improvements that might be upon them, severance and consequential damages and expenses incident to acquisition. The amounts he thus fixed were as follows: for the property in St. Paul $7,645,100.24; in Minneapolis, $4,027,616.17; in Duluth, $3,555,593.93. In the case of the St. Paul and Minneapolis properties the amounts are precisely those adopted by the master in his findings, and to this he adds 5 per cent to cover cost of acquisition and consequential damages. The master was of the opinion that the appraisers of these properties were "fully impressed with their value for railroad purposes" and that their appraisement as verified by them before him and modified by the railway company "is a generous valuation, and should be accepted as full railroad value of the terminal properties," and it was so accepted with the addition above stated. With respect to the Duluth property, where the appraisement appears to have rested upon the ordinary values of real estate, the master sets forth as the appraised value, $3,602,443.43, to which he adds 25 per cent, or $900,610.85, "for railway value, cost of acquisition, and consequential damages."

In reviewing the findings, the court below reached the conclusion that

> the master in effect found that the cost of reproduction and the present value of the lands for the terminals in the three great cities, including therein all cost of acquisition, consequential damages, and value for railroad use which he allowed, was only about 30 per cent more than the normal value of the lands in sales between private parties. He found the value of the lands outside the terminals to be only twice their normal value.

From our examination of the evidence we are unable to conclude that the excess stated may be thus limited. What is termed the normal value does not satisfactorily appear. It further will be observed—from the summary of valuations we have set forth in the margin[1]—that the amount thus allowed in item 1 for lands, yards, and terminals, both in and out of the three cities ($21,024,562), was included in the total on which 4½ per cent was allowed in item 30 for "engineering, superintendence, legal expenses," and again was included in the total on which 5 per cent was allowed in item 37 for "contingencies," and, in addition, was included in the total on which 10 per cent was allowed in item 39 for "interest during construction."

These are the results of the endeavor to apply the cost-of-reproduction method in determining the value of the right of way. It is at once apparent that, so far as the estimate rests upon a supposed compulsory feature of the acquisition, it cannot be sustained. It is said that the company would be compelled to pay more than what is the normal market value of property in transactions between private parties; that it would lack the freedom they enjoy, and, in view of its needs, it would have to give a higher price. It is also said that this price would be in excess of the present market value of contiguous or similarly situated property. It might well be asked, who shall describe the conditions that would exist, or the exigencies of the hypothetical owners of the property, on the assumption that the railroad were removed? But, aside from this, it is impossible to assume, in making a judicial finding of what it would cost to acquire the property, that the company would be compelled

[1] See note, p. 690.

to pay more than its fair market value. It is equipped with the governmental power of eminent domain. In view of its public purpose, it has been granted this privilege in order to prevent advantage being taken of its necessities. It would be free to stand upon its legal rights, and it cannot be supposed that they would be disregarded.

It is urged that, in this view, the company would be bound to pay the "railway value" of the property. But, supposing the railroad to be obliterated and the lands to be held by others, the owner of each parcel would be entitled to receive, on its condemnation, its *fair market value* for all its available uses and purposes. *United States* v. *Chandler-Dunbar Water Power Co.*, decided May 26, 1913 [229 U. S. —, *ante*, 667, 33 Sup. Ct. Rep. 667]. If, in the case of any such owner, his property had a peculiar value or special adaptation for railroad purposes, that would be an element to be considered. *Mississippi & R. River Boom Co.* v. *Patterson*, 98 U. S. 403, 25 L. ed. 206; *Shoemaker* v. *United States*, 147 U. S. 282, 37 L. ed. 170, 13 Sup. Ct. Rep. 361; *United States* v. *Chandler-Dunbar Water Power Co.*, *supra.* But still the inquiry would be as to the fair market value of the property; as to what the owner had lost, and not what the taker had gained. *Boston Chamber of Commerce* v. *Boston*, 217 U. S. 189, 195, 54 L. ed. 725, 727, 30 Sup. Ct. Rep. 459. The owner would not be entitled to demand payment of the amount which the property might be deemed worth to the company; or of an enhanced value by virtue of the purpose for which it was taken; or of an increase over its fair market value, by reason of any added value supposed to result from its combination with tracts acquired from others, so as to make it a part of a continuous railroad right of way held in one ownership. *United States* v. *Chandler-Dunbar Water Power Co.* and *Boston Chamber of Commerce* v. *Boston*, *supra.* There is no evidence before us from which the amount which would properly be allowable in such condemnation proceedings can be ascertained.

Moreover, it is manifest that an attempt to estimate what would be the actual cost of acquiring the right of way if the railroad were not there is to indulge in mere speculation. The railroad has long been established; to it have been linked the activities of agriculture, industry, and trade. Communities have long been dependent upon its service, and their growth and development have been conditioned upon the facilities it has provided. The uses of property in the communities which it serves are to a large degree determined by it. The values of property along its line largely depend upon its existence. It is an integral part of the communal life. The assumption of its nonexistence, and at the same time that the values that rest upon it remain unchanged, is impossible and cannot be entertained. The conditions of ownership of the property and the amounts which would have to be paid in acquiring the right of way, supposing the railroad to be removed, are wholly beyond reach of any process of rational determination. The cost-of-reproduction method is of service in ascertaining the present value of the plant, when it is reasonably applied and when the cost of reproducing the property may be ascertained with a proper degree of certainty. But it does not justify the acceptance of results which depend upon mere conjecture. It is fundamental that the judicial power to declare legislative action invalid upon constitutional grounds is to be exercised only in clear cases. The constitutional invalidity must be manifest, and if it rests upon disputed questions of fact, the invalidating facts must be proved. And this is true of asserted value as of other facts.

The evidence in these cases demonstrates that the appraisements of the St. Paul and Minneapolis properties which were accepted by the master were in substance appraisals of what was considered to be the peculiar value of the railroad right of way. Efforts to express the results in the terms of a theory of cost of reproduction fail, as naturally they must, to alter or obscure the essential character of the work undertaken and performed. Presented with an impossible hypothesis, and endeavoring to conform to it, the appraisers — men of ability and experience — were manifestly seeking to give their best judgments as to what the railroad right of way was worth. And doubtless it was believed that it might cost even more to acquire the property, if one attempted to buy into the cities as they now exist, and all the difficulties that might be imagined as incident to such a "reproduction" were considered. The railroad right of way was conceived to be a property *sui generis*, "a large body of land in a continuous ownership," representing one of the "highest uses" of property, and possessing an exceptional value. The estimates before us, as approved by the master, with his increase of 25 per cent in the case of the Duluth property, must be taken to be estimates of the "railway value" of the land; and whether or not this is conceived of as paid to other owners upon a hypothetical reacquisition of the property is not controlling when we come to the substantial question to be decided.

That question is whether, in determining the fair present value of the property of the railroad company as a basis of its charges to the public, it is entitled to a valuation of its right of way not only in excess of the amount invested in it, but also in excess of the market value of contiguous and similarly situated property. For the purpose of making rates, is its land devoted to the public use to be treated (irrespective of improvements) not only as increasing in value by reason of the activities and general prosperity of the community, but as constantly outstripping in this increase, all neighboring lands of like character, devoted to other uses? If rates laid by competent authority, state or national, are otherwise just and reasonable, are they to be held to be unconstitutional and void because they do not permit a return upon an increment so calculated?

It is clear that in ascertaining the present value we are not limited to the consideration of the amount of the actual investment. If that has been reckless or improvident, losses may be sustained which the community does not underwrite. As the company may not be protected in its actual investment, if the value of its property be plainly less, so the making of a just return for the use of the property involves the recognition of its fair value if it be more than its cost. The property is held in private ownership, and it is that property, and not the original cost of it, of which the owner may not be deprived without due process of law. But still it is property employed in a public calling, subject to governmental regulation, and while, under the guise of such regulation, it may not be confiscated, it is equally true that there is attached to its use the condition that charges to the public shall not be unreasonable. And where the inquiry is as to the fair value of the property, in order to determine the reasonableness of the return allowed by the rate-making power, it is not admissible to attribute to the property owned by the carriers a speculative increment of value, over the amount invested in it and beyond the value of similar property owned by others, solely by reason of the fact that it is used in the public service. That would be to disregard the essential conditions of the public use, and to make the public use destructive of the public right.

The increase sought for "railway value" in these cases is an increment over all outlays of the carrier and over the values of similar land in the vicinity. It is an increment which cannot be referred to any known criterion, but must rest on a mere expression of judgment which finds no proper test or standard in the transactions of the business world. It is an increment which, in the last analysis, must rest on an estimate of the value of the railroad use as compared with other business uses; it involves an appreciation of the returns from rates (when rates themselves are in dispute) and a sweeping generalization embracing substantially all the activities of the community. For an allowance of this character there is no warrant.

Assuming that the company is entitled to a reasonable share in the general prosperity of the communities which it serves, and thus to attribute to its property an increase in value, still the increase so allowed, apart from any improvements it may make, cannot properly extend beyond the fair average of the normal market value of land in the vicinity having a similar character. Otherwise we enter the realm of mere conjecture. We therefore hold that it was error to base the estimates of value of the right of way, yards, and terminals upon the so-called "railway value" of the property. The company would certainly have no ground of complaint if it were allowed a value for these lands equal to the fair average market value of similar land in the vicinity, without additions by the use of multipliers, or otherwise, to cover hypothetical outlays. The allowances made below for conjectural cost of acquisition and consequential damages must be disapproved; and, in this view, we also think it was error to add to the amount taken as the present value of the lands the further sums, calculated on that value, which were embraced in the items of "engineering, superintendence, legal expenses," "contingencies," and "interest during construction."

By reason of the nature of the estimates, and the points to which the testimony was addressed, the amount of the fair value of the company's land cannot be satisfactorily determined from the evidence, but it sufficiently appears, for the reasons we have stated, that the amounts found were largely excessive.

Finding this defect in the proof, it is not necessary to consider the objections which relate to the sources from which the property was derived or its mode of acquisition, or those which are urged to the inclusion of certain lands which it is said were not actually used as a part of the plant; and we express no opinion upon the merits of these contentions.

The property other than land, as the detailed statement shows, embraced all items of construction, including roadbed, bridges, tunnels, etc., structures of every sort, and all appliances and equipment. The cost of reproduction new was ascertained by reference to the prices for such work and property. In view of the range of the questions we have been called upon to consider, we shall not extend this opinion for the purpose of reviewing this estimate, or of passing upon exceptions to various items in it, as their disposition would not affect the result.

The master allowed the cost of reproduction new without deduction for depreciation. It was not denied that there was depreciation in fact. As the master said, "everything on and above the roadbed depreciates from wear and weather stress. The life of a tie is from eight to ten years only. Structures become antiquated, inadequate, and more or less dilapidated. Ballast requires renewal, tools and machinery wear out, cars, locomotives, and equipment, as time goes on, are worn out or discarded for newer types." But it was found that this depreciation was more than offset by appreciation; that "the roadbed was constantly increasing in value"; that it "becomes solidified, embankments and slopes or excavations become settled and stable and so the better resist the effects of rains and frost"; that it "becomes adjusted to surface drainage, and the adjustment is made permanent by concrete structures and rip-rap"; and that in other ways, a roadbed long in use "is far more valuable than one newly constructed." It was said that "a large part of the depreciation is taken care of by constant repairs, renewals, additions, and replacements, a sufficient sum being annually set aside and devoted to this purpose, so that this, with the application of roadbed and adaptation to the needs of the country and of the public served, together with working capital . . . fully offsets all depreciation and renders the physical properties of the road not less valuable than their cost of reproduction new." And in a further statement upon the point, the "knowledge derived from experience" and "readiness to serve" were mentioned as additional offsets.

We cannot approve this disposition of the matter of depreciation. It appears that the master allowed, in the cost of reproduction, the sum of $1,613,612 for adaptation and solidification of roadbed, this being included in the item of grading, and being the estimate of the engineer of the state commission of the proper amount to be allowed. It is also to be noted that the depreciation in question is not that which has been overcome by repairs and replacements, but is the actual existing depreciation in the plant as compared with the new one. It would seem to be inevitable that in many parts of the plant there should be such depreciation, as, for example, in old structures and equipment remaining on hand. And when an estimate of value is made on the basis of reproduction new, the extent of existing depreciation should be shown and deducted. This apparently was done in the statement submitted by this company to the Interstate Commerce Commission in the Spokane Rate Case in connection with an estimate of the cost of reproduction of the entire system as of March, 1907. See 15 Inters. Com. Rep. 395, 396. In the present case, it appears that the engineer of the state commission estimated the depreciation in the property at between eight and nine million dollars. If there are items entering into the estimate of cost which should be credited with appreciation, this also should appear, so that instead of a broad comparison there should be specific findings showing the items which enter into the account of physical valuation on both sides.

It must be remembered that we are concerned with a charge of confiscation of property by the denial of a fair return for its use; and to determine the truth of the charge there is sought to be ascertained the present value of the property. The realization of the benefits of property must always depend in large degree on the ability and sagacity of those who employ it; but the appraisement is of an instrument of public service, as property, not of the skill of the users. And when particular physical items are estimated as worth so much new, if in fact they be depreciated, this amount should be found and allowed for. If this is not done, the physical valuation is manifestly incomplete. And it must be regarded as incomplete in this case. *Knoxville* v. *Knoxville Water Co.* 212 U. S. 1, 10, 53 L. ed. 371, 378, 29 Sup. Ct. Rep. 148.

Apportionment of values. As the rate of net return from the entire Minnesota business (interstate and intrastate) during the test year was 6.021 per cent on a valuation of $90,204,545, and would be greater if computed upon a less value, we are brought to the question whether the methods of apportionment adopted are so clearly appropriate and accurate as to require a finding of confiscation of property used in the intrastate business.

The apportionment of the value of the property, as found, between the interstate and intrastate business, was made upon the basis of the gross revenue derived from each. This is a simple method, easily applied, and for that reason has been repeatedly used. It has not, however, been approved by this court, and its correctness is now challenged. Doubtless, there may be cases where the facts would show confiscation so convincingly in any event, after full allowance for possible errors in computation, as to make negligible questions arising from the use of particular methods. But this case is not of that character.

In support of this method, it is said that a division of the value of the property according to gross earnings is a division according to the "value of the use," and therefore proper. But it would seem to be clear that the value of the use is not shown by *gross* earnings. The gross earnings may be consumed by expenses, leaving little or no profit. If, for example, the intrastate rates were so far reduced as to leave no net profits, and the only profitable business was the interstate business, it certainly could not be said that the value of the use was measured by the gross revenue.

It is not asserted that the relation of expense to revenue is the same in both businesses; on the contrary, it is insisted that it is widely different. The master found that the revenue per ton-mile in the intrastate business, as compared with the revenue per ton-mile in the interstate business, was as 1.4387 to 1.0000. And, on his assumption as to the extra cost of doing the intrastate business, he reached the conclusion that the cost per ton-mile in proportion to the revenue per ton-mile in the intrastate business, as compared with the interstate business, was as 1.7377 to 1.0000. It is contended, according to the computations, that only a little over 10 per cent of the entire net revenue of the test year ($5,431,514.66) was made in the intrastate business, and that 90 per cent thereof was made in the interstate business; but approximately 21 per cent of the total value of the property was assigned to the intrastate business.

If the property is to be divided according to the value of the use, it is plain that the gross-earnings method is not an accurate measure of that value.

In *Chicago, M. & St. P. R. Co.* v. *Tompkins*, 176 U. S. 167, 44 L. ed. 417, 20 Sup. Ct. Rep. 336, the court below had found the value of the plaintiffs' property in South Dakota to be $10,000,000, and had divided it between the interstate and intrastate business, according to the gross receipts from each. Mr. Justice Brewer, in delivering the opinion of the court, after referring to the result reached, said:

Such a result indicates that there is something wrong in the process by which the conclusion is reached. That there was, can be made apparent by further computations, and in them we will take even numbers as more easy of comprehension. Suppose the total value of the property in South Dakota was $10,000,000, and the total receipts both from interstate and local business were $1,000,000, one half from each. Then, according to the method pursued by the trial court, the value of the property used in earning local receipts would be $5,000,000, and the per cent of receipts to value would be 10 per cent. The interstate receipts being unchanged, let the local receipts by a proposed schedule be reduced to one fifth of what they had been, so that instead of receiving $500,000 the company only receives $100,000. The total receipts for interstate and local business being then $600,000, the valuation of $10,000,000, divided between the two, would give to the property engaged in earning interstate receipts in round numbers $8,333,000, and to that engaged in earning local receipts $1,667,000. But if $1,667,000 worth of property earns $100,000, it earns 6 per cent. In other words, although the actual receipts from local business are only one fifth of what they were, the earning capacity is three fifths of what it was. And turning to the other side of the problem, it appears that if the value of the property engaged in interstate business is to be taken as $8,333,000, and it earned $500,000, its earning capacity was the same as that employed in local business — 6 per cent. So that although the rates for interstate business be undisturbed, the process by which the trial court reached its conclusion discloses the same reduction in the earning capacity of the property employed in interstate business as in that employed in local business, in which the rates are reduced. *Id.*, pp. 176, 177.

The value of the use, as measured by return, cannot be made the criterion when the return itself is in question. If the return, as formerly allowed, be taken as the basis, then the validity of the state's reduction would have to be tested by the very rates which the state denounced as exorbitant. And, if the return as permitted under the new rates be taken, then the state's action itself reduces the amount of value upon which the fairness of the return is to be computed.

When rates are in controversy, it would seem to be necessary to find a basis for a division of the total value of the property independently of revenue, and this must be found in the use that is made of the property. That is, there should be assigned to each business that proportion of the total value of the property which will correspond to the extent of its employment in that business. It is said that this is extremely difficult; in particular, because of the necessity for making a division between the passenger and freight business, and the obvious lack of correspondence between ton-miles and passenger-miles. It does not appear, however, that these are the only units available for such a division; and it would seem that, after assigning to the passenger and freight departments, respectively, the property exclusively used in each, comparable use-units might be found which would afford the basis for a reasonable division with respect to property used in common. It is suggested that other methods of calculation would be equally unfavorable to the state rates, but this we cannot assume.

It is sufficient to say that the method here adopted is not of a character to justify the court in basing upon it a finding that the rates are confiscatory.

Apportionment of expenses. As already stated, it was held in dividing the freight operating expenses, that the cost of doing the intrastate freight business was two and one-half times that of doing the interstate freight business. That is to say, the division of expenses was made according to ton-miles, interstate and intrastate, after the intrastate ton-miles had been increased two and one-half times.

The substantial question is whether the proof established this extra cost with that degree of certainty which is requisite to support a decree invalidating the state rates.

It appeared that the cost of intrastate business was not kept separately or set up in the accounts or statistics of the company.

The president of the company testified as to his judgment in the matter, which was based, in the absence of such accounts, upon the general facts of operation. His testimony was supported by that of other eminent railroad men, who testified in the Great Northern and Minneapolis and St. Louis cases. The elements entering into the greater expense of doing intrastate business were defined to be: that the average haul was shorter, being (in the case of the Northern Pacific) 104.52 miles for intrastate transportation as against 485.3 miles for interstate transportation; that the state business had to be handled twice at terminals; that the local short-haul business used most valuable terminal facilities in order to obtain its proper handling from the larger distributing centers, and used those facilities to a greater extent for the tons handled than did the longer through business; that the amount of clerical and warehouse labor in connection with the local business was much greater than in the case of the long-haul through business; that the chances of damage were greater in the short-haul business because of the greater number of individual transactions; that in the short-haul business there was an excess of equipment for loading and unloading; that local or way freight trains were "loaded lighter"; that the wear and tear on the local trains was greater because of frequent stopping and starting; that there was increased switching, resulting in greater damage to equipment and tracks; that the local train was generally on the road more hours than a through train, and therefore consumed more coal; that in the smaller stations the amount of shifting was large; that many of the local trains carried passengers, involving two stops at each station, one for passengers and the other for the local freight work; that the manner of operation of local trains increased the chances of injury to employees; that the short-haul business moved irregularly and spasmodically, and that its facilities were worked at their full capacity only for limited periods.

From these considerations, which were elaborated in the testimony, the witness reached the conclusion that the "so-called local short-haul intrastate business costs anywhere from three to six or seven times as much as the so-called long-haul through interstate business." In the Great Northern Case, the witnesses expressed the opinion that the extra cost of intrastate freight was three or four times greater than that of the interstate freight. One witness said that it would be from four to six times. These estimates, it is understood, had relation to the cost per ton mile.

The appellants do not dispute that business carried for short distances on local trains is more expensive than the handling of other business, but it is insisted that this is due solely to the different train service that it receives. It is said that all through trains start from divisional points and run from one end of the division to the other without stop; that the local trains are made up of cars carrying business destined for points intermediate the termini of the division, and take up all traffic originating at the intermediate stations; that the word "local," as applied to these trains, is not synonymous with intrastate, but that the local trains carry a large part of the interstate traffic, both in receiving and distributing it; and that by far the greater part of the extra cost of the local train service is properly chargeable to interstate business. It is also insisted that so far as this extra expense can be charged to interstate business, it is adequately met by the additional revenue of that business, which per ton mile, as compared with the interstate business, is as 1.4387 to 1.0000.

To establish these propositions, and to meet the testimony of the complainants' witnesses, the appellants introduced an elaborate series of calculations, made by a professional accountant, which were deduced from the results of an extended examination of the records of the companies. The witness made computations as to the character of the freight on each road, dividing it between through and local freight upon each operating division, and then subdividing it between intrastate and interstate freight. It is contended by the appellants that these calculations are sufficient to show that in the case of the Northern Pacific, about 91 per cent of the freight on through trains was interstate and about 9 per cent intrastate, and that on the local trains the interstate freight amounted to 68.67 per cent, and the intrastate, 31.33 per cent. Calculations of this witness were also introduced, showing his division of the total expenses between the passenger and freight business, and then in each department between the interstate and intrastate business; and by means of these, it was estimated that, under the rates in question (assuming them to have been applied to the business of the fiscal year ending June 30, 1907, to which the calculations were directed), the net profits on the intrastate business as a whole would have been slightly more than 6 per cent upon an amount equal to the share of property value attributed to that business by the master's estimate and apportionment of total value.

These computations are assailed by the appellees as inaccurate and as based upon erroneous estimates. We shall not go into the details, and, for the present purpose, we may assume that the appellees are right in their criticism.

Our conclusions may be briefly stated. The statements of the complainants' witnesses as to the extra cost of interstate business, while entitled to respect as expressions of opinion, manifestly involve wide and difficult generalizations. They embrace, without the aid of statistical information derived from appropriate tests and submitted to careful analysis, a general estimate of all the conditions of transportation, and an effort to express in the terms of a definite relation, or ratio, what clearly could be accurately arrived at only by prolonged and minute investigation of particular facts with respect to the actual traffic as it was being carried over the line. The extra cost, as estimated by these witnesses, is predicated not simply of haulage charges, but of all the outlays of the freight service, including the share of the expenses for maintenance of way and equipment assigned to the freight department. And the ratio, to be accurately stated, must also express the results of a suitable discrimination between the interstate and intrastate traffic on through and local trains respectively, and of an attribution of the proper share of the extra cost of local train service to the interstate traffic that uses it. The wide range of the estimates of extra cost, from three to six or seven times that of the interstate business per ton mile, shows both the difficulty and the lack of certainty in passing judgment.

We are of opinion that, on an issue of this character, involving the constitutional validity of state action, general estimates of the sort here submitted, with respect to a subject so intricate and important, should not be accepted as adequate proof to sustain a finding of confiscation. While accounts have not been kept so as to show the relative cost of interstate and intrastate business, giving particulars of the traffic handled on through and local trains, and presenting *data* from which such extra cost as there may be, of intrastate business, may be suitably determined, it would appear to have been not impracticable to have had such accounts kept or statistics prepared, at least during test periods, properly selected. It may be said that this would have been a very difficult matter, but the company, having assailed the constitutionality of the state acts and orders, was bound to establish its case, and it was not entitled to rest on expressions of judgment when it had it in its power to present accurate *data* which would permit the court to draw the right conclusion.

We need not separately review the findings with respect to the division of passenger expenses, as the same considerations are involved, with the distinction, however, that the extra cost attributed to the intrastate business is relatively small as compared with that charged to intrastate freight. And, in view of the conclusions reached on the controlling questions we have considered, we express no opinion with respect to the method adopted in dividing expenses between the passenger and freight departments.

For the purpose of determining whether the rates permit a fair return, the results of the entire intrastate business must be taken into account. During the test year the entire revenue, as found, from the intrastate business, passenger and freight, amounted to $2,897,912.26. All the rates in question were in force save the commodity rates, and it is further found that the loss that would have accrued in intrastate commodity business, by the application of the commodity rates which were under injunction, would have amounted to $21,493.67.

As neither the share of the expenses properly attributable to the intrastate business, nor the value of the property employed in it, was satisfactorily shown, and hence it did not appear upon the facts proved that a fair return had been denied to the company, we are of the opinion that the complainant failed to sustain his bill.

2. *Great Northern Railway Company.* The master found that at the time this suit was brought the par value of the stock of the company was $149,577,500, and of bonds, $83,119,939; total, $232,697,439. On June 30, 1908, the par value of the stock was $209,962,750, and of bonds, $97,955,939.39; total, $307,918,689.39. The property upon which these securities and their value in the market are based includes, it is found, a very considerable amount not devoted to the public service.

The balance sheet of the company of June 30, 1908, showed the book valuation of the entire system employed in the public service to amount to $319,681,815. The master held that various items were included which were not properly allowable as a part of the cost, and deducting these, there remained as the book-showing of the total amount expended in construction and equipment, $295,401,213. The Minnesota track mileage was found to be practically 32.59 per cent of the total mileage, and upon this basis, the amount assignable to the state of the total cost, as stated, amounted to $96,271,255.

The master found that the cost of reproduction new of the entire system was $457,121,469.[1] The value of the portion of the system in Minnesota was separately found, on the basis of reproduction new, to be $138,425,291. The net profits of the company during the test year from its Minnesota business, interstate and intrastate, were $8,180,025.11, equal to 5.909 per cent upon this estimated value.

The items entering into the estimate are the same in character as those set forth in the estimate of the value of the property of the Northern Pacific Company.[2]

Included in this reproduction cost was an allowance, for "lands for right of way, yards, and terminals," of $25,172,650.80, as follows:

St. Paul, appraisement of Read, Watson, and Taylor	$6,433,348.00
Add 5 per cent for cost of acquisition and consequential damages .	321,667.40
Minneapolis, appraisement of Elwood, Barney, and Ridgeway .	11,619,765.00
Add 5 per cent for cost of acquisition and consequential damages .	580,968.15
Duluth, appraisement of Stryker, Mendenhall, and Little . .	713,280.00
Add 25 per cent for railroad value, cost of acquisition, and consequential damages	178,320.00
Total value of terminals	19,847,366.55
Lands outside of terminals	5,325,284.25
Grand total	25,172,650.80

The appraisements thus referred to, adopted by the master with the additions stated, were made by the appraisers in the three cities who were employed in the case of the Northern Pacific company. The valuations were made at the same time, and upon the same basis, as the corresponding valuations in that case, and are open to the same objections. In the company's estimate of the value of the lands outside these cities, the amount

[1] This did not include the interest of the company in the Spokane, Portland, & Seattle Railroad, or lines under construction.

[2] See p. 691.

stated as the market value was largely increased to obtain the "right of way value"; with respect to lands in agricultural sections, the "market value" was generally multiplied by 3; and of the total amount of the estimate of the company the master allowed 75 per cent, as in the Northern Pacific Case.

In addition, 4½ per cent of the aggregate land values, as found, was allowed in the item for "engineering, superintendence, legal expenses," and the further allowance of 16 per cent of these land values was made in the item of "interest during construction" (4 per cent for four years).

In the physical valuation estimated on the basis of the cost of reproduction new, the master made no deduction for depreciation, while, on the other hand, there was included under the item of grading the sum of $3,219,642 for adaptation and solidification of roadbed. The engineer of the state commission estimated the depreciation in the property at approximately $13,000,000.

What has already been said in the case of the Northern Pacific Company with respect to estimates of value, the apportionment of value, the testimony as to the extra cost of doing the intrastate business, and the division of expenses between interstate and intrastate business, is equally applicable here.[1] In these respects there is no material distinction between the two cases, and the same conclusion must be reached in both.

3. *Minneapolis & St. Louis Railroad Company.* This case presents distinct considerations. The lines of this company consist of about 1028 miles of track, of which 396 miles are operated under lease or trackage rights. Of its owned mileage (632 miles) approximately 60 per cent is in the state of Minnesota. The master thus describes it:

It runs south from the inland cities of St. Paul and Minneapolis to Des Moines, with a branch to Storm Lake, Iowa, and a branch to the South Dakota grain fields. Along its entire line it comes in sharp competition

[1] The total revenue received by the Great Northern during the fiscal year 1908, from its intrastate business, passenger and freight, was $4,641,829.58; and it was found that the loss that would have been sustained by the application of the enjoined commodity rates to the intrastate commodity traffic would have amounted to $87,261.43.

with strong intersecting railroad lines, and while, as before stated, it subserves a useful public purpose and is operated in response to public demand, it can be maintained only by the exercise of the highest economy and watchfulness in its operation, and to succeed must be given greater latitude than is necessary with respect to the more favorably located and prosperous lines of railway.

The less favorable situation of the road is fully recognized by the appellants, who object to its being regarded as affording a fair test of the sufficiency of the rates. They say that its "total mileage and the geographical location" are such "that it cannot be taken as typical of the railway situation in Minnesota"; and they insist that "the important and material questions are raised by the showing made in the Northern Pacific and Great Northern Cases." And the appellees, on their part, assert that "it cannot be seriously contended that the rates complained of are sufficient to yield any reasonable return on a proportionate value of the property used in the conduct of the business covered by the rates"; that the net income of the road "from all sources is scarcely sufficient to pay interest on its outstanding bonds"; that "the value of the property is greatly in excess of the par value of the bonds"; and that, as it seems to the appellees, "this company must earn more money or go into the hands of a receiver, within a comparatively short time."

The main facts are: The par value in 1908, of its stock and bonds, was $30,011,800, divided as follows: stock, $10,000,000 (preferred, $4,000,000, common $6,000,000); bonds $20,011,800. It appeared that no dividends had been paid on the common stock since 1904. The annual interest charges amounted to $952,583.

The book cost of its property, after deducting items disallowed by the master, was $28,574,225; and this, if divided according to mileage, would give to Minnesota as its share, $17,127,390. The mileage basis of division, however, fails to take account of the fact that the property in Minnesota has a greater relative value.

The master found the total value of the property in Minnesota on the basis of the cost of reproduction new to be $21,608,464.

In this estimate there was included the sum of $5,999,397.90 for lands, yards, and terminals. Of this amount $4,556,298 was allowed for the lands in Minneapolis on the estimate of the same appraisers who had been employed in that city by the other companies; and to this the master added 5 per cent. The lands outside these terminals were valued at $1,215,285.

The net earnings of the entire system after paying only operating expenses and taxes, from 1903 to 1909, were found to be as follows: 1903, $1,398,895.30; 1904, $1,229,524.49; 1905, $1,277,870.96; 1906, $1,511,961.99; 1907, $1,419,822.54; 1908, $1,220,862.21; 1909, $1,286,494.08.

The net earning of the company on all its business in Minnesota, interstate and intrastate (involving any use of the property valued as stated), after paying only operating expenses and taxes, were, during the same period: 1903, $1,222,941.77; 1904, $1,052,478.74; 1905, $1,054,853.35; 1906, $1,109,260.56; 1907, $895,977.66; 1908, $742,377.46; 1909, $794,472.58. The reference in each case is to the fiscal year ending on June 30.

It thus appears that the net return from the entire Minnesota business in 1907 was about 4.14 per cent on the estimated value of the property ($21,608,464) in Minnesota; in 1908, less than 3.5 per cent; and in 1909, less than 3.7 per cent.

The master made his computations, with respect to the return permitted under the rates in question, upon the operations of the fiscal year ending June 30, 1907. The class rates had been effective from November 15, 1906, and the passenger fare act from May 1, 1907. It was estimated by the master that the additional loss, which would have accrued in the interstate business if these rates had been in force during the entire fiscal year ending June 30, 1907, and if, in addition, the commodity rate act, which was enjoined, had been applied to the intrastate traffic of that year, would have amounted to $131,358, thus making a very serious reduction in a return already inadequate; and his conclusion was that the rates in question were plainly confiscatory.

It is not necessary here to reproduce the computations, as we are satisfied, after a careful examination of the evidence, that while the methods of estimating value, and of apportionment, which have been disapproved in the discussion of the cases of the other companies, are subject to the same objections in this case, so far as they have been employed, the margin of error which may be imputed to them is not sufficiently great to change the result. The net return from the entire business in Minnesota, interstate and intrastate, fell to $742,000 in the fiscal year ending June 30, 1908, and it is plain that the latter amount would have been largely reduced had the commodity rate act been enforced. In view of the actual results of the business in the state, and the clearly established facts with respect to the conditions of traffic upon this road, the conclusion cannot be escaped that the rates prescribed by the acts and orders of Minnesota would not permit a fair return to this company.

Without approving, therefore, the methods of calculation which have been adopted, but recognizing the peculiar situation of this road, and the undoubted effect of the rates in question upon its revenues, we are of the opinion that the decree, so far as it rests upon the confiscatory character of the rates as applied to this company, should be affirmed. In the desire, however, to prevent the possibility that the decree may operate injuriously in the future, we shall modify it by providing that the members of the Railroad & Warehouse Commission, and the attorney general of the state, may apply at any time to the court, by bill or otherwise, as they may be advised, for a further order or decree, whenever it shall appear that, by reason of a change in circumstances, the rates fixed by the State's acts and orders are sufficient to yield to the company reasonable compensation for the services rendered.

The decrees in Numbers 291 and 292 are reversed and the cases remanded with directions to dismiss the bills respectively without prejudice.

The decree in Number 293 is modified as stated in the opinion, and, as modified, is affirmed.

Mr. Justice McKenna concurs in the result.

XXVI

THE REGULATION OF RAILWAY RATES UNDER THE FOURTEENTH AMENDMENT[1]

I

In 1873 the Supreme Court of the United States, in the first decision[2] that involved the construction of the Fourteenth Amendment, limited its application in a way that must have surprised both those who had advocated and those who had opposed its adoption on the floor of Congress. The court held that the privileges and immunities of citizens of the United States protected by the amendment were not the general privileges and immunities of citizens, but only those special privileges and immunities that belonged to citizens of the United States as such, — the right to come to the seat of government, to assert claims against the national government, to transact business with it, to seek its protection, to share its offices, to have free access to its seaports, subtreasuries, land offices, and the courts of justice of the several states, to demand its care and protection over life, liberty, and property when on the high seas or in the jurisdiction of a foreign government, to assemble and petition for redress of grievances, and to have the writ of habeas corpus; to use the navigable waters of the United States, and to enjoy all rights secured by treaty with foreign nations, to change citizenship from

[1] From the *Quarterly Journal of Economics*, 1912, pp. 389–424.

[2] Slaughter House Cases, 16 Wallace, 36.

It may not be amiss to quote the language of that part of the first section of the Fourteenth Amendment which is here under consideration:

> No state shall make or enforce any law which shall abridge the privileges or immunities of citizens of the United States; nor shall any state deprive any person of life, liberty, or property without due process of law; nor deny to any person within its jurisdiction the equal protection of the laws.

The reader need hardly be reminded that this Amendment was made after the Civil War, being ratified in 1868.

one state to another with the same rights as other citizens of that state. Important as these rights are, they are not the ordinary everyday rights that closely affect the citizen. For these he was left to the protection of the states. Though the actual decision related only to one clause of the amendment, the opinion of Mr. Justice Miller, who spoke for the court, intimated strongly that the clause forbidding the states to deprive any person of life, liberty, and property without due process of law, and to deny to any person within its jurisdiction the equal protection of the laws, was intended to protect against unjust discrimination the negro race only.

Three years later, however, in the Granger cases [1] (1876) it was taken for granted that the scope of the latter clause of the amendment was broader, and that it protected not merely those of the negro race, but all persons. The court in fact followed the dissenting opinions of Justices Field and Bradley, not the dictum of the prevailing opinion of Justice Miller.

The Granger cases settled the authority of the state legislatures to control the charges of a business affected with a public interest. Some of the language used by the court went far in denying any right of the court to interfere. It was said distinctly that though the power conceded to the legislature was liable to be abused, the people must resort for protection against abuses to the polls and not to the courts. It was conceded that under some circumstances, but not under all, statutory regulations might deprive the owner of his property without due process of law; but it was held that the amendment did not change the law; "it simply prevents the States from doing that which will operate as such a deprivation."

The question of rates seemed by these decisions determined to be a legislative, not a judicial question. Six years later [2] the court held that a railroad company whose board of directors was by the charter authorized to establish rates could not as against

[1] *Munn* v. *Illinois*, 94 U. S. 113 (1877). *Chicago, B. & Q. R.R. Co.* v. *Iowa*, 94 U. S. 155. *Peik* v. *Chicago and N.W. Railway Co.*, *Lawrence* v. *Same*, 94 U. S. 164. *Chicago, M. & St. C. R.R. Co.* v. *Ackley*, 94 U. S. 179. *Winona & St. Peter R.R. Co.* v. *Blake*, 94 U. S. 180. *Stone* v. *Wisconsin*, 94 U. S. 181.

[2] *Ruggles* v. *Illinois*, 108 U. S. 526 (1883).

a general law of the state exact more than three cents per mile per passenger. The reasoning was put on a narrow basis, involving only the construction of the charter. The power granted was to determine the rates by by-laws; the power to pass by-laws was limited to such as were not repugnant to the laws of the state, and hence it was held that the by-laws could not fix a greater rate than was permitted by the general legislation; "grants of immunity from legitimate control," said the Chief Justice, "are never to be presumed."

The states soon began to avail themselves of the power to control business affected with a public interest. The first important case concerning the limitation of their powers arose in California.[1] It decided that the rates of a water company might be fixed by a county board in which the water company was not represented, although the charter of the company provided for its representation. The court expressly reserved the question what might be done in case the municipal authorities did not exercise an honest judgment or fixed a price manifestly unreasonable. Two years later,[2] it was decided that railroad charges might be fixed by a Railroad Commission, although charters provided that the companies themselves might fix the tolls and charges. The legislature of Mississippi, by legislation subsequent to the charters, created a Railroad Commission with power to revise rates and increase or reduce them as experience and business operation might show to be just. It was argued that the legislature by the provision in the charters had surrendered the power of control over fares and freights. It was conceded that the rates must by the rule of the common law be reasonable, and the court held that the state was left free to act on the subject of reasonableness within the limits of its general authority as circumstances might require. "The right to fix reasonable charges has been granted," said Chief Justice Waite, "but the power of declaring what shall be deemed reasonable has not been surrendered. If there had been an intention of surrendering this power, it would have been easy to say so; not having

[1] *Spring Valley Water Works* v. *Schottler*, 110 U. S. 347 (1884).

[2] Railroad Commission Cases, 116 U. S. 307 (1886).

said so, the conclusive presumption is there was no such intention." The court, however, was careful to guard against an inference that the power of regulation was without limit. "The power to regulate," it was said, "is not a power to destroy, and limitation is not the equivalent of confiscation. Under pretense of regulating fares and freights, the State cannot require a railroad corporation to carry persons or property without reward; neither can it do that which in law amounts to a taking of private property for public use without just compensation, or without due process of law."

The statute was held not to be in conflict with the due process clause and the equal protection clause of the Fourteenth Amendment. "General statutes fixing maximum rates," it was said, "do not necessarily deprive the railroad company of its property contrary to the amendment." The importance of the qualifying word "necessarily" appeared in subsequent decisions when it was held that such statutes might sometimes be void. The decisions thus far were in favor of public control, and against review by the courts.

II

Four years later, in the Minnesota Rate Cases,[1] the court took a position hard to reconcile with what was said in *Munn* v. *Illinois* and the succeeding cases. The Minnesota Commission had ordered a reduction of rates for transportation of milk from three cents to two and a half cents a gallon; and for switching cars from $1.25 and $1.50 per car to $1.00 per car. The railroads resisted and, upon application to the state courts, a mandamus was issued to put in force the rates fixed by the commission. The Supreme Court reversed this action. Justice Blatchford rested the reversal upon the fact that the decision of the railroad commission was made a finality under Minnesota law; he said that the commission could not be regarded as clothed with judicial functions or possessing the machinery of a court of justice. "The question of the reasonableness of a rate of charge for

[1] *Chicago, M. & St. P. Railway Co.* v. *Minnesota*, 134 U. S. 418 (1890). *Minneapolis Eastern Railway Co.* v. *Minnesota*, 134 U. S. 467 (1890).

transportation by a railroad company, involving as it does the element of reasonableness both as regards the company and as regards the public, is eminently a question for judicial investigation, requiring due process of law for its determination. If the company is deprived of the power of charging reasonable rates for the use of its property, and such deprivation takes place in the absence of an investigation by judicial machinery, it is deprived of the lawful use of its property and thus in substance and effect, of the property itself, without due process of law and in violation of the law of the Constitution of the United States; and in so far as it is thus deprived, while other persons are permitted to receive reasonable profits upon their invested capital, the company is deprived of the equal protection of the laws."

The court seemed by this language to decide that the question of rates was always a judicial question, and not, as had been held before and has been held since, a legislative question; that it could therefore be settled by a judicial tribunal only; that if a railroad company was not allowed to charge reasonable rates, its constitutional rights were violated; and that it was entitled to reasonable profits in the same sense as other persons not engaged in a public calling. It is difficult to see how the right to profit as individuals not engaged in a public calling can be consistent with the right of the state to regulate the rates of those engaged in such a calling. The opinion, carried to its logical conclusion, would substitute the courts for the commission as final arbiter; and in effect would throw the whole burden of rate making upon the judicial machinery. No wonder the opinion did not command the unanimous voice of the court. Justice Miller concurred in the result, but upon the ground that the commission had applied to the courts to enforce their order; that in substance this was asking the courts to determine that the order was reasonable, and hence the court had the right and duty to inquire into the reasonableness of the tariff of rates.

Justice Bradley, speaking for himself and Justices Gray and Lamar, dissented. He pointed out that the decision practically overruled *Munn* v. *Illinois* and the railroad cases decided with it; that the question of the reasonableness of a charge, so far from being a judicial question, was preëminently a legislative one involving considerations of policy as well as of remuneration; that in practice it had usually been determined by the legislature by fixing a maximum in the charter of the company or afterwards if there were no binding contract; that the question only became judicial when the legislature enacted simply that rates should be reasonable, thus necessarily submitting the question what was in fact reasonable to the judicial tribunals; but that the legislature might itself or by its commission fix the rates; and that for that purpose their decision was final, unless they so acted as to deprive parties of their property without due process of law; but that a mere difference of judgment as to amount between the commission and the companies without any indication of intent on the part of the commission to do injustice, did not amount to a deprivation of property. The real difference between Justice Blatchford and Justice Bradley was as to the question presented in a rate case. According to the former it was: "is the rate a reasonable one, and such as would afford the same profit as could be realized by one not subject to regulation?" According to the latter it was: "is the rate so unreasonable as to be arbitrary and amount to confiscation of property rather than mere regulation of a rate?" The difference is striking and fundamental. If the legislature had the right to regulate rates, as had been settled in the Granger cases, then the property of the railroads was qualified by that public right, and there could be no deprivation of such qualified property as long as the legislature confined itself to fair regulation and did not undertake to confiscate under the guise of regulation. The view of the minority has finally prevailed.[1]

Justice Bradley in the course of his opinion took occasion to speak of the relations between the courts and the legislature. His words are worth quoting:

> It is always a delicate thing for the courts to make an issue with the legislative department of the government, and they should never do so if it is possible to avoid it. By the decision now made we declare, in effect, that the judiciary, and not the legislature is the final arbiter in the regulation

[1] *Atlantic Coast Line* v. *No. Car. Corp. Comm.*, 206 U. S. 1 (1907).

of fares and freights of railroads and the charges of other public accommodations. It is an assumption of authority on the part of the judiciary, which, it seems to me, with all due deference to the judgment of my brethren, it has no right to make.

The decision of the Court in the Minnesota Rate cases, it was further pointed out, gave a new extension to the meaning of the words "due process of law." Justice Blatchford's language must mean that due process of law requires judicial procedure "with the forms and machinery," to quote his language, "provided by the wisdom of successive ages for the investigation judicially of the truth of a matter in controversy." Long before this decision the court had held in an elaborate opinion by Mr. Justice Curtis [1] that the same words in the Fifth Amendment did not necessarily imply a regular proceeding in a court of justice or after the manner of such courts; and this view had been adopted and applied in the construction of the Fourteenth Amendment. The difficulty of Mr. Justice Blatchford's view becomes apparent if it is applied to the taking of the property of the citizen by taxation, by assessments for public improvements, or by administrative measures under the police power; or to restraint of the person made necessary by our immigration laws. "In judging what is due process of law," said Mr. Justice Bradley, "respect must be had to the cause and object of the taking, whether under the taxing power, the power of eminent domain, or the power of assessment for local improvements, or none of these: and if found to be suitable or admissible in the special case, it will be adjudged to be due process of law; but if found to be arbitrary, oppressive and unjust, it may be declared to be not 'due process of law.'"

The decision in the Minnesota Rate case inevitably led to repeated efforts to secure review by the courts of rates fixed by statute or the orders of public commissions.

After an unsuccessful effort by a friendly litigation to have a particular rate declared unreasonable,[2] the question next arose in the great case of *Reagan* v. *Farmers' Loan & Trust Co.*,[3]

[1] *Murray's Lessee* v. *Hoboken Land and Improvement Co.*, 18 How. 272 (1856).

[2] *Chicago & Grand Trunk Railway Co.* v. *Wellman*, 143 U. S. 339 (1892).

[3] 154 U. S. 362 (1894).

noteworthy because it was the first successful effort to enjoin the enforcement of rates fixed by a commission.

The question was squarely raised, for the defendant denied the power of the court to entertain the inquiry at all, and insisted that the fixing of rates for carriage by a public carrier was a matter wholly within the power of the legislative department of the government and beyond examination by the courts. To this the court through Mr. Justice Brewer answered:

> The province of the courts is not changed, nor the limit of judicial inquiry altered, because the legislature instead of the carrier prescribes the rates. The courts are not authorized to revise or change the body of rates imposed by a legislature or a commission; they do not determine whether one rate is preferable to another, or what under all circumstances would be fair and reasonable as between the carriers and the shippers; they do not engage in any mere administrative work; but still there can be no doubt of their power and duty to inquire whether a body of rates prescribed by a legislature or a commission is unjust and unreasonable, and such as to work a practical destruction to rights of property, and if found so to be, to restrain its operation.

The complainants challenged the tariff as a whole and the court's inquiry was limited to its effect as a whole. The facts were thus stated by the court:

> The cost of this railroad property was $40,000,000; it cannot be replaced to-day for less than $25,000,000. There are $15,000,000 of mortgage bonds outstanding against it, and nearly $10,000,000 of stock. These bonds and stock represent money invested in the construction of this road. The owners of the stock have never received a dollar's worth of dividends in return for their investment. The road was thrown into the hands of a receiver for default in payment of the interest on the bonds. The earnings for the last three years prior to the establishment of these rates were insufficient to pay the operating expenses and the interest on the bonds. In order to make good the deficiency in interest the stockholders have put their hands in their pockets and advanced over a million of dollars. The supplies for the road have been purchased at as cheap a rate as possible. The officers and employees have been paid no more than is necessary to secure men of the skill and knowledge requisite to suitable operation of the road. . . . The actual reduction by virtue of this tariff in the receipts during the six or eight months that it has been enforced amounts to over $150,000.

Upon these facts the Court said:

A general averment in a bill that a tariff as established is unjust and unreasonable, is supported by the admitted facts that the road cost far more than the amount of the stock and bonds outstanding; that such stock and bonds represent money invested in its construction; that there has been no waste or mismanagement in the construction or operation; that supplies and labor have been purchased at the lowest possible price consistent with the successful operation of the road; that the rates voluntarily fixed by the company have been for ten years steadily decreasing until the aggregate decrease has been more than fifty per cent; that under the rates thus voluntarily established, the stock, which represents two-fifths of the value, has never received anything in the way of dividends, and that for the last three years the earnings above operating expenses have been insufficient to pay the interest on the bonded debt, and that the proposed tariff, as enforced, will so diminish the earnings that they will not be able to pay one-half the interest on the bonded debt above the operating expenses; and that such an averment so supported, will, in the absence of any satisfactory showing to the contrary, sustain a finding that the proposed tariff is unjust and unreasonable, and a decree reversing it being put in force.

In deciding whether a tariff is so unreasonable and unjust as practically to destroy the value of the carrier's property, it is of course essential to fix the standard or principle upon which that value is to be determined. Upon this question the Reagan case is indecisive. Some of the language suggests that cost of the property is the proper measure of its value; other language, cost of replacement; and still other language, present value. The question was left for discussion in the later cases.

The Reagan case had dealt with the effect of the tariff of rates as a whole. Similar questions arose in *St. Louis and San Francisco Railway* v. *Gill*,[1] where it was decided that the correct test was the effect of the rates on the whole line of the carrier's road, and not the effect upon that portion which was formerly a part of one of the consolidating roads; that a company cannot claim the right to earn a net profit for every mile of road, nor attack as unjust a regulation which fixes a rate at which some part would be unremunerative; that the earnings of the entire line must be estimated as against all its legitimate expenses

[1] 156 U. S. 649 (1895).

under the operation of the act within the limits of the state. The last qualification presents a new difficulty, — that of severing a railroad into parts divided by the imaginary state lines. The later effort to segregate intrastate and interstate business has led to difficult problems still in process of solution. The Gill case was a suit for a penalty, and the court in referring to Justice Miller's statement in the Minnesota Rate cases that the rates were binding until judicially determined to be void, added that in cases where the legislature itself fixed the rates, a bill in equity was impracticable because there was no public functionary or commission which could be made to respond, and the companies, if they were to have any relief, must have the right to raise the question by way of defense to an action for penalties. This remark was unnecessary to the decision, since the result of the case on the facts was against the carrier. The remedy by injunction to restrain legal officers of the state from prosecuting, came later.

The same principle that applies to the case of a carrier, applies also to a turnpike company. In *Covington, etc., Turnpike Company* v. *Sandford*,[1] the Court held that the facts that the tolls for several years prior to 1890 had not admitted of dividends greater than 4 per cent on the par value of the stock; that the proposed reduction would so diminish the income of the company that it could not maintain its road, meet its ordinary expenses, and earn any dividends whatever for stockholders, showed that the constitutional rights of the turnpike company were violated. Justice Harlan was careful to say that a mere failure of the rates to suffice to earn four per cent on the stock would not justify holding the rates to be void. "It cannot be said," he added, "that a corporation is entitled, as of right, and without reference to the interests of the public, to realize a given per cent upon its capital stock. . . . The public cannot properly be subjected to unreasonable rates in order simply that stockholders may earn dividends." In dealing with the question how the reasonableness of rates was to be ascertained, the court was not very satisfactory. The inquiry was said to involve a consideration of the

[1] 164 U. S. 578 (1896).

right of the public to use the road on paying reasonable tolls, and also of the reasonable cost of maintaining the road in good condition for public use, and the amount that may have been really and necessarily invested in the enterprise. It was held that there might be other circumstances, not then necessary to state; that each case must depend upon its special facts; and justice might require different rates for different roads. In short, the opinion merely holds that rates must be reasonable and fair both to the public and the company and must not be so low as practically to deprive the company of its property. No standard was fixed, and the case decided only that the particular rates infringed the constitutional provision. The language of the court indicates that it is the actual and necessary investment of the company that is to be considered. This seems to mean the actual necessary cost as distinguished from cost of replacement or present value.

The results reached up to this point may be thus summarized. State enactments or regulations establishing rates that will not permit of the carrier earning such compensation as under all the circumstances is just to it and the public, infringe the provisions of the Fourteenth Amendment; and the question whether rates are so unreasonably low as to deprive the carrier of its property cannot be conclusively determined by the legislative authority of the state, but may be the subject of judicial inquiry.

III

These general principles do not go far to solve the question in a particular case. The decision in the Nebraska Maximum Rate cases[1] took a further step. It was contended on behalf of the state that the compensation to be allowed the carrier after payment of operating expenses was purely a question of public policy to be determined by the legislature and not by the courts. "It cannot be successfully contended," said counsel for the state, "that so long as the rate fixed pays something above operating expenses to the corporation for the carrying of property, it

[1] *Smyth* v *Ames*. *Smyth* v. *Smith*. *Smyth* v. *Higginson*, 169 U. S. 466 (1898).

amounts to the taking either of the use or of the property." "It must follow then, that, so long as the rate fixed by the law will pay the operating expenses when economically administered, and something in addition thereto, the power of the court ends, and the extent to which rates must produce profits is one of political policy." In short, the contention was that the right of property in a railroad consisted in the title and possession and the privilege to operate it economically, with the right to such additional compensation, however small, as the legislature chose to allow from time to time. The successful maintenance of this proposition would plainly have ended the control of the courts over the subject. It went to the very root of the matter. It might logically be contended that a property right that was subject to legislative regulation, as settled by the Granger cases, was not taken away when the legislature did in fact regulate; but it was nevertheless true that the power to regulate was not a power to destroy. The case involved really a definition of the word "property" as applied to a common carrier; and in view of the earlier decisions, the Court very naturally answered the contention of counsel by saying:

> The idea that any legislature, State or Federal, can conclusively determine for the people and for the courts that what it enacts in the form of law, or what it authorizes its agents to do, is consistent with the fundamental law, is in opposition to the theory of our institutions. The duty rests upon all courts, Federal and State, when their jurisdiction is properly invoked, to see to it that no right secured by the supreme law of the land is impaired or destroyed by legislation. This function and duty of the judiciary distinguishes the American system from all other systems of government. The perpetuity of our institutions and the liberty which is enjoyed under them depend, in no small degree, upon the power given the judiciary to declare null and void all legislation that is clearly repugnant to the supreme law of the land.

The definition of "property" becomes, therefore, in the last resort a matter for the courts.

The Nebraska case involved also the question of rates within a state over railroads extending through other states. It was said that rates reasonable in Iowa might be unreasonable in Nebraska since the density of population, and hence of traffic, might be greater in the former, while the cost of construction and maintenance might be less. It was held that the reasonableness of rates on traffic wholly within the state must be determined without reference to the interstate business done by the carrier or to the profits derived from it.

The argument that a railroad line is an entirety; that its income goes into, and its expenses are provided for out of a common fund, and that its capitalization is on its entire line, within and without the state, can have no application where the State is without authority over rates on the entire line, and can only deal with local rates and make such regulations as are necessary to give just compensation on local business.

Whether the attempt thus made to sever the intrastate from the interstate business can be carried out successfully is a question involved in later litigation and not yet settled. It involves a determination of the proportion of value of plant and cost of traffic to be attributed to the lines within the state. In view of the interaction of the various elements of cost and of revenue within and without the state upon each other, the problem is most difficult, and may prove possible of solution only by an approximation.

The Court in the Nebraska case considered also the question on what amount the railroads were entitled to earn a revenue. The companies contended that they were entitled to such rates as would enable them at all times, not only to pay operating expenses, but also to meet the interest regularly accruing upon all outstanding obligations and to justify a dividend on all their stock; less than that, it was said, would deprive them of property without due process of law. The Court held, however, that this contention practically excluded from consideration the fair value of the property used, omitted the right of the public to be exempt from unreasonable exactions, would justify the railroad in trying to earn interest on bonds in excess of its fair value and dividends on fictitious capitalization. The court was still indefinite in laying down the basis of the valuation on which earnings might fairly be had. It said the rights of the public would be ignored if rates were exacted without reference to the fair value of the property used for the public or the fair value of the services rendered. But these two bases of calculation are far from leading to the same result. To base rates upon the value of the property, involves the value of the plant in its entirety and the net result of all the rates on thousands of items. To base them upon the value of the services rendered, involves a consideration only of particular items and may involve a consideration of the value of the services to the shipper. The two methods are incommensurate. What the court decided was that the basis of all calculations as to the reasonableness of rates must be the fair value of the property used; that in order to ascertain that value, the original cost of construction, the amount expended in permanent improvements, the amount and market value of the bonds and stock, the present as compared with the original cost of construction, the probable earning capacity of the property under the particular rates prescribed, and the sum required to meet operating expenses, are all matters for consideration, to be given such weight as may be just and right in each case. Justice Harlan was careful to add: "We do not say that there may not be other matters to be regarded in estimating the value of the property."

Many of these elements required and have received and are destined to receive further definition and analysis. What other elements are to be considered may never be finally settled, so infinitely various are the circumstances that distinguish each case as it arises.

The Court soon had occasion to apply the rule, and the opinion shows no greater certainty in the basis of valuation.[1] A water company insisted that the court should consider the cost of the plant, the annual cost of operation including interest on money borrowed and reasonably necessary to be used in constructing the same; the annual depreciation of the plant from natural causes resulting from its use; and a fair profit to the company either by way of interest on the money expended for the public use, or upon some other fair and equitable basis. All these matters the court conceded ought to be taken into consideration, but it held that the basis of calculation was defective in not requiring the real value of the property and the fair value in themselves of the services rendered to be taken into consideration.

[1] *San Diego Land Co.* v. *National City*, 174 U. S. 739 (1899).

The opinion, however, points to no more definite rule. "What the company is entitled to demand," says the Court, "in order that it may have just compensation, is a fair return upon the reasonable value of the property at the time it is being used for the public." This adopts present value as the standard, but leaves unsettled how the reasonable value of the property is to be ascertained, and what is a fair return.

The opinion in the next case[1] sought to make a distinction between public service companies and companies which without any intent of public service have placed their property in such a position that the public has an interest in its use. As to the first class, Justice Brewer said the owner intentionally devoted his property to the discharge of a public service, and undertook that which is a proper work for the state, and might be said to accept voluntarily all the conditions of public service which attach to like service performed by the state itself. As to the second class the owner placed his property in such a position willingly or unwillingly, that the public acquire an interest in its use, but he submits only to those necessary interferences and regulations which the public interests require. Of the former it was said that since the state was not guided solely by a question of profit but might conduct the business at a loss having in view a larger general interest, so perhaps an individual who had shown his willingess to undertake the work of the state might be held to perform that service without profit. The suggestion was put in the form of an interrogation, since it was confessedly unnecessary in the pending case to determine the question. It seems to conflict with *Smyth* v. *Ames*, and the Court has never yet decided that the legal right of regulation goes to this extent. The decided case involves a corporation of the other class, which was not doing the work of the state, was not performing a public service, and had acquired from the state none of its governmental powers. The business was that of a stock yard at Kansas City. The business was held to be so affected with a public interest, being at the gateway of a great commerce of which it was an important if not a necessary adjunct, that its charges like those

[1] *Cotting* v. *Kansas City Stock Yards Co.*, 183 U. S. 79 (1901).

of a grain elevator were subject to public regulation. But the Court said the

business in all matters of purchase and sale is subject to the ordinary conditions of the market and the freedom of contract. He (the owner) can force no one to sell to him, he cannot prescribe the price which he shall pay. . . . If under such circumstances he is bound by all the conditions of ordinary mercantile transactions, he may justly claim some of the privileges which attach to those engaged in such transactions. And while he cannot claim immunity from all state regulation, he may rightfully say that such regulation shall not operate to deprive him of the ordinary privileges of others engaged in mercantile business.

The difference in practical result suggested in the opinion is that in the case of a business affected with a public interest although not devoted to the public service, the state's regulation of charges is not to be measured by the aggregate of profits determined by the volume of business, but by the question whether any particular charge to an individual dealing with him is, considering the service rendered, an unreasonable exaction.

The question is not how much he makes out of his volume of business, but whether in each particular transaction the charge is an unreasonable exaction for the services rendered. He has a right to do business. He has a right to charge for each separate service that which is reasonable compensation therefor, and the legislature may not deny him such reasonable compensation, and may not interfere simply because out of the multitude of his transactions the amount of his profits is large. Such was the rule of the common law even in respect to those engaged in a quasi public service independent of legislative action. In any action to recover for an excessive charge, prior to all legislative action, who ever knew of an inquiry as to the amount of the total profits of the party making the charge?

The distinction suggested by Justice Brewer and his expressions with reference to the subject are interesting and suggestive; but the opinion was not the opinion of the court. Six out of nine judges assented to the judgment upon the ground that the Kansas statute violated the Fourteenth Amendment because it applied only to one stock-yards company, and not to other corporations engaged in like business in Kansas, and therefore denied to that company the equal protection of the laws. They were careful to say that they expressed no opinion upon the question whether it deprived the company of its property without due process of law. This, and not Justice Brewer's elaborate opinion, expresses the view of the court. Under the facts of the case it amounted to saying that the answer was doubtful as to the question whether rates that enabled a company to earn 5.3 per cent on the value of the property used for stock-yards purposes, instead of about 10 per cent previously earned, amounted to depriving it of property without due process of law; the propriety of any rate of return was not decided.

The suggestion that a public service company, doing the work of the state, might properly do it for an unremunerative rate bore fruit in the Minnesota Coal Rate case.[1] That case is important because it sustained an unremunerative rate upon coal fixed by the state commission. The ruling is in conflict with the reasoning of *Smyth* v. *Ames* (the Nebraska cases) and the court recognizes the necessity of explaining the distinction. It says that while the reasonableness or unreasonableness of rates for intrastate traffic must be determined without reference to the interstate business, it does not follow that the companies are entitled to earn the same percentage of profits on all classes of freight carried. This hardly justifies the conclusion that the carrier may be compelled to carry some goods at a loss; for if so, the power to select those goods involves a power to discriminate quite at variance with fundamental principles; if the railroad can be compelled to carry coal at a loss, it may also be compelled to carry other goods at a loss; and since it is entitled to a fair return upon the whole business, this loss must be made up by the imposition of a heavier rate on other goods than would naturally fall thereon; the public authorities are then permitted to discriminate against some shippers and in favor of others, a discrimination which has always been condemned, and was held to be illegal by the New Jersey Supreme Court,[2] upon the ground that carriers were engaged in a public employment, three years before the United States Supreme Court decided the Granger cases.

[1] *Minneapolis & St. Louis R'd Co.* v. *Minnesota*, 186 U. S. 257 (1902).

[2] *Messenger* v. *Pennsylvania R.R.* 700, 407 (1873).

The court in the Minnesota Coal Rate case sought to justify the losing rate upon the ground that for purposes of ultimate profit and of building up a future trade, railways carry both freight and passengers at a positive loss. No doubt such is the fact, and if railways were to be left free to fix rates according to their own pleasure, and to discriminate at their pleasure between shippers, the practice of sowing seed to reap a future crop might be permissible. The difficulty is that considerations of that kind are not reducible to a legal rule, but involve considerations of business policy.

It is not only difficult to determine how much of the value of an entire railroad shall be attributed to the portion within a state, but since even that portion is used in part for intrastate and in part for interstate traffic, the value of the property used for local and for through traffic must also be determined; and since all the business is done by the same men, with the same equipment, the total cost of conducting the business must also be apportioned. As might be expected from the intricacy of the problem, the results thus far reached are not satisfactory. In the Gill case it was held that every mile need not pay; from which it would seem to result that the system must be treated as an entirety, and that losses on local traffic might be balanced by profit on through traffic or vice versa. *Smyth* v. *Ames* decided the contrary, and made necessary the determination of the proper basis for apportionment of value and cost. The South Dakota case [1] rejected gross receipts as a proper basis for the apportionment. The other basis suggested is that of the volume of traffic determined according to ton mileage. The tendency of the more recent cases in the lower Federal courts seems to be in the direction of apportioning cost and value according to gross receipts. The question is still unsettled in the Supreme Court. In the Florida Phosphate cases,[2] the court leaned to the ton-mile basis, at least as far as concerns the cost of doing the business.

[1] *Chicago, M. & St. P. Ry.* v. *Tompkins*, 176 U. S. 167.

[2] *Atlantic Coast Line* v. *Florida*, 203 U. S. 256 (1906). *Seaboard Air Line* v. *Florida*, 203 U. S. 261 (1906).

The question to be decided when the protection of the Fourteenth Amendment is invoked, is whether the rates as a whole afford a sufficient return, or are so low as to amount to confiscation. When, as in the South Dakota Coal case or the Florida Phosphate cases, the rate upon a single article only is involved, it is impossible to determine the effect of that single rate upon gross or net returns on the entire traffic, and hence impossible to prove that the rate fixed is so low as to amount to confiscation. Such was the result in the Florida Phosphate cases, and it is quite conceivable that the court might be forced to decide that one unremunerative rate after another was not in conflict with the property right of the carrier, until an entire schedule of unremunerative rates might have been sustained. In the Phosphate cases the question did not arise, since the rate permitted exceeded the average receipts per ton per mile under the previous tariff. But the possibility of the result I have indicated illustrates the danger of the decision in the Minnesota Coal case, that a carrier may be required to carry a particular commodity at an unremunerative rate.

IV

The reasonable value of the property used was by 1903 pretty well recognized as the proper standard upon which returns may be earned. In *San Diego Land & Town Co.* v. *Jasper*[1] the Court said: "It no longer is open to dispute that under the Constitution what the company is entitled to demand, in order that it may have just compensation, is a fair return upon the reasonable value of the property at the time it is being used for the public." That standard is adopted as against a standard based on actual cost, less depreciation. Actual cost, selling price, valuation for taxation, may all be evidence of the actual value. But actual value may sometimes be enhanced by the fact that the plant is larger than is needed. Is the company entitled to earn a revenue on an unnecessary expenditure? To this question, the Court answers, no. Upon the value as fixed by the local board, rates

[1] 189 U. S. 439 (1903).

were fixed with the intention of securing a yield of 6 per cent. The court found no sufficient evidence that this rate was confiscatory. But the local board had fixed the rates as if the water company supplied the whole 6000 acres outside the city for which the works were intended. In fact it supplied less, and its receipts were therefore less than the supervisors estimated. The result might give the appellant less than 6 per cent on the value of the plant. But the court said that if the plant was built for a larger area than it could supply, the Constitution did not require that two-thirds of the contemplated area should pay a full return. The case is therefore important because it holds that a failure to pay six per cent on present value is not necessarily decisive of the question whether rates are confiscatory so as to violate the constitutional provision. The present value on which the company is entitled to a return is only the present value of what is reasonably necessary for the public service.

A water company in California[1] was incorporated under a statute which empowered the county board of supervisors to regulate rates, but not to reduce them so low as to yield to stockholders less than 1½ per cent a month on the capital actually invested. After the company had invested about a million dollars in its plant, a new statute empowered the supervisors to so adjust the rates as to yield not less than 6 nor more than 18 per cent per annum upon the value of the property actually used and useful for the supply of water. The court held that there was no contract the obligation of which was impaired, and that even if there was a contract, the legislature might alter or amend the original statute under its reserved power. For our present purpose the important point decided is that it is not a confiscation nor a taking of property without due process, nor a denial of the equal protection of the laws, to fix water rates so as to give an income of six per cent upon the then value of the property actually used, even though the company had prior thereto been allowed to fix rates that would secure to it 18 per cent upon the capital actually invested. The right of property of a water company

[1] *Stanislaus County* v. *San Joaquin and King's River Canal and Irrigation Co.*, 192 U. S. 201 (1904).

under the California statute, so far as it is protected by the Fourteenth Amendment, is no more than a right to earn 6 per cent on present value, regardless of actual investment or previous statutory provisions permitting a larger return.

The method of determining present value still remains to be settled. To ascertain the value of tangible property, such as lands or buildings, for the purpose of determining the just compensation required to be made when it is taken for public use, has always been a sufficiently difficult question. To ascertain the value for the purpose of determining whether a schedule of rates is confiscatory is more difficult still.

In the Knoxville Water Company case,[1] the value had been based on cost of reproduction, to which there was added $10,000 for organization and promotion expenses, and $60,000 for value as a going concern. The court declined to decide upon the propriety of including these two items in the estimate, and expressly reserved them for consideration when the question necessarily arose. The Knoxville case turned upon the failure of the court below to make a proper deduction for depreciation arising from age and use. It was held that the water company was not entitled to value an old plant as if it were a new one. The more interesting question was as to the right of the company to add to the present value of its plant the cost of what had been lost through destruction or obsolescence, and what had been impaired in value although still in use. There was little discussion of the question in the opinion, no doubt because the circumstances of the particular case did not call for discussion. The court held that it was the duty of the company to use enough of its earnings to keep its plant good, before coming to the question of the amount of its profits, and that if it failed to keep its investment unimpaired, whether because it declared unwarranted dividends on over-issues of securities, or because it failed to exact proper prices for its output, it could not enhance the present value of its property by the addition of the costs of its mistakes. The question is likely to arise, as it has already in some cases, in a more difficult form, where fruitless but necessary

[1] *Knoxville* v. *Water Co.*, 212 U. S. 1 (1909).

experiments have been made, or plant has become obsolete in a rapidly advancing industry before it could possibly be made good out of current earnings. It arose before the Interstate Commerce Commission, in the converse case where the corporation, in order to reduce its apparent rate of earnings, sought to charge against current earnings the cost of betterments from which it was likely to profit for years to come. The Supreme Court approved the ruling of the Interstate Commerce Commission and held that the instrumentalities that are to be used for years should not be paid for by the revenues of a day or year.[1] A public service company cannot use more money in a year than is required for actual depreciation, and carry the excess as an addition to capital for the purpose of estimating the amount on which it is entitled to dividends, in determining whether a rate is confiscatory.[2] Novel questions of this character will arise with increasing frequency, and require the most careful consideration. Like most other questions in every department of the law, they are in their origin rather questions of fact than questions of law, although in course of time the rules become settled and thus become rules of law. In their origin, and as yet, many questions are questions of sound business management and engineering science. The law prescribes reasonable returns upon a reasonable valuation. What is a reasonable return and what is a reasonable valuation must vary with the circumstances of each particular case.

The basis of present value adopted in the Knoxville Water Company case was cost of reproduction less an allowance for depreciation in order to make up the difference between the value of new and old. Such a basis in the case of land, especially in a growing city, tends to make the cost of reproduction exceed the original cost, and in the case of railroads especially is almost sure to make present value greatly in excess of cost to the companies. It has therefore been contended with much ingenuity and force that the basis for rate regulation should not exceed the capital actually invested. In *Willcox* v. *Consolidated*

[1] *Illinois Cent. R.R.* v. *Inter. Com. Comm.*, 206 U. S. 441 (1907).

[2] *Louisiana R.R. Comm.* v. *Cumberland Tel. Co.*, 212 U. S. 414 (1909).

Gas Co.,[1] it was argued that one gas company should not be permitted to charge more than another for the sole reason that movements of population, uninfluenced by either company, had caused the site of its plant to be more valuable if vacated and sold; for it was said that although the fortunate company was entitled to obtain the full value of the land when sold, the unrealized profit meanwhile did not represent profit used in the manufacture and distribution of gas, but rather represented wealth which the manufacture and distribution of gas keeps out of use. This argument seems sound. The circumstances of the case did not call for an answer by the court. It did, however, distinctly reject the basis of actual cost even in the case of land. It held that the value of the property must be determined as of the time when the inquiry was made regarding rates; that the company was entitled to the benefit of any increase of value. That is in harmony with the general rule of law which permits the owner of real estate to profit by any increase in the value of his land. Obviously, however, if we are to uphold the rule that a public service corporation is entitled only to a reasonable return and that the public are entitled to be served at reasonable rates, we must apply the rule of reasonableness to the amount of the investment, as was done in the San Diego Water case. The Court recognized this, for it said there might be an exception to the rule where the property had increased so enormously in value as to render a rate permitting a reasonable return upon such increased value unjust to the public. This makes the reasonableness of the amount allowed for value of the property depend on the reasonableness of the rate to the public; but since the rate must afford a reasonable return to the company also, we are at once reasoning in a circle. The basis suggested by Mr. Whitney, in his argument as counsel, seems a better one, — that the value allowed should be the estimated cost of replacing the land in use with other land capable of accomplishing the same result. Probably no one would contend that if a gas company had been so fortunate as to locate its works at the corner of Broad and Wall Streets, and its land had attained the enormous value that there

[1] 212 U. S. 19 (1909).

prevails, it should be entitled to a return from its gas sales on the present value of the site. Prudent management would require removal to a less expensive site better adapted for the business.

The more difficult question that arose in the Gas Company case was the valuation of the franchise. As to the general question of the propriety of including the value of the franchise in the valuation of the property, the opinion gives little light. All that was decided was that it was proper to include in the valuation, the value attributed with the consent of the state to the franchises at the time of the consolidation of the companies, upon which investors had relied; and that it was wrong to hold, as the court of first instance did, that the value of the franchise had increased in the same ratio as the value of the tangible property. When it came to the general question, the Court said that to allow for increased value of the franchise was too much a matter of pure speculation and also opposed to the principle upon which such valuation should be made. Whether the Court meant merely that the evidence in the particular case was not sufficiently certain to justify the increased valuation, or whether it meant that upon principle the valuation of the franchise ought not under ordinary circumstances to be included, the opinion leaves in doubt.

The court calls attention to the fact that the franchise was subject to the legislative right to so regulate the price of gas as to permit no more than a fair return upon the reasonable value of the property. It would have been but a step to hold that to base the return to the company upon the value of such a franchise would be impossible, since the value of the franchise in turn depended on the rates. The two being dependent, one on the other, neither could furnish a substantial basis for fixing the other. As Judge Savage well said in a case in Maine,[1] "to say that the reasonableness of rates depends upon the fair value of the property used and that the fair value of the property used depends upon the rates which may be reasonably charged seems to be arguing in a circle." There is, however, as he points out, a sense in which the value of the franchise must be considered. It is the franchise, the right to operate and if possible to earn a dividend, that makes

[1] *Brunswick & T. Water District* v. *Maine Water Co.*, 59 Atl. Rep. 537 (1904).

the difference between a lot of junk, — old rails, pipes, and the like, — not worth recovering from their situation in and upon the ground, and a completed plant, railroad, water works, gas works, as the case may be. This is a part of the value of a going concern, the allowance for which the court refused to pass upon in the Knoxville Water Co. case. Even though the franchise is revocable, the fact that the plant has a legal right to exist gives added value to the physical structures. The value of a rightfully existing structure which may be lawfully used is very different from the value of the same structure without the legal right to use it for the purpose for which it was assembled. Quite recently, in the valuation of the Omaha Water Works,[1] the court has expressly approved an appraisal of the value as a going concern. "The difference between a dead plant and a live one," said Justice Lurton, "is a real value, and is independent of any franchise to go on, or any mere good will as between such a plant and its customers."

Although ordinarily the value of a franchise is not enhanced by the prospective profit from any particular schedule of rates, there is an exception where by reason of a contract protected by the contract clause of the Federal constitution, the corporation may continue to charge specified rates for a definite time.[2] The courts insist on finding the elements of a contract as they would between individuals. There must be an agreement upon sufficient consideration. Where the contract is made by a municipality, there must be legislative authority in the municipality to make the contract; and such legislation is construed strictly in favor of the public; authority to fix and determine rates does not authorize a municipality to make a bargain by which it ties itself

[1] *Omaha* v. *Omaha Water Co.*, 218 U. S. 180 (1910).

[2] *Los Angeles* v. *Los Angeles City Water Co.*, 177 U. S. 558 (1900); *Detroit* v. *Detroit Citizens Street Railway Co.*, 184 U. S. 368; *Cleveland* v. *Cleveland City Ry. Co.*, 194 U. S. 517 (1904); *Cleveland* v. *Cleveland Electric Railway Co.*, 201 U. S. 529 (1906); *Vicksburg* v. *Vicksburg Water Works Co.*, 206 U. S. 496 (1907). See also *New Orleans Water Works Co.* v. *Rivers*, 115 U. S. 674 (1885); (sustaining an exclusive right to supply water); *New Orleans Gas Co.* v. *Louisiana Light Co.*, 115 U. S. 650 (1885); (sustaining an exclusive right to supply gas); *Walla Walla* v. *Walla Walla Water Co.*, 172 U. S. 1 (1898).

up for the future.[1] Another exception may be suggested, — the investment by present owners in reliance upon the continuance or value of the franchise. To what extent, if at all, this element may enter into the calculation has not been expressly decided, nor does the Gas Company case settle the question. It settles indeed that under some circumstances such allowance must be made; but no attempt is made to define the circumstances with precision.

The Court held that the Gas Company case was not one for the valuation of good will because the complainant had a monopoly in fact and the consumer must take gas from it or go without; he must resort to the old stand whether he would or no. The Court held also that there was no particular rate of compensation which must in all cases and in all parts of the country be regarded as sufficient for capital invested in business enterprises; the amount of risk, the locality where the business is conducted, the rate expected and usually realized there upon investments similar in character, were all mentioned as factors, and it was held that under the circumstances of the gas business in the city of New York, six per cent was a proper return.

The element of wages of superintendence, which Mr. Whitney in his argument conceded must be covered by the returns to the company, was left out. In one sense this is not a return upon capital but wages of labor, and if it were possible for earnings due to the skill with which the business is managed to be secured to those alone whose skill produced the result, perhaps no more need be said. Practically, however, the earnings depend in part, sometimes in large part, not upon the skill in actual present-day management, but upon the satisfaction with which the public has been served in the past, perhaps by men long since dead. Given equal and reasonable rates, one company will be able to earn large dividends, and another perhaps unable to pay its way; and this result may be due not to any less efficient management,

[1] *Freeport Water Co.* v. *Freeport City*, 180 U. S. 587 (1901); *Danville Water Co.* v. *Danville City*, 180 U. S. 619 (1901); *Rogers Park Water Co.* v. *Fergus*, 180 U. S. 624 (1901); *Knoxville Water Co.* v. *Knoxville*, 189 U. S. 434; *Home Telephone Co.* v. *Los Angeles*, 211 U. S. 265 (1908).

but merely to the fact that one has been long in satisfactory operation while the other is new and not yet in vogue. The greater earnings of the one may even be due to the mere caprice of fashion. But to whatever cause it is due, difficulty will arise unless allowance be made, either by increasing the capital valuation on which the company is permitted to earn a return, by way of a valuation of a going concern or the value of the probability of an already assured income, or else by allowing an additional return on the valuation minus this increment, by way of extra compensation for the greater skill or the greater satisfaction with which it serves the public. Even in the case of so close a monopoly as the Gas Company in New York City, it is not impossible that some of its earnings may have been due to this cause; for although it had a monopoly of the supply of gas through pipes in the streets, it may have had competition, in the supply of light, heat, and power, from the electric companies. Although legally permissible, it would often be impracticable to cut down rates to a level that would afford a fair return to one company upon a valuation that failed to take into account the element of value of a going concern or an assured income, without ruining its weaker competitor. In some cases such lowering of rates would prove inadvisable, especially in the case of railroads. One road may through fortunate investments, the discovery of valuable minerals along its route, the opening of fertile territory, and a rapid increase of population, prove a highly profitable investment; another at the same rates may barely pay its way; yet to cut down rates on the prosperous road so as to reduce its high dividends to a normal level, would emphasize and accentuate the advantage already possessed by those along its line over those along the line of the less prosperous road. Either the prosperous road must be allowed to earn a higher return upon the valuation or the valuation must allow for these elements.

Up to the present time, the United States Supreme Court has not been called upon to decide what elements are proper to be considered in determining the present value of a plant of a public-service company. That the value of the plant as a going concern, not only ready for business but with business actually established, is greater than the bare cost of reproduction of the physical plant, is recognized by cases in other courts. It must be so, leaving out of view altogether the element of good will, which in the case of a strict monopoly ought to be disregarded. A going concern has necessarily expended money in various ways aside from the cost of physical plant in order to get going. The cost of promotion of the enterprise, of corporate organization, of obtaining the necessary franchises, permissions, and consents, of securing the necessary connections with other companies by rail or wire; the cost of experiments necessary in every new industry, and the often rapid substitution of improved appliances before the cost of the old can have been recouped out of earnings; the cost of developing the business including the oft-times necessary loss attending the incomplete stage of the plant, or the introduction of new appliances and methods; the cost of financing the enterprise, including interest on capital sunk before any returns begin to come in, — all go to make up the cost of a complete going plant, and are all expenses that a new enterprise must needs incur.

The United States Supreme Court has not as yet been called upon to analyze the costs of operation and to decide what items of cost of operation ought to be included in the annual charges before the profit can be ascertained. Professor Wyman has dealt with the subject in a satisfactory way [1] and the scope of this article does not call for its further discussion.

The question presented by a schedule of rates under the Fourteenth Amendment is whether the schedule permits a fair return upon a reasonable valuation or is so low as to amount to confiscation. This involves different considerations from those involved when the only question is the propriety of the rate on a single article. It cannot be foretold what effect a change of certain rates, for example on coal or gas, will produce on the net revenue of the business as a whole. This difficulty has been met by the adoption of a tentative course, leaving it for time

[1] Wyman on Public Service Corporations, § 1150 *et seq.*

and experience to determine whether constitutional rights have been infringed.[1]

A most serious difficulty is presented by our dual form of government. It is beyond the scope of the present discussion to treat the numerous cases dealing with the commerce clause, and the question what is interstate and what is intrastate commerce. The net return to a railroad company, — and it is to railway traffic that the questions most frequently relate, — depends on the relation between its income from whatever source derived and its outgoes whether for the conduct of interstate or intrastate business. The two are inextricably intermingled, and the problem of preserving the rights and powers of both the state and the federal governments is one of the problems of the future.

Francis J. Swayze

[1] *Willcox* v. *Consolidated Gas Co.*, 212 U. S. 19; *Northern Pacific R'y* v. *North Dakota*, 216 U. S. 579.

XXVII

THE ENGLISH RAILWAY AND CANAL COMMISSION OF 1888[1]

WHILE the law providing for the Commission of 1873 passed both Houses of Parliament with comparative ease and received but little opposition from the railway interest, the law of 1888 developed by small degrees, and met much opposition. The report of the Committee of 1881 had stated that a permanent railway tribunal was necessary.[2] Railway Commission legislation was introduced regularly between 1882 and 1886. In 1885 the nine principal railways submitted bills to Parliament embodying a general classification and a rearrangement of their maximum rates. But the protests of the traders led to the withdrawal of these measures. The defeat of the government in 1886 on the Irish Question prevented any further action at that time. In 1887 a regulative measure, which in some respects resembled the legislation of the following year, passed the House of Lords.

So far as the form of the Commission is concerned, the most important changes introduced by the legislation of 1888 were the court organization of the Commission and the limitation of the right of appeal. Under the old organization the Commission was considered to be in the same position as any inferior court, and might be prohibited from proceeding in matters over which it had no jurisdiction.[3] Now, by giving the Commission a definite

[1] From the *Quarterly Journal of Economics*, Vol. XX, 1905, pp. 1–55. The author was the expert employed by the Canadian Government in 1902 to draw up its Report upon Railway Rate Grievances and Regulative Legislation. British Railway Statutes and Regulations are reprinted in full in Hearings before the Senate (Elkins) Committee on Interstate Commerce, 1905, Vol. V, Appendix, pp. 133–264. [2] Report of Select Committee on Railways, 1881, Part I, p. iii.

[3] *Toomer* v. *L. C. D. Ry. Co. and S. E. Ry. Co.*, 3 Ry. and Canal Traffic Cases, 98.

court organization and by making its decisions final on questions of fact, much strength was added.

The new legislation provided for a Commission of five members, composed of two lay and three *ex-officio* members. The *ex-officio* members are superior court judges, one for England, one for Scotland, one for Ireland. The active Commission at any one time has a membership of three, the two lay commissioners presided over by the designated superior court judge of the country in which the Commission is sitting.[1] While the judges who serve on the Commission are appointed for terms of five years, the lay commissioners hold office on a good-conduct tenure. The old provision whereby one of the lay commissioners was to be "of experience in railway business" was continued; and Mr. Price, the railway member of the former Commission, was reappointed. The qualification of the other lay commissioner was not specified. To this position Sir Frederick Peel, whose training was legal and who had been a member of the Railway Commission in 1873, was appointed. The lay commissioners were admonished of their judicial functions, for in their letters of appointment they were informed, "Doubtless you will feel that the judicial nature of your office is also incompatible with any active engagement in political controversies."

In every possible way the fact was emphasized that the Commission was a court, and therefore not concerned with rate making. The control of matters pertaining to rates was divided. Powers in regard to conciliation of rate difficulties were given to the Board of Trade. When the provision placing the revision of maxima and of classification in the hands of the Board of Trade was under consideration, an amendment to place such revision in the hands of the Commission was negatived.

The Act of 1888, while it repealed portions of the railway regulative acts already in existence, did not codify the portions remaining. Consequently there are still in effect sections of the

[1] The draft legislation of 1887 had provided a cumbrous arrangement whereby the judicial commissioner was to preside when a question of law was involved, while in other matters his attendance was to be invited by the lay commissioners, "if it was expedient for the better performance of the Commission's duties."

Railway Clauses Consolidation Act, 1845, the Railway and Canal Traffic Act, 1854, the Regulation of Railways Act, 1868, and the Regulation of Railways Act, 1873. Since 1888 jurisdiction in regard to actual rates has been given by an Act of 1894 ; while, under a law of 1904, the powers of the Commission in regard to private sidings have been made more definite by an interpretation of the "reasonable facilities" clause of the Act of 1854.[1]

While the jurisdiction given by the Act of 1888 embraces a variety of functions, the most important of which are undue preference, facilities for traffic, traffic on steamboats, through rates, rate books, terminals, legality of rates, provisions relating to private branch sidings, and references under the Board of Trade Arbitrations Act, 1874, the most important matters from the standpoint of the traders are (*a*) terminals, (*b*) reasonable facilities, (*c*) through rates, (*d*) undue preference, (*e*) control over actual rates.

Terminals, Reasonable Facilities and Through Rates

The history of the terminal question is a long and involved one. When the earlier railways were chartered, the "canal toll" idea prevailed. For a time carriers, already in existence, quoted through rates over the railway lines, making such arrangements as they deemed proper in regard to payments for special services and for station terminals. It was not long, however, before the railways controlled the forwarding business, and complaint soon arose. The railways claimed the right, in addition to the powers given them under their maximum rates, to make charges for additional services and for terminals.[2] The traders contended that the maximum rates covered all that the railways were

[1] For detail concerning the unrepealed sections, see Woodfall, The New Law and Practice of Railway and Canal Traffic, etc., Appendix A.

[2] The question of terminals has come up in the United States. The charter of the Pittsburg & Connellsville Railway gave it the right to charge tolls. It was decided it had the right to charge terminals as well. *National Tube Works* v. *Baltimore & Ohio R.R.* (Penn.), 28 Am. and Eng. R'd Cases, 13.

legally empowered to collect. It was concerning the station terminals, however, that the keenest contention existed. The Select Committee of 1882 had recommended that terminal charges should be recognized, but that they should be subject to publication by the companies, and that in case of challenge they should be sanctioned by the Railway Commission.[1] A clause to this effect was contained in the regulative measure introduced by Mr. Chamberlain in 1884. In a decision of the Court of Queen's Bench in 1885 the right of the railways to collect terminals was definitely recognized.[2] But the traders did not recognize this decision as final; for, because of a technical condition, it was impossible to carry the case before the higher courts. While the legislation of 1888 was in committee, various attempts were made to place the control of terminals under the Railway Commission, as well as to provide that in every case the maximum rates should include terminals. But the government took the position that terminals were legally established, and so they were given explicit recognition. *

The Act of 1888 had recognized terminals. The Provisional Orders Acts gave them definite form. The matter was finally passed on by the Commission in 1891 in a decision which upheld that of 1885.[3] Justice Wills, who gave the decision in the former terminal case, was at this time the judicial member of the Commission. On appeal the decision of the Commission was upheld. While the question of the legality of terminals has thus been settled, there still remains the question of the right of the trader to be exempt from the payment of terminals under special conditions. This question is of especial interest

[1] Select Committee on Railways, 1882, pp. v and xvii.

[2] *Hall* v. *London, Brighton, & South Coast Railway*, 15 Q. B. D. 505. This overruled a decision of the Railway Commission. A discussion of the question from the traders' standpoint will be found in Hunter, The Railway and Canal Traffic Act, 1888, pp. 38–50. See also British Railways and Canals, by "Hercules," chap. ii (a pro-trader brochure, published in London in 1885). A summary of the railway point of view will be found in the address of Mr. Pope, Q.C., representing the London & Northwestern Railway before the Board of Trade, October 29, 1889, reported in *Railway News*, November 2, 1889, pp. 778–780. See also Grierson, Railway Rates, English and Foreign, pp. 93–106.

[3] *Sowerby & Co.* v. *Great Northern Ry. Co.*, 7 Ry. and Canal Traffic Cases, 156.

in connection with the mining and manufacturing districts, where the establishments furnishing and receiving freight are usually situated on private sidings or on private railways. The importance of these sidings is shown in the fact that, while at the Sheffield freight station the tonnage in 1900 was 580,000, at a near-by siding it was 1,100,000. In 1894 the Commission was given jurisdiction in claims for exemption from payment of terminal charges at sidings when it was alleged that the services had not been performed. Under the provision of the Act of 1888, requiring the railway to distinguish conveyance from terminal charges, it had been held that the responsibility of the railway might be discharged by stating that the whole payment was for a conveyance rate.[1] But the Court of Appeal decided in 1897 that it was incumbent on the railway, in such a case to prove that it did not charge for terminals.[2] The Commission has power to allow a rebate from sidings charges without proof that any definite amount of terminal is included in the rate. A *prima facie* case for such a rebate is made out, if it is shown that, in respect of similar traffic between substantially the same termini, and passing over substantially the same routes, a sidings trader who does not require or use any terminal accommodation or services is charged the same amount as a trader who uses the station.[3] But the latter rate must not be simply a paper rate.[4] In calculating the amount of the rebate, it has, in general, been the practice of the Commission to follow the rule in Pidcock's case; i.e., to assume that the service charges are in the same proportion to the rates actually charged as the maximum service charge would be to the sum of the maximum rates, — i.e., the maximum rate and the maximum terminals.[5]

[1] *New Union Mill Co.* v. *Great Western Ry. Co.*, 9 Ry. and Canal Traffic Cases, 160.

[2] *Salt Union, Ltd.* v. *North, Staffordshire Ry. and Others*, 10 Ry. and Canal Traffic Cases, 179.

[3] *Vickers, Sons & Maxim, Ltd.* v. *Midland Ry. and Others*, 11 Ry. and Canal Traffic Cases, 259.

[4] *Cowan & Sons* v. *North British Ry.*, 11 Ry. and Canal Traffic Cases, 271.

[5] *Pidcock* v. *Manchester, Sheffield & Lincolnshire Ry.*, 9 Ry. and Canal Traffic Cases, 45.

The through-rate clause of the Act of 1888 provides that through rates, stating the amount, route, and apportionment of the rate, may be proposed by a railway, a canal company, or a trader. In case of dispute regarding the rate or its apportionment the matter is brought before the Commission. In apportioning the through rate, the commissioners are to consider the special circumstances of the cases, and are not to compel any company to accept lower mileage rates than it may for the time legally be charging for like traffic, carried by a like mode of transit on any other line of communication, between the same points, being the points of departure and arrival of the through route.

Reasonable facilities in general must be such as can reasonably be required of the railway company, due allowance having been made for the way in which the service is already performed.[1] Similarly, in a reduced through rate there must always be considered whether there is a commensurate advantage to the railway company.[2] *Prima facie*, it is against public interest to interfere with vested legal rights, unless some compensation or equivalent is given. There must, therefore, be evidence both of public interest and reasonableness in favor of the rate and route sufficient to outweigh the former considerations.[3] The fact that two competing routes will tend to make either company treat the traders more reasonably is a consideration bearing on the question of public interest.[4] At the same time the Commission will not grant a through rate which creates unhealthy competition.[5] If there are grounds for the Commission granting something claimed as a proper facility for using railways, an objection grounded on its inconvenient consequences to railway companies

[1] *Newry Navigation Co.* v. *Great Northern Ry.* (Ireland), 7 Ry. and Canal Traffic Cases, 176.

[2] *Plymouth Incorporated Chamber of Commerce* v. *Great Western Ry. & L. & S. W. Ry.*, 9 Ry. and Canal Traffic Cases, 72; 10 *Ibid.* 17.

[3] *Didcot, Newbury & Southampton Ry.* v. *Great Western Ry. & L. & S. W. Ry.*, 9 Ry. and Canal Traffic Cases, 210.

[4] *Plymouth, Devonport & S. W. Ry.* v. *Great Western Ry. & L. & S. W. Ry.*, 10 Ry. and Canal Traffic Cases, 68.

[5] *Didcot, Newbury & Southampton Ry.* v. *L. & S. W. Ry. and Others*, 10 Ry. and Canal Traffic Cases, 17.

by reason of arrangements made by themselves will not be sufficient reason for not granting it.[1] The particular circumstances of the proposed route and rate must be considered. The reasonableness of a rate over a proposed route is not to be measured by an existing rate over an alternative route, even if the rate over the latter route may be reasonable.[2]

Incident to granting a through rate, a through booking (ticketing) arrangement may also be made.[3] While the Commission has not attempted to lay down any general principle on which through rates are to be apportioned, it will consider any special expenses in construction or special charges a company may have been empowered to make.[4] It is not clear that the Commission has power to rescind a through rate once established under the Act of 1888.[5] So far no such action has been taken.

In the claims made by canal and by dock companies to obtain through rates, considerable emphasis has been laid upon the technical interpretation of the word "railway." Thus it was decided in 1897 that the powers the Manchester Ship Canal possessed to construct railways on its quays, although these railways were simply for its own service, constituted it a railway company. In 1901 the action of the Commission in approving a through-rate arrangement for a dock company was overruled on the ground that the railways possessed by the dock company did not constitute a railway within the meaning of the act.[6] In

[1] *Corporation of Birmingham & Sheffield Coal Co., Ltd.* v. *Manchester, Sheffield & Lincolnshire Ry., Midland Ry., & L. & N. W. Ry.*, 10 Ry. and Canal Traffic Cases, 62.

[2] *Didcot, Newbury & Southampton Ry., etc.* v. *Great Western Ry., etc., ut supra.*

[3] *Didcot, Newbury & Southampton Ry.* v. *Great Western Ry. & L. & S. W. Ry.*, 10 Ry. and Canal Traffic Cases, 1.

[4] *Forth Bridge & North British Ry. Co.* v. *Great North of Scotland Ry. & Caledonian Ry.*, 11 Ry. and Canal Traffic Cases, 1. This would cover, for example, "bonus mileage," or an arbitrary, in the case of an expensive bridge.

[5] *Great Northern Central Ry.* (Ireland) v. *Donegal Ry.*, 11 Ry. and Canal Traffic Cases, 47.

[6] *London and East India Docks Co.* v. *Great Eastern Ry. & Midland Ry.*, 11 Ry. and Canal Traffic Cases, 57. This was a majority decision, Peel dissenting. The decision of the Court of Appeal was given by Mr. Justice Wright, who was a member of the Commission when the Manchester Canal case was decided. He distinguished the cases.

1903 a further application of the same company, subsequent to its acquisition of a short railway with which it had made connections, was refused on the ground that the difficulties of exchange of traffic did not justify the granting of such an application.

The Commission has looked at each through-rate case by itself. It has refrained from proposing a through rate. It has limited its action to the acceptance or rejection of the proposed through rate as brought before it. The power to propose through rates has been of little value to the traders. Normally, they have not been possessed of the exact knowledge necessary to the making of a through rate, with the result that they have been successful only in one out of five applications. The following summary gives details with reference to the through-rate applications formerly acted upon by the Commission :

Year	By Canal Company		By Dock Company*		By Railway Company*		By Traders		By Municipal Corporation and Traders	
	Granted	Refused	Granted	Refused	Granted	Refused	Granted	Refused	Granted	Refused
1895 . .	2	–	–	–	–	–	1	1	–	–
1896 . .	1	–	–	–	1	–	–	–	–	–
1897 . .	1	–	–	–	3	–	–	–	–	1
1898 . .	–	–	–	–	–	–	–	–	–	–
1899 . .	–	–	–	–	2	1	–	–	–	–
1900 . .	–	–	–	–	–	–	–	–	–	–
1901 . .	–	–	–	–	–	–	–	–	–	–
1902 . .	–	–	1	–	–	–	–	–	–	–
1903 . .	–	–	–	2	–	–	–	2	–	–

* No action prior to 1895.

Undue Preference

The question of "undue preference" has long engaged attention in England. Complaints were made during the investigations of 1882 that many anomalies existed in domestic rates. Thus London sugar refiners complained that, while Greenock was double the distance from given points, sugar was being carried to these points at the same rates as were given to London.[1] But it was against low import or *preferential* rates, which intensified the competition to which different industries were subjected, that special attention was directed.[2] The Act of 1873 had left much to the discretion of the Railway Commission in dealing with the question of undue preference. In the parliamentary discussions of 1887 and 1888 there were constant complaints of preferential rates. It was stated that no general measure dealing with railway traffic could be considered satisfactory which did not prevent preferential rates in favor of foreign products.[3] The government held, however, that no difference should be made between English merchandise and foreign merchandise because of origin.[4]

The undue preference section of the Act of 1888 provides that where, for the same or similar services, lower rates are charged to one shipper than are charged to another, or any difference in treatment is made, the burden of proof that such actions do not constitute an undue preference shall be on the railway. In considering whether the action complained of constitutes an undue preference, the commissioners are to consider "whether such lower charge or difference in treatment is necessary for the purpose of securing in the interests of the public the traffic in respect of which it is made. *Provided that no railway company shall make, nor shall the commissioners sanction, any difference in the tolls, rates, or charges made for or any difference in the treatment of home and foreign merchandise in respect of the same or similar services.*"[5] The final clause of the

[1] See evidence of J. H. Balfour Browne before the Select Committee of 1882, explanatory of the factors involved, answers to questions 1297 and 1298.

[2] In addition to the evidence bearing on this point contained in the Select Committee Report of 1882, see also detail in the Report of the Royal Commission on Depression of Trade and Industry, 1886.

[3] Motion of Earl of Jersey, Hansard, 1888, third series, Vol. 322, p. 1796. This was defeated by a vote of 72 to 45.

[4] Lord Salisbury, Hansard, 1888, third series, Vol. 323, p. 1052.

[5] I have italicized this so as to bring out the distinction of treatment between home and foreign traffic. In the bill, introduced in 1887, clause 25 provided that the commissioners were to consider whether the difference in charges or treatment was necessary "for the purpose of securing the traffic in respect of which it was made." The vague phrase, "in the interests of the public," contained in the legislation of 1888, was placed in the Bill of 1887 by amendment.

section prohibits a higher charge for similar services, for the carriage of a like description and quantity of merchandise, for a less than is charged for a greater distance on the same line of railway. The concluding clause of the section is not only wider than the "long and short haul" clauses of the American statute, it is also much wider than the prohibition hitherto existing in English legislation. An attempt was made by the railway interest to have a "long and short haul" clause placed in the legislation. It was argued that where a question of preferential rates came up, the comparison should in fairness to the railway be made with traffic carried over the same portion of the line.[1] It was held, however, that the consideration of this matter could safely be left to the discretion of the Commission.

Complaints concerning undue preferences have occupied a prominent place before the Commission. Broadly speaking, the subject-matter of these falls under the headings of: (*a*) *differential rates*, concerned with disparities in domestic rates and including as subheads export rates, group rates, and rebates in respect of quantity; (*b*) *preferential rates*, concerned with disparities between home and import traffic. Before 1888 inequalities of charges for like services were only *prima facie* evidence, and the burden of proof was on the complainant: now it is on the railway. In the earlier decisions no rule is apparent. Each case was considered by itself. A decreased rate to develop a particular traffic in a particular district was an undue preference. The mere fact preference existed was not sufficient: it must be shown to be "undue" and "unreasonable." Differences in rate might be allowed where there were differences in the cost of conveyance.[2]

[1] The proposal was voted down, both in Grand Committee of the House of Commons and in the House itself. The motion will be found in Hansard, 1888, third series, Vol. 329, p. 452. The statement of Mr. Acworth, Hearings before the Committee on Interstate Commerce of the United States Senate, etc., 1905, Vol. III, p. 1851, that there is in the Act of 1888, a "long and short haul" clause — "the short distance included in the long distance" — is evidently attributable to the fact that he had not a copy of the act before him.

[2] For a summary of the law on this point, prior to 1888, see Woodfall, *op. cit.*, pp. 77–82. See also Darlington, Railway Rates, chap. iv.

Additional points have been made under the present Commission. A contract to give exclusive use of a given station to a particular colliery is an undue preference, as are also lower tolls given by a navigation company to prevent a large dealer moving his business.[1] Normally, similar charges should be made for similar services.[2] An unreasonable preference is a question of fact, and no general principle will be laid down.[3] Competition is a circumstance to be taken into consideration, and the extent to which it is to be considered is a question of fact, not law.[4] There can be no mathematical equality in regard to the charges or advantages between places which are outside of a group and the different members of a group. Competition and convenience to the neighborhood are to be considered as affecting the justifiability of a group rate.[5]

On the question of differential rates the Commission has reversed itself. As has been indicated, the Commission is empowered to consider whether the rate complained of "is necessary for the purpose of securing in the interests of the public the traffic in respect of which it is made." In 1890[6] complaint was made that lower rates on grain and on flour were given from Cardiff to Birmingham than from Liverpool to Birmingham. The distances were respectively 173 and 98½ miles. The railway company contended that this was on account of competition and that the lower rate was necessary (1) in its own interest, (2) in the interests of the public. Direct inland communication

[1] *Rishton Local Board* v. *Lancashire & Yorkshire Ry.*, 8 Ry. and Canal Traffic Cases, 74; *Fairweather and Others* v. *Corporation of York*, 11 Ry. and Canal Traffic Cases, 201.

[2] *Timm & Son* v. *Great Eastern Ry.*, *Lancashire & Yorkshire Ry.*, *and Others*, 11 Ry. and Canal Traffic Cases, 214.

[3] *Per* Lord Herschell in *Pickering Phipps and Others* v. *London & N. W. Ry. and Others*, on appeal, 8 Ry. and Canal Traffic Cases, 100, 101; *Inverness Chamber of Commerce* v. *Highland Railway Co.*, 11 Ry. and Canal Traffic Cases, 218.

[4] *Pickering Phipps*, case cited, p. 87. Group rates are authorized by Section 29 of the Act of 1888. See in this connection the important decision given in *Denaby Main Colliery Co.*, *Ltd.* v. *M. S. & L. S. Ry.*, 11 App. Cas. 97.

[5] *Pickering Phipps*, *etc.*, 87–88.

[6] *Liverpool Corn Traders' Association* v. *London & N. W. Ry.*, 7 Ry. and Canal Traffic Cases, 125.

exists between Bristol and Birmingham by way of the Severn river and canal navigation. There is also a combined sea and rail route.

Justice Wills pertinently said Parliament had dealt with the matter of undue preferences with a "faltering hand." It had left to the Commission the responsibility of deciding many things which would more naturally have been laid down in legislation.[1] The somewhat inchoate nature of the undue-preference clause is, however, more correctly attributed to its compromise origin. While it was intended, in a general way, that the phrase "in the interests of the public" should protect the interests of the consumers, Justice Wills was undoubtedly correct in saying that Parliament had no clear idea of what it meant. He considered that the "public interest" must be something wider than that of one of the two localities concerned, and stated that he could not see that any important "public interest" would be affected if the traffic in grain and flour should have to seek some other route from Cardiff to Birmingham.[2] The action of the railway in engaging in such competition created artificial conditions which interfered with the natural course of trade. Sir Frederick Peel put this point still more strongly: "A traffic which differs only from other traffic in being competitive can have no such a distinction made in its favor, however necessary a lower charge may be to meet the competition, or however much it may be to the benefit of the company to secure the traffic." The attempt of the railway to compete with the "natural advantages" of the traffic which went from the Severn ports[3] by sea and rail, or by inland water navigation, to Birmingham was unjustifiable. His general reasoning rested on the assumption that the low rail rate from Cardiff gave "little or no profit," and that therefore a penalty was being placed on Liverpool in the "highly remunerative rate" it paid.[4]

The unsatisfactory position taken by this decision in regard to the effect of competition, and the extent to which this was

[1] P. 137. [2] Pp. 136–138.

[3] These are Cardiff, Portishead, Avonmouth, Bristol, and Sharpness.

[4] Pp. 140, 141.

to be taken into consideration, was, however, apparently justified by the decisions on the matter. While the law was confused and contradictory, the leading decision — Budd's case — ruled water competition out of consideration.[1] The effect of water competition on the undue-preference clause was brought up again in 1892.[2] Complaint was made of an undue preference in flour and grain between the Severn ports and Birmingham, on the one hand, and Birkenhead and Birmingham, on the other. While the rate from Birkenhead to Birmingham, a distance of 98 miles, was 11*s.* 6*d.*, the rate from Bristol to Birmingham, a distance of 141 miles, was 8*s.* 6*d.* The railway contended that the apparent anomaly was attributable to water competition. Both a majority and a minority decision were given. In the dissenting opinion, delivered by Sir Frederick Peel, it was held that, while the evidence justified low rates from the Severn ports, at the same time the Birkenhead rate should be reduced so as to give a lower mileage rate. The majority opinion upheld the railway position. The rates complained of were attributable to effective competition, maintained by a competing railway and by water competition. The existing inequality in rates was necessary to give the section of country around Birmingham the advantage of the supplies both from the Severn ports and from Birkenhead. Justice Wills stated that in the former decision he had construed "public interest" too narrowly. The public intended was the public of the locality or district. Any considerable portion of the population in general as opposed to an individual or an association was sufficient.[3]

While it is contended that one principle was applied in the first Corn Traders' case, because the amount of traffic affected

[1] *Budd (P. O.)* v. *L. & N. W. Ry.*, 4 Ry. and Canal Traffic Cases, 394. The cases bearing on this subject are dealt with by Justice Wills in his decision. See also Lord Herschell in *Pickering Phipps*, *infra*, 104, 105. See also Butterworth and Ellis, A Treatise on the Law relating to Rates and Traffic on Railways and Canals, etc., pp. 168–170.

[2] *Liverpool Corn Traders' Association* v. *Great Western Ry.*, 7 Ry. and Canal Traffic Cases, 114.

[3] *Liverpool Corn Traders' Association* v. *Great Western Ry.*, 7 Ry. and Canal Traffic Cases, 127.

was small, and that a different principle was applied in the second case because the amount of traffic affected was large,[1] it would appear that the change of position was, in reality, attributable to a decision in a case appealed from the Commission in 1891.[2] In this the construction of "public interest" had been involved. It was contended that a difference in rate complained of was not necessary for the purpose of securing the traffic in the public interest, and that the railway in making such a rate was seeking its own interest, not that of the public. This attempt to exclude the railway interest from "public interest" was denied by Lord Herschell. The point which should be considered, he stated, was not only the legitimate desire of the railway to obtain traffic, but also whether it was in the interest of the railway to secure this traffic rather than abandon it. The legislature, he continued, had recognized that there were cases where the traffic could not be obtained if the lower rate was raised, and where at the same time it would be unfair to demand as a condition of obtaining the traffic a reduction of the higher rate.[3] By judicial construction "public interest" has thus come to mean the controlling power of effective competition on particular rates. Undoubtedly there was a desire, when the legislation was under consideration in Parliament, to give the phrase a narrower construction. In 1887 it was stated that the railway, in carrying traffic on a rate competitive with sea-borne traffic, must show that there was a distinct public interest involved. The fact that some additional profit was obtained by engaging in such traffic was not sufficient.[4]

The "long and short haul" question comes before the Commission but seldom. When it does, it is not treated, as in the United States, as a form of preference demanding exceptional

[1] See Boyle and Waghorn, The Law relating to Railway and Canal Traffic, Vol. I, p. 4; also evidence of Mr. W. M. Acworth, Committee on Interstate Commerce, etc., 1905, Vol. III, p. 1849.

[2] *Pickering Phipps and Others* v. *L. & N. W. Ry. and Others*, 8 Ry. and Canal Traffic Cases, 83.

[3] *Pickering Phipps, etc.*, 102 and 103.

[4] See statement of Lord Salisbury, Hansard, 1887, third series, Vol. 314, p. 332.

treatment. The Commission has recognized effective competition as a justification of a lower rate for the longer distance. Where a higher rate is charged for the shorter than for the greater distance, the less being included in the greater, the Commission has held that, in the absence of effective competition at the longer distance point, such an arrangement is not justifiable, and that the shorter distance point should share on a mileage basis in the low rate given to the longer distance point.[1] The effect of competition has also been recognized in the case of export traffic. In 1903, in the Spillers & Bakers case, a low "shipment" rate was held necessary to obtain traffic. It was considered impossible to raise this rate, and the dissimilarity of circumstances did not warrant a comparison of the higher domestic rate with the lower export rate.[2] In 1904 a briquette manufacturing firm claimed that it was unduly prejudiced, since it paid the domestic rate on its raw material, while the manufactured product came into competition abroad with coal carried on a low export rate. The Commission upheld the principle of export rates, and further found that the railway was under no obligation to regulate its charges with reference to the ultimate competition complained of.[3]

From an early date English railway law has held that wholesale rates for large shipments do not constitute an undue preference. So early as 1858 in Nicholson's case, a leading case, it was decided that carrying at a lower rate in consideration of large quantities and full train loads at regular periods was justifiable, provided the real object was to obtain a greater profit by reduced cost of carriage. In taking this point of view, it was recognized that various shippers would necessarily be excluded from the advantage of the low rate granted on such conditions.[4] In the decisions of the Commission of 1873 it was recognized

[1] *Timm & Sons* v. *N. E. Ry., Lanc. & York Ry., and Others*, 11 Ry. and Canal Traffic Cases, 214.

[2] *Spillers & Bakers, Ltd.* v. *Taff Vale Ry.;* 20 The Times L. R. 101.

[3] *Lancashire Patent Fuel Co., Ltd.* v. *L. & N. W. Ry., Great Central Ry., and Others.* A summary will be found in the *Railway Times*, August 13, 1904.

[4] *Nicholson* v. *Great Western Ry.*, 5 C. B. (N. S.) 366. The test of the agreement complained of will be found in the footnotes to pp. 382–408. See also *Evershed* v. *L. & N. W. Ry.* (1877), 2 Q. B. Div. 267.

that lower rates might be given because of train-load shipments or of ability to load a greater weight into trucks.[1] The general justification of such arrangements has been recognized by the present Commission.

An example from a case decided in 1900 will indicate the nature of the arrangement.[2] A rebate of 3*d.* per ton from the established rate was to be made on condition that a minimum shipment of 25,000 tons of coal a year was guaranteed, and that the arrangement should last for five years. The Commission has, in various cases, held such rebates excessive.[3] The ground taken has been that the rebate is justified by a reduction in cost to the company, and that the rebate should not be in excess of the saving to the company. It is obvious that such a practice as this has dangers connected with it. A considerable number of complaints have been directed against the excessive advantages obtained by Messrs. Rickett, Smith & Co. under their rebate arrangement with the Midland Railway. In one case, though the evidence is contradictory, there are the earmarks of a secret rebate.[4] While the decisions of the old Commission recognized bulk of traffic as a justification for reduction of rates, the policy of the present Commission has not been clear cut. In some cases it has recognized quantity as a justification for a rebate.[5] But it has in other cases attempted to confine cost to mere economies of bookkeeping, attributable to more prompt settlements, etc.; [6] and it has expressed the dictum that rebates in respect of quantity would justify a differentiation of charges in so many cases that

[1] E.g. *Ransome* v. *Eastern Counties Ry.* (No. 2), 1 Ry. and Canal Traffic Cases, 109; *Girardot, Flinn & Co.* v. *Midland Ry.*, 4 Ry. and Canal Traffic Cases, 291; *Greenop* v. *S. E. Ry.*, 2 Ry. and Canal Traffic Cases, 319.

[2] *Daldy and Others* v. *Midland Ry. and Others*, 10 Ry. and Canal Traffic Cases, 305.

[3] E.g. *Charrington, Sells, Dale & Co.* v. *Midland Ry. Co.*, 11 Ry. and Canal Traffic Cases, 222; *Wallsall Wood Colliery Co.* v. *Midland Ry.*, *Railway Times*, July 25, 1903.

[4] *Charrington, Sells, Dale & Co.*, *ut supra*, p. 229.

[5] *Daldy and Others*, *ut supra*, p. 310. See also *Hickelton Main Colliery Co.* v. *Hull & Barnsley Ry.*, *Railway Times*, July 25, 1903. In this case the consideration of the lower rate was a minimum of 38,000 tons per annum.

[6] E.g. *Charrington, Sells, etc.*, *ut supra*, 230.

the rule against preference would be in danger of disappearing, "and the small trader would be in a more helpless position than the position in which he now is."[1]

While the traders recognize the value of export rates, and the effects of competition thereon, the conditions which affect the import rate are often neglected, and the low rail rates given on imported goods are often attributed to the stupidity, if not turpitude, of the railways in preferring home to foreign goods. When the Act of 1888 provided that the Commission should not "sanction any difference . . . in the treatment of home and foreign merchandise in respect of the same or similar services," it was claimed that this absolutely forbade preferential rates, and that the home traffic would therefore be carried at the same as that of foreigners.[2] Notwithstanding this enthusiastic prediction there is at present a reiterated demand for a select committee to investigate the question of preferential rates.

The discussion of preferential rates in England has proceeded along lines familiar to every student of the effects of water competition on railway rates. "Why," asks one, "if they (the railways) can carry at a profit from foreign countries, can they not carry home produce at the same rate?"[3] If the London & Northwestern carried a train load of meat from Liverpool to London at 25*s*. because it was American, it should be able to do the same wherever the meat came from.[4] "*Ex hypothesi* they (the railways) already got a profit out of the produce they carried, . . . and what they would have to do was to put the English farmer and producer on the same footing as the foreigner."[5]

The question of preferential rates was brought before the Commission in 1895 in an exceedingly important case, which

[1] E.g. *Charrington, Sells, etc.*, *ut supra*, 231.

[2] Waghorn and Stevens, Report upon the Proceedings of the Inquiry held by the Board of Trade, 1889 and 1890, pp. 12 and 106. This report to the Lancashire and Cheshire, Devon and Cornwall, and Irish Conferences (traders' organizations), was published at Manchester in 1890. It contains a searching but extremely acrid and biased examination of the railway position.

[3] Lord Henniker, Hansard, 1885, third series, Vol. 315, p. 412.

[4] Mr. Mundella, Hansard, 1888, third series, Vol. 329, p. 413.

[5] Mr. Chamberlain, Hansard, 1888, third series, Vol. 339, p. 445.

lasted eight days.[1] Complaint was made that the railway charged lower rates from Southampton docks to London on the following goods of foreign origin — wool, hay, butter, cheese, lard, hops, fresh meat, bacon, hams — than it charged on similar articles of home origin, which were normally carried a shorter distance, and that the services rendered in respect of the foreign traffic were not less than those rendered for the home traffic in the proportion that the rates were lower. A few examples will serve to show the nature of the disparity complained of: —

Station	Distance Traveled	Rates on Fresh Meat, Hay, and Hops to London		
		Rate for Meat	Rate for Hay	Rate for Hops
Southampton docks	76 miles	17*s.* 6*d.*	5*s.*	6*s.*
Southampton town	76 "	26*s.* 3*d.*	9*s.* 8*d.*	20*s.* 10*d.*
Alton	45 "	9*s.* 2*d.*	7*s.* 4*d.*	20*s.*
Botley	76 "	27*s.* 6*d.*	9*s.* 8*d.*	22*s.* 7*d.*

Back of the complaint lay a competition of ports for foreign traffic. The London docks were in competition with the Southampton docks, which were owned by the London & Southwestern Railway.[2] Competition existed between the all water route to London and the water and rail route *via* Southampton.

At first the railway endeavored to justify the apparent anomalies on the grounds that the rates complained of were made on the basis of water competition, and that, besides, they were balances of through rates. But the Commission ruled that such matters could not be considered in evidence under the provisions of the Act. Under these conditions the railway had to fall back on the unsatisfactory standard of cost of service. It was shown that the rates for the home traffic covered a variety of services — e.g., receiving, weighing, loading, covering,

[1] *Mansion House Association on Railway and Canal Traffic for the United Kingdom* v. *London & Southwestern Railway*, 9 Ry. and Canal Traffic Cases, 20.

[2] When these docks were acquired by the railway in 1892, it was anticipated they would be a formidable competitor of the London docks. For information descriptive of the highly developed facilities for handling traffic at the Southampton docks, see *Railway Age*, July 1, 1904; *Railway News*, January 7, 1905.

superintendence, provision of station accommodation, switching — which were not included in the rate on the foreign goods. The foreign merchandise was less valuable, less liable to damage, more easily and expeditiously handled, could be dealt with at times more convenient to the railway, always in larger quantities, and generally in a much more economical manner. On account of better baling, to cite one example, three tons of foreign hops could be loaded into a truck that would hold only two and a half tons of English hops.

The traders contended that such conditions of traffic as regularity and quantity, while admitted, were not capable of being included in the "similar services" spoken of in the undue preference section. Their contention was in substance that, while there might be differences in the case of home traffic because of dissimilarity of circumstances, in the case of the foreign traffic it was intended that there should not, on any account, be any difference in favor of foreign goods.

Had the contention of the traders been successful, it would have established a principle. But the decision of the Commission, which has been claimed as a victory by both parties, was of a compromise nature, and proceeded on the careful lines already laid down that undue preference is a matter of the facts of the particular case. The articles with which the decision concerned itself were hops, fresh meat, and hay. These were the only articles in which there was any considerable traffic from the stations intermediate between Southampton and London. The rates quoted on the other articles were simply "paper" rates. Sir Frederick Peel, who decided on the facts, held that the differences between the home and the import rates on meat, hops, and hay were not justified.[1] While his colleagues accepted this opinion, it was with hesitation. They both had doubts as to the alleged preference on meat,[2] and justly so. The average consignment of foreign meat from Southampton was 37 tons. In a period of seventeen months 10,638 tons of meat were shipped in 286 consignments. On the other hand, from Salisbury, the leading English meat center concerned, 231

[1] Mansion House case, pp. 38, 39. [2] *Ibid.*, pp. 32 and 43.

tons in 825 consignments were shipped in the same period. It is apparent that, where the whole series of costs would be so different, the Commission strained the idea of cost of service to the breaking point, and in doing so favored the home producer.

The decision was based on the idea, manifestly correct, that it was the intention of the statute to eliminate competition from the factors to be considered. At the same time the majority of the Commission are satisfied that the real factor controlling the rate situation in this case is water competition. As was said by Justice Collins, there was "no reason or principle in leaving out of account the fact of a rival route by rail or water from the point of departure to the point of arrival in the case of goods from abroad and taking it into account, as it clearly may be taken into account, where the comparison is between home goods only."[1]

This unsatisfactory decision, which cost the traders £2000 in law costs, obtained no general principle for the traders, and at the same time forced the railways to depend upon the artificial justification of cost of service. While the decision is of such a nature that in a case where there is real competition of home and foreign products a different verdict might be given, no further action in regard to preferential rates has been taken before the Commission. In 1899 the question of preferential rates was brought before the Board of Trade under the conciliation clause, but no satisfactory agreement could be obtained.[2]

It was Mr. Chamberlain who introduced into the legislation the clause under discussion. The agitation in regard to preferential rates has been given an added vigor by his preferential trade movement. Back of much of the outcry concerning preferential rates is a hazy protectionism. The support Mr. Chamberlain has obtained, for example, in the iron and steel industry is in considerable part due to preferential rates on iron and

[1] Mansion House case, p. 32. See also the statement of Lord Cobham in *Didcot, Newbury & Southampton Ry. Co.* v. *Great Western Ry. & L. & S. W. Ry.*, 9 Ry. and Canal Traffic Cases, 210.

[2] Case 16, Seventh Report of the Board of Trade, under Section 31 of the Act of 1888.

steel products, although the matter is complicated by the export rates given by the railways of competing countries.[1]

The control over docks by railway companies, which was objected to at an earlier date as a source of discrimination,[2] has been increasing of recent years. The railways have found it necessary to obtain control not only of docks, but also of steamer lines connecting with the Continent, in order to obtain the through rates which are necessary, if the import and export traffic are to balance, and thus permit a more economical use of rolling stock.[3] Complaint is made that the railways are spending large sums in erecting docks and warehouses at ports in order to encourage foreign trade, thereby still further increasing the number of preferential rates. The provisions of the Act of 1888 with reference to the right of the traders to have through rates from foreign points distinguished into their domestic and foreign portions are somewhat ambiguous. In the Southampton case the traders were unable to ascertain the foreign portion of the rate. As a result of this condition, an attempt was made in 1904 to obtain a provision in a special railway act, requiring that the railway should distinguish on its rate books, in the case of imports on a through rate, the portions attributable to (1) land carriage abroad, (2) dock, harbor, and shipping charges abroad, (3) conveyance by sea, (4) dock, harbor, and shipping charges at the British port, (5) railway charges in the United Kingdom. This was voted down by 103 to 79 on the ground that it was unfair to pick out a particular company in connection with what was a general matter.[4]

[1] See *Report of the Tariff Commission* (Chamberlain), 1904, Vol. I: The Iron and Steel Industry, under heading "Preferential Rates." *Contra*, see "British Railways and Goods Traffic: Is Preference given to Foreign Products?" (A. Dudley Evans, *Economic Journal*, March, 1905).

[2] Section 27 of the draft Report of the Select Committee of 1882, p. xxviii.

[3] The practice of consigning goods on through rates is increasing. At the same time Continental railways — e.g. those of Belgium — refuse to make through rates, except with railway companies. As to the alleged evil effects of such arrangements, see remarks of Mr. Hanbury, president of the Board of Agriculture, Hansard, 1902, fourth series, Vol. 108, p. 1640. See also Boyle and Waghorn, *op. cit.*, Vol. I, p. 304.

[4] Lancashire and Yorkshire Railway Bill. For text of the Instruction, see Hansard, 1904, fourth series, Vol. 131, p. 1473.

The farmers of the United Kingdom are subject to competition from many points. To cite but a few examples: Algerian fruit and vegetables, French hops, Danish butter and eggs, compete with the home products. The hop rates complained of when President Hadley wrote still exist. Not only do the English farmers complain of preferential rates, there is also complaint from Ireland that the existing rate basis discriminates against Irish eggs, butter, and bacon. It should be noted, although such a consideration is ruled out by the Railway Commission, that the low rates complained of are balances of through rates. It costs about £10 for freight charges to place one ton of Algerian fruit or vegetables in London. In fruit shipments the foreigners have had the advantage that a considerable number of the British growers are not giving sufficient attention to grading and packing and, in general, to the requirements of consumers. The following may be taken as examples of the complaints in regard to Danish competition: —

	DISTANCE (mixed route)	RATE PER TON	
		Butter	Eggs
Esbjerg (Denmark) to Birmingham	553 miles	47*s.* 6*d.*	58*s.* 8*d.*
Armagh (Ireland) " "	358 "	42*s.* 6*d.*	50*s.*

The apparent disparity of rates on a distance basis disappears when it is remembered that on the Danish products there is a long water haul, and that there is also the difference between a car-lot and a less than car-lot basis. The Danish rates are quoted on minimum consignments of ten tons, while the Irish rates are based on three hundredweight.

The more enlightened English farmers recognize the effects of water competition. They know that it would not benefit them to have the through rate raised, as it would simply mean that the foreign produce would move more cheaply by an all water route. When the London & Southeastern Railway in 1887 placed foreign hops on the same rate basis as domestic hops, the result was that the former moved by water to London.

The English producer was injuriously affected by the increased competition which lowered the price. At present approximately 90 per cent of the Continental produce imported by way of Boulogne and Calais goes by water to London. While the farmers recognize the superior facilities for handling foreign goods, they at the same time consider that the disparity between home and foreign rates is too great.[1]

Some part of the complaint in regard to preferential rates is attributable to misunderstandings in regard to rate conditions as well as to a lack of initiative on the part of the farmers. The Royal Commission on Agriculture stated in 1897 that, while coöperation among farmers was necessary in order to obtain lower rates, this matter could not be helped on by legislation.[2] But little has been done by the farmers to accomplish this.[3] While there is much unorganized complaint in regard to agricultural rates, the farmers are presenting very little evidence before the Departmental Committee, which is at present investigating the matter. The railways have been more willing than the farmers to coöperate. For forty years the London & Northwestern has been collecting small consignments of agricultural produce along its lines. These it forwards in bulk, delivers them to the London salesmen, pays market dues, collects the proceeds from the salesmen, and forwards the balance to the shippers. The London & Southwestern, which does a large business in package freight, undertook recently to supply the farmers along its lines with copies of Pratt's *The Organization of Agriculture.* All of the railways have been active in giving special rates to encourage agricultural shipments.[4] But, while

[1] E.g. evidence of W. W. Berry, a prominent hop grower of Kent, before the Royal Commission on Agricultural Depression, 1897, answers to questions 49,190, 49,226, 49,258. See also statement of Mr. Sinclair, Hansard, 1904, fourth series, Vol. 136, p. 295.

[2] Final Report, p. 529.

[3] See statement of the president of the Board of Agriculture, Hansard, 1902, fourth series, Vol. 108, p. 1639.

[4] For full detail concerning the special arrangements made by British railways in this regard, see Railway Rates and Facilities, copy of correspondence between the Board of Agriculture and Fisheries and the Railway Companies of Great Britain, etc., 1904. A large number of details bearing on the question of

the Danes are shipping produce into England on relatively low rates, which are the result of coöperation, 70 per cent of the domestic agricultural shipments on the Northeastern Railway are below three hundredweight, and 90 per cent fall below one ton.

Control over Actual Rates

In dealing with the rate policy of the Commission, a distinction must be made between the period prior to 1894 and that subsequent thereto. Though it had been stated in 1872 that legal maximum rates afforded but little real protection to the public,[1] the system was continued by the Act of 1888. While the work of the Board of Trade, as embodied in the Provisional Orders Acts, meant in all cases the systematization and in many cases the reduction of the maxima, the outcome was not satisfactory to the traders, some of whom wanted a general reduction of rates, regardless of the cost to the railways. The change of status in regard to *reasonable* rates introduced by the Act of 1888 was more apparent than real. The former Railway Commission had stated that, in addition to there being a necessity that rates charged should be within the maximum, there was also the added requirement that they must be reasonable.[2] No legal action had been taken, however, in regard to this matter. Two judicial decisions given in 1883 and in 1887 seemed to uphold the position that a maximum rate sanctioned by Parliament was conclusively reasonable.[3] But the statements in these decisions are simply dicta, since the question of reasonableness of rates was not directly involved. The Act of 1888, however, settled that the maximum rate was conclusive of reasonableness.[4]

preferential rates will be found in Pratt's Railways and Their Rates. This book has come to hand since the material contained in this section was set up.

[1] Report of the Joint Select Committee on Railway Companies Amalgamation, 1872, p. xxxiv.

[2] Fourth Report of the Railway Commissioners, p. 6, Section 14.

[3] See *Manchester, Sheffield & Lincolnshire Co.* v. *Brown*, 8 App. Cas. 715, and *Great Western Railway Co.* v. *McCarthy*, 12 App. Cas. 218. In the latter case Lord Watson took the position, "*Prima facie*, I am prepared to hold that a rate sanctioned by the legislature must be taken to be a reasonable rate."

[4] See Act of 1888, Section 24, Subsection 6 and Subsection 10. Report of Board of Trade, 1890, on Classification of Merchandise Traffic, etc., p. 17.

At the outset of its work the only way in which the Commission was brought in touch with rates was through the provisions concerned with undue preference and with through rates. The Commission will not state beforehand that a rate is preferential.[1] One of the commissioners, Sir Frederick Peel, has taken the position that certain powers over actual rates were given to the Commission. He has construed the statement in the "undue preference" clause which directs the commissioners to consider "whether the inequality cannot be remedied without unduly reducing the rate charged to the complainant" to give a power of reducing the higher rates.[2] Concerning this interpretation there is some doubt. Justice Wills holds that the words in question do not confer any rate-making power, but simply indicate the circumstances to be considered.[3] In an Irish case in 1897, in which the question of distributive rates was involved, it was held that the rate to a shorter distance point should be 3*d.* per ton less than the rate to the longer distance point; but no attempt was made to determine the longer distance rate.[4] In 1900 a temporary reduction of a canal toll was directed.[5] However, it cannot be said that these decisions have established the power of the Commission to reduce rates under the undue preference clause. Sir Frederick Peel also holds that the Commission may fix a through rate, no matter what the railways concerned may have agreed upon. While this matter has not been passed on, the weight of opinion is against such an interpretation.[6] It would appear, although this also has not been passed upon, that the Commission has no power to test the

[1] *In re* Taff Vale Ry. Co., 11 Ry. and Canal Traffic Cases, 89.

[2] Note his dissenting opinion in the Liverpool Corn Traders' Association case in 1892.

[3] Select Committee on Railway Rates and Charges, 1893, answer to question 8268.

[4] *Carrickfergus Harbor Commissioners and Others* v. *Belfast Northern Counties Ry.*, 10 Ry. and Canal Traffic Cases, 74.

[5] *Fairweather & Co. and Others* v. *Corporation of York*, 11 Ry. and Canal Traffic Cases, 201.

[6] Evidence before Select Committee of 1893, answers to questions 7963, 7964, 7966. See also the extremely guarded statement of Justice Wills before the same committee, answer to question 8264.

reasonableness of an established through rate. While the Commission has power to fix a through rate, if the parties do not agree, it would appear, although this is a moot point, that it has no power to apportion such a rate.[1] The Commission stated explicitly in 1895 that it had no power under the Act of 1888 to inquire into the reasonableness of a particular rate.[2] The various reductions of rate which have been ordered in connection with the workmen's trains applications are given under an entirely different jurisdiction.[3]

In the matter of group rates there has been some conflict between the English and the Irish decisions. The former regard competition and convenience as the most important factors. The latter lay more stress on distance. The appeals from the Commission have settled that competition is as important a factor in connection with rates as geographical position.

The question of the reasonableness of particular rates was suddenly brought before the Commission in 1894. The adjustments necessary in putting into force the rates under the revised maxima were great. The fact that fully one half of the traffic is carried on exceptional rates, which are below the class rates, still further complicated matters.[4] At the same time there was an apparent desire on the part of some of the railways to give the traders an object lesson in regard to the disadvantages of the legislative intervention which had brought some maxima below the actual rates formerly charged. And so the maximum class rates were published as the actual rates effective January 1, 1893. The outcry which followed quickened the work of adjustment, and led to an undertaking on the part of the railways that the rate increase should not be more than 5 per cent. But this

[1] This point was raised in the Forth Bridge case, 11 Ry. and Canal Traffic Cases, 5, but was not passed upon.

[2] *West Ham Corporation* v. *Great Eastern Ry.*, 9 Ry. and Canal Traffic Cases, 15.

[3] E.g. *In re London Reform Union* v. *Great Eastern Ry.*, 10 Ry. and Canal Traffic Cases, 280. See Ferguson, Railway Rights and Duties, pp. 206, 207.

[4] For detail concerning these rates, see "Report on the Question of Slow Freights (England)," by Henry Smart, *Bulletin of the International Railway Congress*, July, 1904.

did not prevent the enactment of a piece of panic legislation, passed hurriedly and without due consideration.[1] By this act it was provided that, where rates were directly or indirectly increased after December 31, 1892, they were *prima facie* unreasonable. The fact that the rate complained of was within the maximum was not to be a justification of the increase. The Commission was given power to deal with complaints arising under this act, subject to the provision that an application was first to be made to the Board of Trade. Over seventeen hundred complaints were brought before the Board of Trade between the date of the passage of the act and the end of February, 1895.

In the investigations leading up to the Provisional Orders legislation the traders had all along been desirous of having the actual rates serve as maxima.[2] The evident intention of the majority of the members of the Select Committee of 1893 was that the rates in force at the end of 1892 should be the maxima.

In taking up the new functions imposed by the revolutionary Act of 1894, the Commission had a full appreciation of the difficulties of the new jurisdiction. Justice Collins said, "I cannot suppose that Parliament intended to take the management of these great trading companies [the railways] out of the hands of the practical men who work them, and to place it in the hands of the Railway Commissioners." The Commission had no intention to exercise a rate-making power. It was its intention to construe the legislation strictly. In the interpretation of the statute there was, however, a difference of opinion between the commissioners. Lord Cobham held that the Commission was not competent, of its own knowledge, to say whether a rate was reasonable or not. "No tribunal, however expert, would undertake to say that a 6*s.* 6*d.* rate for the carriage of coal from Derbyshire to London is reasonable, but that 6*s.* 9½*d.*

[1] A mass of detail pro and con will be found in the evidence attached to the Report of the Select Committee of 1893. See also Mavor, "The English Railway Rate Question," *Quarterly Journal of Economics*, April, 1894; Acworth, The Elements of Railway Economics, pp. 147–154.

[2] E.g. speech of J. H. Balfour Browne, already cited, p. 171. Evidence of Marshall Stevens before the Select Committee of 1893, answers to questions 2448 and 2518.

is unreasonable." The legislature had, however, given a standard of reasonableness in the rate of 1892, and the rate could not be increased above this unless good reasons were shown.[1] In endeavoring to obtain some definite standard of measurement of reasonableness, the Commission ruled out all reference to competition, or to that more inclusive system, charging what the traffic will bear.[2] The opinion of the traders, that the rates in force at the end of 1892 should be maximum rates, received a partial support from Lord Cobham, who held that the fact that a rate had not been increased prior to 1892 created a strong presumption against the railway because it had not increased the rate when it had the unchallenged right to do so;[3] but Justice Collins held that conditions prior to 1892 could be considered, and that the reasonableness of a rate was to be tested by conditions existing or apprehended before the legislation came into force.[4] Later decisions have taken into consideration conditions subsequent to 1894.[5] There still remained the question of the criterion of reasonableness. Justice Collins held that this should be cost of service. Reasonableness, he held, must be measured by reference to "the service rendered and the benefit received." This, in his opinion, pointed to cost of service as the base, because "the service rendered and the benefit received were unaffected by the prosperity or misfortune of the parties to the contract."[6] This squared with the views of the traders, who held that the true basis of a rate was cost of service.[7] The fact that the legislation provided, in the first

[1] *Derby Silkstone Coal Co., Ltd.* v. *Midland Ry.*, 9 Ry. and Canal Traffic Cases, 107.

[2] E.g. *Charlaw and Sacriston Collieries Co.* v. *Northeastern Ry.*, 9 Ry. and Canal Traffic Cases, 140. In *Black & Sons* v. *Caledonian Ry., etc.*, 11 Ry. and Canal Traffic Cases, 176, the Court of Sessions refused, on appeal, to grant the process which would enable the railway companies to investigate the books of the applicants to see what their profits had been during a given period.

[3] Derby Silkstone Coal Co. case, p. 130.

[4] *Ibid.*, p. 111.

[5] E.g. *Black & Sons*, *ut supra*.

[6] Derby Silkstone case, p. 113. The decision in this regard is based on *Canada Southern Ry. Co.* v. *International Bridge Co.*, 8 App. Cas. 731, 732.

[7] E.g., letter of Sir James Whitehead, president of the Mansion House Association, London *Times*, December 22, 1892; also speech of J. H. Balfour Browne, *ut supra*, p. 257.

instance, a rate of an antecedent period as a criterion of reasonableness would seem to show an intention of ruling out in the present rate any consideration of what the traffic would bear; for, if charging what the traffic would bear, in the present, were admitted as a present criterion of reasonableness, it is difficult to see how the past rate could serve as a standard of reasonableness, when, presumably, what the traffic would bear was something essentially different.

The increases in rates complained of, which have for the most part arisen in connection with coal traffic, have in a number of cases been indirect, attributable to decreases in the allowance made for wastage in the coal traffic, etc. The criterion the Commission has found it necessary to adhere to — cost of service — has tied it down to an arbitrary arrangement. To meet this condition, the railways have had recourse to technicalities savoring, in some instances, of subterfuge. It one case it was alleged that the increase complained of was attributable to an increase in the cost of cartage as distinguished from conveyance charges. The former fell under terminal services, over which the jurisdiction of the Commission was limited.[1]

No general principle has been established in the unreasonable-rate cases. The railways had claimed the right in 1893 to increase the rates by 5 per cent as compared with the rates in force in 1892. While the traders never recognized the validity of this claim, the Board of Trade by 1898 had accepted this arrangement as justifiable. The important Smith & Forrest case, which came up in 1899, was intended to test this arrangement.[2] Complaint was made by the oil refiners of Liverpool and Manchester that an increase of 5 per cent was unreasonable. The increase was in part direct, in part indirect, attributable to decreases in cartage rebates. The matters involved were pertinent to the whole freight traffic of the United Kingdom, and affected future

[1] *Mansion House Association, etc.* v. *L. & N. W. Ry.*, 9 Ry. and Canal Traffic Cases, 174. See especially the remarks of Lord Esher in the appeal proceedings, pp. 199, 200.

[2] *Smith & Forrest* v. *L. & N. W. Ry. and Others*, 11 Ry. and Canal Traffic Cases, 156.

as well as past rates. The railways introduced statistical evidence showing that, because of various increases in cost, particularly in the case of labor, expenses were 5.1 per cent higher in 1892 than in 1888 and 6.3 per cent higher in 1898 than in 1892. The railways desired to carry the comparisons back to 1872, when many of the old rates had been fixed; but the Commission considered 1888 a sufficiently remote date, and comparisons were made with the conditions of 1891. It was found that an increase of 3 per cent would be justified. The Commission has thus shown its intention to look at each case by itself. If a 5 per cent increase should be found justifiable in a particular case, it would not necessarily have any bearing on a later decision.

The desire of the Commission not to engage in any rate-making experiments has kept it from making any statements as to general rates. It has concerned itself with the reasonableness of particular rates. The Commission has painstakingly endeavored to get at the cost involved. The decisions have been compromises. Where decisions have been against the railways, damages have been awarded on the basis of the difference between the increase and what was deemed a justifiable increase; and the railways have been ordered to desist charging the unreasonable rates. In a recent case an attempt was made to obtain an expansion of the unreasonable-rate jurisdiction.[1] It was contended that it was unreasonable to increase a rate, although the increased rate was still below the point to which it had been decreased in 1894. The Commission did not, however, pass upon this question. It is apparent that, if such a contention were accepted, still more rigidity would be introduced into the system. The traders' anticipations as to the effect of the Act of 1894 have been nullified by the willingness of the Commission to consider conditions antecedent to the legislation. The whole position, it must be recognized, is an exceedingly artificial one. While the position taken by the Commission is strained and unsatisfactory, it is difficult to see, when it was specifically referred back to the conditions of

[1] *Millom & Askam Hematite Iron Co.* v. *Furness Ry. and Others*, reported in *Railway Times*, January 21, 1903.

1892, what other method it could have adopted. By acting as it has, a degree of elasticity has been retained for the process under the legislation which it otherwise would not have possessed.[1]

It was objected at the outset, that the judicial member would dominate the Commission, owing to the difficulty of distinguishing between law and fact. It has happened, however, that in the performance of their duties the lay members determine on questions of fact. At the same time, while the opinion of the *ex-officio* commissioner is final on a point of law, the lay members also form and express their opinions.

The government has throughout considered the requirement that one member of the Commission shall "be experienced in railway business" to mean that he shall have been a railway director or a railway manager.[2] Exception has been taken to this by the traders. To the attempt to obtain a business representative on the Commission, in addition to a railway representative, the railways are not opposed. It is from the government that the objection has come. Mr. Mundella, when president of the Board of Trade, said he would be glad to appoint a "really" business man who should be an impartial authority, fairly representative of the trading class. Mr. Mundella had stated that the Commission as then constituted was generally unsatisfactory.[3] An attempt was made by the traders in 1894 to so amend the legislation that one of the commissioners should be "experienced in trade or commerce." This was not pressed beyond the first reading.[4] Mr. Bryce, who succeeded Mr. Mundella, held, however, that no such restriction as his predecessor had favored

[1] The criticism directed against the Commission by Grinling, in British Railways as Business Enterprises, pp. 161–163, contained in Ashley's British Industries, is not wholly justified.

[2] Mr. Price, before his appointment to the Commission of 1873, had been chairman of the Midland Railway. Viscount Cobham, who succeeded Mr. Price in 1891, had been deputy chairman of the Great Western. On Viscount Cobham's resignation, early in the present year, he was succeeded by Mr. Gathorne-Hardy, who had been deputy chairman of the Southeastern.

[3] Hansard, 1894, fourth series, Vol. 28, pp. 792, 793.

[4] The text of this bill will be found in the *Railway Times*, June 16, 1894, p. 782. See also Report of the Select Committee of 1893, p. xiii.

should be placed on the choice of the government. The desire to have a commercial representative is still active. Believing that the commissioners should be assessors, possessed of expert knowledge, rather than judges, the traders have urged that the terms of the commissioners should not exceed ten years, so that there might be an opportunity to keep constantly in touch with actual conditions.

Looking at conditions as they are, it is apparent that the presence of a railway representative on the Commission has meant that those appearing before it have been more careful to give essential details. There is no real cause for complaint, from the traders' standpoint, concerning the services which the lay members have performed. The railway representative, for example, in the enforcement of the legislation of 1894 has followed very closely the ideas favored by the traders. Sir Frederick Peel has been willing to give a broad construction to the legislative provisions concerned with control of rates.

The average English trader asks for a process which shall be "short, sharp, and decisive." And to him the process of the Commission has undoubtedly been unsatisfactory. As a minimum, six weeks elapse between the filing of the application and the decision of the case.[1] In a number of cases more than a year has elapsed between the initial hearing and the decision. In some cases the delays are attributable to adjournments in order to permit the obtaining of more evidence.[2] In other cases delays have been caused by an endeavor to get the parties to settle the questions in dispute. When cases are appealed, there are further delays. While one case has been decided on appeal within two months after the decision of the Commission, the usual period is from six months to one year.

Notwithstanding the assumption in 1887, that giving a *locus standi* to governing bodies and to traders' associations would cause much litigation, the number of complaints is not great.

[1] The Rules of Procedure of the Commission allow twenty-one days after the filing of the application for the filing of replies.

[2] E.g. the important case of Spillers & Bakers, etc., was heard first December 9 and 10, 1903. It was then adjourned for further evidence, and was decided in July, 1904.

In the period 1889–1903 there have been, on the average, fifty applications a year; but many of these have been of minor importance. In the same period there have been on the average twenty-three decisions a year. But here there are many cases where one decision covers a group of identical cases.[1] Complaint has been made of the small number of days on which the Commission sits. In the nine years, 1896–1904, the average period the Commission has sat annually as a court is thirty-two days. This, it is true, is exclusive of the days when the Commission has sat to consider applications for sanctioning working agreements between railways, the time taken up in connection with the administrative duties of the Commission, and the days on which the registrar of the Commission has inquired into damages and interlocutory proceedings which would otherwise come before the commissioners acting as a court. Of these no record is kept; but, after making all allowance, it is apparent that the Commission is not overworked. It is apparent, however, as has been recognized by the traders themselves, that the mere enumeration of the number of days on which the Commission has sat is no criterion of its usefulness.[2]

The Commission is criticised on account of its expense. This criticism is, however, directed only to a slight extent against its cost of maintenance.[3] It is the expense of obtaining a decision that the critics have in mind. In recommending a limitation of the right of appeal, the committee of 1882 intended to limit expense. By providing for the intervention of the Board of Trade in various matters, the legislation of 1888 hoped that the expense of proceedings might be kept down. The attempt of the legislation of 1894 to lessen expense, by providing that costs should not be granted by the Commission, except in cases where the claim or the defense is frivolous or vexatious, was intended to obviate the burden of the fees of the railway lawyers falling

[1] See Table I, on p. 793.

[2] In this connection see the statement of Sir B. Samuelson, who was very active, on the traders' side, in the steps leading up to the legislation of 1888. Hansard, 1883, third series, Vol. 278, p. 1887.

[3] In 1903 the cost of maintenance of the Commission amounted to £6497.

on the trader, when defeated in a case. The admittedly high expenses are not attributable to the fees of the Commission, which are moderate,[1] but to the development of a technically equipped Railway Commission Bar. It was early seen that the necessary prominence of the lawyers employed would make the process relatively expensive. The same conditions existed in connection with the Commission of 1873. In the body of lawyers found practicing before the Commission are many whose names are prominent in the Parliamentary bar, — a practice whose fees are high. The legal work before the Commission has tended to fall into the hands of a relatively small number of practitioners.[2] Prior to 1894 it was the practice to allow costs for two lawyers, unless when some especially technical matter was involved.[3] Since 1894 there have been, on the average, two lawyers on each side in the traders' cases. Under these conditions the expense, in a case contested before the Commission, runs from £150 to £200 a day. The individual trader is able to lessen his expense where, as in the sidings' rent cases, a group of traders bring action on a common set of facts. Only in one case has a rate matter been presented before the Commission by the complainant himself; and he was unsuccessful. The judicial members of the Commission are opposed to the complainants appearing in person. While it is true that in one case, which was settled before trial, the total court costs to the complainant were £1; and these, with his other expenses, were reimbursed to him by the railway, it is apparent that those who

[1] See Railway and Canal Commission Procedure, Schedule III, Woodfall, *op. cit.* See also Senate Committee on Interstate Commerce, *ut supra*, Vol. V, Appendix B, p. 220. The Commission fees in rate cases, as a maximum, do not exceed £5.

[2] In the 58 traders' cases covered by the reported decisions down to 1902, 68 lawyers took part. Mr. J. H. Balfour Browne, K.C., who is the dean of the traders' legal forces, appeared in 41 cases; Mr. C. A. Cripps, in 36; Mr. E. Moon, in 31. In all there were 32 lawyers who appeared in more than three cases. Eight of these appeared in more than ten cases each. The leaders have not practiced exclusively on one side. For example, Mr. C. A. Cripps, who has appeared in 30 cases for the railways, has appeared in 6 cases on the traders' side.

[3] The registrar is the taxing officer of the Commission. See appeal from his decision in this connection in *Glamorganshire County Council* v. *Great Western Ry.*, 9 Ry. and Canal Traffic Cases, 1.

are aggrieved in small matters cannot afford to come before the Commission.[1] There have not been the migratory sessions of the Commission which the traders favor. The sessions are held in the capital cities of the countries concerned. It is cheaper to have the cases taken to the technically equipped lawyers in the capital cities than to have these come to the cases in local centers. If the case involves any matter of considerable moment, the contest has to be carried on against the Railway Association. This being so, the complaints have to be fought out by firms, groups of traders, trade associations, Chambers of Commerce, local governing bodies.[2] The cost of a suit before the Commission is, under these conditions, about the same as before any other high court.[3]

In view of the expense attaching to suits before the Commission, it has been urged that the power possessed by the Board of Trade under the Act of 1873 to institute proceedings before the Railway Commission should be utilized. While the railways would not object to the Board of Trade presenting before the Commission matters arising under the conciliation procedure of the Board, where its decisions have not been accepted by the railways, it has been held that this would interfere with the efficiency of the conciliation clause. The government has held that to make a government department public prosecutor in cases before the Railway Commission would savor rather of persecution than of prosecution.[4] One exception has been made to this general rule. In 1899 the Irish Department of Agriculture was empowered in its act of organization to present rate grievances before the Commission at the public expense. So far

[1] See evidence of T. Middleton before the Royal Commission on Agricultural Depression, 1897, answer to question 2361.

[2] One of the most interesting trade associations is the Mansion House Association, founded in 1889. It represented, before the Board of Trade in 1889–1890, 209 public and local authorities, 174 commercial and agricultural organizations, besides a large number of individuals.

[3] While the limitation of appeal reduces the expense, the powers of the Court of Appeal to grant costs in Commission cases is not affected by the legislation of 1894.

[4] Hansard, 1883, third series, Vol. 278, p. 1901, statement of Honorable Joseph Chamberlain.

there has been only one such case, in 1902. In this the Board of Agriculture was successful.

The Associated Chambers of Commerce urged in March, 1904, that, with a view to cheapness and expedition, the local county courts should be used in cases between the railways and the traders. This suggestion is especially intended to cover the case of the small trader. In one form or another it has been under discussion since the early nineties. Cases affecting railways already come before the county courts from time to time.[1] While the county court method of procedure might work fairly well in local matters, it is apparent that this procedure is unfitted for matters of more general interest. There would also be a defect in that the way is open for a lack of expedition. Appeals may be taken on points of law or equity from the decisions of the county court. In the consideration of these appeals the high courts are empowered to draw inferences of facts. Exceedingly small matters are appealed at present. In 1904 one appeal was concerned with an alleged overcharge of 11½*d.* on a railway journey.[2] It has been suggested, however, that the cost of appeals under the proposed jurisdiction should, where the appeal is by a railway, be borne by the railway.[3]

When the Act of 1894 was under discussion, it was claimed that the legislation was defective, in that it had not restored the right possessed prior to 1888 to challenge the reasonableness of all rates. To the proposition to confer rate-making power on the Commission the government was strongly opposed. It considered that "to ask the Railway Commission, or any tribunal, to consider what is a reasonable rate would be to give them no firm ground on which they could stand."[4] Back of all the criticism directed by the trader against the Commission there is in

[1] E.g. cases arising under Section 5 of the Railway Rates and Charges Act of 1891. This section is concerned with special charges that may be made by railways for special services.

[2] *Ashton* v. *Lanc. & Yorkshire Ry.*, 2 K. B., 1904, 313.

[3] Waghorn and Stevens, *op. cit.*, p. 65.

[4] Statement of Honorable James Bryce, president of the Board of Trade, in an interview with the deputation on railway rates and charges, June 15, 1894, *Railway Times*, June 23, 1894.

reality a desire that the rate-making power should be exercised. But, while the desire exists, there is a lack of unanimity as to the means to use to accomplish this. In this uncertainty some are looking to the Board of Trade.

The Board of Trade was given jurisdiction, under the Act of 1888, to deal with rate grievances through a conciliation process modeled on that contained in the Act to Regulate Commerce. It is also empowered to attempt to settle complaints about unreasonable rates. The operation of the Board of Trade under its conciliation jurisdiction is recognized as having met with a considerable degree of success.[1] Agreements have been obtained in about one third of the cases brought before it. By the explanations it obtains from the railways the board is also able to settle incipient rate grievances. The process is simple and inexpensive. When a complaint is made, the railway is communicated with, so that a statement of its position may be obtained. If the matter cannot be settled by correspondence, an attempt is made to arrange a meeting at the Board of Trade between the complainant and a railway representative. Here the matter is taken up in an informal manner. Isolated cases have dragged on a year without a decision, but normally some settlement is obtained much more promptly. Complaints varying from an overcharge of 2*d.* on a lawn mower to questions concerned with preferential rates come before the board. In 1900 it was able to obtain a reduction in distributive rates affecting five hundred towns in England and in Ireland. Since 1888 over eleven hundred cases have been brought before the board.[2] Approximately one half of these were presented in the period 1899–1903. The table on the following page shows the result of the more important applications.

There were, then, under these headings satisfactory agreements in about one fifth of the applications made.

[1] This is admitted by so strong an advocate of the rate-making power as Mr. W. A. Hunter. See an article of his "Railway Rates and the Common Weal," *New Review*, Vol. VIII, p. 341.

[2] This is exclusive of over 1900 unreasonable-rate complaints dealt with by a special official prior to 1899.

Principal Applications, 1899–1903	Seventh Report		Eighth Report	
	Settled	Unsuccessful	Settled	Unsuccessful
Classification	4	9	2	12
Delays in conveyances, facilities, etc.	15	15	4	5
Facilities and tolls on canals . . .	2	4	—	—
Rates, differential	9	18	—	10
Rates, preferential	—	2	—	—
Rates, through rates obtained . .	2	7	2	4
Rates, through rates, reduction of .	2	2	—	1
Rates, unreasonable, reduction of .	37	82	18	29
Rebate, cartage	6	3	3	2
Rebate, station terminals	1	—	—	—

While the conciliation work of the Board of Trade has met with a fair degree of success in smaller matters, it has failed when larger matters have had to be dealt with. In Pidcock's case, which later came to the Railway Commission, there was involved the right of the complainant to receive rebates in respect of terminal services not performed at his sidings. The matter dragged on for seventeen months, and finally the railways stated they would take the matter to the Commission, although in the opinion of the Board of Trade the "matter was of no such intricacy or difficulty as to make the arbitrament of a more elaborate tribunal essential to a just decision."[1] The railways will not recognize the conciliation procedure in any matter which involves legal right. With a view to simplifying procedure the Act of 1888 provides that, when a trader desires to obtain a through rate, a preliminary hearing before the Board of Trade is necessary. However, since the determination of the board on such a matter has no legal effect, the preliminary hearing has become simply a perfunctory matter. The Board of Trade is unwilling to express an opinion; while the railways are unwilling to take any position that may be used against them before the Commission.

When the rate increases of 1893 were under discussion, the Mansion House Association proposed, on behalf of the traders,

[1] Fourth Report of the Board of Trade of Proceedings under Section 31 of the Railway and Canal Traffic Act, 1888, p. 6.

to accept the decision of the Board of Trade on these rates if the railways would also pledge themselves to accept the decision. But to this the railways would not agree. To the attempt to give the Board of Trade power over rates the railways are strongly opposed. This position is also supported by the Board of Trade itself. It has constantly claimed that the strength of the conciliation procedure of the board is wholly attributable to lack of compelling power. It is averse to any increased jurisdiction over rates being conferred upon it. It also believes that, if a new rate tribunal is organized, it should, while equipped with a commanding personnel, be of the "advisory" type.

Table I[1] indicates that, from the traders' standpoint, the most important matters brought before the Commission are sidings' rent charges, preference, unreasonable rates, charges for services at sidings, and reasonable facilities. Attention has already been directed to the importance of sidings' traffic in British railway working. For many years the small traders engaged in retailing coal had been using the trucks as storage warehouses. The railways objected to their sidings being crowded with loaded trucks. The colliery owners, to whom the rolling stock belonged, also objected. Formerly the railways had charged demurrage charges based on the average time a truck was detained on a siding. In 1895 the railways decided to charge demurrage based on the actual time a truck was detained on a siding over and above the time necessary to unload it. Since 1895 many applications dealing with this arrangement have been brought before the Commission. Some have come up under the heading of legality of rates, others under the heading of unreasonable rates. The complaints in regard to charges for services at sidings are attributable to the fact, already sufficiently explained, that in the English railway system there are various special charges over and above the conveyance rate. As is indicated in Table I, 779 applications have been made to the Commission.

The preventive effect of the Commission is in part measured by the details given in Table II.[2] A special example will make

[1] P. 793, *infra*. [2] P. 793, *infra*.

the preventive effect clearer. In 1902 some forty-seven cases, which were brought before the Commission alleging that the Midland Railway was unduly preferring a prominent colliery, such favor being to the detriment of the complainants, were settled before trial. In all, 219 cases have been settled or withdrawn. Formal action has been taken in 346 applications,[1] leaving approximately one third of the applications concerning which there is no further record.

There has been only three cases in the history of the Commission in which anything savoring of a secret rebate has been brought before it. The work of the Commission, in so far as rates are concerned, has been almost entirely concerned with freight traffic. The Act of 1888 makes no direct provision for action in regard to passenger rates. It has, however, been settled in decisions arising out of the Commission's action that it has, as an incident of a through-rate arrangement, power to order through booking (ticketing) of passengers. It has also power to deal with passenger facilities under the question of "reasonable facilities." Of the rate cases formerly argued before the Commission the traders have won not far from three fifths. The tendency of the Commission has been to give compromise decisions. Not only have there been compromises as between the contending parties, there have been compromises as between the opinions of the commissioners themselves. In the Rickett, Smith case, in which the point involved was an increase in rates, Justice Collins thought all the increase was justifiable, Lord Cobham thought none of the increase was justifiable, Sir Frederick Peel occupied an intermediate position, and his opinion prevailed. Both in the traders' cases and in the cases between railways the Commission has been attempting to have the parties arrive at satisfactory settlements, without final action on its part. In some cases, when the parties have agreed, the Commission, in accepting the agreement, has incorporated it in its final order.

[1] This includes a large number of group decisions; i.e. where one decision covers identical facts in a set of cases, consent decisions, cases where a settlement arrived at by the parties is embodied in an order of the Commission, dismissal of applications, etc.

The presence of a judge on the Commission has meant a strict constructionist point of view in regard to the law. In general, powers have not been implied. Early in the history of the Commission Justice Wills said nothing could be more mischievous than to strain legislation to cover facts that had been left out of it. In 1892 the same judge, in speaking of a statute, said, "The legislature had reasons of its own, good, bad, or indifferent, which have nothing to do with me." In one case, however, where a railway had closed a branch railway, and pulled down the railway station, the Commission required, with much hesitation on the part of the judicial member, that the railway should give the reasonable facilities asked for; and this of necessity involved the rebuilding of the railway station. This implication from the law of 1854 was promptly overruled.[1]

Undoubtedly the presence of a judge on the Commission has made the relations with the higher courts more harmonious than was the case with the Commission of 1873. There has not been that tendency, so conspicuous in the relations of the Federal courts to the Interstate Commerce Commission, to regard the Commission as an amorphous interloper. In one case, it is true, the Scotch Court of Sessions claimed that, if a decision as to fact depended upon a conclusion in law, then there could be an appeal. This line of argument, which, if followed, would soon undermine the finality of the Commission's decisions on questions of fact, has not been adopted; and there has been a ready recognition by the courts of the finality of the Commission's decisions on questions of fact. The result of this is seen in the attitude of the courts to the decisions of the Commission. Down to 1904 there have been, as is indicated in Table III, thirty-eight appeals. The Commission has been overruled in four cases, while in two others it has been sustained in part and reversed in part. The decisions of the Commission in the traders' cases have more finality than in the cases between railways. While nine tenths of the applications before the Commission have been concerned with traders' rights, there have been only eighteen appeals in

[1] *Darlaston Local Board* v. *L. & N. W. Ry.*, 8 Ry. and Canal Traffic Cases, 216.

the traders' cases; while there have been fifteen appeals in cases where railways alone or railways and dock companies have been concerned.

From the standpoint of the trader a question of importance is the willingness of the railway to obey the orders of the Commission without fighting the matter to the last ditch. While, on the whole, the railways have been loyal to the decisions of the Commission, examples may be found on both sides. In 1902 the railway reconsidered its first intention to appeal the Charrington, Sells case. The result was that a large number of cases, in which the same set of facts was involved, were settled out of court. The London & Northwestern, as a result of the decision in the first Corn Traders' case, gave up the attempt to compete for the traffic with which the case was concerned, and readjusted its rates accordingly. On the other hand, it was necessary, in the case which the Mansion House Association won from the same railway in 1896, to have supplementary proceedings before the Commission in 1897 before the cessation of some of the rates complained of was obtained. The involved uncertainties of English railway law have also played their part. The railways have been able, acting within the law, but depending upon legal, not commercial, conditions, to modify the redress given by the Commission. In 1889 a decision, under the undue-preference clause, found that existing rates were interfering with the distributive business of the Irish town of Newry. Two years later complaint was made because one of the rates complained of had been raised. The railway successfully justified this, on the ground that the section of road, on which there was an increase of rate, was expensive to work on account of cost of gradients, etc. In 1900 the firm of Cowan & Sons, paper manufacturers, failed in an application to the Commission for a rebate on sidings' charges. In retaliation for this application the railway company, which for twenty-eight years had delivered coal at the private siding of the firm in question, refused any longer to deliver coal at the siding. While the railway was at the same time delivering coal at the sidings of adjacent competing firms, it delivered the coal for the Cowans at a near-by station, and they had to haul it *back* to their siding. The decision of the Commission in favor of the Cowans was overruled. It was held that the arrangement between the railway and the trader in this case was a purely voluntary arrangement, creating no prescriptive rights against the railway. It was not till 1904 that legislation, bringing such sidings within the facilities clause of the Act of 1854, and thus supporting the Commission's decision, was passed.

The Commission, whenever there is an identity of facts, — e.g., in many of the sidings' rent cases, — has dealt with cases in groups, giving a decision which covers a set of cases. The unwillingness of the courts to give the decisions of the Commission a more general effect has assisted in tying the decisions down to the facts of a particular case. In October, 1901, the Commission decided that certain coal rates charged by a number of Scotch railways were unreasonable. The rates were discontinued, as regards the complainants, in December of that year. Three other traders, who were subjected to the same rates, but who had not been parties to the suit, later brought action in the courts for damages because the railways had continued to charge them the rates complained of. The court held, however, that the decision of the Commission had no general effect. Although the rates had been found unreasonable, the court would take no cognizance of this unless they were also illegal.[1]

The functions committed to the Commission are extremely diverse. While it has, with evident innuendo, been called the Traders' Court, it has, in addition to dealing with rate matters, an extensive jurisdiction in regard to arbitration of matters referred to it by the Board of Trade; e.g., differences between railways involving such matters as running rights, number of trains under a running arrangement, arrangements in regard to connection in a through train service over a connecting line, division of expenses between the owning and the controlling company, differences between the Postmaster-General and railways in regard to postal payments, questions arising in connection

[1] *Lanarkshire Steel Co., Ltd.* v. *Caledonian Ry.*, 11 Scots Law Times Reports, 407, 408. A preliminary decision of the court had held that the Commission's decision was of general effect. *Ibid.*, 225.

with the introduction of improved brakes, complaints in regard to the water supply of London. In addition it serves as a court of appeal from the Board of Trade in cases arising out of the rules made by the Board of Trade under the railway labor acts, and has alternative jurisdiction in the workmen's trains applications. In addition to jurisdiction under special acts the Commission exercises functions finding their legal sanction in some nineteen general acts.

Not only are there complaints at present in regard to preferences on imported products, there are also complaints concerning the rates and facilities given home products. Complaint is especially active in the case of Irish agricultural products. Comparisons, unfavorable to domestic rates, are constantly being made with foreign rates. The question of shipments on "owner's risk" rates gives rise to many complaints. The criticism of the Commission on Agriculture of 1897, that the rate regulative legislation has not given clear effect "to the intentions of Parliament,"[1] is general among the traders. That the Commission has not accomplished much that was expected of it is a patent fact. Its procedure has not met the case of the small trader. At the same time the rate regulative procedure that accomplishes all that is expected of it is not absent from England alone. The Commission, it must be remembered, was organized, not to reduce rates or to intervene actively in matters of rate regulation, but as a court to settle differences. As a court, it has performed its functions. While there was, at the outset, some tendency on the part of the judicial members to look at matters from a legal standpoint rather than from the standpoint of facts, the tendency has been, in more recent years, to meet the conditions rather than to bend the conditions to meet preconceived theories. On questions of railway law the Commission has been, on the whole, more in touch with the facts than the ordinary law courts. While the expense attaching to litigation before the Commission is readily apparent, it may be queried in how far there is a justification for expecting either a cheap settlement or a settlement, at the public expense, of important business matters. So far as

[1] Final Report, paragraph 526.

England is concerned, the attempts to obtain cheap settlements, in the face of the existing involved body of railway law, would mean, if successful, results of little worth.

In the United States the Federal courts have recognized the debt of the Act to Regulate Commerce to the English regulative legislation. But, when comparison is made of the constitution and functions of the English Commission with those of the Interstate Commission, differences at once appear.

The English Commission is a court. The American Commission has the functions of a referee or special commissioner. The former has final decision in regard to fact and a limitation on the right of appeal, with the result that appealed cases are normally settled within a year. The latter has no finality of decision in regard to fact, and appeals from its decisions have taken from two to nine years to decide. While the English Commission has been overruled in the period ending 1904, wholly or partly, in six out of thirty-eight appeals, the American Commission has, in approximately the same period, been overruled in twenty-nine out of thirty-eight appeals.[1] While the Interstate Commerce Commission has, practically from the outset, claimed, as a necessary implication from the language of its enabling statute, an amendatory rate-making power, the English Commission, organized as a court, has, almost without exception, kept aloof from making implications extending its jurisdiction, and has denied any intention to exercise a rate-making power. While the members of the American Commission hold on a limited tenure and the Commission is a bipartisan organization, the tenure of the lay commissioners in the English Commission is for good conduct, there is a pension on retirement, no question of bipartisan organization enters in, and the provision is made that one of the commissioners shall have technical knowledge of railway affairs. The judicial members of the English Commission are assigned to it for five years; but during the period they are not engaged in the Commission work they perform their regular duties as judges of the high court.

[1] See Table III. See also Appendix D, Vol. V, p. 331, Hearings of Committee on Interstate Commerce, etc., 1905.

In the details of the regulative policy which has developed under the Commissions, resemblances and differences appear.[1] The English regulative policy is not in harmony with that of the United States in regard to the extent to which competition is to be considered as a justification of rate anomalies. While the English legislation eliminates competition in the case of import rates, the American position, as established in the Import Rate case, states that competition is to be considered as affecting both import rates and domestic rates. In the case of domestic rates the English Commission at first would not recognize competition as the justification of an anomalously low rate basis unless a well-defined "public interest" was thereby served. Later it accepted the same view as was set forth in the United States in the Alabama Midland case; namely, that competition is one of the matters which may lawfully be considered in making rates. The grievance of secret rebates, one of the central evils in the United States, is practically nonexistent in England. There is no provision other than that of the undue preference clause to cover such a grievance. In both countries the principle that undue preference is a question of fact has been accepted. While the United States has singled out a particular form of preference for special treatment under the "long-and-short-haul" clause, England has allowed more elasticity by placing the matter under a general clause. On the question of the justifiability of granting wholesale rates in respect of quantities larger than car-load lots, the American decisions have been contradictory. The lower courts have shown a tendency to accept the decision in Nicholson's case, but in the Party Rate case the Supreme Court established as the law that a discrimination in respect of quantity, even if allowed to all doing the same amount of business, is to be considered from the standpoint of public policy and the effect of such an arrangement upon trade competition.[2] In so deciding

[1] There is no recognition, in the working of the English Commission, of results arrived at in the regulative policy of the United States.

[2] *I. C. C.* v. *Baltimore & Ohio Rd. Co.*, 145 U. S. 263. This upholds the general position taken at an earlier time by the Interstate Commerce Commission in *Providence Coal Co.* v. *Providence & Worcester R. Co.*, 1 I. C. C. Decisions, 363. See also Judson, The Law of Interstate Commerce and its Federal Regulation, p. 194.

there has been accepted as a principle what is, so far, only a tendency in the English regulative policy.

The dissimilarities of the matters dealt with by the two Commissions will be seen by referring to Table I. The items common to the two Commissions are legality of rates, unreasonable rates, reasonable facilities, and undue preference.[1] In all, about one half of the applications made to the English Commission are concerned with matters of a kind coming before the American Commission.

The English Commission has used two sets of rate principles: competition as an important factor in differential rates, export rates, and in general in the home side of undue preference; cost of service in regard to preferential rates, and unreasonable rates. This has been in great degree attributable to the legislation. The traders have desired free trade in exports, not in imports. Admitting that there has been a certain *judicial* bias in favor of the cost-of-service principle, it is at the same time apparent that legislation, like that of 1894, which makes a past rate the *prima facie* criterion of reasonableness rules out the possibility of considering present competition. The defects of the legislation of 1894 are its own. The Commission has made the legislation less unworkable than could have been expected.

A considerable part of the desire to control and lower actual rates in England pertains to that hysterical belief in England's industrial decadence which has found some favor in recent years. A considerable part of the criticism arises from the endeavor to prove, on the basis of foreign statistics not properly comparable with English statistics, that English rates are unduly high. Some rearrangements in the Commission's machinery would, however, effect improvements. An arrangement whereby, when a question of principle is established in a decision of the Commission as distinct from a mere finding on facts, the enforcement should be placed in the hands of the Board of Trade

[1] I omit sidings' rent (demurrage) charges, because the conditions under which these arise in England differ entirely from those existing in the United States.

instead of leaving it as a question of possible dispute to be fought out in individual cases, would effect an improvement. A closer articulation of the conciliation procedure of the Board of Trade with the process of the Commission, whereby the findings of the former would have a status before the latter, would also be expedient. The Commission is becoming more and more a technical court, whose decisions are modified by an attempt to obtain settlements rather than legal decisions. Notwithstanding the criticism directed against it, it is difficult to see how, considering the peculiar geographical, industrial, and railway conditions it has faced, the Commission could have accomplished more than it has done.

S. J. McLean

Leland Stanford Jr. University

TABLE I

SUBJECT-MATTER OF APPLICATIONS DEALT WITH BY THE COMMISSION, 1889–1903[1]

	1889	1890	1891	1892	1893	1894	1895	1896	1897	1898	1899	1900	1901	1902	1903
Board of Trade (Prevention of Accidents Act, 1900)	–	–	–	–	–	–	–	–	–	–	–	–	–	6	26
Classification	–	–	–	–	–	–	–	–	–	–	1	–	–	–	1
Facilities, reasonable	3	8	3	3	1	6	–	1	4	2	2	5	4	4	3
Postmaster-General, applications concerning	–	–	–	–	–	–	–	–	–	2	2	2	–	1	–
Preference, undue	3	4	5	4	5	5	4	6	–	1	6	3	97	10	8
Rates, distinction of	2	3	–	–	–	–	–	1	–	–	–	–	–	–	–
Rates, legality of	–	2	–	1	–	–	–	2	–	–	–	2	–	–	–
Rates, through	–	–	–	–	–	2	13	4	3	3	6	2	1	–	–
Rates unreasonable	–	–	–	–	–	1	63	10	2	24	–	–	3	–	1
Sidings, rent (demurrage)	–	–	–	–	–	–	–	6	–	–	25	3	–	108	91
Sidings, rebate from sidings' charge	–	–	–	–	–	1	6	3	–	4	9	8	6	–	3
Sidings, services on, charges for	–	–	–	–	–	–	1	4	5	1	–	2	–	23	24
Terminal charges	–	1	–	–	–	1	–	1	–	–	–	–	–	–	–
Trucks, rebates because not supplied	–	–	–	–	2	–	–	–	1	–	–	–	–	–	–
Railways, differences under special acts, etc.	3	10	1	2	4	5	3	7	6	3	3	4	2	1	2
Railways, working agreements approved	3	2	5	5	2	–	2	2	2	–	1	2	3	1	–
Workmen's trains applications	–	–	–	1	–	–	–	–	–	23	1	3	–	1	–
Water Act, Metropolitan (1897), applications	–	–	–	–	–	–	–	–	–	2	–	2	–	–	–
Miscellaneous	–	–	1	2	1	2	3	3	1	2	–	1	1	1	1

TABLE II

CASES WITHDRAWN OR SETTLED EITHER IN COURT OR OUTSIDE, 1889–1903[1]

	1889	1890	1891	1892	1893	1894	1895	1896	1897	1898	1899	1900	1901	1902	1903
Facilities, reasonable	1	–	–	2	–	1	1	–	2	2	–	4	1	3	2
Postmaster-General, applications concerning	–	–	–	–	–	–	–	–	–	1	–	–	–	–	–
Preference, undue	–	–	1	–	2	2	2	–	2	2	2	–	–	2	15
Rates, legality of	–	1	–	–	–	–	–	2	3	–	–	–	–	–	–
Rates, through	–	–	–	–	–	–	–	1	2	–	1	1	–	1	–
Rates, unreasonable	–	–	–	–	–	–	2	16	20	19	8	1	4	30	–
Sidings, rent (demurrage)	–	–	–	–	–	–	–	2	2	–	–	–	–	1	1
Sidings, rebate from sidings' charge	–	–	–	–	–	–	1	2	1	3	2	3	1	–	–
Sidings, services on, charges for	–	–	–	–	–	–	–	1	2	–	–	1	–	–	–
Railways, differences under special acts, etc.	–	–	1	–	1	1	–	2	–	2	–	1	–	–	–
Workmen's trains applications	–	–	–	–	–	–	–	–	–	12	1	3	1	–	–
Water Act, Metropolitan (1897), applications	–	–	–	–	–	–	–	–	–	–	1	–	–	–	–
Miscellaneous	–	–	–	–	–	2	–	2	1	–	–	1	1	–	–

[1] In various cases a number of points are dealt with. In constructing the table, I have selected the most important point in each case.

TABLE III

Cases Appealed from the Railway and Canal Commission, 1889–1904[1]

Year	Name of Case	Appealed by	Point Involved in Appeal	Result
1890	*Taff Vale Ry. Co.* v. *Barry Docks & Ry. Co.*	Defendant	Differences under special act	Com. sustained.
1891	*Sowerby & Co.* v. *Great Western Ry. Co.*	Plaintiff	Terminal charges	" "
1891	*Rhymney Ry. Co.* v. *Bute Docks Co.*	"	Facilities between parties	" "
1892	*Pickering, Phipps, et al.* v. *L. & N. W. Ry. et al.*	"	Undue preference	" "
1892	*Liverpool Corn Traders' Ass'n* v. *Gt. W'n Ry.*	"	Undue preference	" "
1894	*Northeastern Ry.* v. *Scarborough & Whiby Ry.*	"	Construction of working agreement	" "
1894	*Darlaston Local Board* v. *L. & N. W. Ry.*	Defendant	Reasonable facilities	" overruled.
1895	*Mansion House Ass'n* v. *Gt. Wt'n Ry.*	"	Unreasonable rates	" sustained.
1896	*Greenwood & Sons* v. *Lanc. & Yorkshire Ry.*	"	Rebate on sidings' charges	" "
1896	*Watson, Todd & Co.* v. *Midland Ry. & L. & N. W. Ry.*	Plaintiff	Terminal rebates	" "
1896	*Mansion House Ass'n* v. *L. & N. W. Ry.*	Defendant	Unreasonable rates	" "
1896	*Didcot, N. & S. Ry.* v. *Gt. W'n Ry. & L. & S. W. Ry.*	"	Through booking of passengers	" "
1897	*Northeastern Ry.* v. *North British Ry.*	Both parties	Running rights	" "
1898	*Salt Union* v. *North Staffordshire Ry.*	Defendant	Rebate on sidings' charges	" "
1898	*Gt. Northern Ry.* v. *N. E. Ry. & N. B. Ry.*	"	Differences under special act	" "
1899	*Huntingdonshire County Council* v. *Simpson*	"	Reasonable facilities	" "
1900	*Postmaster-General* v. *Corp'n of London*	"	Telegraph connections	" "
1900	*Postmaster-General* v. *Corp'n of Glasgow*	"	Telegraph connections	" "
1900	*Forth Bridge* v. *N. B. Ry., Gt. N. Ry., et al.*	Plaintiff	Through rates	" "
1900	*L. T. & S. Ry.* v. *Gt. Eastern Ry.*	"	Differences between railways	" overruled.
1901	*Cowan & Sons* v. *North British Ry.* (No. 2)	"	Rebates on sidings' charges	" sustained.
1901	*Black & Sons* v. *Cal. Ry., N. B. Ry., & G. & S. W. Ry.*	Defendants	Application for details of plaintiffs' profits to use in suit	" "
1901	*Cowan & Sons* v. *North British Ry.* (No. 3)	Defendant	Reasonable facilities	" { sustained.[2] overruled.[2]
1901	*Huntington et al.* v. *Lanc. & Yorkshire Ry.*	Plaintiff	Ownership of a siding	" sustained.
1901	*Rhymney Ry.* v. *Great Western Ry.*	"	Differences between parties	" "
1901	*Gt. Western Ry.* v. *Metropolitan Ry.*	Defendant	Differences between parties	" "
1902	*Crompton & Co.* v. *Lanc. & Yorkshire Ry.*	"	Rebate on sidings' charge	" { sustained.[2] overruled.[2]
1902	*Vickers, Sons & Maxim* v. *Midland Ry. et al.*	"	Rebate on sidings' charge	" sustained.
1902	*London & India Dock Co.* v. *Gt. Eastern Ry. & Midland Ry.*	Defendants	Power to propose through rate	" overruled.
1902	*Lanc. Brick & Terra Cotta Co.* v. *Lanc. & Yorkshire Ry.*	"	Connection of siding with railway	" "
1902	*Gt. Western Ry.* v. *Metropolitan Ry.*	Defendant	Difference between parties	" sustained.[2]
1902	*Mold & Denbigh J'n Ry.* v. *L. & N. W. Ry.*	Plaintiff	Difference between parties	" "
1902	*Abram Coal Co.* v. *Gt. Central Ry.*	Defendant	Undue preference	" "
1903	*London & India Docks* v. *Midland Ry. & Gt. Eastern Ry.*	Plaintiff	Refusal of proposed through rate	" "
1903	*Great Western Ry.* v. *Postmaster-General*	"	Compensation for mail	" "
1903	*Ackers, Whitley & Co.* v. *Gt. Central Ry.*	Defendant	Undue preference	" "
1904	*North British Ry.* v. *Caledonian Ry.*	"	Running rights	" "
1904	*Lancashire & Yorkshire Ry.* v. *Wright*	Plaintiff	Point of law	" overruled.

[1] The official report of cases for 1904 is not yet available.

[2] In part.

XXVIII

RAILWAY REGULATION IN FRANCE[1]

THE railway policy of France is based on the view that railways should be exploited, not by the State, but by strong independent companies under strict government control. National purchase has again and again been considered, but has always been rejected. When last it was proposed in the French Parliament that the State should buy out four of the large railway companies, one hundred Chambers of Commerce voted against, and one only for, the proposal. While the companies are encouraged to earn large profits,[2] they are never allowed to compete with one another, or to invade one another's territory, and their arrangements for sharing traffic or earnings constantly receive official sanction. The State has refrained from dictating their tariffs, and confined itself to exercising a veto over those which they propose. Under the Railway Conventions of 1883, as under those of 1859, the government has no power either to fix or to alter rates. The proposal of a rate must emanate from one of the companies, but before taking effect it has to be approved by the Minister of Public Works.

The official machinery by which this control over rates is exercised consists of three parts: a salaried corps of expert officials for gathering information; a large nonsalaried committee made up of high officials, members of the legislature, and representatives of the business community, to give advice

[1] From the *Quarterly Journal of Economics*, Vol. XX, 1906, pp. 279–286. Further details are given in translations from Colson's "Abrégé de la Législation des Chemins de Fer, etc.," in Hearings before the Senate (Elkins) Committee on Interstate Commerce, 1905, Vol. V, Appendix, pp. 265–297.

[2] M. Pelletan, in his report of May 12, 1889, pointed out that French railway shares paid from 10 to 24 per cent of their original cost; since then there have been some increases in dividends.

based on that information; and, lastly, the Minister who acts on that advice.

The permanent officials who investigate and report on all questions concerning rates number 68, and cost the State 400,000 francs a year; that is, 10 francs for each kilometer of railway at present in operation.[1] Of this amount 258,500 francs represent the salaries of the chief experts, 32 in number.[2] At their head, receiving 20,200 francs a year, is the Director of Commercial Supervision (*Directeur du Contrôle Commercial*), who studies the tariffs and commercial workings of all the French companies. Under his orders are the General Supervisors of Commercial Exploitation (*Contrôleurs Généraux de l'Exploitation Commerciale*), each of whom has similar duties in respect to a single railway, receives 11,400 francs a year, and is assisted in his work by one Principal Inspector and several Special Inspectors. To each railway is assigned one Principal Inspector (*Inspecteur Principal*) of Commercial Exploitation, receiving 8000 francs a year, and from three to five Special Inspectors (*Inspecteurs Particuliers*), each of whom receives from 6500 to 5500 francs a year. These inspectors are all under the orders of the General Supervisor in charge of that particular railway.

There is at the Ministry of Public Works a bureau of Railway Direction, one of the divisions of which investigates tariffs and charges, and the head of which is known as the Director of Railways (*Directeur des Chemins de Fer*). This high official acts as counselor to the Minister on all points connected with railway administration.

But the Minister's chief adviser is the Consultative Committee of Railways (*Comité Consultatif des Chemins de Fer*) over which he presides, and which examines questions of rates as well as all others affecting the relations between the railway companies and the State. The organization of this Committee has been several times changed. In its present form, which

[1] The 40,000 kilometers "of general interest" are alone to be counted, since tariffs of local lines are, as a rule, passed upon by the prefects of the several departments.

[2] M. Sibille's Report on Budget of 1905 (*Ch. des Députés*, No. 1962), pp. 148, 183.

dates from 1898, it has 100 unpaid members, 10 *ex officio* and 90 appointed for two years by the President of the Republic. The present membership consists of 36 government officials (6 *ex officio*), 34 members of the legislature (4 *ex officio*), and 30 men holding no political office. A combination is thus secured of administrative, legislative, and general opinion.

Among the officials are the Director General of Customs, a brigadier general on the general staff, the Directors of Forests, of Agriculture, of Commerce, and of Labor, the Director of Roads, Navigation and Mines, the Director of Commercial Supervision, the Director of Railways, and five other members of the Council of State. Among these last is M. Picard, well known as the author of the two principal works on French railways, who, as vice chairman, presides over the Committee in the absence of the Minister; while M. Colson, another member, is almost equally well known for his book, Transports et Tarifs, and for the articles on Transportation which he contributes to the *Revue Politique et Parlementaire.* Both these officials have heretofore filled the post of Director of Railways.

Among the Deputies MM. Baudin, Barthou, Bourrat, and Sibille, and among the Senators M. Waddington, are specially conversant with railway problems, the first two being ex-Ministers of Public Works, and the three others having written elaborate reports on various railway questions.

In the general group we find twelve presidents or members of Chambers of Commerce (Paris, Lille, Hâvre, Lyons, Bordeaux, and Marseilles being among the cities represented), six presidents or members of national Agricultural Societies, two workingmen, the Governor of the Bank of France, seven business men or civil engineers, two of whom represent internal navigation, one judge, and one representative of the International Railway Congress. This last member, M. Griolet, is also vice chairman of the Railway du Nord, and is the only railway official belonging to the Consultative Committee.[1]

[1] For further particulars, see J. de la Ruelle, Contrôle des Chemins de Fer (Paris, 1903), p. 218, and for the names of present members, see Annuaire du Min. des Travaux Publics, 1905, p. 34.

General meetings of the Committee are seldom held, most of its business being transacted by its "permanent section," a subcommittee of 40 members (4 *ex officio*, 36 annually chosen by the Minister), which meets at least once a week. This "section" comprises twelve Senators and Deputies, six representatives of commerce, industry, and agriculture, three civil engineers, two workingmen, and the member of the Railway Congress, besides sixteen of the government officials. Matters of importance may be referred to the whole Consultative Committee by the Minister, or by the Vice President either on his own initiative or upon the request of five members of the "section."

When a company wishes to introduce a new rate or to change an old one, the regular procedure is the following. The text of the proposed rate must be posted up or otherwise advertised in the company's stations, and sent to the Minister of Public Works, to the Director of Commercial Supervision, to the Prefects of departments, and to the Chambers of Commerce of districts affected by the rate. The Chambers of Commerce and the Prefects are expected to forward to the Minister in writing any protests or comments which they may wish to make.

The proposal is then carefully examined by the General Supervisor of Commercial Exploitation in charge of the railway proposing the rate, whose duty it is to report thereon. In this task he is assisted by the Principal Inspector and the several Special Inspectors of the railway in question. These officials are instructed personally to inform themselves as to the needs of trade and the views and wishes of business men. Having done so, they prepare a written report, which must embody "a thorough discussion of the prices proposed, and a comparison between them and other tariffs in force on the French railways at the various shipping points with which this traffic competes."[1] The report is submitted to the Director of Commercial Supervision, who transmits it with or without revision to the Minister of Public Works. As soon as these documents reach the Minister he lays them before the Consultative Committee. If this Committee makes a favorable report, the Minister approves the

[1] Ministerial Circular of July 16, 1880.

rate, and it usually goes into effect within fifteen days from that date. Thus on March 25, 1904, a proposed addition to one of the special tariffs of the Railway de l'Ouest was duly advertised. It was officially approved on the 11th, and took effect on the 26th of April, 1904.[1] No rate can become operative until one month after having been advertised. In order to keep the public fully informed, the text of the proposal and that of the ministerial approval are published in the *Journal Officiel.*

The ministerial sanction given to any rate may be withdrawn at any time, and, in accepting a rate proposed, the Minister may attach to his approval certain conditions to which the company must assent before the rate can take effect. A passenger rate cannot be increased till it has been in force three months, nor a freight rate till it has been in force one year.

The interval between the proposal and the approval of a rate, which is normally one month, is sometimes a great deal longer. Should it, however, be necessary to put a rate into immediate effect, the Minister often grants a provisional "homologation," whereby the rate becomes at once available pending its formal consideration and approval.

The French tariffs that have been thus approved are published in the two large folio volumes of the *Recueil Chaix*, a revised edition of which is issued quarterly. The edition bearing date July, 1905, but not actually issued till last September, has 1712 pages in the volume containing the tariffs for slow freight, and 980 pages in that containing the rates for fast freight and passengers. These manuals would be less bulky if they embodied only the tariffs of the large companies, but they also include the rates of all the light railways, narrow-gauge lines, and tramways throughout France. In the intervals between the editions of this work newly approved rates are published in a special weekly bulletin, as well as in the *Journal Officiel.* Thus the authorized railway tariffs are at all times readily accessible to the French public.

Since the French regard railway tarification from a commercial standpoint, their tariffs, like those of England and the

[1] *Journal Officiel,* April 3 and 25, 1904.

United States, are based on the so-called "value" system, which consists in charging such rates as the traffic will bear. Their system of classification would take too long to explain. Suffice it to say that, in compliance with the demands made by the government in 1879, the classification and description of freight was made uniform on all the French railways by their reformed tariffs approved between August, 1884, and December, 1890. At the same time the number of reduced tariffs and special rates was much cut down, and the *Recueil Chaix* considerably simplified. Since those reforms, however, the large family of special rates has continued to multiply, under the pressure of commercial needs, though the Consultative Committee is on principle opposed to them, and seeks, whenever possible, to procure in their stead reduced kilometric scales of rates drawn up on the Belgian differential plan, and applicable in any direction and on any line of the given railway.

In sanctioning a special rate, the Committee almost always insists, as a condition of approval, that intermediate stations shall also be entitled to it, and that a special rate, say from Toulouse to Orleans, shall be enjoyed as far as Orleans by goods shipped from Toulouse to points beyond Orleans.

The Minister of Public Works having no power to fix rates, the principal function of the Consultative Committee is to check unjust, discriminating, or capricious tarification, and thus by degrees to produce throughout France an equitable system of rates. It often suggests to the companies what changes it deems desirable, and, though it can only suggest, yet the possession of its veto often enables it, when granting one of the companies' requests, to gain its own point as a *quid pro quo*. This influence is all the stronger because the authority vested in the Minister, and through him in the Consultative Committee, covers not only the commercial (i.e., rate-making), but also the technical and financial[1] sides of railway administration.[2]

[1] E.g. no railway company can issue bonds without the assent of the Consultative Committee and of the Minister.

[2] It is clearly to the companies' interest not to offend an authority on which they are in so many ways dependent. A different system of administration, interfering only in commercial matters, would be far from having the same influence (Colson, Transports et Tarifs, 1898, p. 350).

The Committee always declines to indorse any special rate savoring of undue preference or discrimination; for instance, a rate in favor of goods produced by a particular factory or of materials ordered by a particular contractor. It also rejects any rate calculated to draw away traffic from any other French railway or to ruin the business of coasting steamers or canal boats. Thus in April, 1899, a special rate of 15 francs on mineral waters shipped to Paris was requested by the P.-L.-M. Company. This rate was approved in April, 1900, but, the canal men of Roanne having pointed out that it was ruining them, the approval was withdrawn on August 24, 1901.

The Committee endeavors to adjust the tariffs enjoyed by competing industrial centers in such a way as to secure to each the natural advantages of its location. If, however, a particular place or industry has long had the benefit of certain special rates, and has thus acquired a quasi-vested right to them, the Committee will not allow them to be abolished without stipulating that they shall be reëstablished, "if within a year their disappearance gives rise to well-founded complaints."

A good illustration of the manner in which the Committee may obtain concessions from the companies is furnished by the negotiations leading up to the approval on October 27, 1900, of the new tariff of Accessory Charges (*Frais Accessories*). The companies had for twenty-five years been urging that the registration fee for luggage should be raised to 15 centimes, while the Committee still insisted on maintaining it at 10 centimes. The Committee also wished that the companies should guarantee to the consignor of freight using the lines of several companies the route offering the cheapest combination of rates, even when not demanded by him, as they had been doing since 1883 for the consignor of freight using the lines of a single company. The companies, on the other hand, had been anxious to suppress certain special rates affecting about 1350 kinds of freight. The matter was settled by a compromise, in which the companies waived their claim for the 15-centime registration fee, and consented to guarantee the cheapest route in the manner mentioned, while the Committee advised the Minister to sanction the suppression of the special rates on the ground that they were practically obsolete.[1]

In Algeria and in the Regency of Tunis the service of commercial supervision has been organized in a manner practically identical with that above described, and proposals of rates are referred either to the Minister of Public Works in Paris or to the Resident-General in Tunis. This latter personage is assisted by a consultative committee of eight or ten members most of whom are officials connected with the administration of the Regency.

W. H. Buckler

Johns Hopkins University

[1] Arrêté du 27 October, 1900, Impr. Nat., 1902.

XXIX

RAILROAD OWNERSHIP IN GERMANY[1]

* * * * * * * *

THE Prussian railway administration was reorganized on April 1, 1895.[2] Previous to that time there had existed two distinct official bodies, or "resorts," immedately below the minister of public works. The latter was then, and is now, the executive head of the railway administration, and the two bodies subordinated to him were known as Eisenbahndirektionen and Eisenbahnbetriebsämter, respectively, the one having direct charge of the operation of the railways and the other performing purely administrative functions. Of the Direktionen there were 11, and of the Betriebsämter 75. The functions of both of these have now been consolidated in the royal State railway directories, of which 20 have been created,[3] with their seats at Altona, Berlin, Breslau, Bromberg, Cassel, Cologne, Danzig, Elberfeld, Erfurt, Essen, Frankfurt a. M., Halle a. S., Hannover, Kattowitz, Königsberg, Magdeburg, Münster, Posen, St. Johann-Saarbrücken, and Stettin. Each directory is composed of a president, appointed by the King, and the requisite number of associates, two of whom, an Ober-Regierungsrath and an Ober-Baurath, may act as substitutes of the president under the direction of the minister. Each directory has complete administrative control over all the railways within its limits, although the subordinate civil administrative organs of the State, such as the Oberpräsident, Regierungspräsident, and Landrath, have certain powers in the granting of concessions, police regulations,

[1] From *Annals of the American Academy of Political Science*, 1897, Vol. X, pp. 399–421. *Ibid.* Vol. XIX, March, 1907, is another good description.

[2] Only a few minor changes have been introduced since.

[3] Since this was written (1897) the Hessian railways have been associated with the Prussian and the number of directories increased to 21.

etc. The directory decides all cases arising out of the action of special and of subordinate branches of the administration; and, representing the central administration, it may acquire rights and assume responsibilities in its behalf. The directories may be characterized as general administrative organs, one of whose great functions is the proper coördination of all the parts of the railway system.

Below and subordinated to them are special administrative organs, upon whom falls the duty of local adaptation and supervision. There are 6 classes of these local offices, and their names indicate in a general way their functions: operating, machine, traffic, shop, telegraph, and building offices or Inspektionen, as they are called. Shortly before the new system went into operation the minister of public works issued special business directions for each class of offices. The contents of each of these ministerial orders may be grouped under 3 heads: (1) the position of the office in the railway service; (2) its jurisdiction in matters of business; (3) general provisions. To give a detailed analysis of the functions of the local offices is out of the question here. It should be added, however, that all phases of the service, whether from the point of view of the railways or of the public, are carefully provided for. Thus one of the foremost duties —"die vornehmste Aufgabe"— of the local traffic office is to maintain a "living union" between the railway administration and the public. For this purpose the chief of the office is in duty bound, by means of numerous personal interviews and observations, to inform himself concerning the needs of the service in his district, to investigate and to remedy complaints and evils without delay, and to take such measures as will secure the most efficient service. It is also one of his duties to inform the public concerning the organization and administration of the railways, so as to avoid idle complaints. This single provision in the rules governing one of the local offices illustrates the spirit of them all.

Private railways, which before April 1, 1895, had been supervised by a special railway commission, are now subject to the jurisdiction of the president of a directory and his alternates.

This was another step toward greater unity in the system. The directories upon whom the supervision of the private roads devolves are those at Altona, Berlin, Breslau, Cassel, Cologne, Elberfeld, Erfurt, Essen, Frankfurt a. M., Halle, Hannover, Königsberg, Magdeburg, Münster, St. Johann-Saarbrücken, and Stettin. As there are 20 directories, and only 16 supervise private railroads, it is evident that jurisdictions for private roads are not identical with those of directories. Nor does each directory have an equal number of miles of private or State roads within its jurisdiction. This depends largely upon the geographical distribution of the railways and upon the intensity of the traffic. Thus, the Berlin directory supervises 587 kilometers of State roads, while Halle has 11,884 kilometers. The other directories lie between these two extremes. It may be added that on April 1, 1895, the private roads represented together only 2200 kilometers (not including Anschlussbahnen, and 71 kilometers rented to private parties) against 27,060 kilometers[1] of State roads, of which 10,479 kilometers contained two or more tracks.

All Prussian railways, then, whether State or private, are subject to the jurisdiction of a carefully graded administrative system — local, intermediate, and central — each part of which is connected with every other part in such a manner that, without interfering with the ability to act promptly in cases of emergency, every act not only finds its responsible agent, but the central organ can also make its influence felt in the remotest branch of the system and at the same time not transcend its responsibility to the public.

Advisory councils and other bodies. Whether we regard the interests of the railways and of the public as identical or not, there are certainly times when harmony between the two does not exist. This may be due to the failure of each to understand the other, or to some wrongful act which one of them may have committed. Whatever the cause, if such circumstances do arise any organ which can promptly and prudently remove the friction performs an admirable service in the interests of public traffic. Such an agent is found in Prussia in the advisory councils and

[1] Increased to 37,161 kilometers by the close of 1900.

other bodies which coöperate with the legally responsible parts of the railway administration. These councils are created by law, and are required to meet regularly for the purpose of coöperating with the State administration upon all the more important matters pertaining to the railway traffic, especially time-tables and rate schedules.

The first German advisory council was organized in the federal domain of Alsace-Lorraine. Through an impulse given by the chamber of commerce of the city of Mülhausen a conference between the representatives of the chambers of commerce of Alsace-Lorraine and the general imperial railway directory at Strassburg was held at Mülhausen on October 21, 1874. Organization, composition, and functions of the council were agreed upon during the first session. Originally its membership was confined to the chambers of commerce of Alsace-Lorraine, but later representatives of the various agricultural and industrial bodies were also admitted. All matters falling within the domain of at least 2 chambers of commerce could be brought before the council.

The proceedings of this conference made such a favorable impression upon the federal railway commissioner that he attempted, although without immediate success, to induce the other German railways, both State and private, to assist in this movement toward a closer union and a better understanding between the commercial and railway interests by instituting similar councils. The circular letter of the commissioner, addressed to the railways on January 11, 1875, is one of the most significant steps in the development of the councils.

"This arrangement," says the letter, "primarily strives to establish an intimate connection between the places intrusted with the administration of the railways and the trading classes. It will keep the representatives of the railways better informed as to the changing needs of trade and industry and maintain a continued understanding between them; and, on the other hand, it will impart to commerce, etc., a greater insight into the peculiarities of the railway business and the legitimate demands of the administration, and consequently, by means of earnest and moderate action, it will react beneficially upon both sides through an exchange of views."

This statement sounds the keynote of the whole movement. For a time the railways were not very ready to respond, and the movement made little progress until the policy of the State to purchase private railways was about to be inaugurated. The Prussian Landtag made its approval of the first bill for the nationalization of railways dependent upon certain wirthschaftliche Garantien (economic guarantees) which it demanded of the Government. A resolution to this effect was adopted by the Landtag in 1879. The ministry of trade and industry had already taken active steps during the previous year. In 1880 a bill embodying the motives of the resolution of the Landtag was introduced, and after having undergone various changes and modifications was approved and published as the law of June 1, 1882.

Prussia was thus the first, and, up to the present time is the only,[1] country in which advisory bodies of this nature were placed upon a legal basis. The law is entitled Gesetz, betreffend die Einsetzung von Bezirkseisenbahnräthe und eines Landeseisenbahnraths für die Staatsbahnverwaltung. As the name indicates, it creates a class of advisory boards or councils known as Bezirkseisenbahnräthe (circuit councils), and one national council, called Landeseisenbahnrath. The national council is the advisory board of the central administration, and the circuit councils of the railway directories. Since the reorganization of the railway administration, April 1, 1895, 8 circuit councils have been in existence, with their seats in Bromberg, Berlin, Magdeburg, Hannover, Frankfurt a. M., Cologne, Erfurt, and Breslau. It will be remembered that there are 20 directories, so that a circuit council serves as an advisory board for more than one directory. The national council is composed of 40 members, holding office for 3 years. Of these, 10 are appointed and 30 are elected by the circuit councils from residents of the province or city, representing agriculture, forestry, manufacture, and

[1] Japan and Switzerland have since then established similar councils on a legal basis.

trade, according to a scheme of representation published in a royal decree. Of the appointed members, 3 are named by the minister of agriculture, domains, and forests; 3 by the minister of trade and industry; 2 by the minister of finance; and 2 by the minister of public works. An equal number of alternates is appointed at the same time. Direct bureaucratic influence is guarded against by the exclusion from appointment of all immediate State officials. The elective members are distributed among provinces, departments, and cities, by the royal order to which reference has just been made, and both members and alternates are elected by the circuit councils. The presiding officer and his alternate or substitute are appointed by the King. In addition, the minister of public works is empowered to call in expert testimony, whenever he may think it necessary. Such specialists, as well as regular members, receive for their services 15 marks (about $3.60) per day and mileage.

The national council meets at least twice annually, and deliberates on such matters as the proposed budget, normal freight and passenger rates, classification of freight, special and differential rates, proposed changes in regulations governing the operation of railways, and allied questions. It is required by law to submit its opinion on any question brought before it by the minister of public works; or, on the other hand, it may recommend to the minister anything which it considers conducive to the utility and effectiveness of the railway service. Its proceedings are submitted regularly to the Landtag, where they are considered in connection with the budget, thus establishing "an organic connection" between the national council and the parliament. In this way the proceedings are made accessible to every one, and an opportunity is given to approve or disapprove what the council does, through parliamentary representatives. The system is one of reciprocal questioning and answering on part of the minister of public works, the national council, and the parliament.

The circuit councils are equally important and interesting. Since January 1, 1895, 9 of these have been in existence. Their membership, which varies considerably with the different councils, was fixed by the minister of public works in December, 1894. Any subsequent modifications which may have been made have no bearing on what we are considering here. At that time the council at Magdeburg had only 24, while that at Cologne had 75 members. The nature of their composition can best be illustrated by presenting an analysis of the membership of one such council. The council of Hannover, comprising the railway directories of Hannover and Münster-Westphalen, seems to be a fair type. In that council we find 1 representative from each of the chambers of commerce of Bielefeld, Geestemünde, Hannover, Harburg, Hildesheim, Lüneburg, Minden, Münster, Osnabrück, Ostfriesland and Papenburg, Verden and Wesel ; 1 representative from each of the following corporations or societies : Society of German Foundries in Bielefeld, German Iron and Steel Industrials in Ruhrort, Craftsmen's Union of the Province of Hannover, Branch Union of German Millers in Hannover, Union of German Linen Industrialists in Bielefeld, Society for Beet Sugar Industry in Berlin, Society for the Promotion of Common Industrial Interests in the Rhine Country and Westphalen, in Düsseldorf, and the Society of German Distillers in Berlin; 4 representatives from the Royal Agricultural Society in Celle; 3 from the Provincial Agricultural Society for Westphalen, in Münster ; 1 from the German Dairy Society in Schladen and Hamburg, the Society of Foresters of the Hartz, the North German Foresters in Hannover, the Union of Forest Owners of Middle Germany in Birnstein, and from the Society for the promotion of Moor Culture in the German Empire ; and, lastly, 1 from the Society of German Sea Fishers in Berlin. This one illustration is probably sufficient to show the thoroughly representative character of the circuit councils. If a circuit comprises railways covering territory of other German States, the chambers of commerce, industrial, and agricultural societies of such territory may also be represented in the council. The minister of public works has power to admit other members, and frequently does so when the nature of the questions upon which the council deliberates makes it desirable. Thus, at a meeting in which the rates on coal and coke — to be noted hereafter — from the Rhenish mining districts to the seashore were to be considered, there were present an Oberpräsident, accompanied by an assessor, a deputy of a Regierungspräsident, a Landrath (these three are civil administrative officers presiding over a province, circuit, and department, respectively), a representative of the Upper Mine Office at Bonn and at Dortmund, of the Royal Mine Directory at Saarbrücken, of the Royal Railroad Directory at Hannover, of the Dortmund and Gronau and Enscheder Railroad Company (private), in addition to the regular representatives and voting members.

The circuit council, as has been indicated above, stands in a relation to the railway directory similar to that of the national council to the minister. The law makes it mandatory upon the directory to consult the circuit council on all important matters concerning the railways in that circuit. This applies especially to time-tables and rate schedules. On the other hand, the council has the right, which it freely exercises, of making recommendations to the directory. In case of emergency the directory may act according to its own judgment independently of the council, but it is required to report all such cases to the standing committee of the council and to the council itself. This provision supplies the elastic element, which enables the railways to meet momentary wants. The standing committee of the council is an important body. It meets regularly some time before the full council holds its sessions, and its proceedings form the basis of the deliberations in the council. The committee receives petitions, memorials, and other communications. The bearers of these are invited to appear before the committee and to advocate their cause. Questions are asked and answered on both sides, and after all the questions have been presented the committee votes upon the petition or request, usually in the form of a resolution adopted by majority vote, recommending the council to accept or reject the demands made in the petitions. The action of the committee is reported on each question by a member designated for that purpose to the full council at its next session. While the decision of the committee is usually accepted by the council, it in no way binds that body. Before the council meets, each member has an opportunity to examine the arguments presented before the committee, and the facts upon which its decisions are based. If the advocates of the petitions before the council present new evidence, or if the recommendations of the committee are shown to be unsound, the council simply reverses the decision of the committee. Of the nature of these petitions I shall speak later.

These advisory councils have spread into Bavaria, Saxony, Württemberg, Hesse, Oldenburg, Mecklenburg-Schwerin, Austria, Italy, Russia, Denmark, Roumania, and, in a much modified form, into France. An examination of the councils in these countries shows the same principle underlying them all — the representation of all the different economic interests in the conduct of the railways. In composition and organization they are much alike. They owe their existence, however, except in Japan and Switzerland, not to law, but simply to administrative orders.

There are still other bodies which, although not created by law and not confined in their activity to Prussia, have long exerted a powerful influence throughout the Empire. Foremost among these stands the Generalkonferenz (general conference). Under its guidance the modern German system of rates, called Reformtarif, has been systematically developed. The general conference meets annually, and discusses matters relating to tariffs, fees, operating regulations, etc. Thus, at a recent meeting the conference disposed of no less than 53 different items, relating mostly to the classification of goods and the adjustment of rates, all of which, as in case of the circuit councils, had been previously considered in subordinate bodies whose deliberations lie at the basis of the proceedings in the general conference. It is composed of members representing all the German railways, and votes are distributed according to the number of miles of road the members each represent, and the total number of votes, increasing, of course, with the growth of the German system. At the meeting referred to, the total number of votes was 322, of which 51 were not represented. Of these 51, 28 belonged to roads having 1, 10 to those having 2, and 1 to those having 3 votes. The Prussian State railways had 139 votes, the Bavarian State railways 28, those of Saxony 16, the State roads of Alsace-Lorraine 11, the State roads of Baden 10, and so on down, the remainder representing the smaller State and private railways. These figures show the predominating influence of Prussia in the conference.

Bodies subordinate to the general conference have already been alluded to. These are the Tarif-Kommission and the Ausschuss der Verkehrsinteressenten (tariff commission and committee of those interested in transportation). The tariff commission is a standing committee whose members represent Prussian State roads, 2 Swiss roads, and 1 of the railways of Mecklenburg. It meets 3 times a year, and occupies itself with petitions and other communications from shippers. The committee of shippers (Verkehrsinteressenten) is composed of members representing agriculture, trade, and industry; and some of the matters brought before it are previously discussed by a subcommittee. Both of these bodies occupy themselves almost exclusively with freight rates and matters immediately connected with them. Out of 23 items brought before them during a 2 days' session in 1893, 22 were deliberated upon in joint session, although each body voted separately. The discussions in these sessions are so thorough that the recommendations made are, in the great majority of cases, approved by the general conference. Those conclusions of the commission which are adopted in the form of a declaratory statement become binding upon members unless protests are made. Subjects discussed in the conference and commission may, and frequently are, brought before the councils.

Among the various railway traffic and rate unions which might be mentioned none have exerted an influence on rates at all comparable to that which has been exercised by the Society of German Railway Administrations. Founded as a Prussian society in 1846, it became in quick succession a national and an international organization, embracing the railways of Germany, Austria, Hungary, Roumania, Luxemburg, Holland, Belgium, Bosnia, and Russian Poland. Both State and private railways are eligible to membership. A series of 8 standing committees covers the special branches of the service, and if extraordinary matters arise they are referred to special committees. Questions upon which the society is to act must be published at least 3 months preceding the meeting. The proceedings have long been published in an official paper, and, through custom, exert a powerful influence. The attainment of uniformity in construction and other matters has been one of its great aims. In Europe the necessity for international uniformity is much greater than with us, and in the domain of freight traffic this has been well attained by means of an international treaty, signed at Berne on October 14, 1890, by diplomatic agents from Belgium, France, Germany, Italy, Luxemburg, Holland, Austria, Hungary, Russia, and Switzerland. It is officially known as the "Convention internationale sur le transport de marchandises par chemins de fer."

The history of this international agreement dates back to 1874, the same year that Mülhausen inaugurated the movement which led to the institution of advisory councils. In that year 2 Swiss citizens, residents of Bâle, directed to the governments of the surrounding States inquiries concerning their willingness to enter into an international freight treaty. Drafts of such a treaty were worked out in both Germany and Switzerland and discussed in a congress at Berne in 1878. This congress submitted the draft of a treaty to the different governments for examination. Many objections were raised and improvements made. Further conferences, dealing also with questions of technical uniformity, were held in 1882 and 1886, and on October 14, 1890, the draft approved by the third congress was formally drawn up as a treaty and approved. The original treaty has been modified and supplemented in various ways, partly by agreements among all these countries and partly by agreements among several of them. Every 3 years, or sooner, if one fourth of the treaty-making States demand it, a general congress must be called together to consider improvements in the agreement.

As its name indicates, the Bernese treaty applies only to international freight traffic. Excepting articles the transportation of which is regularly monopolized by the post offices of the contracting States, the treaty governs all shipments of goods from or through one of the States to another. It provides for uniform through bills of lading, prescribes routes for international traffic, fixes liability in cases of delay and loss, prohibits special contracts, rebates, and reductions, except when publicly announced and available to all, and prescribes certain custom-house regulations. Not the least important feature of the treaty is the creation of a central bureau, organized and supervised by the Swiss Bundesrath, with its seat in Berne. The duties of the bureau are five:

1. To receive communications from any of the contracting States, and to transmit them to the rest of them.

2. To compile and publish information of importance for international traffic, for which purpose it may issue a journal.

3. To act as a board of arbitration on the application of the countries concerned.

4. To perform the business preliminaries connected with proposed changes in the agreement, and, under certain circumstances, to suggest the meeting of a new conference.

5. To facilitate transactions among the railways, especially to look after those which have been derelict in financial matters. After notice has been given by the bureau, the State to which the railway belongs or by whose citizens it is owned can either become responsible for the debts of the road or permit the exclusion of the road from international traffic.

The expenses of the bureau are met by contributions of the contracting States in proportion to mileage.

The original agreement provided that any of the States might withdraw at the end of 3 years, on giving 1 year's notice. No such notice has ever been given. Any violation of the treaty can be punished in the courts, and a judgment having been rendered in one country the courts of the others are bound to assist in its execution, unless the decision conflicts with their own laws. But so far as the question of fact is concerned there is no appeal, and a German court is bound to accept the findings of a court in France. Germany, Austria, Hungary, Russia,

Switzerland, and, to a less extent, France have embodied provisions of the international code in their internal code, thus leading to unification beyond the limits of international traffic. To what extent the Bernese treaty may influence other phases of the national and international laws of the States of central Europe cannot well be foreseen. That States differing widely in forms of government, geographical position, and commercial interests have voluntarily made themselves amenable to a common code of law under these circumstances, again impresses one with the great power and many-sided influence of railways and the healthy development of closer international relations. The code is binding for a domain embracing nearly 3,000,000 square miles and 260,000,000 people. It ranks in importance with the international postal, telegraph, and copyright unions.

Proceedings of advisory councils. The leading features of the Prussian railway administration relating to rates have now been presented. It remains to illustrate by means of a few side lights from the proceedings how a part of the machinery acts. To convey a somewhat detailed view of the workings of the administrative organs directly concerned with the operation of the railways would unduly extend this paper; besides, it would be a little technical and not essential from the economic point of view. So we shall content ourselves with a brief account of some of the deliberations of the advisory and other bodies directly occupied with questions about rates. We shall save time by first obtaining a general idea of the German system of rates, for which purpose the general plan of the German reform tariff is here given:

German Tariff Scheme

1. Fast freight by the piece (express package freight).
2. Fast freight by the car load.
3. Piece goods (less than car loads).
4. General car-load class A 1, in shipments of at least 5000 kilograms.
5. General car-load class B, in shipments of at least 10,000 kilograms.
6. Special tariff A 2, in shipments of at least 5000 kilograms.
7. Special tariff I, II, III, in shipments of at least 10,000 kilograms.

The rates and what pertains to them are officially published in volumes not unlike our monthly magazines. This tariff scheme was first introduced in 1877, and through the influence mainly of the general conference it has become gradually more unified. It is obvious that the price of transportation of goods becomes less as they fall into a class farther down the list. The general car-load classes include goods of higher value not enumerated in any of the special tariffs, while the special tariffs I, II, and III embrace less valuable goods — their value falling by degrees — so that, generally speaking —

Special tariff I includes manufactured goods.

Special tariff II includes intermediate products.

Special tariff III includes raw materials and bulky goods of small value, such as certain waste products of gas factories, tanneries, paper factories, slaughterhouses, etc.

Special tariff A 2 is for goods belonging to special tariffs I and II in consignments below 10,000 and above 5000 kilograms. Goods belonging to special tariff III, but weighing less than 10,000, though at least 5000 kilograms, are transported at the rates of special tariff II. Then there are special rules and rates for such things as explosives, precious metals, vehicles, timber, fish, bees, meat, carrier doves, etc. Questions as to classification and the transference of goods from one class to another often arise. Here is a typical case:

The Chamber of Commerce of Lennep, a Rhenish city, petitioned the general conference to transfer manufactured horseshoes — "raw hoof irons," the Germans say, but which will here be designated simply as "horseshoes" — from special tariff I to special tariff II. A prominent business firm brought the question before one of the railway directories, and from there it was carried before the minister of public works. The minister consulted the permanent tariff commission and the committee of shippers, and finally the question was brought before the advisory councils.

The petitioners asserted that the manufacture of horseshoes was a new industry which, after many costly experiments, had only recently gained a firm foothold; that the trade had been gradually growing, especially with the East, and that consignments had been sent to Russia, Italy, Austria, and other countries. In domestic trade the use of these horseshoes had been promoted by military authorities and street-car companies, because it lessened cost and relieved the blacksmith of much purely mechanical work. It enabled him to do better work more cheaply and with greater uniformity. The charge that it hindered the education of skillful blacksmiths was untrue.

Extensive statistical tables were introduced to show that the life of the industry depended upon the desired change in rates. Horseshoes were subjected to the same rates as fine iron and steel goods, while they properly belonged to intermediate products in special tariff II. Many of the factories were unfavorably located, and it was one of the highest duties of the State to promote industrial activity in regions which lie away from the great channels of trade, if it could be done without too great a sacrifice on part of the public. The desired concessions on part of the railroads would do this. It was unjust for the representatives of the Saxon State railways to assert, as they had done in the tariff commission, that the change in the classification of horseshoes would benefit the Rhenish industry only. Particularistic designs should not be suspected in a movement which was deeply rooted in economic necessities. The representatives of the Bavarian railways had considered fiscal reasons only, but these alone could not be decisive. It would not be businesslike for the State, in order to gain a temporary advantage, to sacrifice the very source of this gain. The railways would fare worse with high rates and a stagnant industry than with lower rates and a prosperous industry, and it was safe to assert that the desired change would, through an increased output, ultimately yield a greater income to the railways. The established system of rates would not be prejudiced; besides, when the question of system is balanced against that of the welfare of an industry the latter should prevail. The nationalization of railways was undertaken not for fiscal, but for economic reasons.

These were the main features of the petition. The petition, together with the records of previous deliberations on the question, was brought before the standing committee of one of the circuit councils, by which the arguments were reviewed and new evidence introduced. Can these horseshoes be classed with rod iron? Are they an intermediate product? Could not plowshares and other articles demand a like change? What is the relation of the proposed change to the competition of Swedish iron? Is it true that the manufacture of horseshoes injures the craft of blacksmiths? Will it lead to a wider use of horseshoes and consequently to an improvement of agriculture? Such were the questions which the committee considered, and in response to which evidence of individuals and of societies was presented and subjected to the most rigid examination by specialists of various classes. From the committee the question went, as all questions considered by the committee do, before the full council, by which the report of the committee was reviewed and the horseshoe problem finally disposed of.

In a similar manner both the committee and council deliberated upon a petition of the Agricultural Society of Rhenish Prussia to place street sweepings in the special class with fertilizers and to reduce rates for shorter distances, because sweepings are used only within from 10 to 20 kilometers of the cities. The sweepings, it was asserted, had considerable value for agriculture, but that the difficulty of disposing of them had led some cities, notably Hamburg, to destroy them, thus depriving agriculture of a valuable agent. The composition and value of sweepings were examined and compared with other fertilizers now available, and the probable effect on the use of these considered. At the same session of the committee the change in time-tables for the summer period was regularly considered. Twenty-eight items were presented by the 14 different members, involving the time and frequency of passenger trains. All propositions which received a majority vote in the committee were brought, of course, before the full council.

In speaking of the composition of circuit councils reference was made to the question of rates on coal and coke. One of the railway directories brought before the standing committee of the circuit council a question first submitted in a petition of the chamber of commerce of Bielefeld and subsequently indorsed, either in part or entire, by other organizations. The petition sought a temporary suspension of rates applicable to coke and coal sent from the Rhenish mining districts to the German seashore and to foreign countries. The suspension was to remain in effect until the prices in the coal market should return to a normal level.

In the consideration of this question the railway directory asked the committee and council to deliver an opinion on each of the following points: (1) Is the level of prices of coke and coal in the Rhenish-Westphalian district an abnormal one? (2) How must the prices of coke and coal be constituted in order that their level may be characterized as normal? (3) Should a permanent or temporary suspension of existing freight rates on coke and coal be recommended in order to effect a reduction of prices within the country? (4) What markets and what rates come into consideration in case of the temporary or permanent suspension of the rates in question? Shall the rates to foreign countries or also the rates to the seashore be changed? (5) What will be the probable effect of the proposed suspension of rates with reference to the sale and the price of coal and coke within the country?

In both the committee and in the council this problem was thoroughly dissected. Naturally there were differences. Abnormal prices were thought to be prices which include an element of profit out of proportion to the other constituents of price. On the one hand, a profit of 40 per cent was shown to exist, which, however, the experts present at once proved to be confined to two specially favored mines. In computations to ascertain the average selling price of coal there was a difference of several marks, which called forth the most rigid examination of the statistics and other evidence upon which the figures were based. The railway authorities showed that in 5 years the outlay for coal for locomotives had risen from 4½ to 7 per cent of their total expenses, while coal was still rising, and the coal men showed that their cost of production had risen because of advances in wages and expenses connected with insurance. It was said that the present low rates for the transportation of coal had been introduced at a time when the coal industry had lain prostrate, and that now all other industries were suffering from the high price of coal, and that this advance in freight rates on coal and coke would check exportation and force down prices at home. A decrease in exportation was deplored by representatives of the German marine. In conclusion, among both the advocates and the opponents of the change, the opinion was expressed that there was reason for rejoicing in the thorough airing which this question had received; that it would lead to a better understanding of actual conditions, and that the coal industry would hereafter be more inclined to give due consideration to the condition of other German industries.

We come now to the consideration of a question which, perhaps even more forcibly than what has just been related, illustrates the comprehensiveness and fair-mindedness with which the railway authorities investigate the problems which affect wide economic interests. It is a petition submitted by the minister of public works to the national council for an expression of opinion. The printed evidence sent to the council alone covers about 500 folio pages. The problem submitted by the minister to the national council was this: Giving due consideration to the financial condition and the financial interests of the State, is it conducive to the general economic interests of the country (1) to introduce special reduced rates for all kinds of manures and fertilizers, irrespective of their nature, and, if so, what rates? (2) to introduce special reductions, and to what extent, for the transportation of (*a*) potassium salts — without discrimination or only "raw salts" — and phosphate; and (*b*) lime, in pieces or powdered, used for fertilization?

This was submitted in October, 1893. During March of that year the Herrenhaus had passed a resolution requesting the Government to introduce reduced special rates for fertilizers, a number of which were specified in the resolution. As stated in support of the resolution, the necessity for it lay in a cheapening of elementary utilities in order to maintain and promote agriculture and to increase the receipts of the railway from the traffic with the interior. The same resolution had previously been adopted by the budget commission of the Landtag.

In response to this resolution the minister of public works sought information from the minister of agriculture, domains, and forests, and all the different agricultural experiment stations as to the occurrence and production of natural and artificial manures in different parts of the country, their price and value in use, and the nature of their application. Various commissions reported on the prices at which different fertilizers could be profitably used on different soils. The agricultural authorities showed where and to what extent these soils existed, and elaborate statistics of the railways and manufacturers told how much had actually been consumed. In this lay the vital issue — the capacity of the land to absorb profitably artificial manures, and the adaptability of the farmer to secure them. The national council said that a simple expression of its appreciation of the great economic significance of the use of both natural and artificial manures was not sufficient, but that an exact and conscientious examination of the effect of existing rates on the widest and most effective use of these was necessary. The deliberations of the committee of shippers, the tariff commission, the general conference, and the evidence submitted through the minister of public works were all thoroughly sifted by the standing committee of the national council before the case went before the full council for its final verdict.

Marbles, slates, and pencils even have been the object of the most serious deliberations of bodies so large and so dignified as the general conference and the national council. A memorial was addressed to one of the railway directories by the marbles, slate, and pencil industry of Thuringia, praying for a detariffization of these articles. The memorial gives a detailed account of the manufacture of marbles, slates, and pencils in Thuringia, and points out the places where it meets competition. It gives the cost of production, output, markets, prices, and the rates of transportation. The conditions of the laboring population are described, and the probable effect of a change in rates on their welfare is analyzed. (One may be pardoned for turning aside to state that the laborers there engaged in the manufacture of slates, although exposed to the danger of completely undermining their health, receive often no more than 12 cents for a day's work of 18 hours.) The railway directory to which the memorial was sent addressed a letter of inquiry to the manufacturer of slates and pencils in Westphalia, whose business would be affected by the competition of Thuringia, calling for information on various points relating to this industry. This reply, together with the memorial and supplementary material, was submitted, through the minister of public works, to the national council.

One cannot read these documents without being impressed with the sincere desire of the railway authorities to do justice to all competitors and at the same time to make such changes as will better the conditions of people like these laborers in Thuringia. Whether or not the benefits arising from a change in rates would really accrue to these people was most carefully considered. The material submitted for consideration in deciding this question, as in case of the preceding questions, furnished evidence on every point which was raised. The moderation with which the petitions are drafted, the high plane upon which the debates are carried on, the thorough conscientiousness and judicial-mindedness with which the arguments are balanced in reaching a decision, all manifest a tone not unlike that of the decisions of our best courts of justice.

Summary and remarks. Prussia began with a general law. In this respect her history is the direct opposite of that of our States. Treating this general law as a nucleus, legislation, royal and ministerial orders and rescripts, and custom have developed two distinct groups of railway administrative organs, each representing distinct sets of interests, yet both working coöperatively. On the one hand we have a group of organs which represents railway interests in particular and which takes the railway point of view. The minister of public works, the railway directories, the general conference and tariff commission, and the Society of German Railways fall into this group, although the two latter stand in a measure on the border line, and none of them are confined exclusively to railway interests. Legal responsibility is fixed in the first two. On the other hand, we have the national and circuit councils with their standing committees and the committee of shippers. These primarily take the social and economic point of view. They are not legally responsible for the conduct of the railways, but act as advisory bodies. They represent all the different interests of the nation, and through them every citizen has not only an opportunity but a right to make his wants known.

The marble and slate industry of Thüringen is relatively insignificant, yet of vital importance to the inhabitants of that section of the country. We have seen how complete an examination the petition of these people received at the hands of the highest authorities of the land. A fair and prompt hearing can be denied to no man, rich or poor. The railways are made real servants. All the administrative, legal, and advisory bodies are organically connected with one another and with the parliament. The lines may be drawn taut from above as well as from below. The elaborate system of local offices makes the system democratic, and the cabinet office and the directories give it the necessary centralization. The system presents that unity which a great business requires, on the one hand; and, on the other, that ramification and elasticity which the diverse and manifold interests of a great nation need for their growth and expansion.

In the formation of the councils the elective and the appointive elements are so well proportioned that it is impossible to "pack" any one of them. In this respect each body is a check on the other. It is easy to reproach the system with "bureaucracy," but to give adequate support to such a stigma would be an impossible task. We need only recall the analysis of the membership of one of the councils. Farmers, dairymen, fishermen, foresters, traders, miners, manufacturers — the long array of human professions have here their representatives. One representative may shape his views according to some particular philosophy of the State. Another will at once restore the balance by presenting the opposite. One member may make extreme statments about some branch of trade or industry. Another will furnish exact information for its refutation. I doubt whether we can find anywhere in the world deliberative or administrative bodies in which the tone and the many-sidedness of the proceedings, the amount and variety of special knowledge displayed, and the logic of the debates present more points of excellence than in these councils and other bodies.

If from the point of view of the railways nothing should come of these proceedings — a most violent assumption — the information brought together would alone make them invaluable. No investigating committee of Congress or legislature ever had a better array of talent in every field at its disposal and under its control than is found in one of these councils or commissions.

It is not my purpose here to present new schemes, or to suggest ways and means by which existing institutions of our own country might be modified to perform similar functions. But let me ask whether, if our coal and iron industry, or fruit and cattle raising, or any other industry, were to receive an examination like that given to the Rhenish coal and coke industry, many things might not be different from what they now are? Imagine a well-organized assembly whose members could speak for the railways, for wheat and cattle, for fruit and steel, for forests and for mines, and is it not probable that the effects anticipated in the circular letter of 1875 would make themselves felt also in the United States? Both our railways and the public have repeatedly gone to extremes because neither understood the other. A system like the Prussian reveals the railways to the public and the public to the railways. It tends to remove blind prejudice and violent measures on both sides. By reflecting accurately the existing conditions, these conferences lead to tolerance, forbearance, and mutual concessions. The conclusions reached often have as salutary an effect on industrial situations as suspended judgments of our courts on defendants. It would be difficult to find in Prussia to-day, among the representatives of any class or interest, objections to the entire railway system which are not relatively insignificant. Both the public and the railways have gained more and more as the system has developed.

It will doubtless have been noticed that in the discussion of the council proceedings the decisions and their effect were not stated. It was my purpose simply to show the nature of the councils, and either a negative or an affirmative vote would throw no additional light on the problem. Without a full presentation of local details it could mean little to state that the council voted to place sweepings into the special tariff with fertilizers.

BALTHASAR H. MEYER

MADISON, WISCONSIN

INDEX

www.ingramcontent.com/pod-product-compliance
Lightning Source LLC
LaVergne TN
LVHW050915080826
845145LV00001B/92

* 9 7 8 1 5 8 7 9 8 0 7 6 3 *